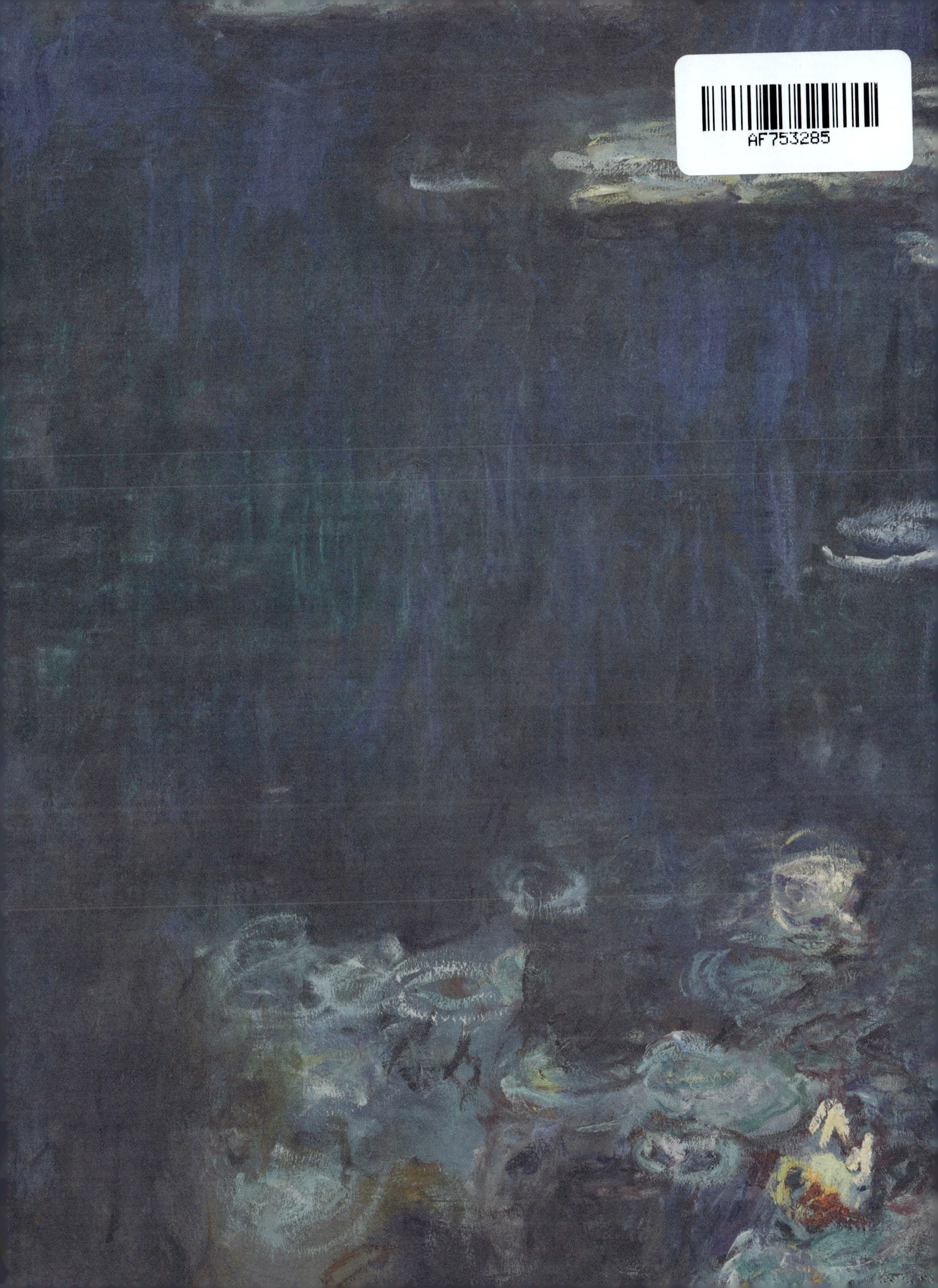

MONET

JEAN-DOMINIQUE REY
DENIS ROUART

WATER LILIES

THE COMPLETE SERIES

We would like in particular to thank Robert Maillard, who was at the origin of the first catalogue raisonné of the *Water Lilies* in 1972, as well as Marie-Christine Decroocq and the Fondation Wildenstein.

TRANSLATED FROM THE FRENCH BY
David Radzinowicz

DESIGN
Amélie Boutry

COPYEDITING
Penny Isaac

TYPESETTING
Thierry Renard

PROOFREADING
Chrisoula Petridis

COLOR SEPARATION
IGS, France

Simultaneously published in French as *Monet: Les Nymphéas*

English-language edition

Éditions Flammarion
82 Rue Saint-Lazare
75009 Paris
France

editions.flammarion.com
@flammarioninternational

24 25 26 5 4 3

ISBN: 978-2-08-020286-4

Legal Deposit: 09/2016

Printed in Slovenia by Florjancic

MONET

JEAN-DOMINIQUE REY
DENIS ROUART

WATER LILIES

THE COMPLETE SERIES

Flammarion

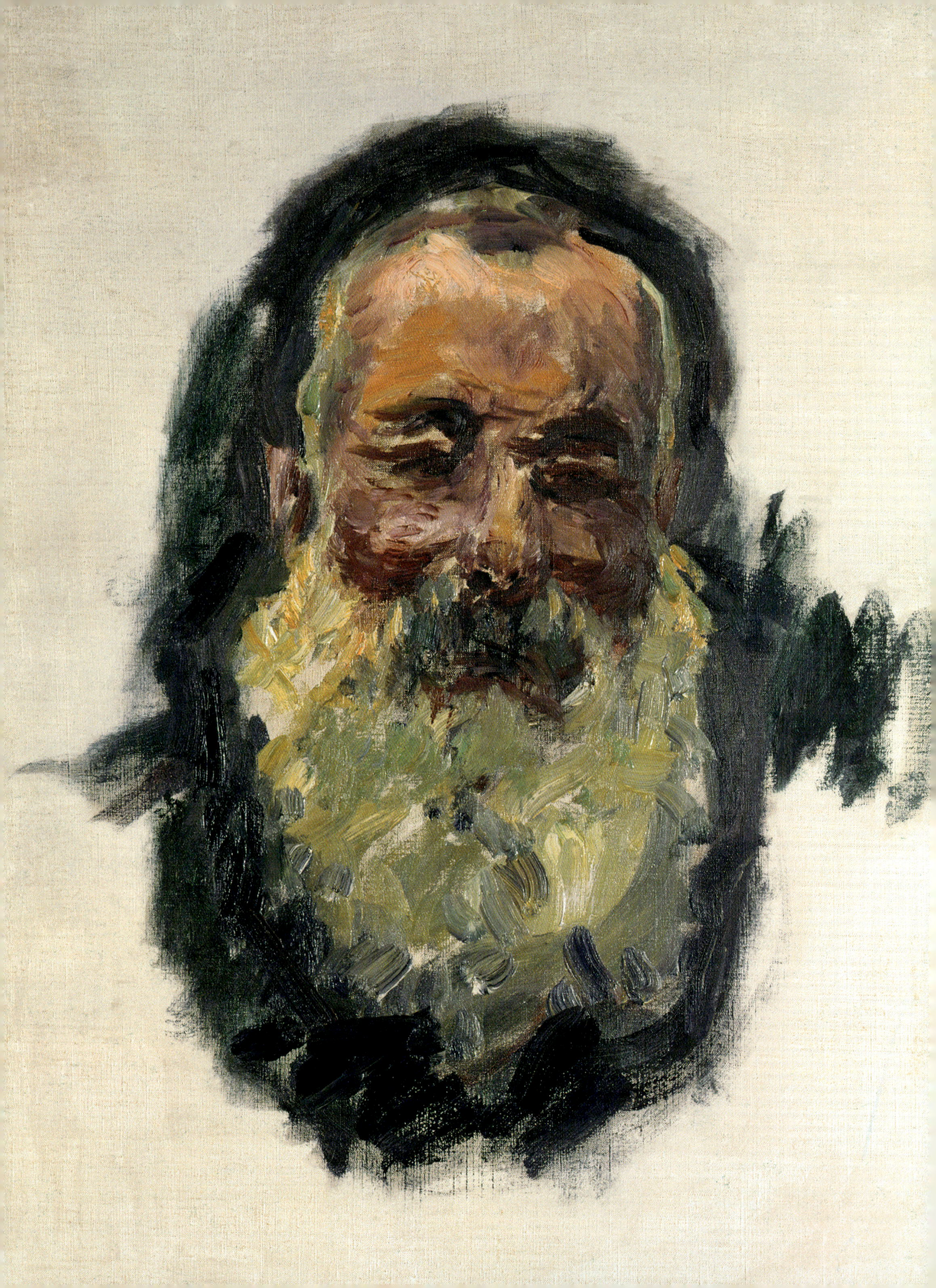

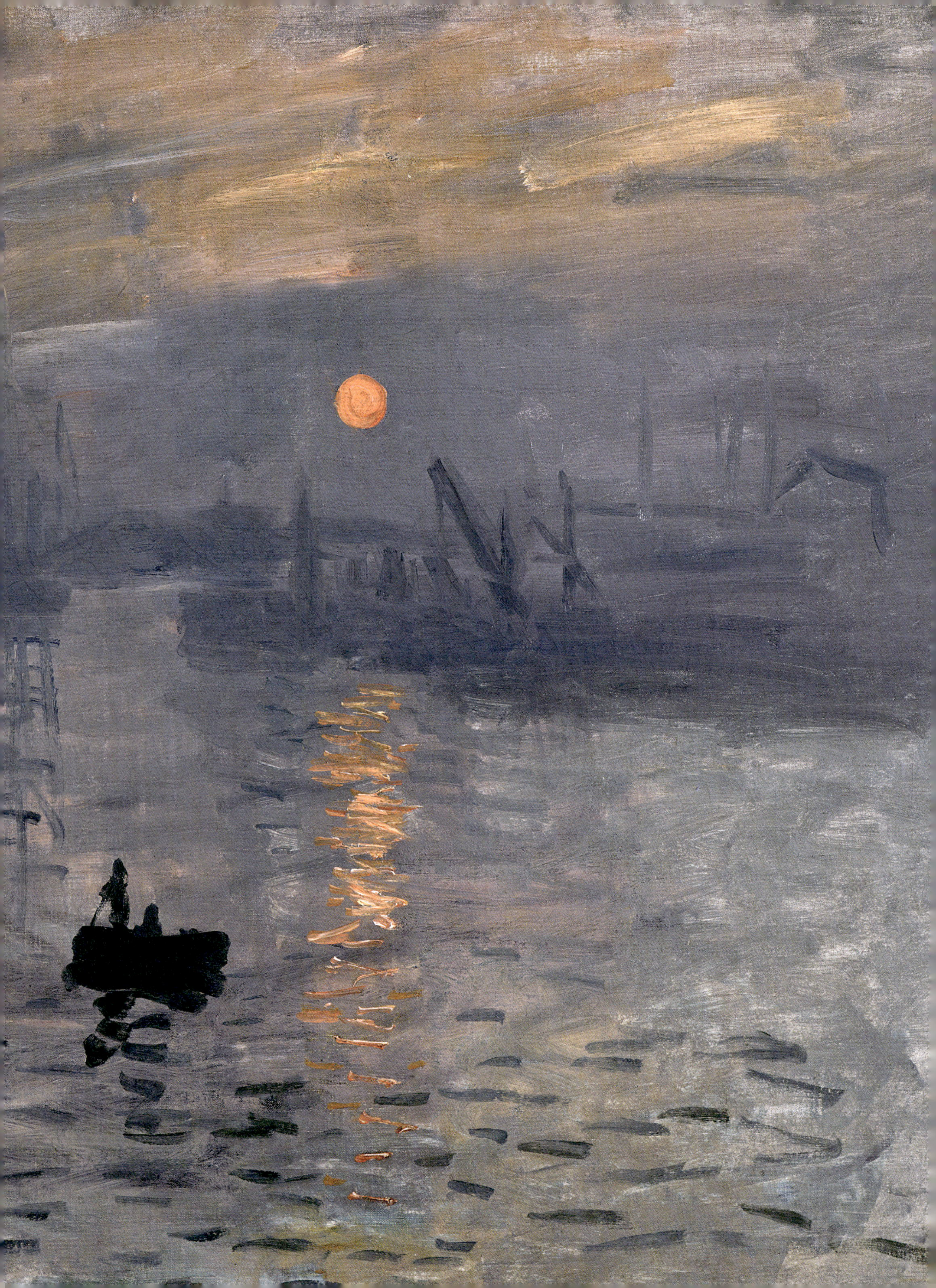

DENIS ROUART

APPEARANCES AND REFLECTIONS

FROM CARICATURE TO PAINTING

The undying love for nature that Monet felt throughout his life dated back to his childhood, as he himself declared to the journalist Thiébault-Sisson in 1900 in an interview published in *Le Temps*: "I am a Parisian of Paris. I was born there in 1840, during the reign of good King Louis-Philippe in a milieu centered on commerce in which the Arts were regarded with disdain. As it was, my childhood was spent at Le Havre where my father had settled in about 1845 the better to pursue his business interests and, as it happened, this childhood of mine was essentially one of freedom. I was born with a lack of discipline. No one was ever able to make me stick to the rules, not even in my youngest days. It was at home that I learned most of what I know now. I thought of my college life as a prison and I could never resolve to spend any time there, even four hours a day, when the sun was inviting, the sea was beautiful and it was so good to run along the cliff-tops in the fresh air or frolic in the sea."

But soon something else attracted the young boy's attention: drawing.

"Until the age of fourteen or fifteen, much to my father's great disappointment, I continued this very irregular but healthy way of life. Somehow, in between, I did acquire the rudiments of a basic education, including some proficiency in spelling. My studies went no further and did not cause me too much trouble, and I was able to combine them with a number of distractions. I illumined the margins of my textbooks, I decorated the blue paper of my exercise books with quite fantastic designs and depicted in the most irreverent manner possible the features in front view or profile of my masters." Little by little, from mere recreation, drawing grew into a vocation.

"I very quickly became adept at this game. At fifteen, I was known by all Le Havre as a caricaturist. My reputation was so well established that I was actually commissioned from all sides for satirical portraits. In consideration of the sheer number of commissions I received, as well as the insufficiency of the allowance I received from my mother, I was prompted, to the horror of my family, to charge a fee for my portraits. I would exact ten to twenty francs depending on the look of the client, and this method went like clockwork. In a month, the number of my customers had doubled and I was able to charge a fixed rate of twenty francs without this reducing demand in any way. Had I continued in this manner, today I would have been a millionaire!

"By this means, I became someone of status in the town. There, along the storefront of the one and only framer to make a living in Le Havre, my caricatures sprawled insolently in rows five or six deep in little gold beading and under glass, like treasured works of art.

PAGE 4
Self-Portrait
1917
27 1/2 × 21 3/4 in. (70 × 55 cm)
oil on canvas
Musée d'Orsay
Paris, inv. RF 2623

PRECEDING PAGE
Impression, Sunrise
(The Port of Le Havre in the Fog)
1872
19 × 24 3/4 in. (48 × 63 cm)
oil on canvas
Musée Marmottan
Paris

FACING PAGE
Water Lilies
1916–19,
59 × 77 1/2 in. (150 × 197 cm)
oil on canvas
Musée Marmottan
Paris, inv. 5164

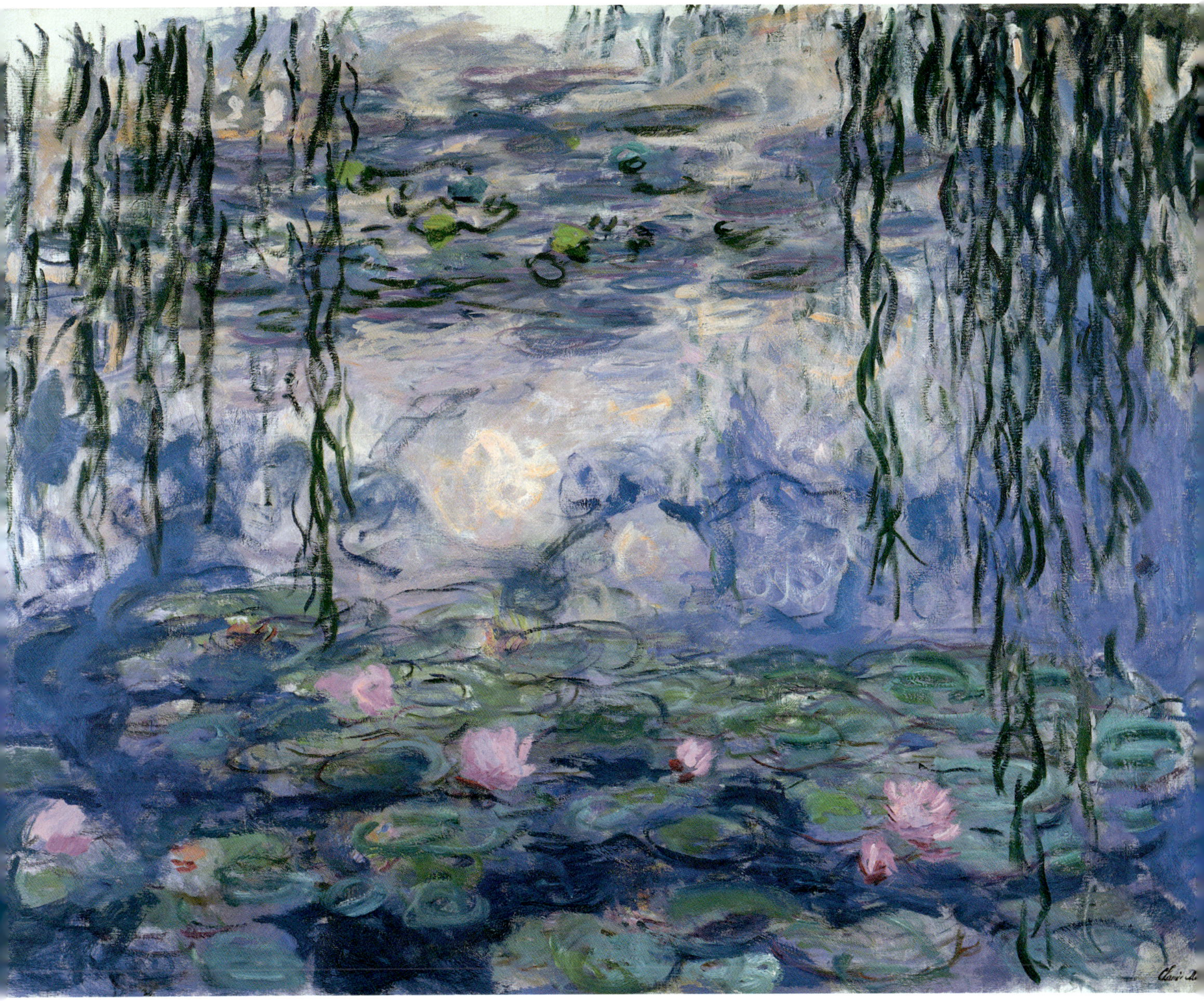

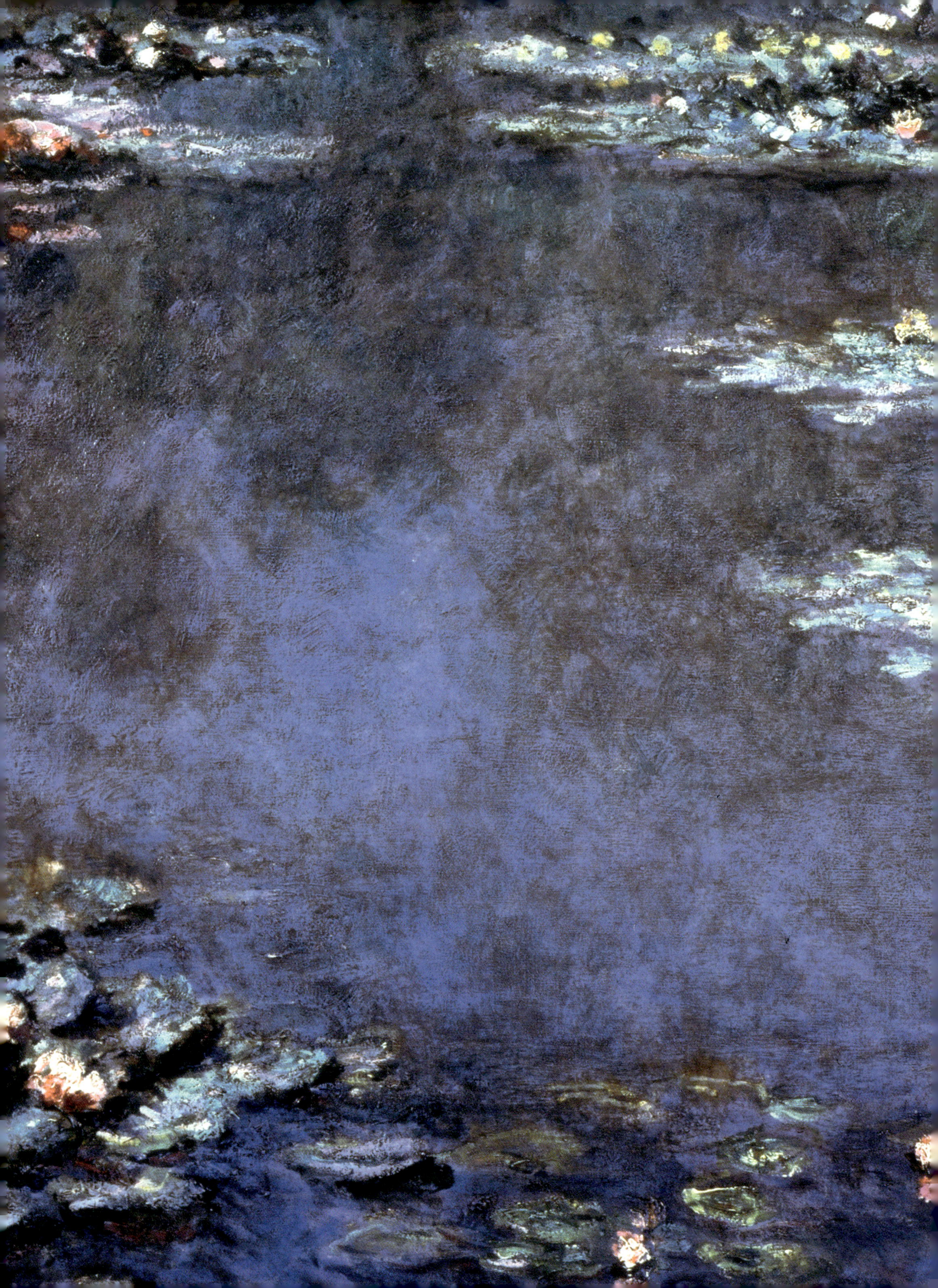

Moreover, when I saw strollers gathering to gape at them with admiration and cry, 'That's What's-his-name!' I felt as if I might burst with pride."

However, his gifts and successes as a caricaturist bore no relation to his love of nature. They were two separate domains and it took the intervention and benevolent insistence of the marine painter Eugène Boudin to convince him to give up caricature.

"I should say, however, that there was a flaw in all this. In this same shop window there hung, often just above my own works, a number of marine scenes that I, along with most of the inhabitants of Le Havre, found revolting. I was so vexed at having to endure such contact that I had no hesitation in belaboring with insults this idiot, this "bastard" Boudin who, thinking himself an artist, had the gall to sign his works. For me, used to Gudin's seascapes—with their arbitrary color schemes, false notes, and tricksy perspectives typical of fashionable artists—Boudin's sincere little compositions, with his little figures so perfectly judged, his neatly rigged boats, his accurate skies and water, drawn and painted solely from nature, held no artistic value for me, and his very verisimilitude seemed suspicious. Hence his paintings inspired me with a dreadful aversion and without even having met the man I loathed him cordially. Often the framer would say: 'You should make the acquaintance of Monsieur Boudin. Despite what they say about him, he knows his job. He's studied in Paris at the Fine Arts School. He could give you some useful advice.' But I resisted, braggart that I was. What could *I* possibly learn from such a ridiculous little man?"

Initially reluctant, the young Claude finally let himself be persuaded by the elder artist to draw and paint from nature: "But Boudin's exhortations did not stick. In the final analysis, I liked the man. He was convinced, sincere, I felt it, but I couldn't stomach his painting, and when he offered to take me to draw in the middle of the fields, I always found some pretext to politely refuse. Summer came; I was free, about, more or less. I could think of no more valid reasons. Worn down, I did as I was bidden. And Boudin, with inexhaustible kindness, undertook to teach me. In time, my eyes were opened, and I really understood nature; and at the same time I learned how to love it. I analyzed its forms with a pencil, I studied it in its colorations."

After six months working from life with Boudin, Monet, now fully determined to become a painter; he felt he should supplement this teaching by studying in a Paris studio. Claude could get round the fact that his father refused to advance him the necessary funds by dipping into the money he had already earned.

Water Lilies
1906
35½ × 36¼ in. (90 × 93 cm)
oil on canvas
private collection

"In effect, I was able to do without it. My purse had been lined long ago. My caricatures had filled it adequately. Often I'd managed to do seven or eight such portraits in a single day. At a louis each, my income had rocketed and I had taken the habit from the start of depositing it with one of my aunts, keeping only insignificant amounts for pocket money. At sixteen, with two thousand francs, one reckons oneself rich! Armed with references acquired through admirers of Boudin who had connections with Monginot, Troyon, and Amand Gautier, I headed without a backward glance to Paris."

Monet's military service in Algeria, where he fell rather seriously ill, caused a gap of almost two years in a life to which he promptly returned—after a convalescence of several months in Normandy, where he became acquainted with Jongkind. The persistence of his desire to follow training in a Parisian school or academy —and enter a stifling world that could offer little to please him—is little short of astonishing. But he did not for all that give up work from nature during the warmer days in the company of Boudin and Jongkind. At that time Boudin took it upon himself to show Monet that "the essential thing is to fix the first impression and that everything that is painted directly from nature possesses a life impossible to obtain by work in studio," prevailing upon his young pupil to produce sketches that demanded "intensity of observation and speed of execution." But was Monet then mature enough to grasp the atmospheric subtleties in which Boudin excelled? The drawings and paintings he executed at that time are cause for doubt, and demonstrate, in any case, a search for solidity that is far removed from the moving fluidity of the seas and skies of his professor. Moreover Boudin was himself entirely conscious of the need for his student to not be limited to his example alone, and to seek out other opinions. "One never gets anywhere in isolation, unless one possesses very powerful dispositions, and even then; one cannot invent an art all alone, in a corner of some province, without criticism, means of comparison, and firm convictions."

Monet's doubts, concerns, and misgivings thus induced him to join up with those of his companions in the studios who shared them—Bazille, Renoir, Sisley—in whose company he examined their predecessors: Corot, and the painters of the Barbizon School, as well as their immediate elders, Courbet, Pissarro, and Manet. The love and deep respect for nature that infused the Barbizon painters could not fail to attract the sympathy of this young team which, however—like Pissarro—seems to have gained more useful lessons from Corot's studies done direct from nature. In the same way, the more specifically visual realism of Manet seems to have exerted a more direct influence on Monet and Bazille that the naturalist realism of Courbet, who was, however, closer to them emotionally.

Water Lilies
1916–19
51 ¼ × 59 ¾ in. (130 × 152 cm)
oil on canvas
Musée Marmottan
Paris, inv. 5098

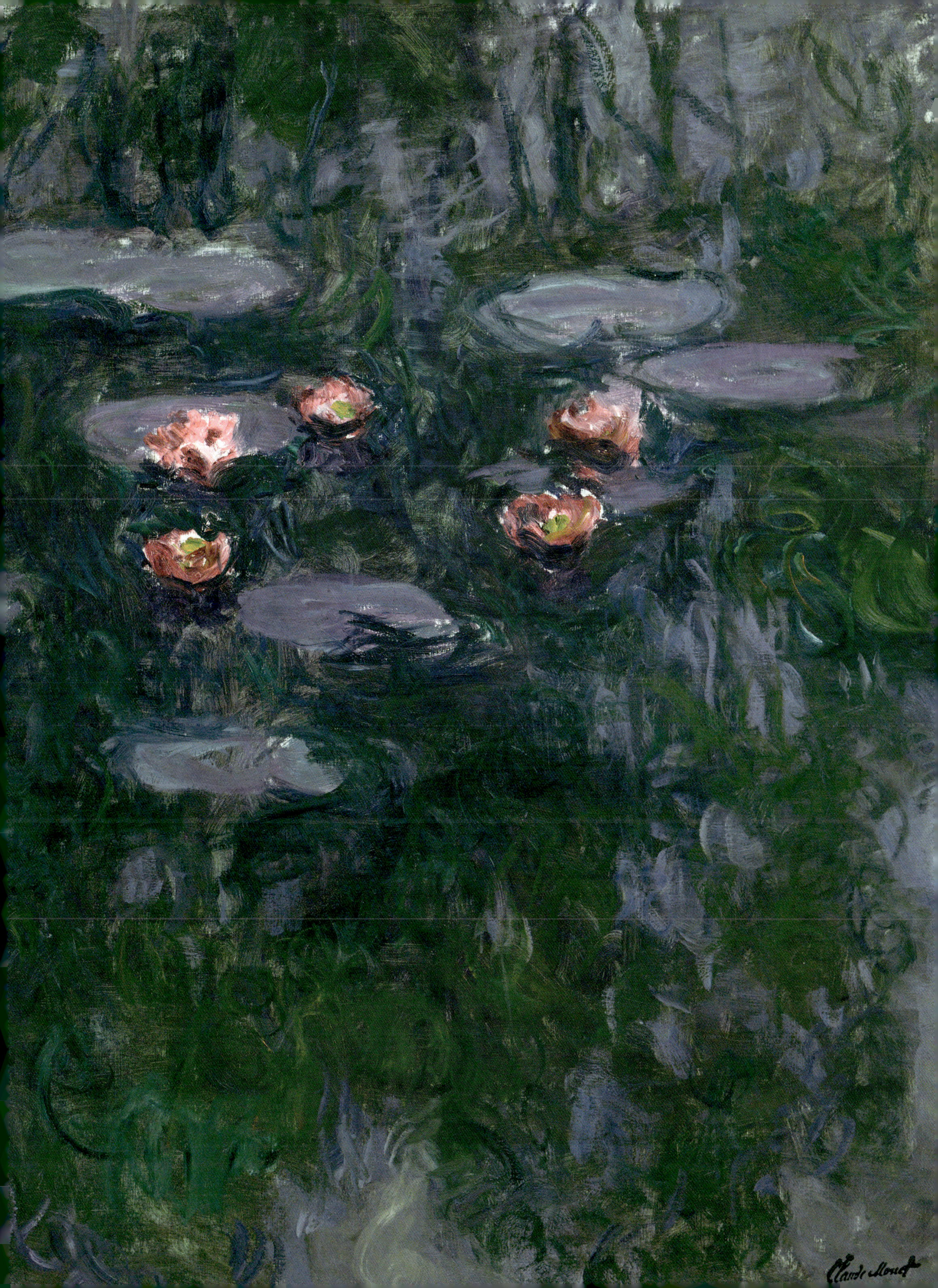
Claude Monet

In point of fact, if the subject of a painting was less significant for Manet than the pictorial realization for which it acted as a pretext, it remains that the primary imperative to produce a valid artistic creation in and by itself was associated in his mind by another, no less imperative need: that of safeguarding the integrity of the visual sensation which had served as its starting point. Succeeding in surmounting the difficulties that the reconciliation of these two, sometimes mutually exclusive goals presented, thanks to a natural faculty for visual synthesis and to the schematic handling it allowed him, Manet managed to express the initial impact of his sensation and fix it in a two-dimensional transposition by way of a diagrammatic approach fostered by his obliviousness to traditional perspective and modeling. Claude Monet and his friends were greatly impressed by this novel and personal style at the exhibition at Martinet's in April 1863, where they could see *Music in the Tuileries Gardens*, *The Spanish Ballet*, and *Lola de Valence*.

The suppression of full modeling and classic perspective, replaced by a crisp opposition between zones of shadow and zones of light, reinforces the clear colors of the plane areas untouched by the stumping typical of academic gradation. The result was a visual power, a youthfulness, a vigor that offered a dramatic contrast to the kind of painting normally seen. Manet's example had a ripple effect on the careers of Bazille and Monet whose works, such as the preparatory drawings and fragments for the large *Déjeuner sur l'herbe* ("Lunch on the Grass", 1865, Musée d'Orsay), the *Women in the Garden* (1866, Musée d'Orsay), and *The Terrace at Sainte-Adresse* (1866, Metropolitan Museum, New York) betray the division into clearly defined patches and the crisp colors juxtaposed against light and shade without gradual transition. But more profoundly, Manet's lead encouraged Claude Monet to become increasingly aware of the negative role played, without the artist even being conscious of it, by previous knowledge of the subject, a familiarity that causes him to paint what he knows is there as much if not more than what he actually sees. This dawning sense was absolutely crucial for Monet.

The vision in flat "cutout" patches was to attenuate over the following years under the influence of Boudin and Jongkind, with whom he continued to work when staying on the Normandy coast, but he endeavored to reconcile it with the search for atmospheric lightness and luminosity, as testified by the firm and schematic character of the seascapes painted in 1867 at Sainte-Adresse. The magnificent results of this compromise over the following years and in 1870 can be seen in the beach scenes at Trouville such as *Camille and Her Sister* (1870, Musée Marmottan) or the *Hôtel des Roches Noires* (1870, Collection J. Laroche). It is feasible to regard this last painting as the masterpiece of an impressionism that, by cleansing its vision of all cerebral baggage, predisposes it to attain pictorial unity through the unity of light. This was the start of all that was to follow. The various paths down which the partisans of the true impressionist spirit were to travel thereafter were little more than the exploitation—pushed to its most extreme consequences—of the potential sparked by this initial interaction.

We now know that the eye does not of itself possess the necessary and sufficient means to obtain an exact idea of its environment. To acquire one, it must appeal for aid from the other senses. In the eye of the newborn, the world presents itself as a luminous block, colorful but not easily comprehended, and it is only by using information received by other senses or faculties that a child can begin to fathom its structure. Such exploration mobilizes the psychophysical activity of the child, who thus from birth adopts the automatic, spontaneous, and quite unconscious practice of seamlessly combining the various contributions. Moreover, the child, like primitive man, is unable to produce a representation of an object simply by looking at it, and can do so only based on what is recorded in his or her memory.

As it is now second nature, this habit has led artists to halfway solutions where there is an unequal balance between vision and knowledge. For his part, Monet directed his attention toward the dogged study of the interplay of light on earth, water, and sky. Such an orientation corresponds to his temperament and personal taste, whose essence was a deep love of natural life in every form apprehensible by the human senses, but with a strong prevalence for the visual developed to the point of an obsessive, all-consuming passion. As the painter explained to Georges Clemenceau in remarks about how he found himself compelled, against every instinct, to paint a study of his young wife Camille on her deathbed: "It is the obsession, the joy, the torment of my days. To the point that one day, finding myself at the bedside of a dead woman who had been and is still dear to me, I surprised myself, my eyes fixed on the tragic temple, in the act of mechanically searching for the succession, the appropriation of the gradations of color that death had just imparted to the motionless face. Tones of blue, yellow, gray, and whatever.... I had come to that." And he concludes: "The desire to reproduce the final image of she who was about to leave us forever is quite natural. But even before the idea dawned on me to record the features to which I was so deeply attached, the organic automatism quivered initially at the shock of the color, my reflexes propelling me, despite myself, in an unconscious operation by which the daily course of my life starts off again. Like the animal turning the millstone."

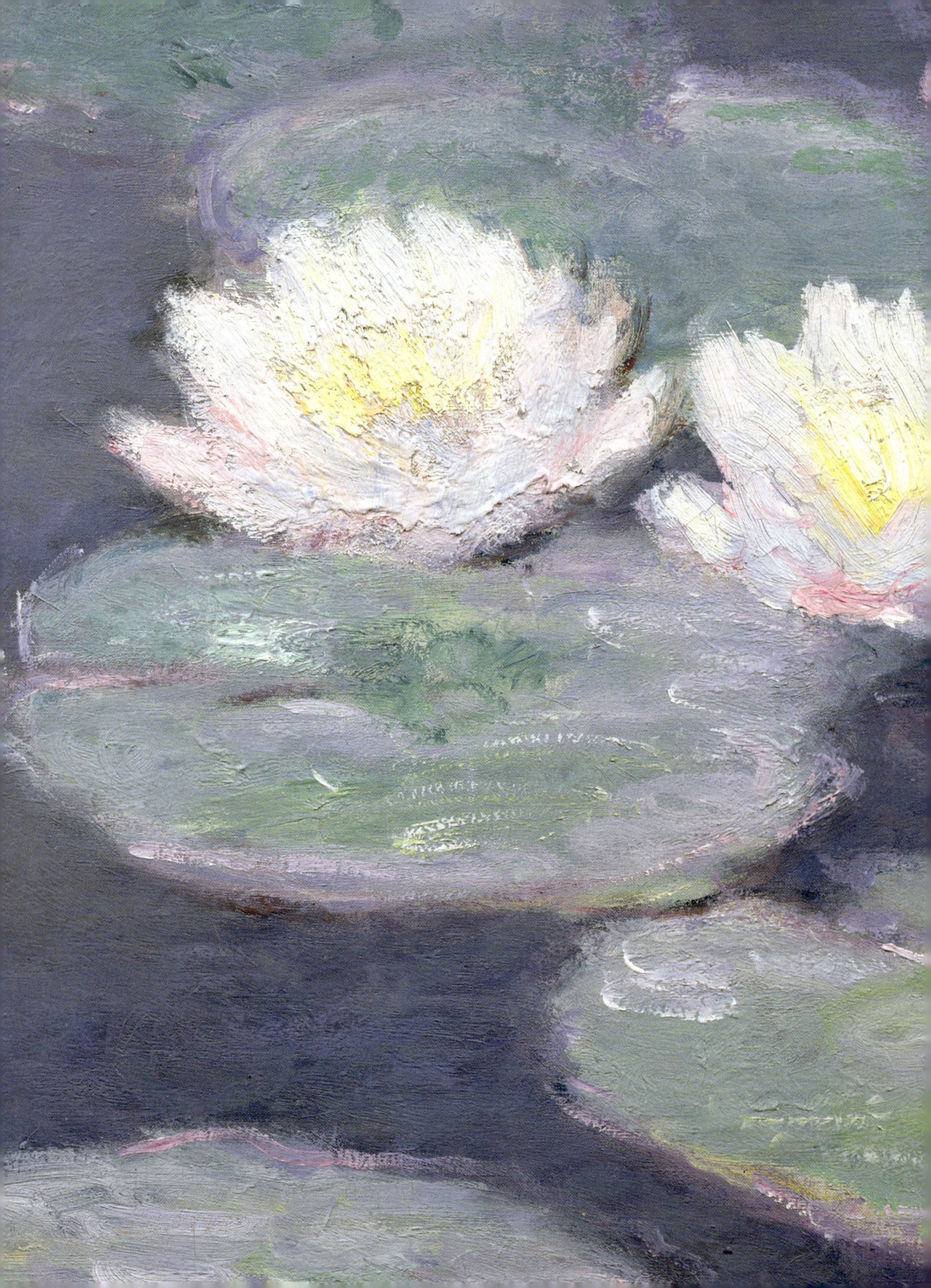

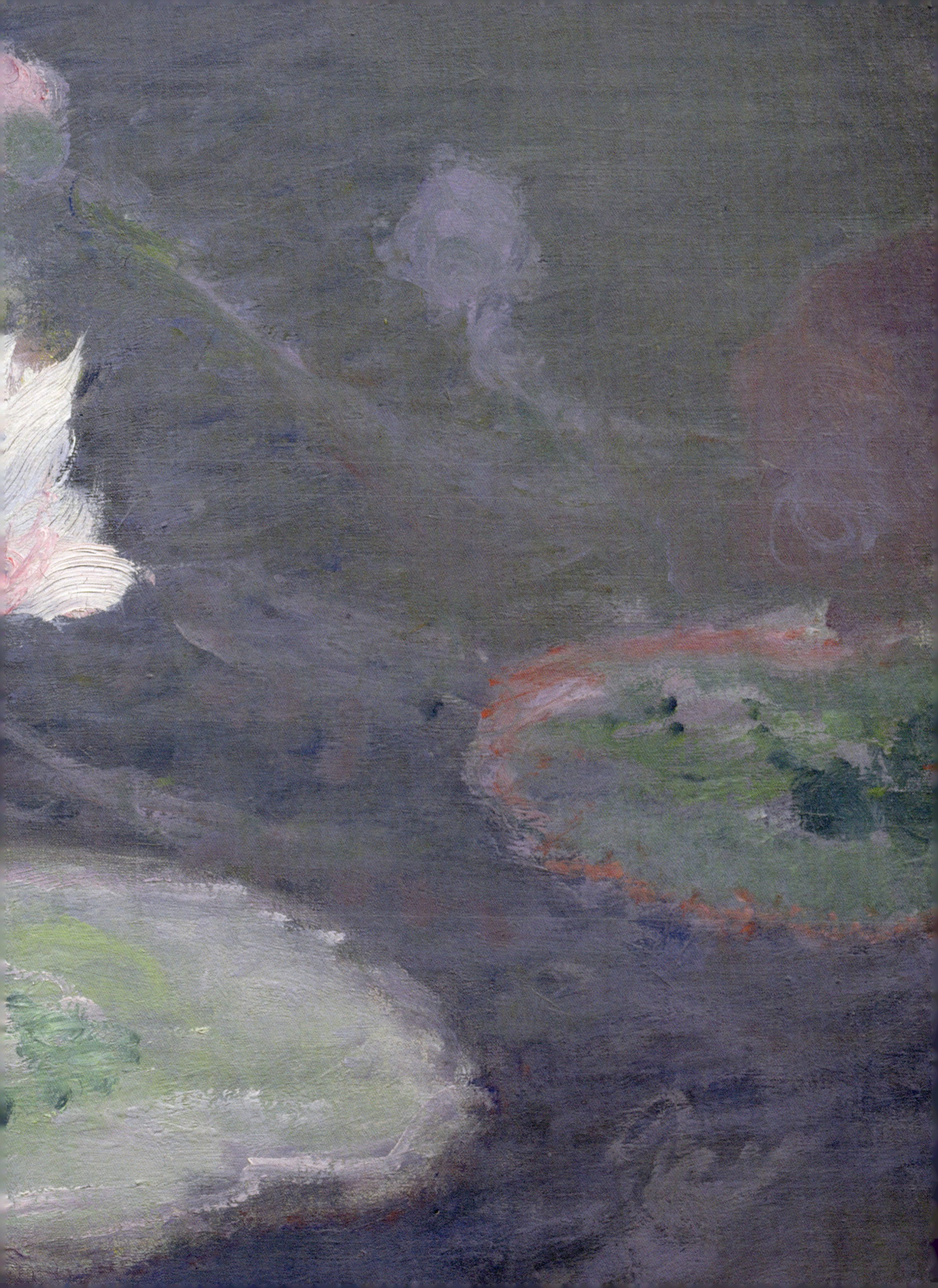

All the same, though deeply committed, Monet's visual explorations never took on a scientific bent, since he was determined to refer solely to his own sensation, unhampered by any preexistent theory or idea. Indeed, guided by his sensibility, the empiricism of this approach meant he eschewed the systematic procedures of a Seurat and the other neo-impressionists, as well as Pissarro (admittedly a temporary recruit). One must note as well Monet's liking for transitory effects and mobile or fluid factors since, without underestimating the role of the plant world, they account for the importance that the sky and the sea held in his work.

MONET AND THE PLANT WORLD

If his liking for nature was crucial for Monet, his childhood in Le Havre directed this taste towards the wide horizon of the sea rather than inland. Regarding school as a prison, he would seize every pretext to absent himself. But instead of taking long walks in the countryside when he played hooky, it was to indulge in what, as he tells us, he loved most: running along the seashore and mucking about in the water. So it was to be expected that, when he left off caricature for painting, his eye drifted instinctively out to the sea and to his immediate surroundings, a tendency naturally encouraged by the example of his elder and initiator in the art, Eugène Boudin. Only in 1863, during a stay in Gleyre's workshop with Bazille, Renoir, and Sisley, did he find himself drawn to venture into the forest of Fontainebleau and paint with his studio chums. They returned over the following years, although Monet spent most of his summers in Normandy, even dragging Bazille along with him. Originally from Montpellier, Bazille wrote to his parents in June 1864: "As soon as we arrived at Honfleur, we were on the lookout for landscape subjects. They were easy to find, because this stretch of country is paradise. There are cows and horses wandering about everywhere. The sea, or rather the wide part of the Seine, provides a delightful horizon to this deluge of greenery."

It is more than probable that the *Farmyard in Normandy* (Musée d'Orsay) dates from this time; heavy and cooped up compared to the *Bas-Bréau Road* (Musée d'Orsay), whose execution and substance are infinitely more fluid and fluent, at least in the leafage, if not the bed in the foreground, and more delicate in its discreet, green-gray color scheme, rather close to Corot. More vigorous and of greater color and value contrast are the two *Pavés de Chailly* (Musée d'Orsay), probably painted in 1865; more personal, they also stand very close to the forest backdrop in the cut-down version of *Déjeuner sur l'Herbe* in the State Hermitage Museum.

PRECEDING PAGE
Water Lilies, Evening Effect
1897–98
28 ¾ × 39 ¼ in. (73 × 100 cm)
oil on canvas
Musée Marmottan
Paris, inv. 5167

FACING PAGE
View of the Water-Lily Pond with Willow
1918–19
59 × 51 ¼ in. (150 × 130 cm)
oil on canvas
private collection

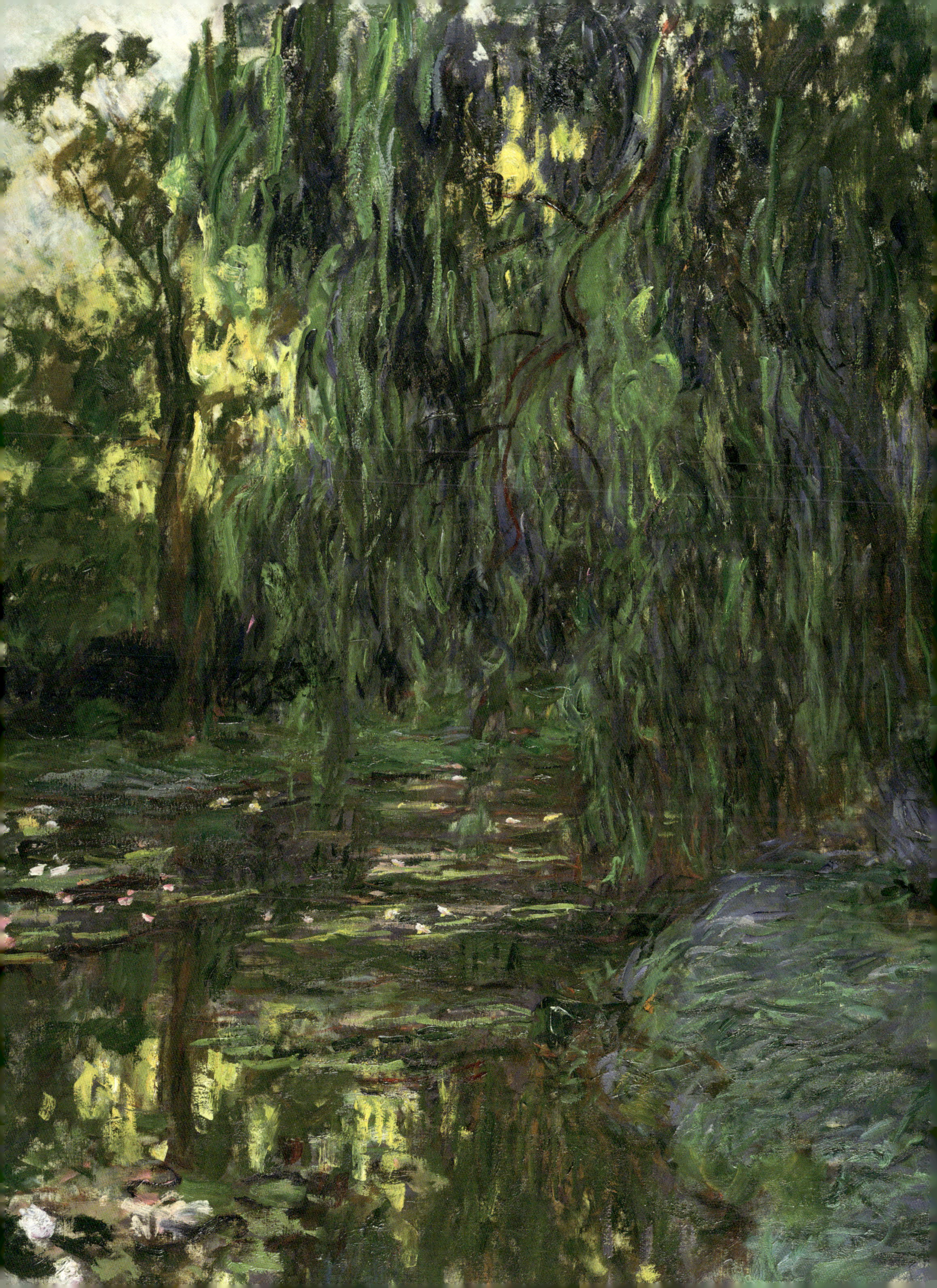

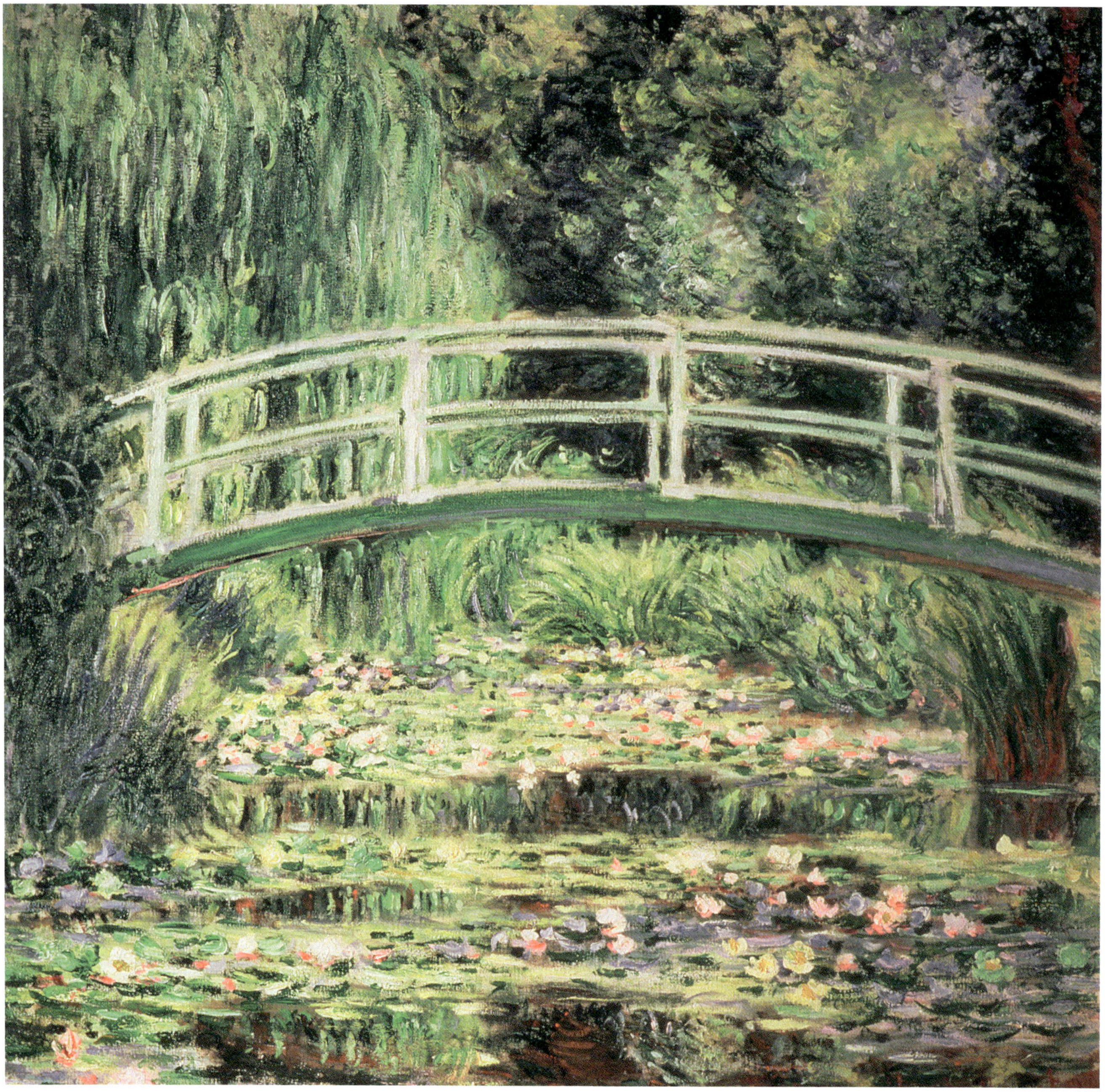

After Bazille left Honfleur in mid-July 1864, Monet joined up with Boudin and Jongkind and seems to have forsaken landscape in favor of marine painting. On the other hand, in spring 1865, from April in fact, he returned to Chailly-en-Bière to execute a project he had long cherished and which he was impatient to set in motion: a *Déjeuner sur l'herbe* of his own, but one that would go further than Manet's because the figures will be taken from a scene from contemporary life and depicted in an authentic, open-air light, instead of posing in a more or less conventional manner and lit in a compromise between exterior and studio. Unfortunately, given the vast size of the planned painting, thirteen feet by nearly twenty (four meters by six), Monet had to abandon working on it *en plein air* and resigned himself to building it up from partial, half-scale studies that had the advantage of being painted from nature. Rolled up and deposited the following winter in the unheated house at Chailly, and prey to damp, the huge canvas could not be exhibited at the Salon of 1866, and Monet was forced to cut down the intact parts he could salvage. The cut-down version at the Hermitage seems to be the work's initial stage, intended to determine the selection of the fragmentary studies that would lead on to the overall composition of the large painting. This is at least the most plausible hypothesis, in spite of the year 1866 that accompanies Monet's signature (who was not above dating and signing his works only when the time came to hang or sell them). In any event, whatever the time scheme, it is the only currently extant fragment that allows a complete idea of Monet's daring project.

He makes no effort to hide his debts to his predecessors, but a distinct personality shows through. As concerned with truth as Théodore Rousseau and the Barbizon painters, he avoids the trap of meticulously reproducing every detail, where precision in the distance betrays the atmosphere as perceived by the senses, which cannot take in near and far-off objects with identical exactitude at the same time. Monet's views are broader and breathe more air; in this they approach Daubigny, but perhaps more still Corot's smaller studies from nature, the schematic tendencies of which are not unrelated to those of Manet. Neglecting the details and condensing his vision, he treats the complex scene of the picnic as a whole, adhering to the overall distribution of the light over the foliage, the tablecloth spread out on the ground, and the seated or standing figures. The picture proceeds by patches of clear color and by value contrasts in light and shade. Monet thus obtains a remarkable unity in lighting that ensures at the same time the homogeneity of the whole picture, proof enough of his enduring fondness for vegetation and capacity to have become a marvelous painter of the forest if he had chosen such a path.

The Water-Lily Pond
1899
35×36¼ in. (89×92 cm)
oil on canvas
Pushkin State Museum of Fine Arts
Moscow, inv. 3309

If in their current state they cannot testify to the overall atmosphere of the piece, the two fragments excised from the painting and the partial half-scale study present the type of handling—in flat patches, highly colored and as if cut out and fitted in like the pieces of a puzzle—if anything to still greater effect. This characteristic manner resurfaced the following year in *Women in the Garden* (Musée d'Orsay), painted at Ville-d'Avray, this time directly in the open air, thanks to a trench into which, when the painter wanted to work on its upper reaches, the painting could be lowered by a system of ropes and pulleys. Hugely interested in this device, Courbet followed Monet's progress assiduously. In the same vein, the *Woman in the Garden* in the Hermitage is touched off with the red spots of a solid mass of flowers, which also sprout in *Garden in Flower* (Musée d'Orsay), made in 1886 or 1887, as well as in *The Terrace of Sainte-Adresse*, in which the beds in flower are also painted in this highly personal fashion which one regrets did not last longer.

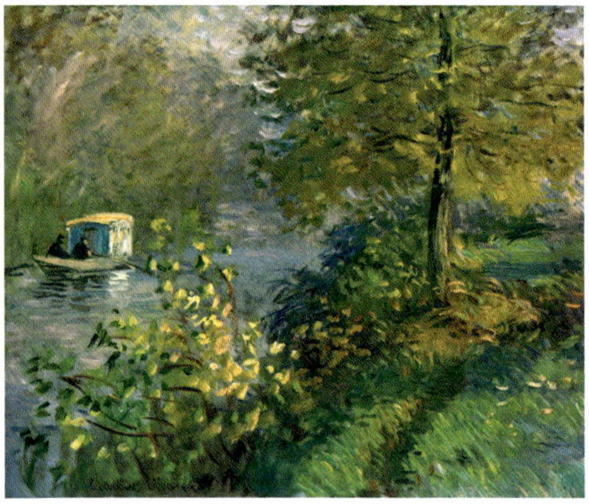

Banks of the Seine, with Monet's Studio Boat,
1874
21¼ × 25½ in. (54 × 65 cm)
oil on canvas
private collection

FACING PAGE
View of the Water-Lily Pond with Willow
1918–19
55 × 59 in. (140 × 150 cm)
oil on canvas
private collection

In effect, from 1867, when placing a *Man with a Parasol* (Kunsthaus, Zurich) in the half-shade of an undergrowth illumined by sunbeams, Monet brushes the décor in broad, free strokes, but laid rather than cut out, though the picture's relationship to Manet still remains undeniable. Thereafter, trees and plants will be little more than one element among the others, occasional or secondary, in his landscapes. Trees might occupy the foreground of *The River* of 1868 (Art Institute of Chicago) and then the middle distance of *La Grenouillère* of 1869, with the river tapering off into the distance, but they form not much more than a backdrop in the version of the same motif perpendicular to the river (Metropolitan Museum, New York). In full sun, there they are treated as a simplified mass. The curtains of trees bordering the water of the Zaan at Zaandam in 1871 and the Seine at Argenteuil from 1872 to 1877 are about the only leafy elements in Monet's landscapes at this period, whether they be various versions of *Bridge at Argenteuil* (Paul Mellon Collection, Washington; Musée d'Orsay) or *Bassin d'Argenteuil* (Musée d'Orsay).

If in Argenteuil Monet somewhat forsook trees, on the other hand he worked a great deal in the garden teeming with flowers in the house that Édouard Manet had obtained for him. There, all is different: the enclosed, limited space of this suburban garden negates distance and brings the motifs nearer, modifying both their scale and, often, their viewing angle. Enchanted particularly by the blaze of flowers in full sunlight, Monet abandons the level and blended handling of *Poppies* (Musée d'Orsay) for more a sharply divided facture of juxtaposed and superposed patches of bright colors.

Déjeuner (1872, Musée d'Orsay) and *The Artist's Garden at Argenteuil* (Art Institute, Chicago) are examples of a sequence of gardens in flower which includes a group of women with sunshades

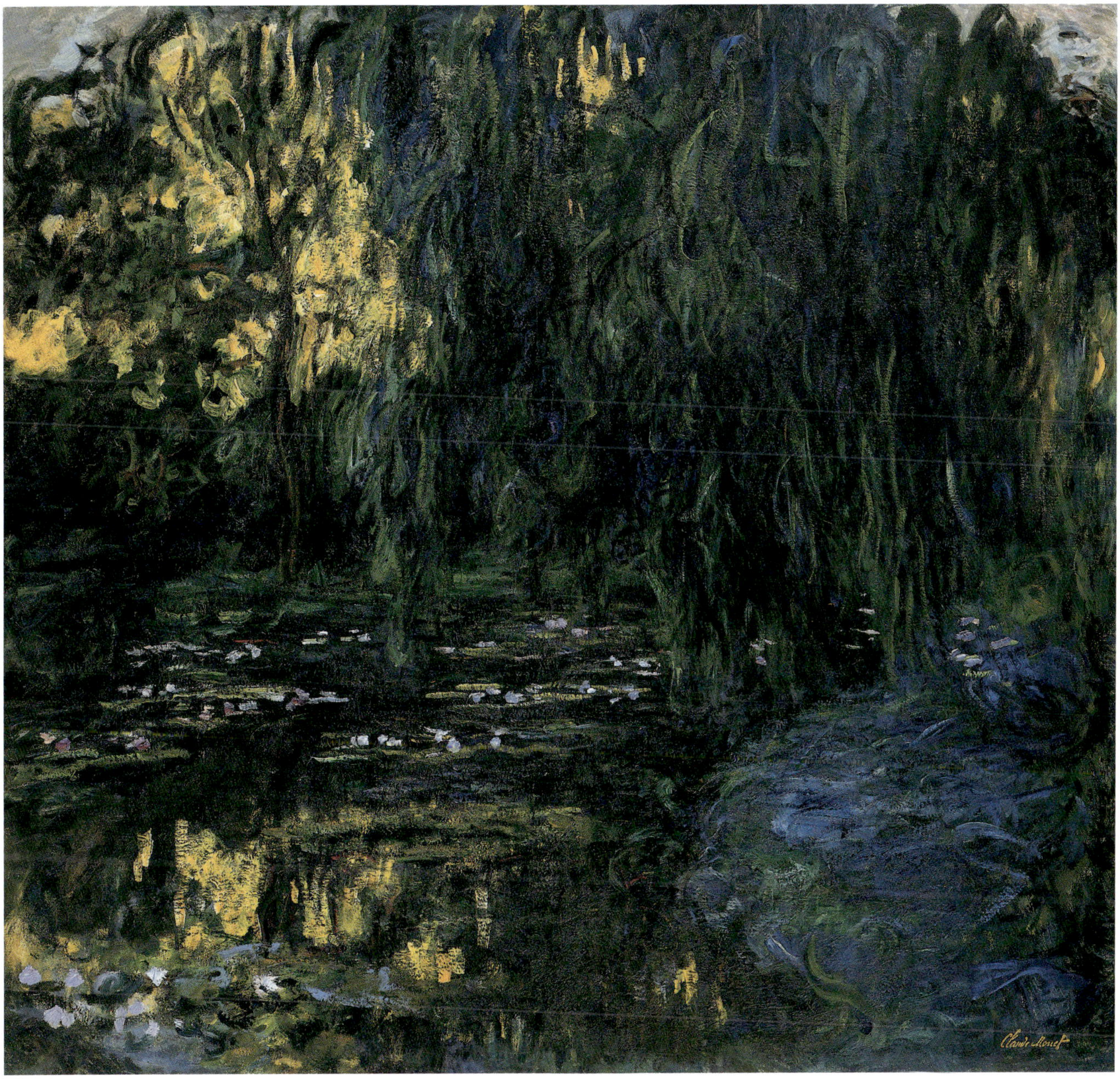
Claude Monet

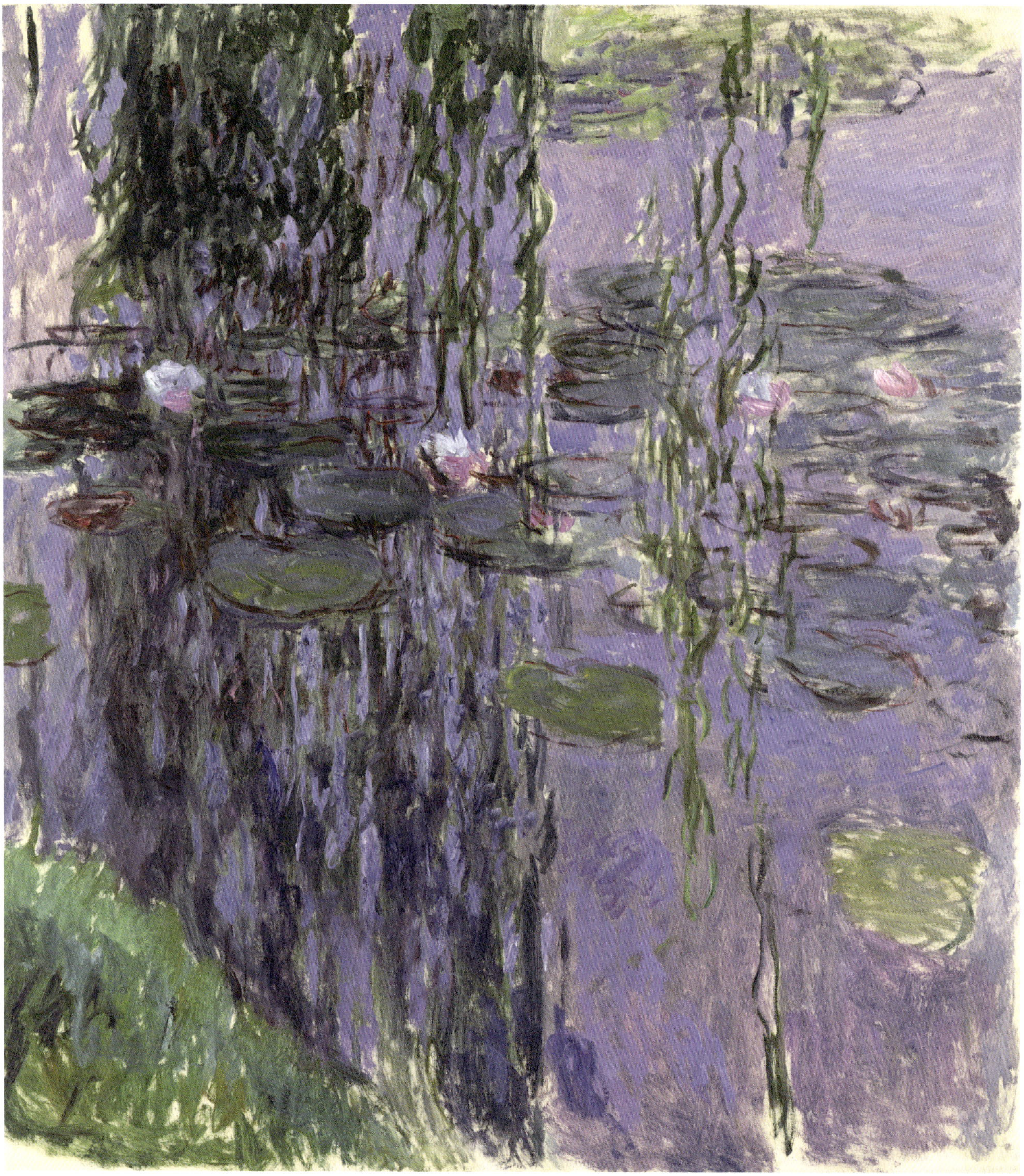

sitting in front of the house (Bührle Collection, Zurich); standing close to a solid mass of gladioli (Detroit Institute of Arts) or rose bushes; sitting reading among wild flowers (1876, David-Weill Collection) or, without sunshade, gathering flowers (1875, Národní Galerie, Prague). In this same horticultural vein, Monet started using diverse brushstrokes that are laid in without being either linked or blended. This evolution is confirmed in 1878 in views of *Parc Monceau* (Metropolitan Museum, New York; private collection, Switzerland), in which even the trees appeared treated in this manner, and its development continued during the Vétheuil period, from 1878 to 1883. Originally the preserve of certain elements, it then tended to gain ground, though without ever becoming all-encompassing or systematic.

A considerable proportion of the plant kingdom is comprised of flexible, light materials that move in the wind: his work was naturally affected by this process. Flowers in gardens, the grasses of the fields, as well as the leafy branches of trees and shrubs, thus take part in a dematerialization in which, generally, only the sky does not take any part; as, for example, in 1881 in *Poppy Field near Vétheuil* (Trüssel Collection, Bern). *The Brook* (private collection, Switzerland) from the same year which, wending its way through the grass and beneath the branches, extrapolates this vision to an exclusively vegetal backdrop. On the chalk cliffs in the Pays de Caux of the following year, the sparse vegetation is limited to grasses that share the picture's surface with the sea and sky. *The Stroll* (Art Institute of Chicago) shows how Monet renders the grass quivering in the breeze by the means of tiny strokes, applied at other times not only to grass, but also to trees and shrubs, as in *The Road at La Cavée, Pourville* (1882).

Monet discovered a very different plant world on the Mediterranean coast when, after an initial sortie in the company of Renoir at the end of 1883, he returned this time alone to work for several months, initially at Bordighera and then at Cap-Martin. Constantly adapting his manner in response to what was in front of him—that is, not only to the light and time of day, but also to the perceivable nature of the elements—he did not treat the dry, stiff vegetation of the local palms and pines in the same fashion as the bowing grasses and foliage of the shores of the English Channel or the Seine Valley. To paint the sumptuous gardens of the Italian villas of Bordighera, he leaves off the fragmented, smaller brushstrokes of Vétheuil and Pourville to take up a more varied execution, better adapted to the more structured forms of the palms, which it underlines rather than vaporizes, and he proceeded in the same manner when it came to tackling the knotty branches and stark needles of the pine trees.

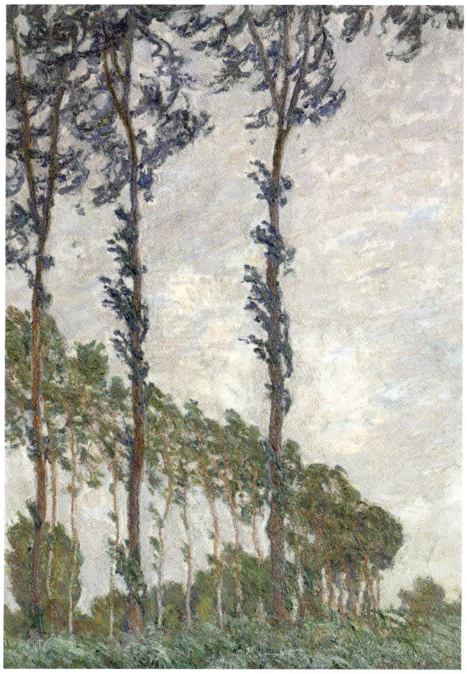

Wind Effect, Poplars Series
1891
39 ¼ × 29 in. (100 × 73.5 cm)
oil on canvas
Musée d'Orsay
Paris, inv. RF 2002-30

FACING PAGE
Water Lilies
1916–19
78 ¾ × 70 ¾ in. (200 × 180 cm)
oil on canvas
Musée Marmottan
Paris, inv. 5117

The light of the south, sometimes veiled in fine weather, can also be raw, encouraging Monet to heighten his tones. If several stands of palm in the valley of Sasso are colored blond and mauve, other isolated palms and even certain gardens are highly colored and accentuate the opposition between cold and hot tonalities, between which various species of plants progress, from the blue of the aloe leaves to the russet of their flowering stems via an entire gamut of greens and yellows. However, many of the pine forests painted at Bordighera or Cap-Martin in pink-bluish harmony are even more strident in tone, and it was probably concerning these that Monet wrote to Paul Durand-Ruel on March 11, 1884: "It'll perhaps make the enemies of blue and pink squeal a bit, because it is precisely this brightness, this fairy-like light that I am trying to render, and those who have never seen, or who do not know how to see, this stretch of country, will complain, I'm sure, of its improbability, though I have in fact underdone the tone: everything is dapple-gray and punch flame."

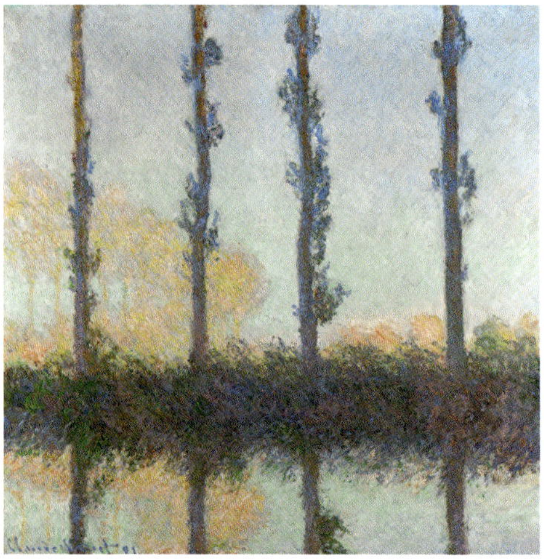

The Four Trees,
1891
32 ¼ × 32 in. (82 × 81.5 cm)
oil on canvas
Mrs H. O. Havemeyer Collection
Metropolitan Museum of Art
New York, inv. 29.100.110

FACING PAGE
Weeping Willow and Water-Lily Pond
1916-19
78 ¾ × 70 ¾ in. (200 × 180 cm)
oil on canvas
Musée Marmottan
Paris, inv. 5125

This chromatic increase in relation to plants continued over the following years: in summer 1885, in the exuberant red of a poppy field close to Giverny at the bottom of a small enclosed valley (Museum of Fine Arts, Boston); then in spring 1886, in Holland, with a succession of tulip fields of a no less explosive red that one can see at the Musée d'Orsay. This poppy red was not attacked again before 1890, when it provides the foreground for the several versions of oat fields painted in various lights. The midground is occupied by the golden yellow of the field itself, framed on the right and wedged in at the bottom by a green wood that leaves a gap on the left leading to the valley; the farther slope of this underlines by its brighter hue the sky's soft blue. An execution adapted to the diverse elements is tempered by a wispiness that confers homogeneity on a landscape typical of the Île-de-France countryside in its harmony of color, its balanced masses, and the peaceful, sun-drenched gaiety of a summer's day.

Monet's passionate concern with the study of light led him to examine each of its variations and effects on the components of a landscape in changing weather conditions, during the course of the seasons, and at different hours of the day. He thus strove to demonstrate to his own and others' satisfaction that the way in which these elements appear to our eyes is due as much to the light they receive as to their own identity. After the theme of the poppies, he tackled the poplars lining the Epte, which attracted his attention due to the contrast between their vertical trunks and the horizontal stretch of the meadow. Several essays in composition, with the curtain of trees seen either front-on or in a row, with or without water in the foreground, resulted in a viewpoint that harmoniously combines horizontals, verticals, and spirals, employing the meandering

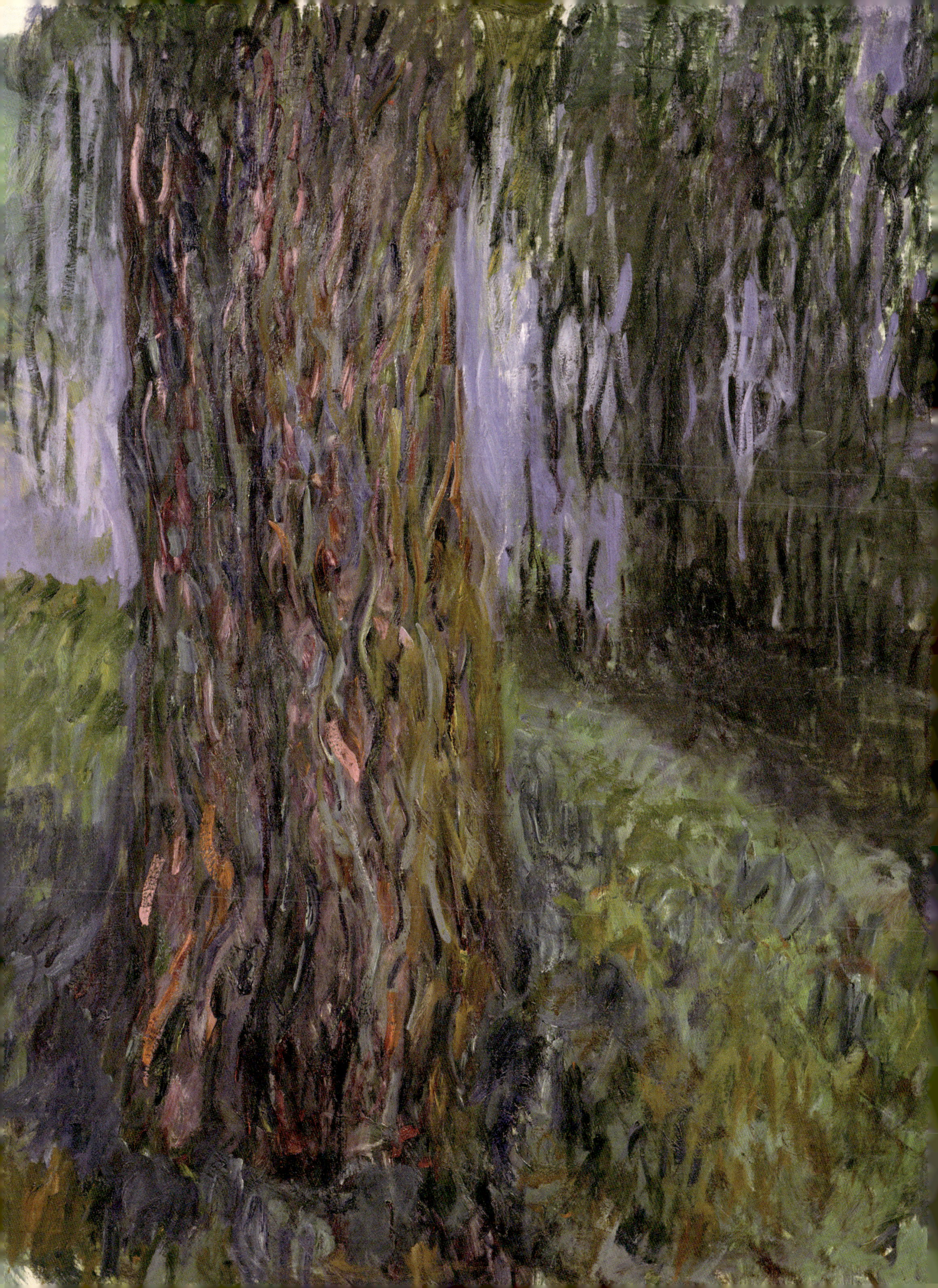

course of the river as a foil that is echoed in the leafy crowns of the poplars that peter off into a zigzag oblique. This motif provides different effects according to the varying color of the leaves in spring, summer, and autumn, but also in the changing light of morning, midday, and evening. Monet persisted with this method in a series of *Haystacks*: he would carry a batch of canvases to his subject, each to be used only during one particular light effect, swapping it for another as this effect disappeared. This optical recording of light was to be systematized still further when he tackled the façade of Rouen cathedral.

Apart from such series, Monet found time to paint various facets of the countryside around Giverny, in which the plant life of the meadows, fields, hedges, and thickets occupies a preeminent place, even when enlivened with figures of girls clothed in bright colors. After 1900, however, he was to work above all on the two gardens that he himself had designed and continued improving with unstinting passion.

SKY AND ATMOSPHERE

If the wash watercolor skies produced by Jongkind appear mobile and transparent, it has to be conceded that the skies in his oil paintings are infinitely less so. Similarly, and just as legitimately, one might advance that Boudin did not attain in his paintings the same effervescence, the same lightness as in the innumerable pastel studies that Baudelaire rightly hailed. This did nothing to prevent him appearing as the "king of skies," as Corot dubbed him, because of both their luminosity and remarkable veracity. It is rather hard to determine exactly the influence of either master on Monet in this particular respect, but it remains undeniable that, in combination, their impact was critical.

Monet did not start competing with his elders in this specialty overnight. His painting of the *Jetty at Honfleur* of 1864 (which at the 1865 Salon was the object of a confusion of his name with Manet's, who was incandescent to see himself being finally and for the first time being feted by press and public alike for a work that was not by him!) was apparently painted under the auspices of Jongkind rather than of Boudin. Its surface is two-thirds occupied by a sky, which was patently Monet's principal concern and on which he lavished the greatest care. The meteorological effect of a sky laden with low clouds, where only a few zones receive the rays of the sun and contrast with those which remain unlit, is partly the cause of the absence of the lightness that the atmosphere usually imparts, but it derives

Water Lilies
1914–17
51¼ × 59 in. (130 × 150 cm)
oil on canvas
Musée Marmottan
Paris, inv. 5085

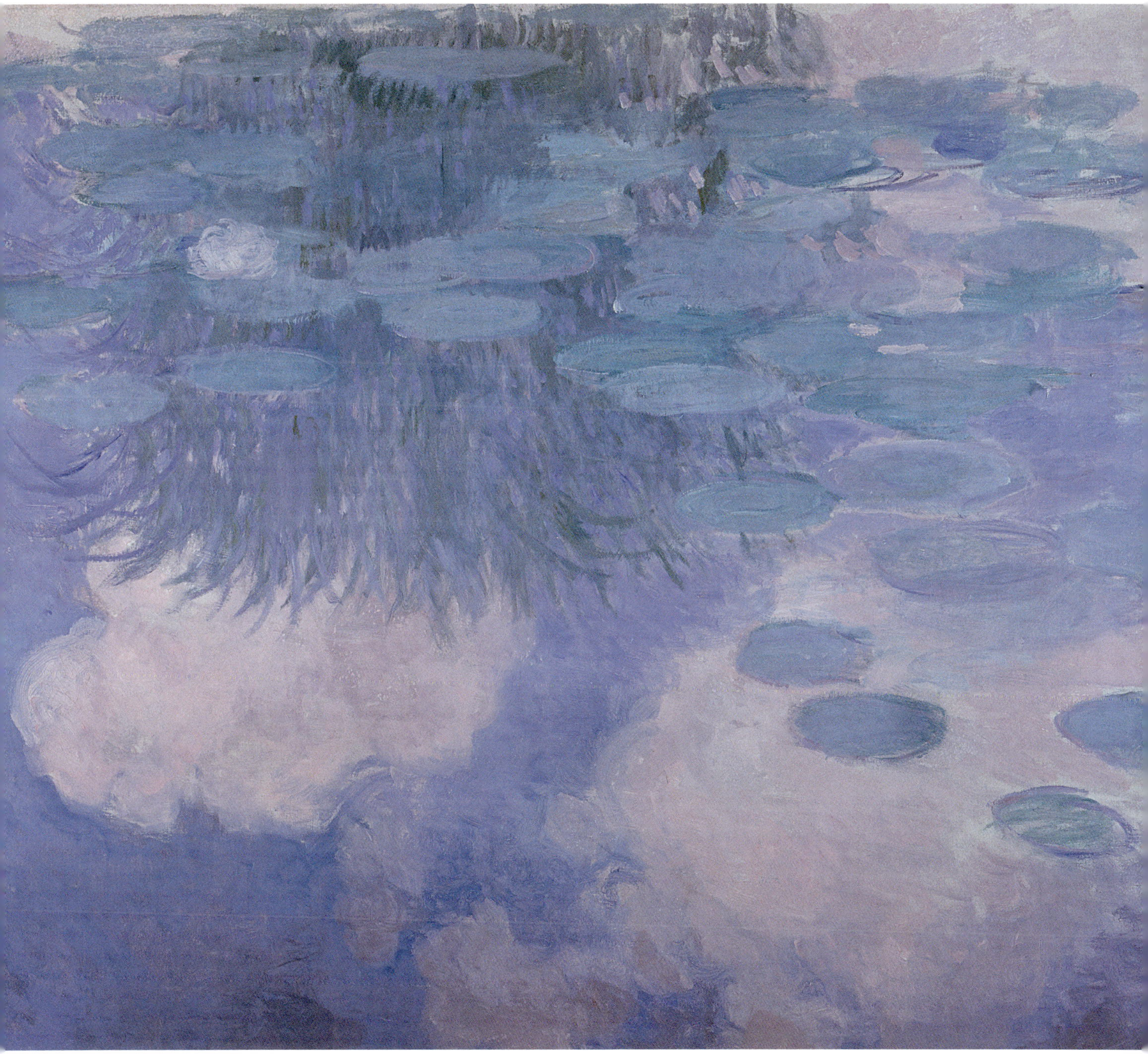

equally from the vigorous and almost brutal facture that is close to Jongkind's oils. The same motif recurred the following year under the title *Mouth of the Seine at Honfleur*, which demonstrates a lighter handling, confirmed in 1866 and 1867 in the skies in the views of Paris and the beaches of Sainte-Adresse. While respecting the characteristics of the various cloud systems, their density, previously a touch forced, is gradually attenuated. Thus Monet, little by little, attained the mobility and the airy lightness of the luminous skies of his Trouville beach views of 1870.

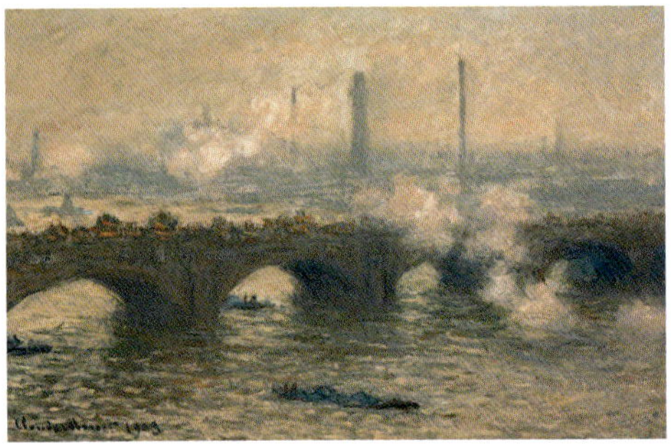

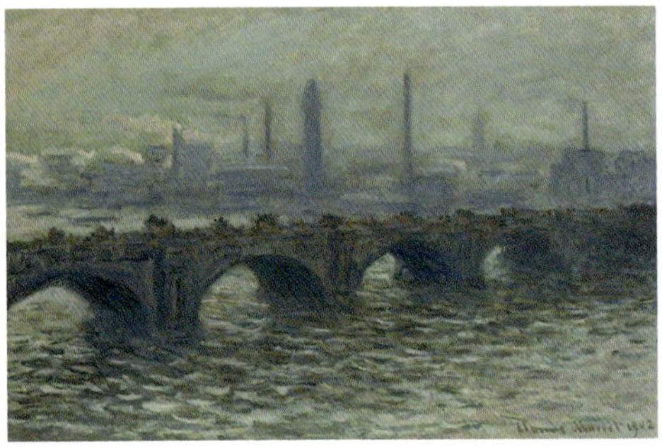

Waterloo Bridge, Gray Day
1903
25 ½ × 39 ¼ in. (65 × 100 cm)
oil on canvas
National Gallery of Art
Washington, inv. 1847

Waterloo Bridge, Foggy Morning
1902
25 ½ × 39 ¼ in. (65 × 100 cm)
oil on canvas
Hamburger Kunsthalle
Hamburg, inv. 1305

FACING PAGE
The Water-Lily Pond, Clouds
1915–26
triptych: each panel 78 ¾ × 167 ¼ in.
(200 × 425 cm)
oil on canvas
Musée de l'Orangerie
Paris, inv. 20100

This fertile period of work ground to a halt with the Franco-Prussian War and the initial defeat of France, when Monet had to flee to England. There he made do with the misty skies of an autumn and winter in London, whose diffuse and veiled light behind the layers of smoke and fog he well knew how to capture.

On his way back from London he traveled through Holland where he stayed in 1871, returning in 1872 and tackling skies whose cloud conditions also varied according to time and season. A splendid example, *View of Zaandam*, with its blue sky strewn with large, sun-drenched white foam, is in the Musée d'Orsay.

That the adjective "impressionist"—with which some sarcastic naysayer baptized the much-scorned art movement launched by Monet—derived from the title *Impression*, given to one of the pictures presented by him at the first exhibition of the group in 1874, was no accident. Indeed, the word does capture the artist's intention, of which the picture thus designated was a characteristic example. Painted in 1872, in it Monet affirmed his desire less to come up with a representation of a view of the port of Le Havre than to express the visual sensation perceived at a given time, in a given atmosphere, and under specific and fleeting lighting conditions. The individual nature of the boats, cranes, and other machines of the harbor tends to vanish in a layer of air materialized by its water-vapor content. Monet exploits this weather phenomenon to distill the entire subject in an atmospheric effect of translucency dappled by sunlight gently veiled in the fog.

Forsaking Normandy, Monet long found a regular source of inspiration in the Seine Valley. He settled initially, in 1871, at Argenteuil, remaining there for six years. This period at Argenteuil was purely focused on the study of water, though this is always associated with other natural elements, together composing a whole. Naturally, the sky continues to find its place, and is often amplified by its being reflected in the river. Never, as is to be expected, occupying the near totality of the picture surface as it does in the Sainte-Adresse marines, nor does the sky here present the ever-varying face of a seascape. It generally appears typical of the Île-de-France on a fine day, characterized by great white plumes of the cumulus in suspension

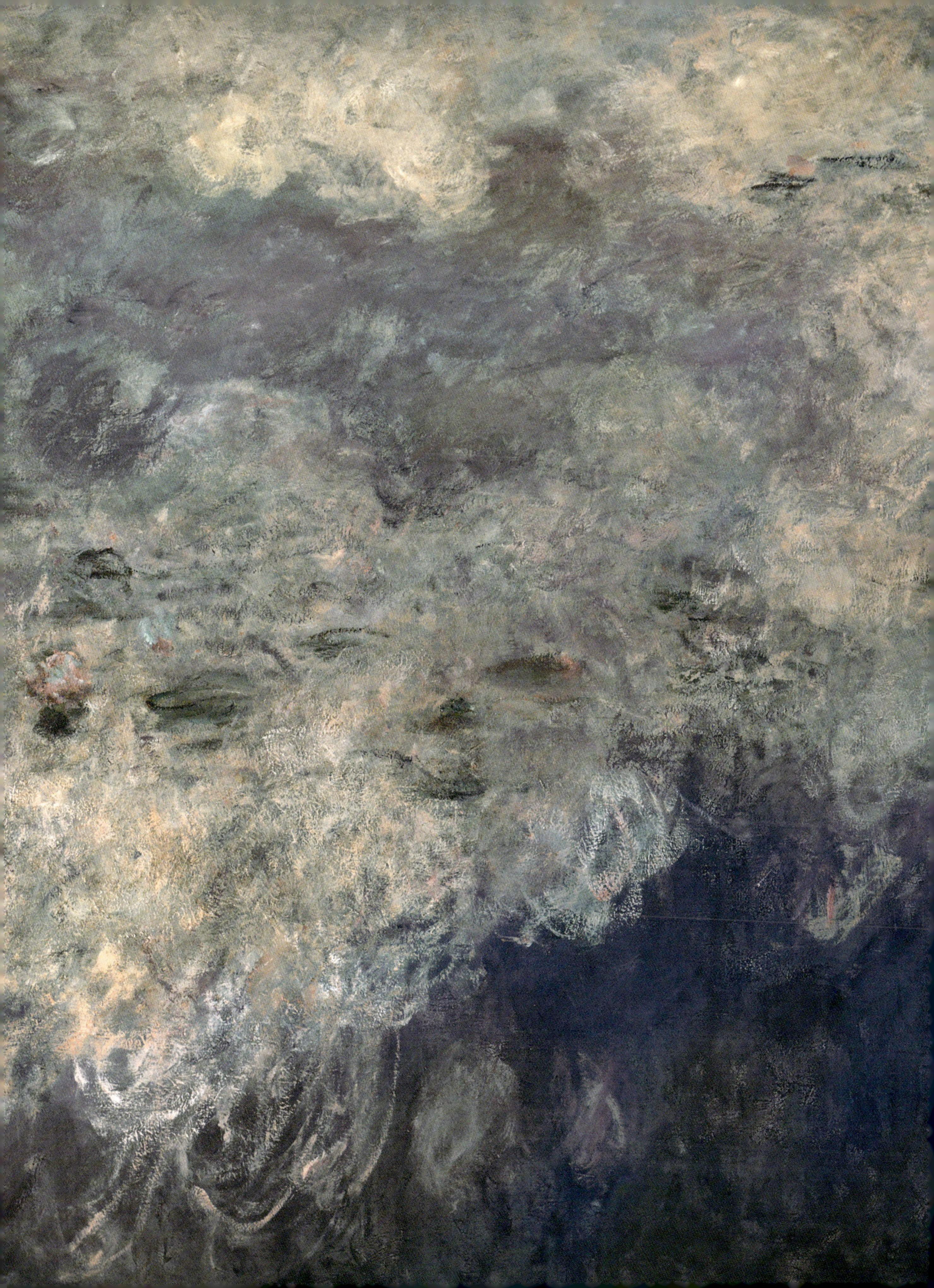

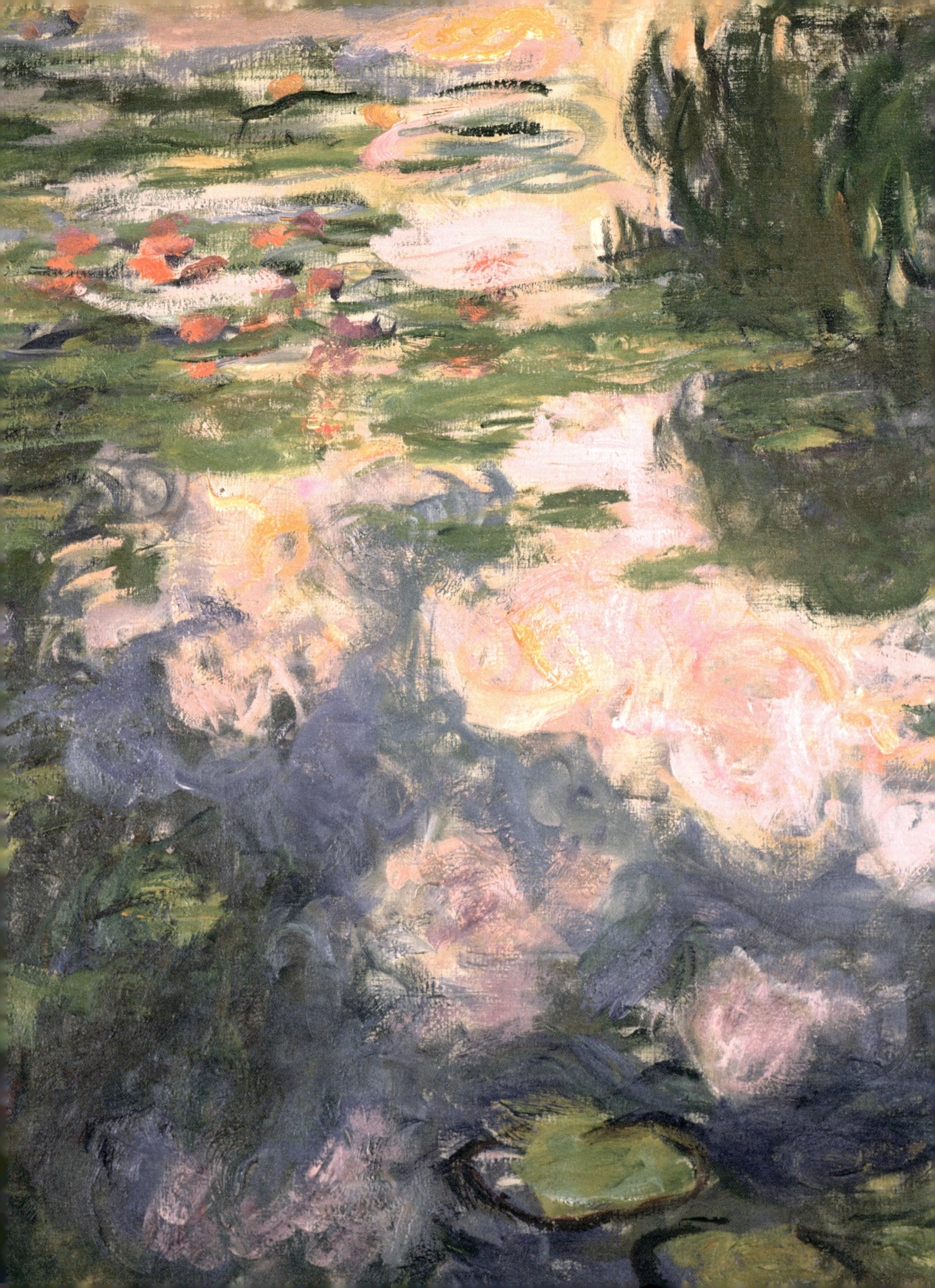

standing out against a blue ground, as in *Bridge at Argenteuil* (1874, Musée d'Orsay) and *The Pool at Argenteuil* (1875, Musée d'Orsay), clouds that Monet treats in a rich, buttery paste that remains smooth in spite of the brush bending as the white is applied. Ceaselessly varying his handling in response to circumstance and adapting it to the effects he desires to render, Monet tackles a regatta at Argenteuil in gray weather (1874, Musée d'Orsay) very differently. Here the sky is treated in brushstrokes of blue and white laid very freely over the gray-white ground of the canvas, with unstable and choppy results. On the other hand, to catch the slightly veiled and diffuse light effect of *Poppies* (1873, Musée d'Orsay), Monet delicately blends in the brushwork (something more often seen in Renoir's work), softening his execution and attenuating the contrasts in a sky that remains nonetheless luminous in spite of its airy wrapping.

It is not illogical to include the artificial clouds of locomotive steam and smoke on which Monet focused particularly in 1876–77 under the heading of atmosphere. Painting *The Train in the Snow* (Musée Marmottan) in the winter of 1875, he had already glimpsed how to utilize the dark gray plume that detaches from the snowy sky only to meld into it, dissolving as it progressively rises. In 1876–77, the same phenomenon provided him with an opportunity to study the more complex and varied ways light fell on and through the spirals of smoke rising from locomotives shunting or standing at the platforms in the Gare Saint-Lazare in Paris. Transparent or opaque, clear or dark in hue, and warmer or chillier than the sky, depending on the light (as Leonardo da Vinci had already observed), to Monet's subtle eye these columns fanning out into enormous capitals and then into large clumps offered an inexhaustible source for observation. Thus, though framed identically, the two views of the station platforms differ as to lighting. The one in the Fogg Art Museum, treated in a generally bluish tonality, presents few contrasts between the roofed and unroofed zones. A sunnier variant in the Musée d'Orsay presents a more marked opposition between the blue smoke untouched by the sun and the white fumes and the rosy clouds outside which are bathed in a warmer glow. This sky, like the rest of the picture, is painted in an opulent and well-worked impasto, thickened by superposed brushstrokes that bestow a certain roughness.

In 1878, obliged to leave Argenteuil, Monet moved to Vétheuil, a village built at a bend in the Seine. His four-year stay there was punctuated, especially toward the end, by forays to the Normandy coast. It was at Vétheuil that the decisive step of dividing up the brushwork so as to express the vibrant halo of

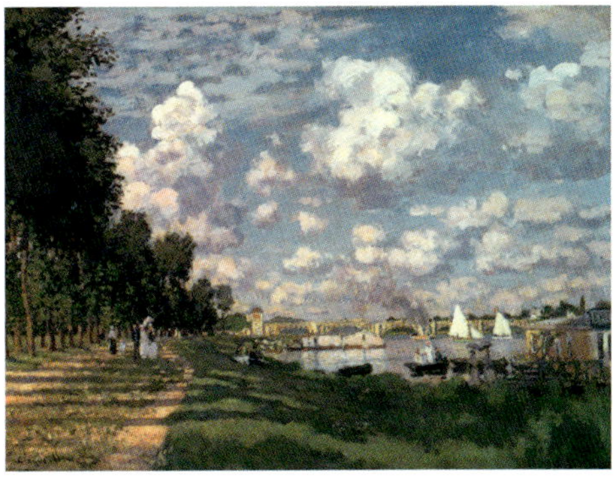

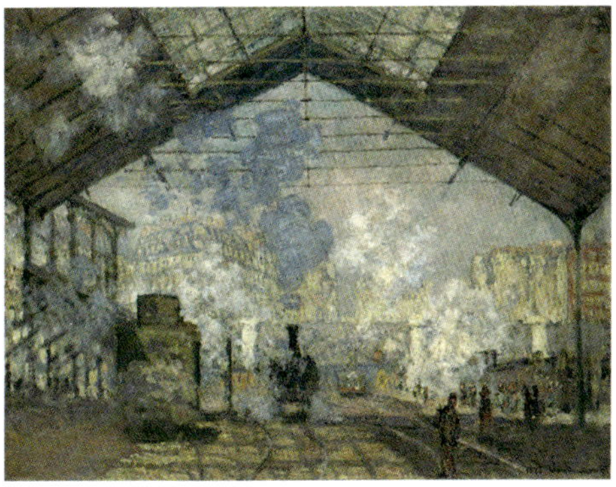

The Pool at Argenteuil
1875
23½ × 31½ in. (60 × 80 cm)
oil on canvas
Musée d'Orsay
Paris

La Gare Saint-Lazare
1877
29¾ × 41 in. (75.5 x 104 cm)
oil on canvas
Musée d'Orsay
Paris, inv. RF 2775

FACING PAGE
The Water-Lily Pond
1917–19
39¼ × 78¾ in. (100 × 200 cm)
oil on canvas
private collection

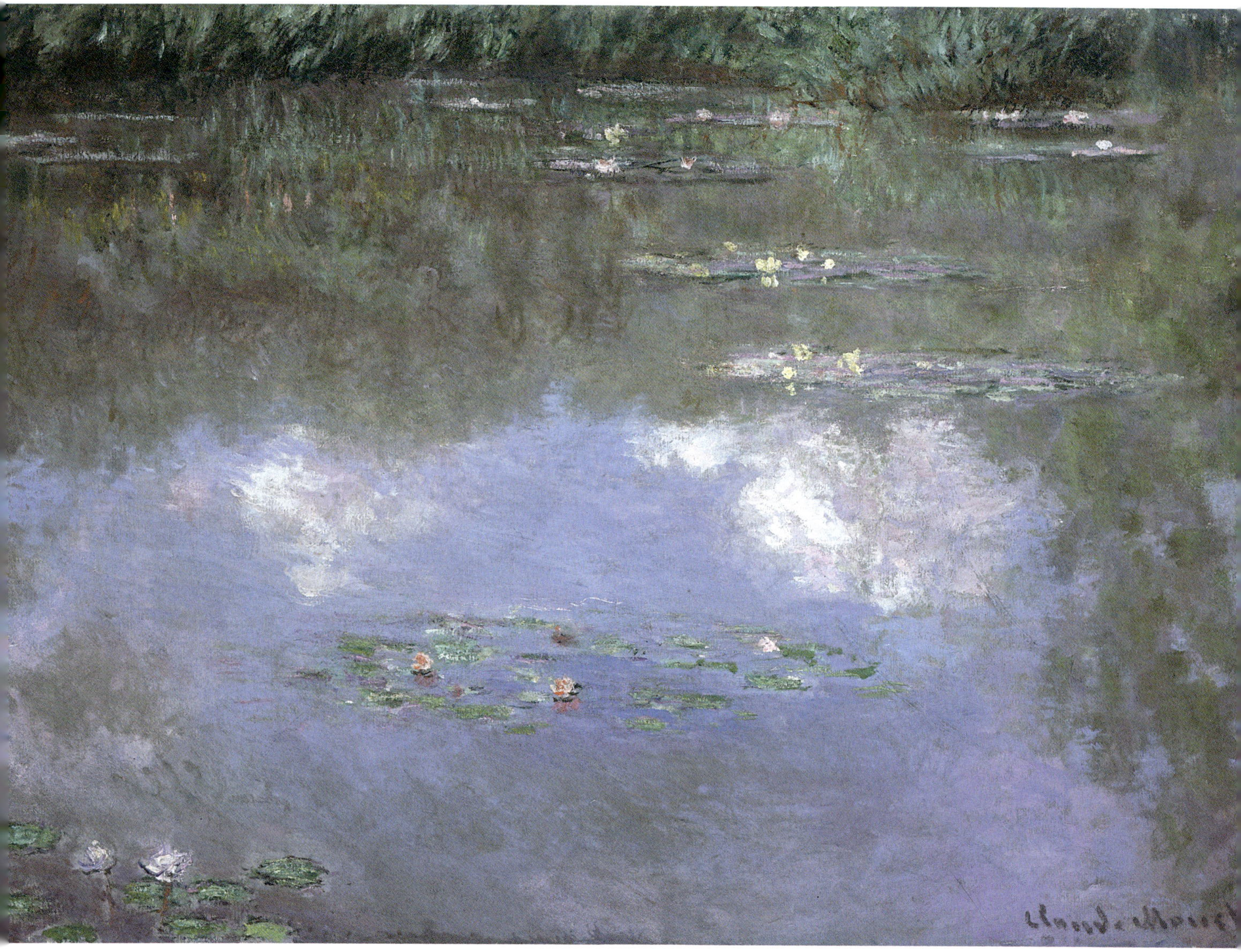

atmospheric light on terrestrial elements was confirmed. But if the clouds are sometimes affected by this treatment, the ethereal vault itself escapes it, the blue color extending in a single layer or else, exceptionally, in broad strokes very different from the broken handling deployed in the rest of the picture. All in all, the skies of Vétheuil are cloudier than those of Argenteuil. Leaving aside the relatively uniform, low and closed-off skies of snowy days, diverse types of clouds make their way through in the valley corridor, dragged, elongated, or shredded by the wind, unless they gather and build up in great round masses. In the first case, the brushwork tends to lengthen horizontally, whereas, in the second, it tends to curve to underline the shape of the clouds. In both, however, the strokes exhibit great freedom and flexibility, in a unified facture at odds with the more compartmentalized approach in the remainder of the painting. That is tangible in works such as *Vétheuil* (1880) from the Osborn Bequest in the Metropolitan Museum, New York.

It is not impossible that the rigors of the winters of 1880 and 1881 had their impact on Monet's evolution due to the particular, freezing light that a hard frost prolonged by sunny skies can communicate to the atmosphere and to nature, as visible in several winter works from Vétheuil such as *Sunbeams and Snow* (National Gallery, London) or *Hoarfrost* (Musée d'Orsay). Shimmering in a bluish or pinkish white, the light is also characterized by the way it spreads everywhere, thereby tending to neutralize the shadows. However, it is from the Vétheuil years that the vision of Monet begins to veer decisively towards an attenuation of the contrast between shade and light. Although he did not actually employ it in the pictures mentioned above, the divided brushwork that he increasingly adopted at that time corresponds to this conception of an all-pervasive light that seeps into everything, even shadow. It seems then at least conceivable that it was in order to capture this diffuse atmospheric illumination that Monet extended it to the series of cliffs in the Pays de Caux painted in 1882. But even there the sky continues to be exception, painted in uninhibited strokes, but laid out in a fluid and light way. This special treatment of the sky, upheld in the Étretat and Belle-Île works, shows how Monet refused to apply any system crudely or uniformly, and that he remained faithful above all to sensation.

Once before, in Argenteuil in 1875, Monet had been tempted by the idea of a female silhouette carrying a sunshade standing out against the sky. Posing his wife and son at the top of a sloping meadow, he positioned himself farther down, viewing them thus from below. The result was a masterpiece. Eleven years later, he approached the same theme in two versions, with his daughter-in-law Suzanne

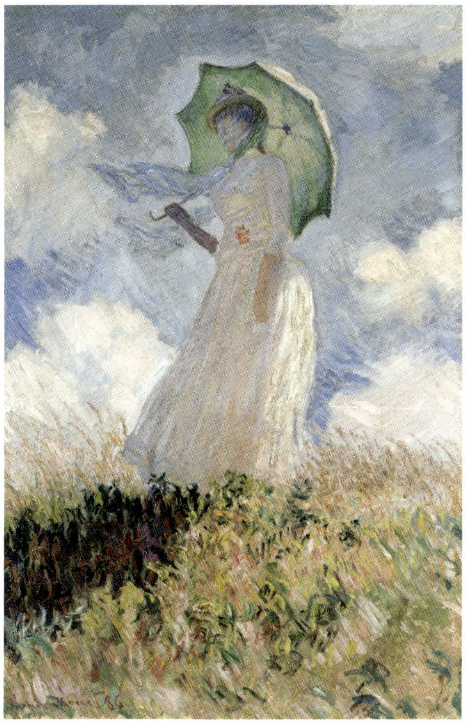

Study of a Figure Outdoors, Woman with a Parasol Turning to the Left
1886
51½ in. × 34¾ in. (131 × 88 cm)
oil on canvas
Musée d'Orsay
Paris, inv. RF 2621

Water Lilies, Water Landscape, the Clouds
1903
28¾ in. × 39¼ in. (73 × 100 cm)
oil on canvas
private collection

Hoschedé as the model and the slope over of Giverny as the pedestal, the grass treated in broad visible strokes, whereas the method used for the woman and the sky is more blended and layered and, with regard to the sky, of airy buoyancy. While *Woman with a Sunshade* is the chosen title for both these pictures, the sky is almost as significant an element. However, the true subject lies in the sea of air and light in which the whole piece bathes.

In the Giverny country views, the sky continues to contribute to the brightness of the pieces, but is sometimes undermined by the trees that mask it, or the masses of flowers that tend to lessen its importance as the eye is drawn to them. Not before the ponds of the *Water Lilies*, where the sky is reflected in water, will it regain a key role.

WATER AND ITS REFLECTIONS

Even if it expresses an unconscious attachment to the mother whose symbol it is, Monet's extraordinary partiality to water cannot be dissociated from his all-embracing love for nature in all its various forms—a fact to which the same symbolic value applies. That as a painter Monet was interested less in water itself than in the images it reflects in its mirror-like surface did not mean that he was fond of it solely as an artist and not as a man. Indeed, if Monet is both a painter and as a visual a creature as it is possible to be, these dispositions did not force him to scrutinize every object with the same intensity. Utterly intent on painting whatever afforded him visual pleasure, his oeuvre is a lengthy exposition of his adoration of the world around him and of life.

The Water-Lily Pond
1917–19
51¼ × 78¾ in. (130 × 200 cm)
oil on canvas
Folkwang Museum
Essen, inv. 343

His childhood in Le Havre aroused and developed his fondness for the sea, and his earliest works, painted in the company of Boudin and Jongkind, directed this taste to the more strictly pictorial domain. His seas follow approximately the same evolutionary curve as his skies, but with differences derived from the respective natures of these two elements. Weighed down by a certain heaviness and an unquestionable opacity in 1864 in the *Jetty at Honfleur*, over the years the waters acquire a lightness and transparency which, in 1866, the sea in *Terrace at Sainte-Adresse* still lacked. It was only rather suddenly in 1867 that the sea appeared more fluid in the many beach scenes then carried out at Sainte-Adresse, such as the one in the Coburn Collection of the Art Institute of Chicago. The shadows of the sailing ships are cut out in schematic patches, which block off the reflection of a sky that lightens the surface of water that is itself layered in the style of Manet, making

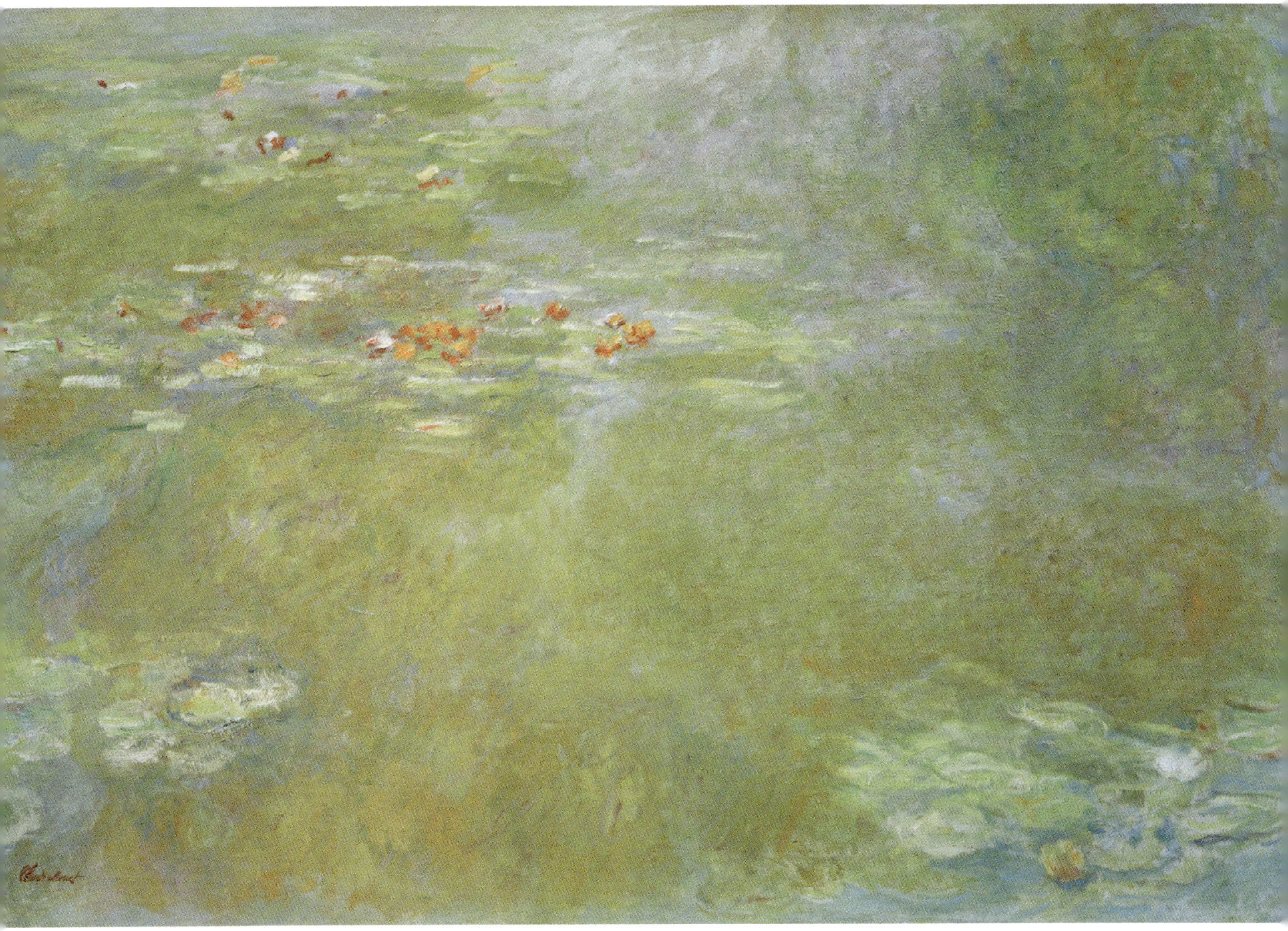

it shine. This fluent manner is confirmed over the following years, right up to the beaches, landing stages, and pools of the port of Trouville in 1870.

Yet previously, in *The River* (Art Institute, Chicago) in 1868, the first work in which he assigns primacy to an image reflected on water, Monet had shown an interest in the fresh variety. Tranquil and almost flat calm, the river reflects an inverted image of the sky and the hill, scarcely deformed by the inevitable but almost imperceptible oscillation of the mass of liquid, which is, however, enough to strip it of all stolid materiality, and create an ill-defined counterpart in which objects are deprived of their precise characteristics. All identity disappears when the wind stirs up the water or wrinkles the surface.

In the view of the bathing spot at *La Grenouillère* (Metropolitan Museum, New York), painted with Renoir at Bougival in summer 1869, it is simply the splashing of the bathers and rowers that breaks the waters into a thousand facets that gleam in the sun and shatter the reflections. Monet expresses this effect in broad, horizontally juxtaposed strokes, detached rather than connected, which exploit the contrasts between those that reflect the light back to the viewer's eye and those that allow it to penetrate the liquid mass.

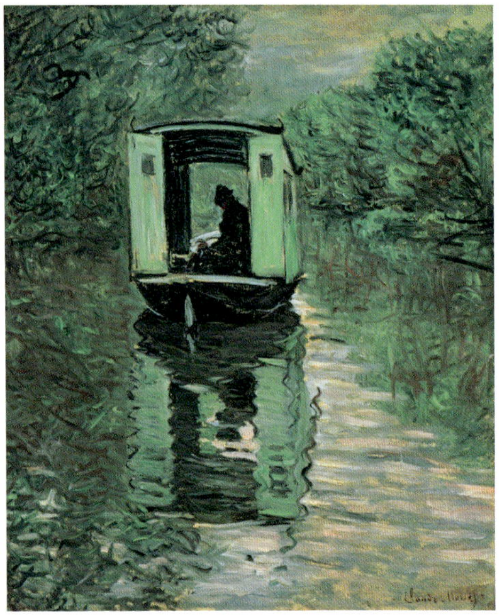

The Studio Boat on the Seine
1876
28 ¼ × 23 ½ in. (72 × 59.8 cm)
oil on canvas
Barnes Foundation
Merion (Pennsylvania), inv. BF730

FACING PAGE
Water Lilies
1904
35 × 36 ¼ in. (89 × 92 cm)
oil on canvas
Denver Art Museum
inv. 4/1935.14

In 1871–72, the generally calm water of the Dutch canals presented Monet with the opportunity to revert, in several canvases of windmills whose image is reflected on the surface of the water, to the more layered technique he had previously employed at Trouville. The same handling reappears in one of the first works to feature sailing ships at anchor in Argenteuil, also dating to 1872. Continuing to 1877, the Argenteuil period sees Monet—as he was always to do besides, and just as for his skies—offering proof of notable objectivity in varying his methods according to the visual appearance of the river. The motionless calm of the waters in a picture of small sailing craft at rest in 1872 calls for a unified and full canvas on which the unmoving hulls and their reflections on the liquid mirror are circumscribed into well-defined patches, the whole in a style still very close to Manet's. Not very different, the stretch of water in *Pleasure Boats* (c. 1873) in the Musée d'Orsay is barely wrinkled by a wave of low amplitude brought out by long, horizontal parallels that striate the luminous reflection of the sky with darker contrasts. The fluid and blended execution here tempers the detachment of the notations; an effect lessened in the broad, rectangular and thick brushwork that conveys the reflection of the blue sky, the white sails, the green trees, and the red huts of *Regattas at Argenteuil* (Musée d'Orsay) painted in 1872 or 1873.

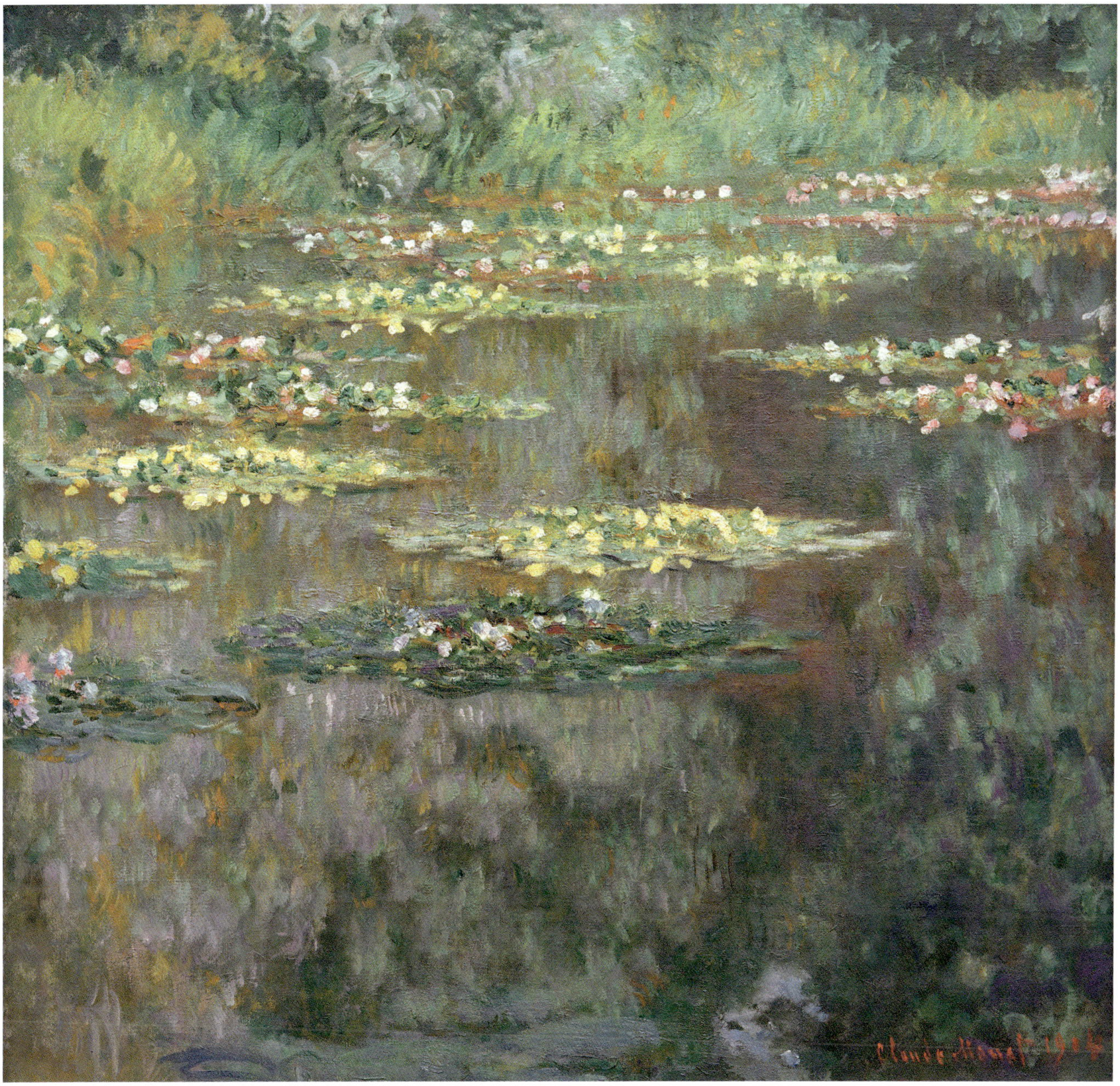

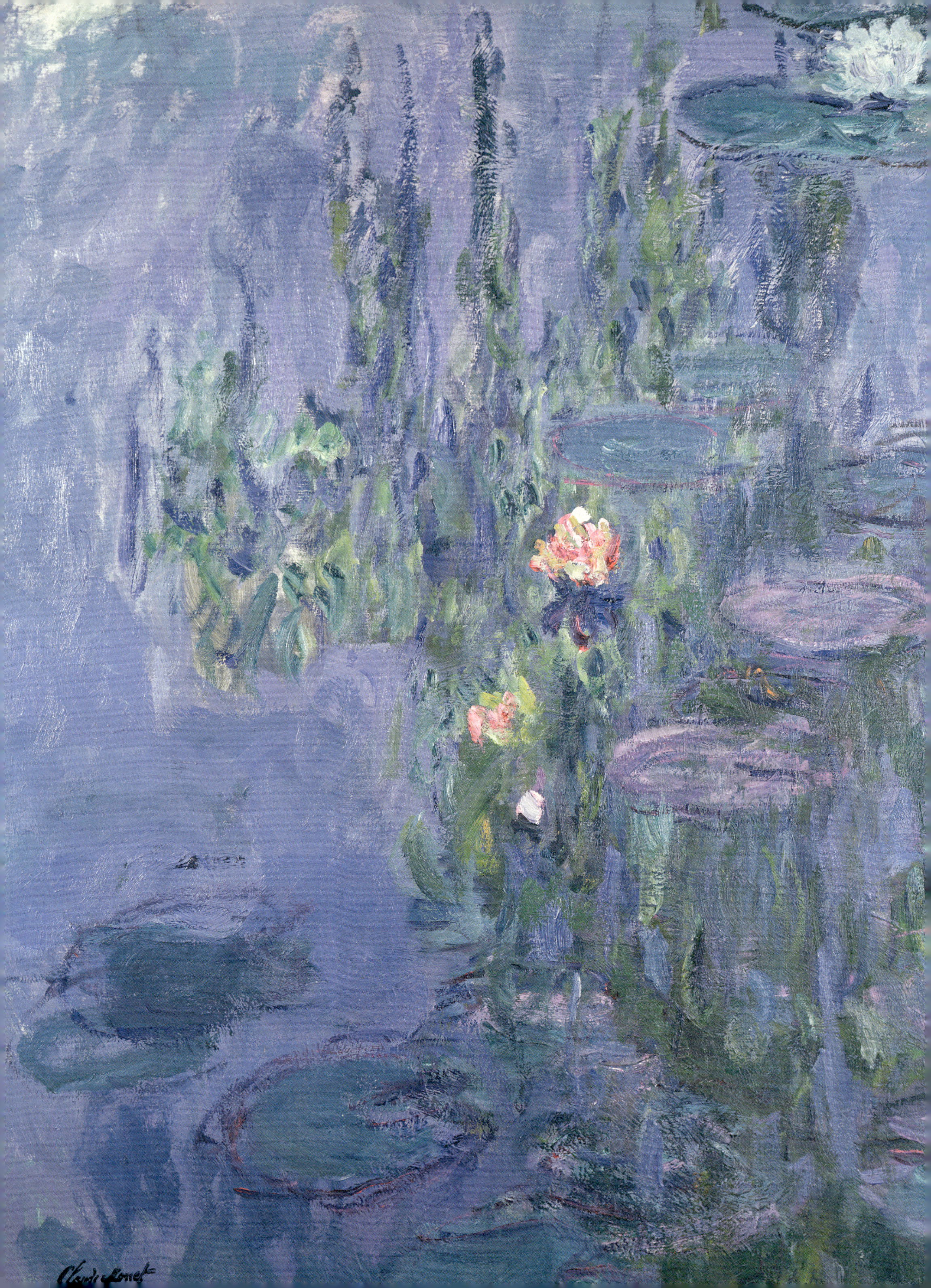
Claude Monet

At a further remove again are those intended to render the gentle lapping of the waters in the *The Bridge at Argenteuil* (Musée d'Orsay), dating to 1874, which reflects a vibrant image of the landscape to the rear, whereas that of the boats and the water in the foreground is painted in a more unified manner. The light touches, laid in like circumflex or grave accents in the *The Railway Bridge at Argenteuil* (Musée d'Orsay), and more still that of *Sailboats, Regattas at Argenteuil* from the Camondo Bequest (Musée d'Orsay), break up the reflected image utterly, in the same way that sharp-topped wavelets whipped up by the wind do in the real world.

It was in seeking to render moving water that Monet thought up the little dab applied with the tip of the brush with which he was soon to capture quivering grasses and leaves, and even—later—air, as it envelops solid masses scintillating under the vibrating effect of an atmosphere bathed in light. The Argenteuil period thus offers a wide range of types of water surface, and thus of the image it reflects, under various weather and light conditions. It also allows us to better trace the process that led Monet to employ a more broken brushwork that he was to extend to elements other than water during the following four years—from 1878 to 1881—that he spent at Vétheuil.

But the stay at Vétheuil was marked by merciless winters that inspired Monet to produce a number of snowy landscapes. In the particular field of water, it provided him in addition with an opportunity to tackle a much less common subject: that of chunks of ice breaking up on the river. It is then a question less of recording changes over the water surface than of studying the contrast between the water and the ice floes riding on it, a contrast Monet underscores by a flat and unified technique employed to capture the smooth and brilliant surface, as against the broad, free impasto with which he treats the ice blocks. *La Débâcle* ("Ice Floes", 1880) in the Gulbenkian Foundation in Lisbon, and the one in the Watson Webb Collection in New York from 1881, exhibit examples of an effect comparable to the one Monet was to deploy twenty years later when he came to tackle the leaves of the water lilies floating over the pond at Giverny.

In the summer period, however, Monet reveled in painting the village of Vétheuil seen from the opposite bank of the Seine, a stretch of water that occupies the entire lower section of a picture divided into three horizontal zones of water, landscape, and sky. In the majority of these views of Vétheuil, the water is treated in small, juxtaposed strokes that often also reappear in the landscape, though they are absent from the sky. The version in the Osborn Bequest in the Metropolitan Museum, New York, is a fine and highly characteristic example.

Water Lilies
1914–17
52 × 33 in. (132 × 84 cm)
oil on canvas
private collection

In summer 1881, Monet stayed for a time on the Normandy coast, returning there over the following years to get to grips with the sea once again as he had somewhat forsaken it over the previous ten years in turning to fresh water. Following Fécamp in 1881 came the series of cliffs of the Pays de Caux in Dieppe, Pourville, and Varengeville in 1882, then Étretat in 1883, 1884, 1885, and 1886; and finally Belle-Île in Brittany (1886). Seldom calm in these climes, the sea was sure to encourage Monet to continue deploying those little comma- or circumflex-like brushstrokes; indeed he developed this technique further. Nonetheless, even then, the treatment never takes on a stereotypical character, because, in adapting to the changing light effects caused by variations in the weather and differing viewing angles, the brushstrokes vary constantly not only in color, but in size, form, and direction. The pointed wavelets caused by a gust of wind seen from afar or from the cliff top at Pourville do not create the same effect as those seen from the water's edge from the base of the rock face at Étretat, since there the nearby wall of chalk against which the breakers strike produces a backwash that dissipates the advancing wave front.

This phenomenon of dissipation reoccurs at Port-Coton, but since the point of view there is rather higher, the situation appears different again. The motif of the Manne Porte at Étretat had already been the subject of a series, with many canvases treated from exactly the same angle but at different hours of the day, the bluish light of the morning alternating with the golden hue of the dying day. Apart from the broad brushwork rendering the water blown about by the wind, and the small strokes corresponding to the lapping of a light breeze, differences in vision and execution also depend on the distance from the subject to the painter's eye. Taking account of such palpable diversity, it would be invidious to analyze Monet's brushwork in any more detail. In effect, the verisimilitude of his seas gleaming in the sun is so diverse that it cannot be due to some systematic and unvarying process; the countless discrepancies transcribed by the artist are simply a translation of the immediate sensory data of the eye.

Water Lilies
1914–17
59 × 78 ¾ in. (150 × 200 cm)
oil on canvas
Neue Pinakothek
Staatsgalerie Moderner Kunst
Munich, inv. 14562

Another fact that should be borne in mind relative to the seascapes produced from 1882 to 1886 is Monet's tendency to increase the impact of the water surface by inclining the plane to the vertical and viewing it from above, as is particularly clear in certain canvases painted from the summit of the cliffs of Pourville or the rocks of Belle-Île. In truth, the elevated banks of the Seine at Poissy had already led Monet to try out a similar experiment in composition in 1882, with *Fishermen in a Boat at Poissy*, in the Österreichische Galerie, Vienna. In this example, the view from above is such that the water surface occupies the whole canvas, much as it was later to do in the *Water Lilies*.

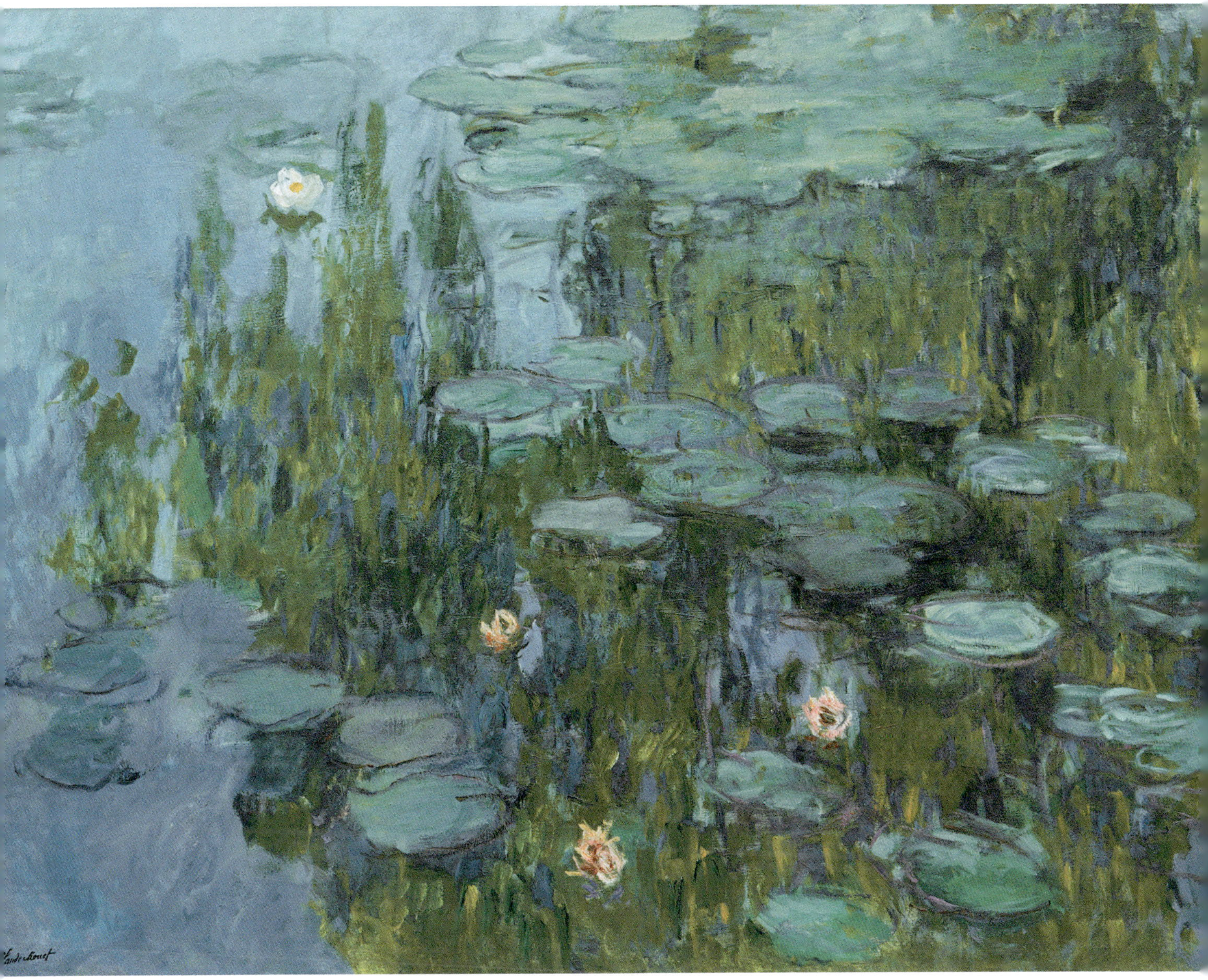

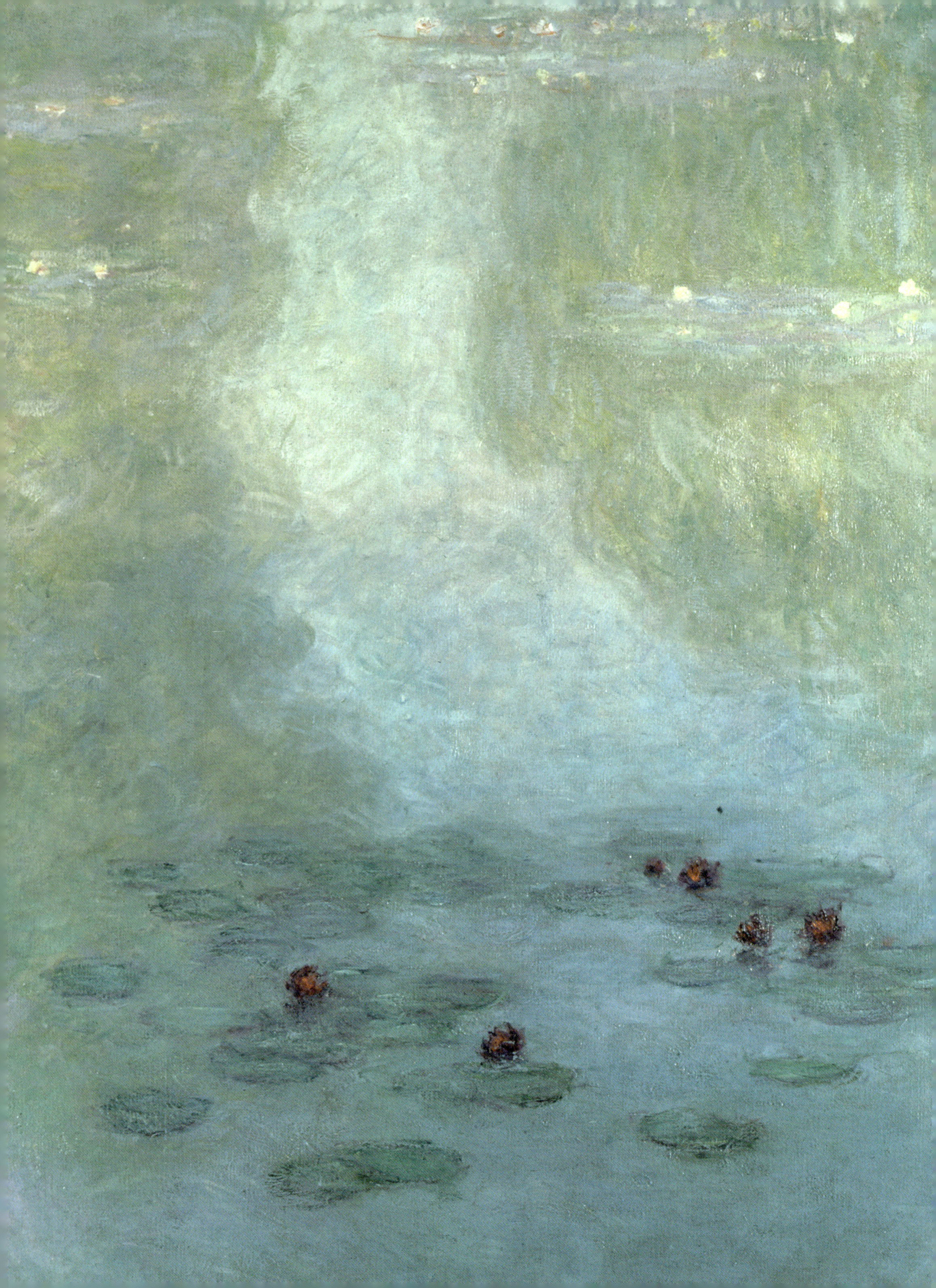

It is also worth noting the coloristic advance appearing at Étretat and more still at Belle-Île, in the juxtaposition of the purple hues of the rock with the blue of the water and their reciprocal interpenetration through the translucent and reflective effect arising from the currents and counter-currents surging between the jagged pyramids of Port-Coton.

Somewhat counter-intuitively, when working at Antibes at the beginning of 1888, Monet was to view the waters of the Mediterranean as far less colorful. Keeping back the most vigorous tones for the trees and roads in the foreground, he held his chromatism in check for the surface of a sea illuminated by reverberation or else veiled in a light fog, or even caught between the two, as in *Antibes Seen from the Salis* in the F. Gould Collection. But the paradox is dissipated by the fact that the specific hue of a fluid is only perceptible to the eye when it is free of reverberated light, since the layer of liquid, being reflective in itself, only reflects the images it receives. This is why—to our eye—water more often appears the color of the sky than its inherent hue. This was something that the public and the Press, in voicing their indignation at the brash blue of the Seine, had failed to take into account when viewing the canvas showing Argenteuil that Manet presented at the Salon of 1875. By eschewing reflections, the bird's-eye view of the Port-Coton pyramids is enough to explain their high color, as is the case in 1889 with certain close-up views of the Petite Creuse at Fresselines.

In many instances, in particular if the surface of the water is slightly rough, ruffled by the wind or disturbed by passing craft, the facets reflecting the light intermix and clash with more absorbent zones, creating a shimmering effect that fascinated Monet, from *La Grenouillère* of 1869 to the Venice of 1908. In views of the Parliament buildings in London (1902–06), the water and the sky take on greater importance than the building, of which only a mere outline is visible in the fog. The fiery ball of the sun piercing the "pea-souper" fog is reflected on the water in a thousand incandescent spangles against a ground unified by the fog into a blue or more or less violet tonality, depending on the time of day and/or the picture concerned. This surprising effect attained an overwhelming lyricism that one might dub romantic were it not to arise from a vision of the world that is not only realistic, but also cosmic.

Once again, it was the glinting light that attracted Monet in the palaces of Venice, where the façades are reflected on the water of the Grand Canal in tremulous, inverted images that dematerialize their structure. Either directly by its rays, or indirectly by its reverberation over the stone frontages, the Mediterranean sun gilds reflections that mix with the Nile green of the waters in supple,

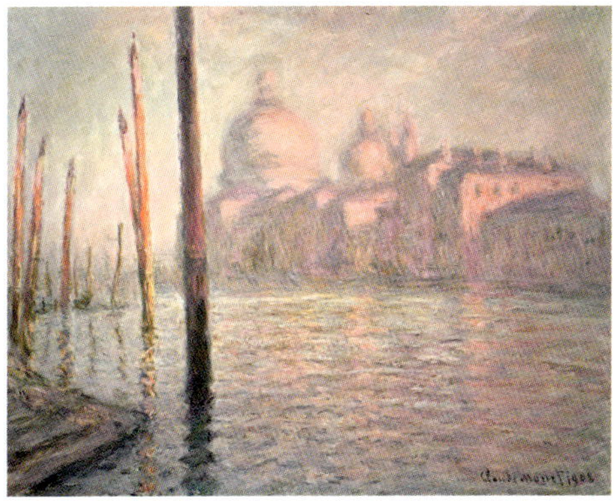

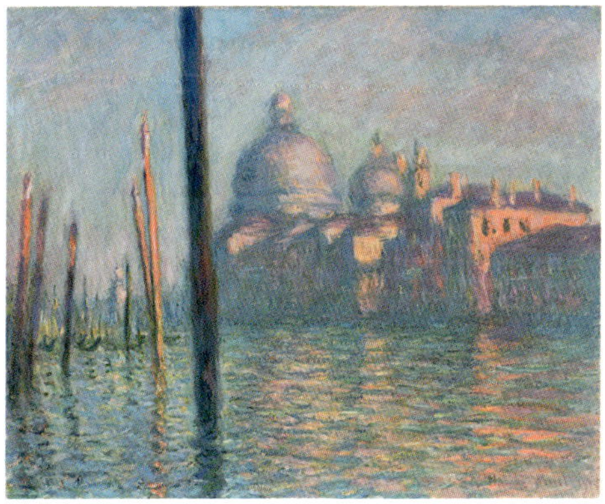

The Grand Canal, Venice
1908
28 ¾ × 36 ¼ in. (73 × 92 cm)
oil on canvas
private collection

The Grand Canal, Venice
1908
29 ¼ × 36 ¼ in. (74 × 92 cm)
oil on canvas
Museum of Fine Arts
Boston, inv. 19.171

FACING PAGE
Water Lilies
1908
39 ¼ × 39 ¼ in. (100 × 100 cm)
oil on canvas
private collection

luminous touches. As against the dramatic character of those in London, the views of Venice are suffused with a peaceful, harmonious, and soothing gaiety.

Between 1890 and 1896, his time monopolized by the series of poppy fields, haystacks, and cathedrals, Monet practically abandoned aquatic subjects. Water recurs, indeed, only in a few of the pictures from the series of *Poplars* painted in 1891, and generally in a narrow band at the bottom of the canvas, as in the example in the Tate, London. Sometimes, however, it takes on greater saliency, in particular in the square picture in the National Gallery of Scotland, Edinburgh, where a stretch of water occupies the lower half of the canvas and reflects a sky diagonally sliced through by the leafy tufts of a band of poplars interacting with their backdrop of clouds; an effect that prefigures the reflections on the pond in the *Water Lilies*.

WATER LILIES

From the simple farmer's house in the middle of an orchard that he had rented in Giverny since 1883 and bought in 1890, Monet created a home fit for an artist. Retaining a few large trees close to the house, as well as his first studio, the orchard was replaced by flowerbeds and soon decorated with arches bearing roses, wisteria, and other climbers. Composed like a palette of plants, Giverny allowed Monet to satisfy simultaneously his fondness for the vegetal and his love of color in canvases, whose luxuriance, though of another order, is that of the *Water Lilies*.

Continuing to improve his garden with flowers, Monet decided to acquire an adjacent meadow that extended beyond the little road and the railway up to an arm of the River Epte. He dreamed of creating a pond supplied by the river in which he intended to grow water lilies. Preserving the aspens already there, he had an irregularly shaped and not very deep pond dug in the middle, which he filled with water lilies and bordered with irises. Nearby, he planted bamboo and weeping willow before lining the avenues with pergolas of climbing plants.

Towards the rear of the plot there runs a diverted brook whose current flattens and stirs a mass of aquatic grasses and freshwater weeds. Fully grown, the various levels of this ensemble of aquatic and land plants constituted a veritable microcosm, around which all his more or less mythical dreams of an earthly paradise might coalesce. Monet considered this water-lily garden part of his oeuvre, as he would a painting, and stated that he had not planted

Water Lilies
1914–17
51¼ × 59 in. (130 × 150 cm)
oil on canvas
private collection

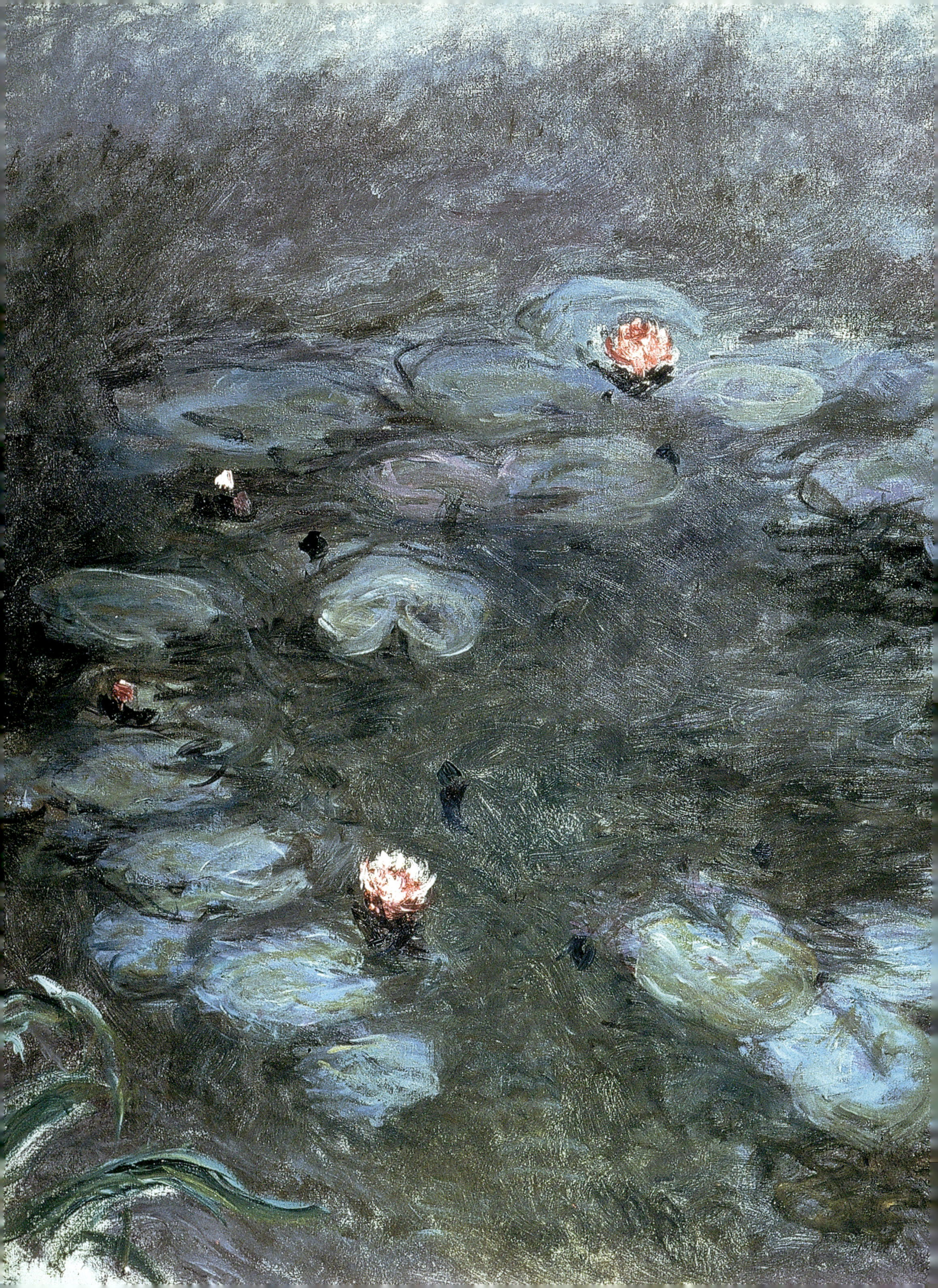

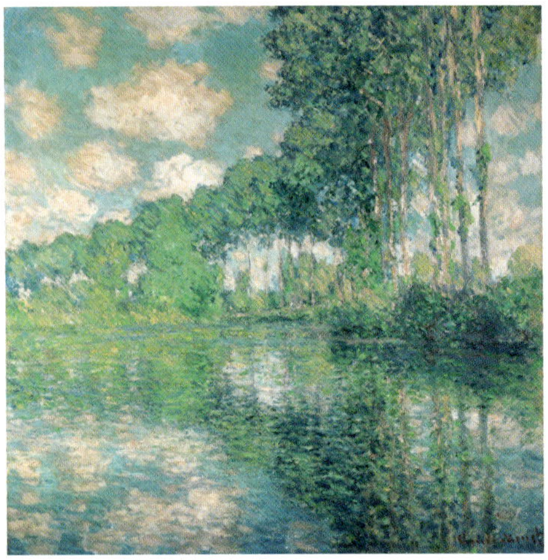

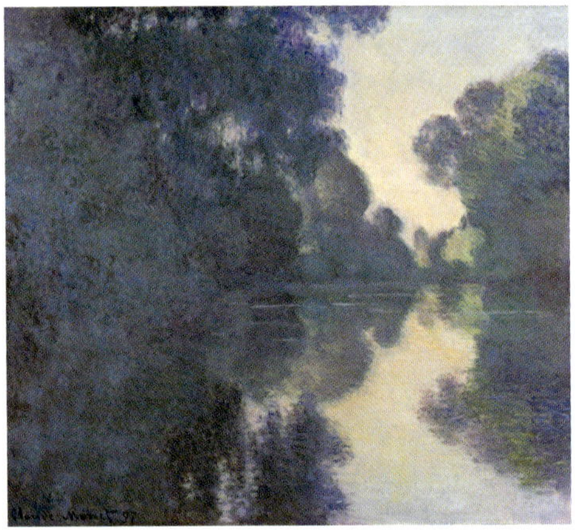

Poplars on the Banks of the Epte
1891, 31¼ × 31¼ in. (79.5 × 79.5 cm)
oil on canvas
National Gallery of Scotland,
Edinburgh, inv. NG 1651

Morning on the Seine near Giverny
1897, 32 × 36½ in. (81.6 × 93 cm)
oil on canvas
Metropolitan Museum of Art
New York, inv. 56.135.4

FACING PAGE
Water Lilies
1905, 35½ × 39¼ in. (90 × 100 cm)
oil on canvas
Museum of Fine Art
Boston, inv. 39.804

it in order to paint it, a desire that dawned on him only afterwards, once the garden had been finished. A few earlier works, though, in their subject matter at least, look like harbingers of the *Water Lilies* series, in particular due to the significant role they allot to a stretch of water or to the inverted motif of the sky and the surrounding trees reflected in it. Without going back to some much earlier works already mentioned, such as *The River* of 1868, wholly centered on the reflected image of a landscape in water, or even to the *Fishermen in Boats at Poissy* of 1882, where the water laps the upper edge of the canvas, but rather keeping to examples from more recent years, it is impossible not to recall the scenes of canoeing on the Epte that Monet painted in 1887.

Admittedly, the subject of these charming nautical scenes is constituted by a group of graceful girls in brightly colored dresses chatting and fishing in boats or rowing in skiffs, but the role played by the water is no less significant for that, the success of the piece indeed deriving essentially from the touching and harmonious echoes between nature and femininity. The rear of the picture of three girls angling (*The Boat at Giverny*, 1887, Musée d'Orsay) being occupied by foliage, the water can hardly take up more than half the canvas. The reflection of the bright figures and the boat, however, accentuates its role considerably. On the other hand, although occupying four-fifths of the surface, the water in *Rowboat on the Epte* in the Museu de Arte in São Paulo, where the reflections are confined to a gleam on the rippling waters, plays a secondary role, consisting primarily in providing a transparent layer over the waving aquatic grasses, as it does in the *Sailboat* in the Musée Marmottan.

The two variants of the same subject of two girls sitting at the stern of a boat (*The Blue Boat* in the Colección Thyssen-Bornemisza, and the one in the National Museum of Western Art, Tokyo) differ only in the former's sunnier atmosphere and the more significant place allotted to water, which occupies the totality of the latter. But this difference is sufficient to considerably increase the role of reflection and to bring the Tokyo example much closer to the ultimate conception of the *Water Lilies*, in which the unique focus is water.

In 1891, at the time of the *Poplar* series, generally painted in a portrait format best suited to the verticality of the slim, parallel trunks, Monet unusually selected a square format for a picture in the National Gallery of Scotland, Edinburgh. The composition relies on the junction, at a point located halfway up the canvas to the left, of the diagonal line of the crown of the trees starting from the top right-hand corner with the inverted oblique of its reflection in the water. It is however obvious that, limited to the rectangle divided by this diagonal, the geometrical schema of the direct image, in isolation,

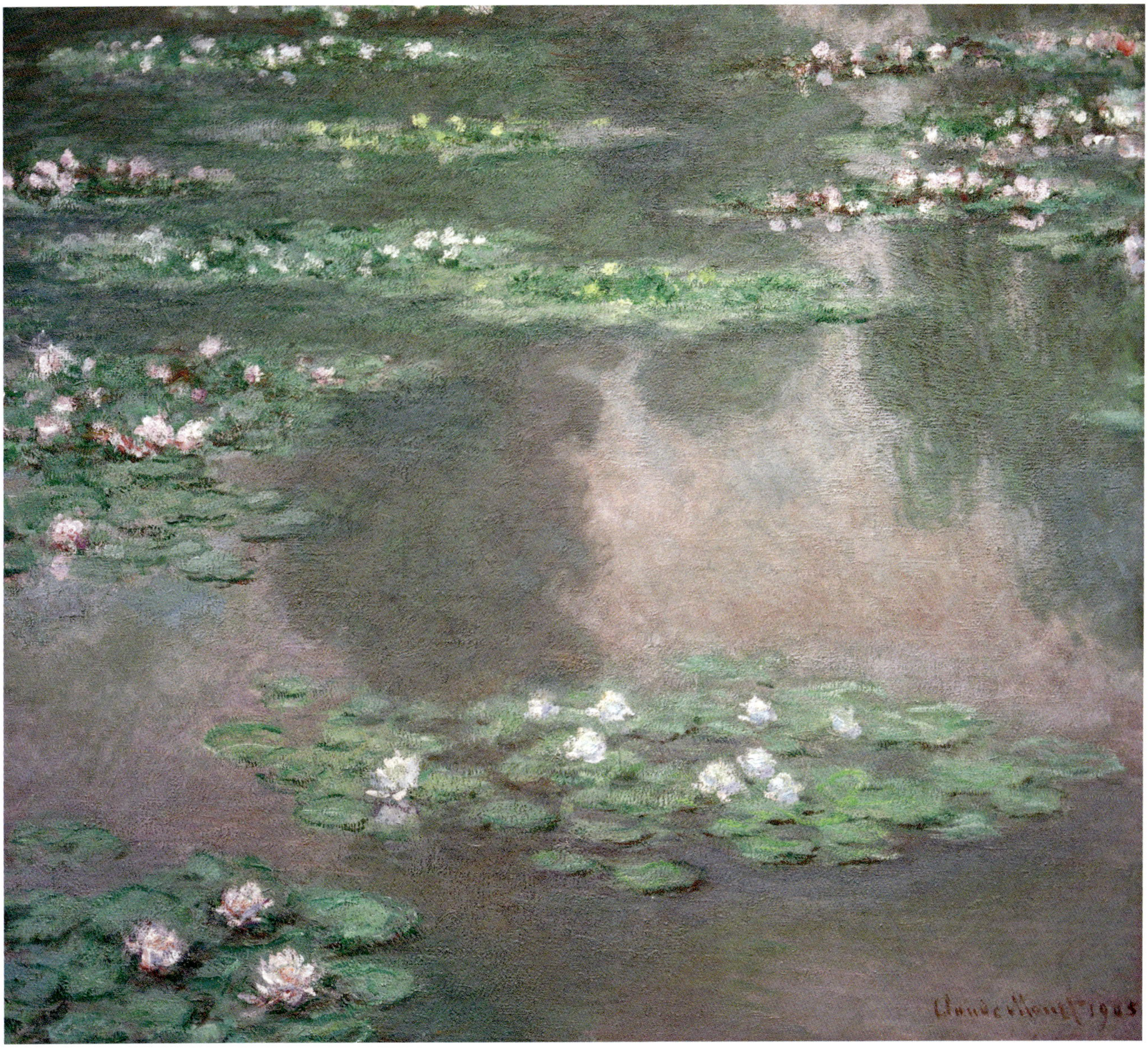
Claude Monet 1905

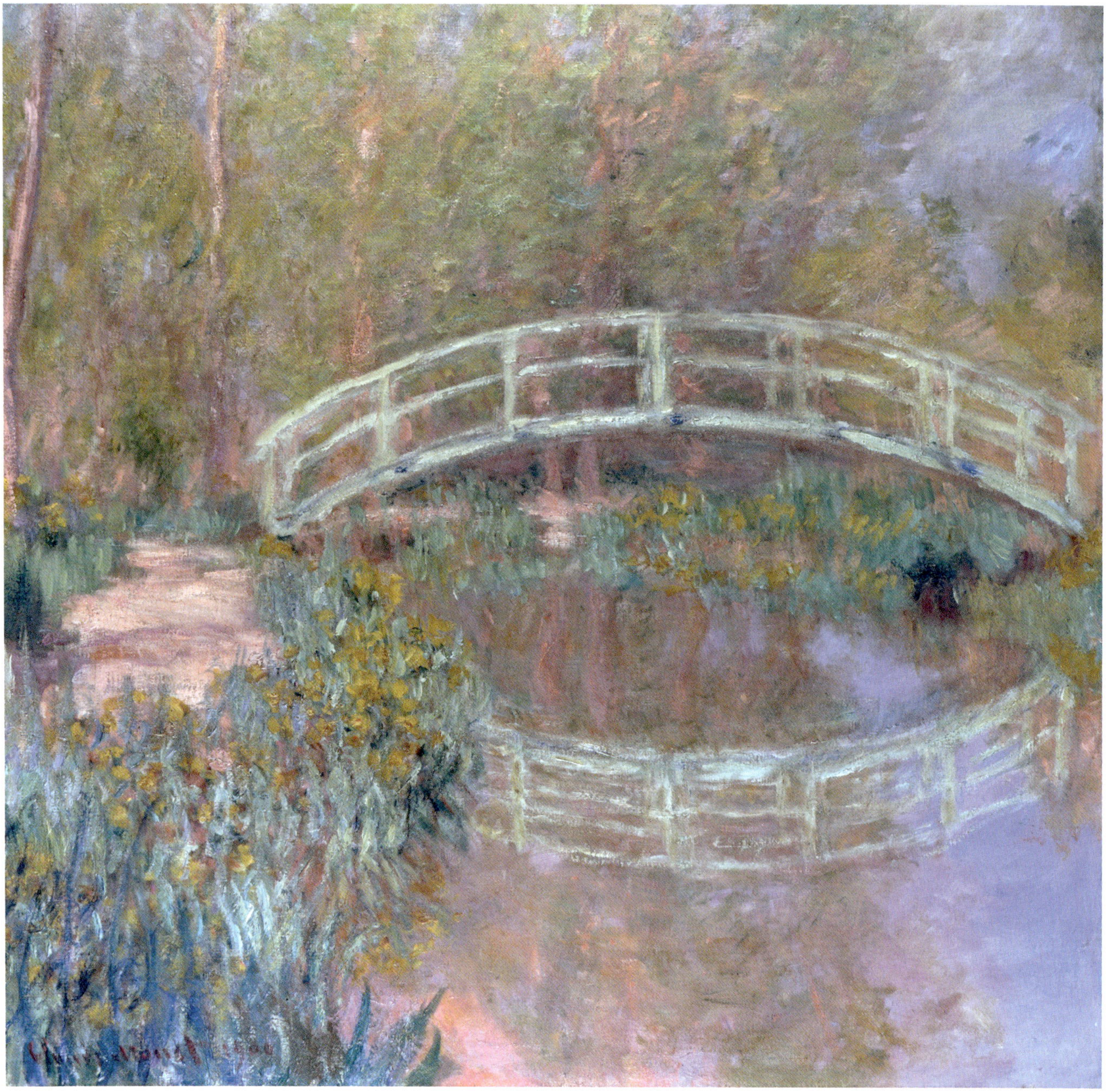

would have been commonplace; the original effect of this arrangement comes from the division of the square surface of the canvas into a pattern of four interlocked right-angled triangles.

In 1897, when doing the *Mornings on the Seine* series, Monet again based his compositions on the opposition and superposition of reflected and direct images, which, due to the misty morning atmosphere, merge seamlessly, appearing in two parts solely because of the fact that the dark masses of the trees against the bright background of the sky seem inverted. Here though, with such sinuously irregular forms, no geometrically minded schema could work. The inverted symmetry of a continuous single image is particularly striking when the unseen meeting point of the image on land with that on water lies exactly mid canvas, generally the case when Monet employed the square shape that he preferred to the landscape format in a *Branch of the Seine* series, very close to *Water Lilies*, as in that in the Museum of Fine Arts, Boston (*Morning on the Seine*, 1897).

In 1890, Monet had already painted the little Japanese bridge spanning the narrowest part of the pond, seen in its totality under its arch scraping the top of the canvas. Then, in 1892, he returned to the motif, centering it in such a way that the arch and its reflection form an ellipse; but it was only in 1898 that he embarked on the actual series of *Water-Lily Ponds*, which was to occupy him for several years.

In a slightly wider than square format, the composition remains virtually identical. The water, planted with water lilies, occupies the lower half of the canvas, and is topped with the arch spanning the channel. The bridge itself emerges from the plants masking the bank on the left from which it springs. The rear of the painting shows trees cut mid-trunk by the upper border of the canvas. As in preceding series, Monet tirelessly repeated the same motif under different lighting conditions, varying from the chillier tonalities of morning to the warmer tones of evening, as shown in the two paintings from the Camondo Bequest in the Musée d'Orsay, *Water-Lily Pond, Green Harmony* and *Water-Lily Pond, Pink Harmony*. It is undeniable that this clever composition is not without connections to the aesthetics of the Modern Style.

From 1904 to 1905 onward, Monet attempted to ascribe a greater role to water, either by standing back farther from the bridge, which is then relegated to the very top of the canvas, or else, contrariwise, by placing himself beyond the bridge and thereby omitting it completely from the visual field. As early as 1904, he started a series conforming to this second approach. This solution is the more radical, since the water surface is here surmounted only by a narrow frieze consisting of grass and the flowers planted on the bank to the rear of the pond.

The Water-Lily Pond, Water Irises
1900
35 × 36¼ in. (89 × 92 cm)
oil on canvas
private collection

In about 1905, Monet even went so far as to eliminate this strip, leaving the entire canvas to water alone. Thanks to the intermediary of the reflection of the sky and the treetops in its mirror surface, he increasingly found that this sufficed for a painting. For this new arrangement, he adopted a rectangular format approximately three feet (one meter) down its longest side that he employed initially, in 1905–06, widthwise. Then, in 1907–08, he began to prefer an upright format that left him greater scope, as it mean that the water could be positioned to the vertical, resulting in a view from above that lessened the effects of perspective and depth. This latter, upright composition presents a singular analogy with that of the views of the *Branch of the Seine* series carried out ten years earlier in a square format. The same effect, of a cascade of light pouring between dark masses of trees that resemble rocky outcrops, recurs in both cases. The relationship lives on in spite of the discrepancy between the single image of the reflection on the pond and the doubled and inverted image of the branch of the Seine, an effect that on the face of it might have introduced a crucial difference between the two subjects. This is because the veil of mist enveloping this stretch of the Seine attenuates both the superposition and inversion, to the point where the image is seemingly continuous. What remains from both is the encounter between a streak of light with some dark, solid masses, which seem more liable to fuse their supple, sinuous, and fluid forms than to come together with any violence.

It is difficult to ascertain exactly when the idea of a vast decorative ensemble devoted to the theme of a waterscape germinated in the mind of Monet. Perhaps he gives us an inkling as early as 1909 to Roger Marx, who—in an imaginary dialogue between him and the artist—had the latter declaring: "I was sorely tempted to decorate a drawing room with this theme of the water lilies: placed up along the walls round which the entire ensemble would wrap, the illusion would have been of an endless whole, of a wave without horizon or shore; nerves overtaxed by work would there relax and follow the reposing example of the stagnant water; and, to the person living there, the room would have offered an asylum for meditation in the middle of a flowery aquarium."

Is this just a premonitory reverie by the writer, or is it an accurate record of what Monet actually said? Perhaps we have to await the oft-quoted conversations between Georges Clemenceau and Claude Monet, which have the famous project at their center? The answer is not clear, but it is certain that the idea progressed in Monet's thinking to the point that he decided to have a new studio built at the top of his garden, big enough to lay out the large number of panels he planned, so allowing him to follow the evolution of the work as a unit day by day. Some six and a half feet (two meters) high, the largest stretchers

Water Lilies, Reflections of Willow
1916-19
52 × 78 ¾ in. (132 × 200 cm)
oil on canvas
Musée Marmottan
Paris, inv. 50999

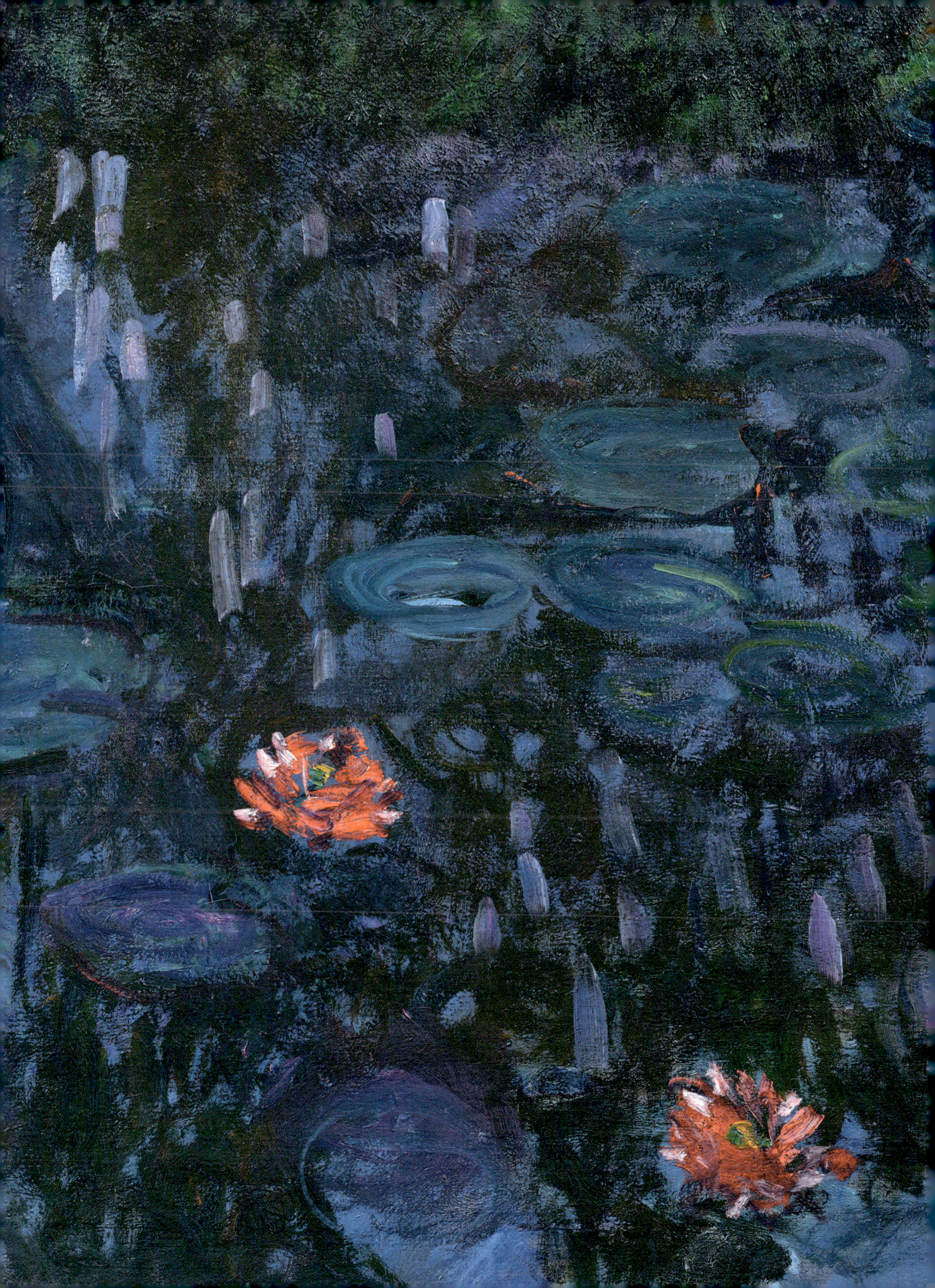

were nearly twenty feet (six meters) long, the medium-sized thirteen feet (four meters), and the shortest, intended for transitions, also six and a half feet (two meters). Mounted on blocks with casters, it was relatively easy to move them about and slide one behind the other when working, as well as when moving backwards and forwards from series to series, as with a stage set.

Working from the motif on smaller, square or rectangular, formats, varying in size between just over three feet to six and a half feet (one to two meters) down the side, Monet carried out all these extremely thorough studies directly from nature. Recopying these partial studies, he then reconstituted the various parts, avoiding both the use of his memory and all gratuitous or arty brushwork. One can only imagine the titanic effort represented by the transposition onto such vast proportions of precise and fleeting light effects, without any deterioration in either its integrity or unity. Such a project was not going be exempt from setbacks, and Monet suffered many periods of material and physical incapacity and discouragement. But the motivation behind his gigantic enterprise always gave him sufficient strength to overcome what were but momentary crises. Only the progressive cataract of 1922, by stopping him from working for a lengthy period and by leaving him uncertain as to the success or otherwise of the operation and its consequences, proved genuinely damaging, though he was lucky enough in time to overcome it and to experience before he died the joy of getting back to work once again.

Entirely committed to a single goal, this final period of Monet's oeuvre constitutes a homogeneous whole, which must be considered as a unit. It is futile to try to identify its stages, since Monet would intermittently return to various panels—and sometimes a long time after starting on them. If it is thus impossible to follow it as it unfolds, in the absence of chronological references, it is less meaningless to take the works themselves as our guide and trace the sense of increasing boldness and freedom, ever-greater ardor and lyricism.

As an example, it cannot be disputed that the great 131-foot (40-meter) group that engulfs the second room in the Orangerie at the Tuileries, with the foreground marked out by weeping willows, still appears dependent on figurative and decorative concerns from which *Sunset* in the first room and the adjacent north panel seem utterly devoid. It is equally possible, though, that this impression does not devolve from chronological factors and is due more to sporadic variations than to a progressive evolution that no evidence can establish.

Nevertheless, as long of course as the works marked by the eye troubles of 1922–23 are excluded, Monet remained faithful until the end to a project that can be summarized as a long visual paean dedicated to the encounter between light and water, and then to the plant world that the latter reveals and to the atmospheric world it reflects.

Corner of the Water-Lily Pond
1918
51¼ × 34¾ in. (130 × 88 cm)
oil on canvas
private collection

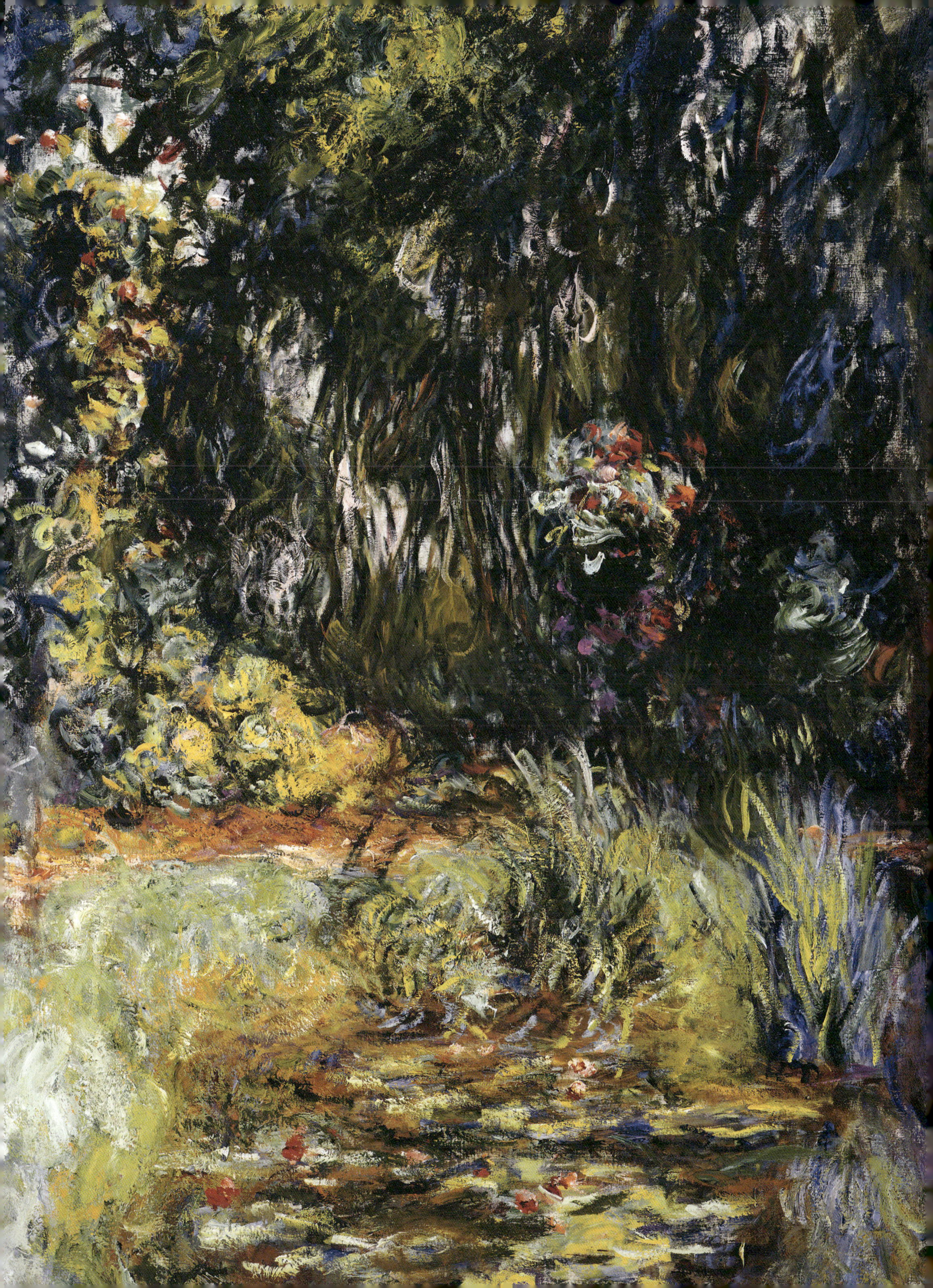

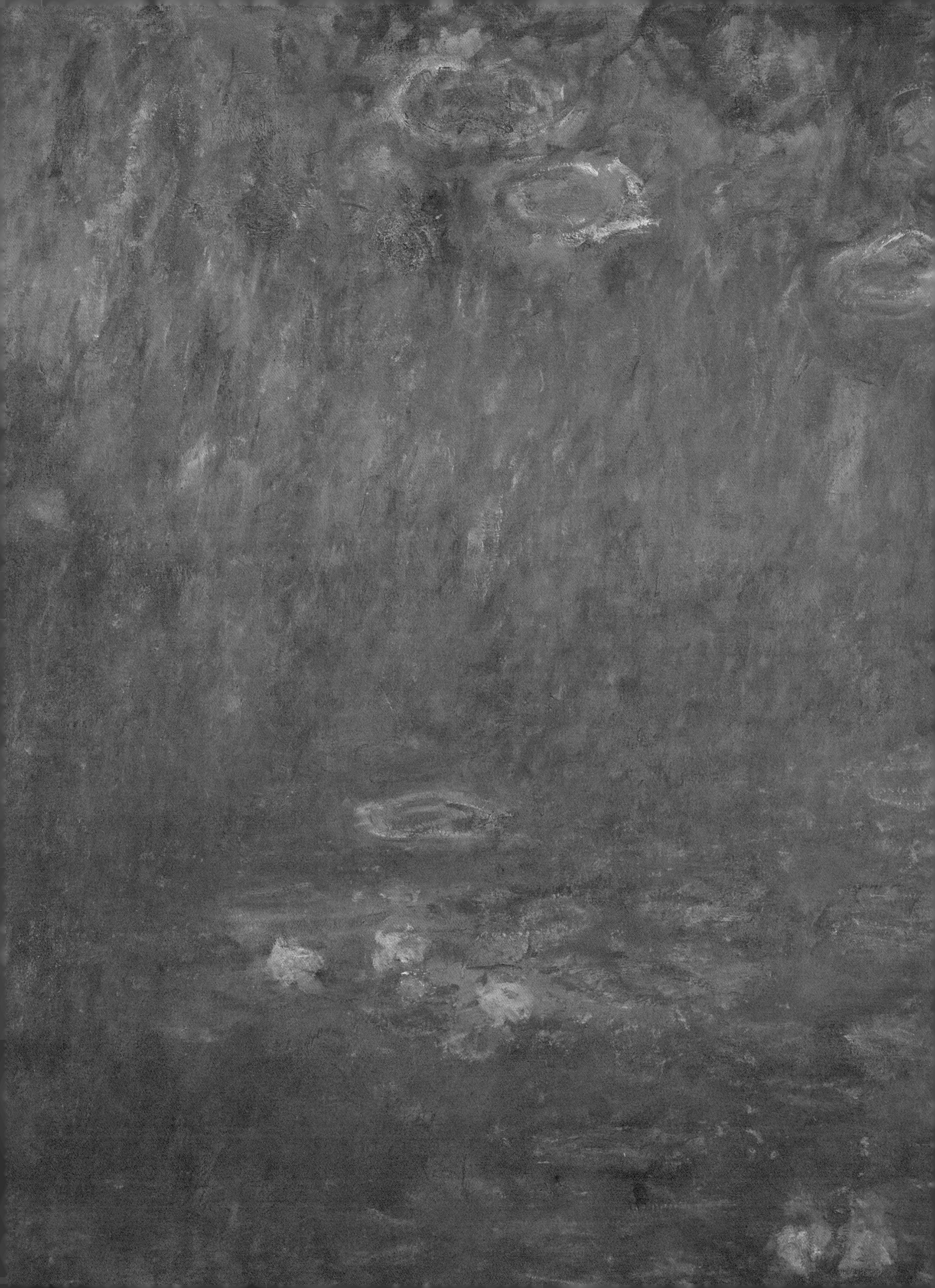

Reinforcing the first-degree contrast between water and the floating islands constituted by the water lilies, there are the second-degree contrasts that each of these two component contains—that is, on the one hand between flat and erect flowers, and, on the other, between those areas of water that absorb and those that reflect light.

The contrast between the green and plain zones with the white or colored patches of the flowers above them is obvious to the eye; that between the areas absorbing the light and those reflecting it is harder to discern, and depends primarily on the unpredictable and relatively elusive distribution of the light itself. However, within the absorbent zone, the underwater stems of the aquatic plants are recognizable by vertical elongation, while, in the reflective area, the images of the sky and the treetops are more difficult to identify at first, although they can generally be made out if sufficient effort is made.

Yet, as the zones of absorption and reflection tend increasingly to interfere with one another, there comes a time when viewers no longer seek to distinguish between them, overwhelmed as they are by the spectacle, which they prefer to savor in its unity. In this they follow the artist himself, who would strive to forget the individual elements corresponding to what he saw. Monet expressed this desire unambiguously on several occasions, in particular to the artist Lilia Cabot Perry, telling her that he did not set to painting without wanting to first unlearn his eye, so that it would seem as if he had never seen the motif before, as if he had been born blind and his eyes were being presented with it for the first time. As he declared: "Whenever you go off to paint, try to forget what objects you have in front of you, a tree, a house, a field or whatever. Think only this: Here is a small square of blue, of pink, a green oval, a strip of yellow, and paint them exactly as they appear to you, the colors and forms exact, until they convey your naive impression of the scene before you."

If the initial impetus came from the stance of Édouard Manet, it is in the late works of Claude Monet, the inventor and formulator of the visual realism that constitutes the very foundation of impressionism, and to which he was always to remain faithful, that the consequences are taken to their extreme; and it is these pieces, with their often hard-to-decode subject that one tends today to think of as abstract. If this point remains polemical, the argument seems to rely partly on an abusive and somewhat erroneous interpretation of the true intentions of Monet, for whom the problem did not lie in the alternative between figuration and abstraction.

The only works of his which, if one did not know their physical cause, might legitimately be envisaged as visionary, are those executed in 1922 during the period of visual impairment caused by the advancing cataract; and then after the eye operation, when he was painting without the correct lenses for his condition. The alteration

The Water-Lily Pond with Willows, Reflections of Trees
1914–18
triptych: each panel 78 ¾ × 334 ¾ in
(200 × 850 cm)
oil on canvas
Musée de l'Orangerie
Paris, inv. 20107

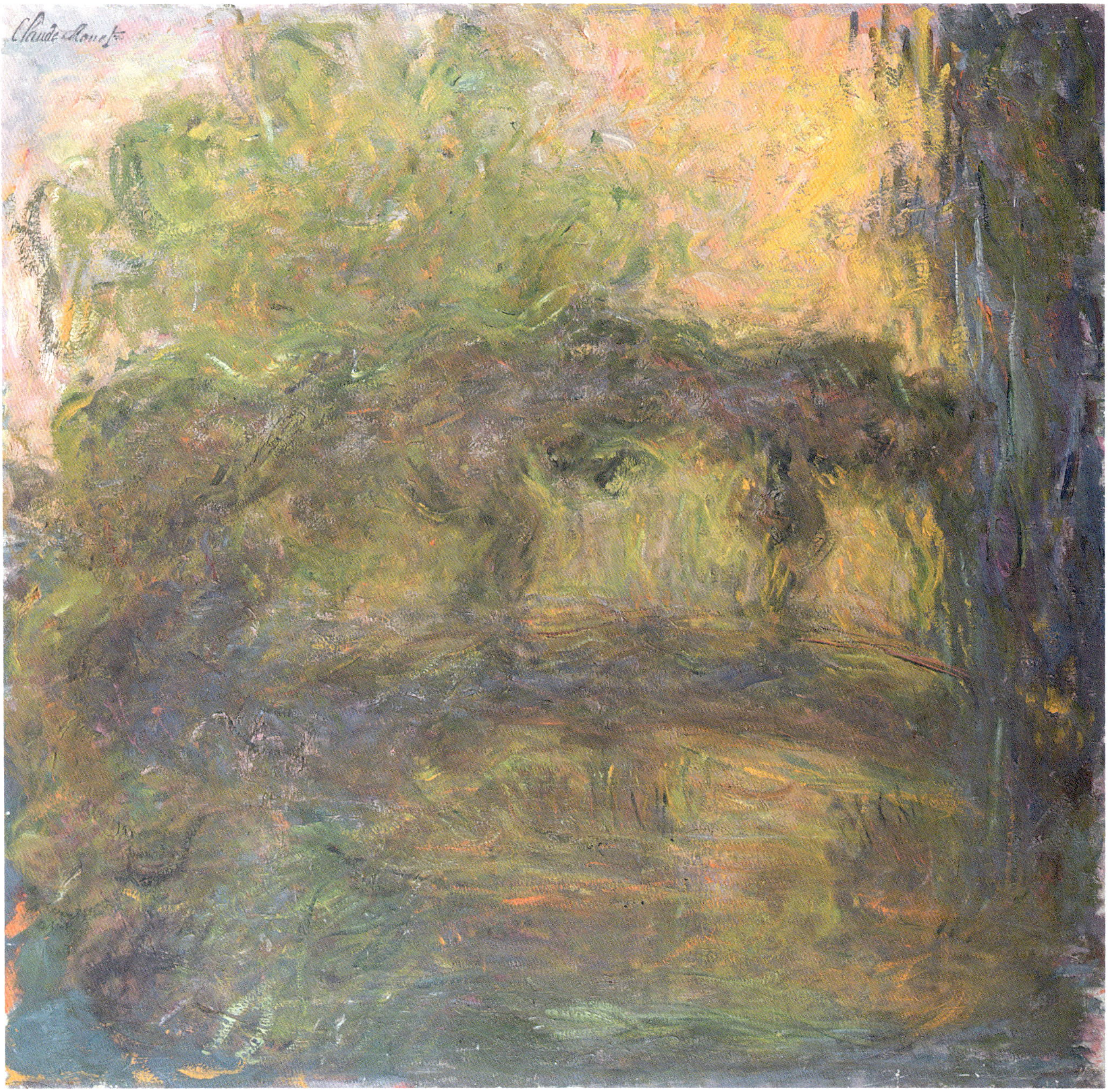
Claude Monet

of colors due to xanthopsia and the imprecision of form due to the lens no longer allowing the eye to focus normally (and in the absence of spectacles) spawned a series of *Lanes with Flowered Arches* (*The Rose Trellises*), *Weeping Willows*, *Houses in Giverny* in the roses, and *Small Japanese Bridges*, characteristic examples of which hang in the Musée Marmottan, and which are genuinely indecipherable for anyone unacquainted, either directly or from other pictures, with the motif that inspired them.

Tormented by the desire to retouch certain pictures intended for the State that he did not regard as fully finished, but conscious in spite of himself of the defective state of his eyesight, he allowed himself to be dissuaded by his entourage and, temporarily leaving aside the *Water Lilies*, started working from nature on the other derivative subjects referred to above. There followed a painful period of ocular readjustment and tentative steps in the painstaking search for the right corrective lenses. When at last, thanks to the science and devotion of an eminent specialist, he had made a satisfactory recovery—at least in the eye that had been operated on—and could see for himself the chromatic anomalies in a group of canvases dominated by a fierce yellow, he was overcome with surprise. At first reproaching his circle for not preventing him from painting in this manner, he then changed his mind and declared that in fact it didn't matter, since nothing could have been done about it and that such a prohibition would anyway have occasioned him unnecessary distress.

Thus we know that his deteriorated vision was neither voluntary nor conscious; but we also learn that, even if he had been made aware of it, he would not have made corrections to what he *saw*. So, far from being visionary works of the imagination, these pictures are, on the contrary, precisely the result of Monet's fidelity to whatever he perceived through his visual organ, even when this was defective. Their starting point was then utterly contrary to that of lyrical abstraction, which is based for its part on plastic creations created in the artist's brain or else produced spontaneously by uncontrolled impulse.

Everything in Monet's oeuvre is authentically experienced and perceived. Nothing results from more or less uncoordinated chance or from the improvisation of an errant imagination. However, such considerations are not to imply that Monet is a figurative painter in the strict sense of the term: far from it. If, from the group of *Water Lilies* of the latter period, the canvases due to Monet's ailment are excluded and we take into account only those carried out under unimpaired visual conditions, self-control and willpower, one finds pieces almost as difficult to decipher as the exceptions, such as the aforementioned work in the first room of the Orangerie, *Sunset*, among others. But there exists a greater quantity of partially figurative and

The Japanese Bridge
1918–24
35 × 36½ in. (89 × 93 cm)
oil on canvas
Galerie Daniel
Malingue, Paris

partially hermetic works that show that here, Monet, guided solely by his sensitivity, no more than anywhere else, was not obeying a pre-established system, and that, as the effects of light presented themselves in a more or less definable manner according to the circumstances, he was no more inclined to avoid this definition if it forced itself upon him than to seek it out if it did not.

It is obvious that the motif of the sky reflected on water presents fewer identifiable elements than *Water Lily* leaves and flowers, and in itself constitutes a theme that favors the absence of representation. As he evolved, it was this that Monet tended increasingly to make the cynosure of his large panels, even if it meant relegating the solid masses of the aquatic plants to the periphery. He shows thus the paramount importance in which he held the most mysterious and astonishing component of the final *Water Lilies* series, and his particular concern to express this visual ecstasy in and for itself, without seeking for it any outside reference or figurative justification.

It would then not be going too far to see Monet as a tachist in some of these very late works. The problem lies in trying to claim him as an abstract and thus assimilate him to the 1950s movement of lyrical abstraction on the other side of the Atlantic, with which, in spite of unmistakable but no better than skin-deep affinities, there remains the fundamental discrepancy of the source of creativity. The production of a visionary imagination or some spontaneous and uncontrolled impulsion should not be confused with one born from an actually experienced visual sensation. This does nothing, however, to undermine the revelation and influence of the *Water Lilies* on subsequent generations.

Not only is Monet a tachist—he is the very first tachist painter. However, his visual tachism expresses something quite different from that spawned by pure imagination. Directly perceived, physically and intensely experienced, it is the authentic expression of an emotion felt by an artist before the living spectacle of light that entranced him and whose modulations of color alone he strove to perceive and record.

The Japanese Bridge
1918–24
35 × 39 ¼ in. (89 × 100 cm)
oil on canvas
Musée Marmottan
Paris, inv. 5093

FOLLOWING PAGE
The Water-Lily Pond
1917–19
39 ¼ × 78 ¾ in. (100 × 200 cm)
oil on canvas
private collection

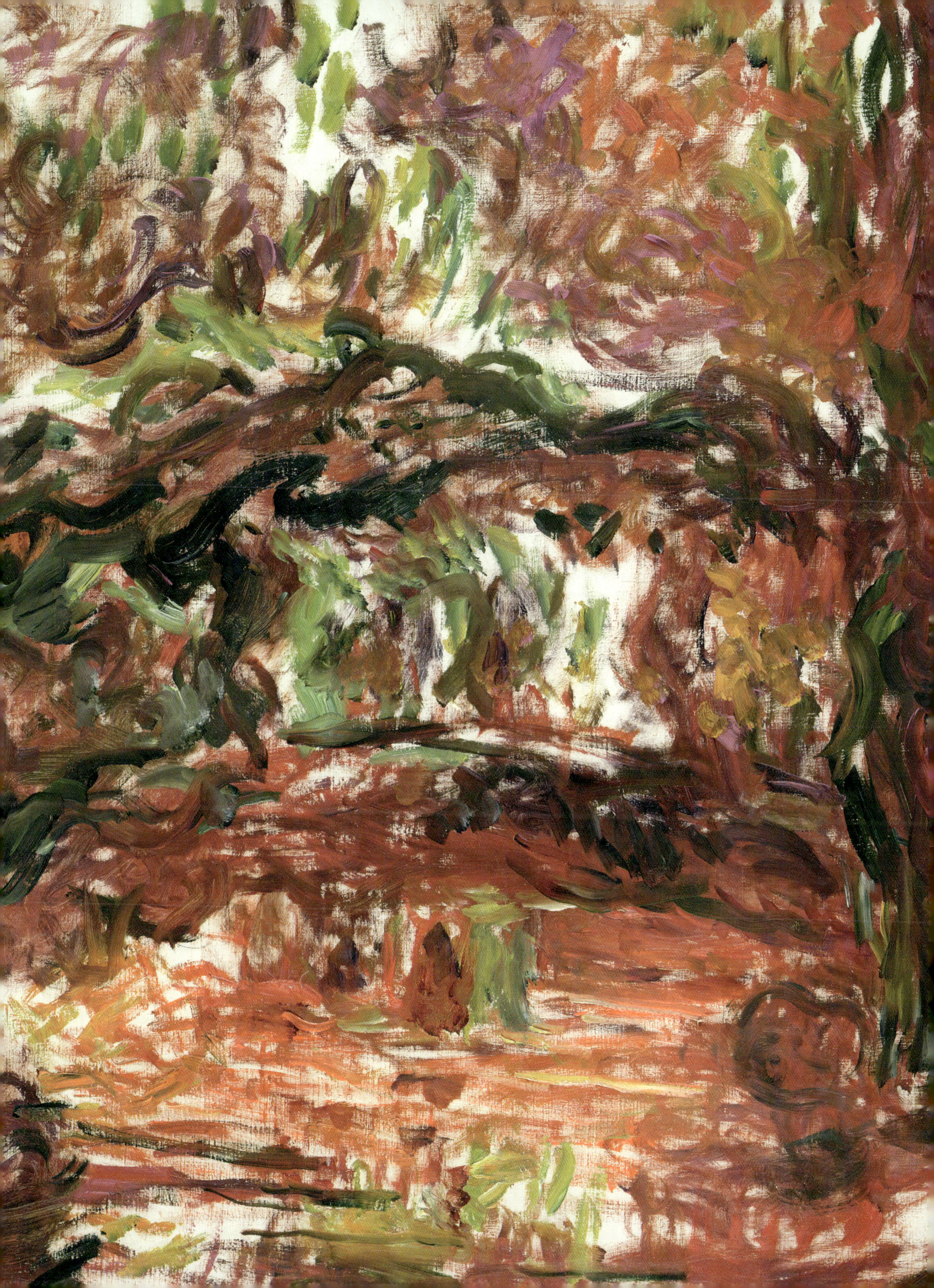

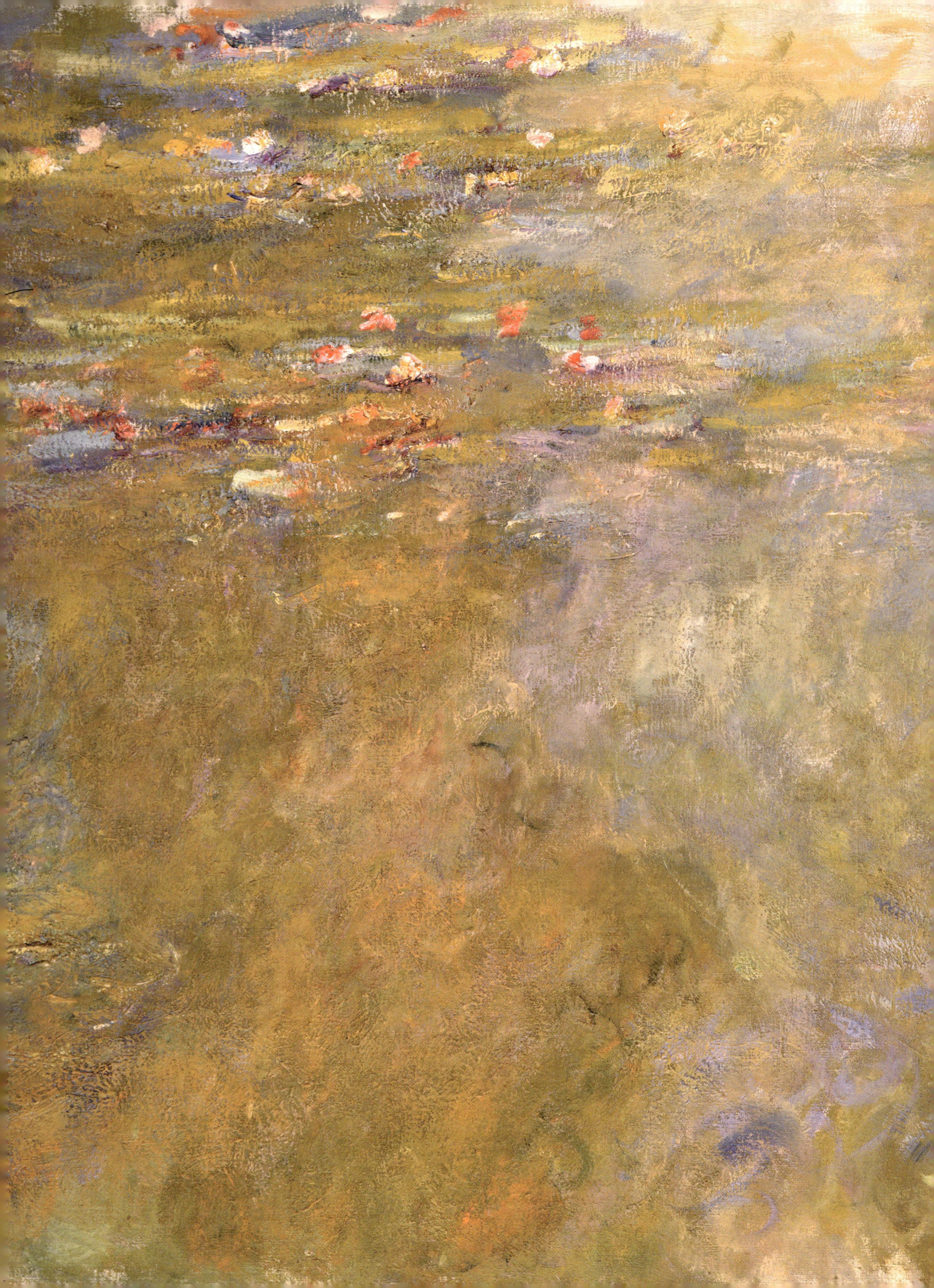

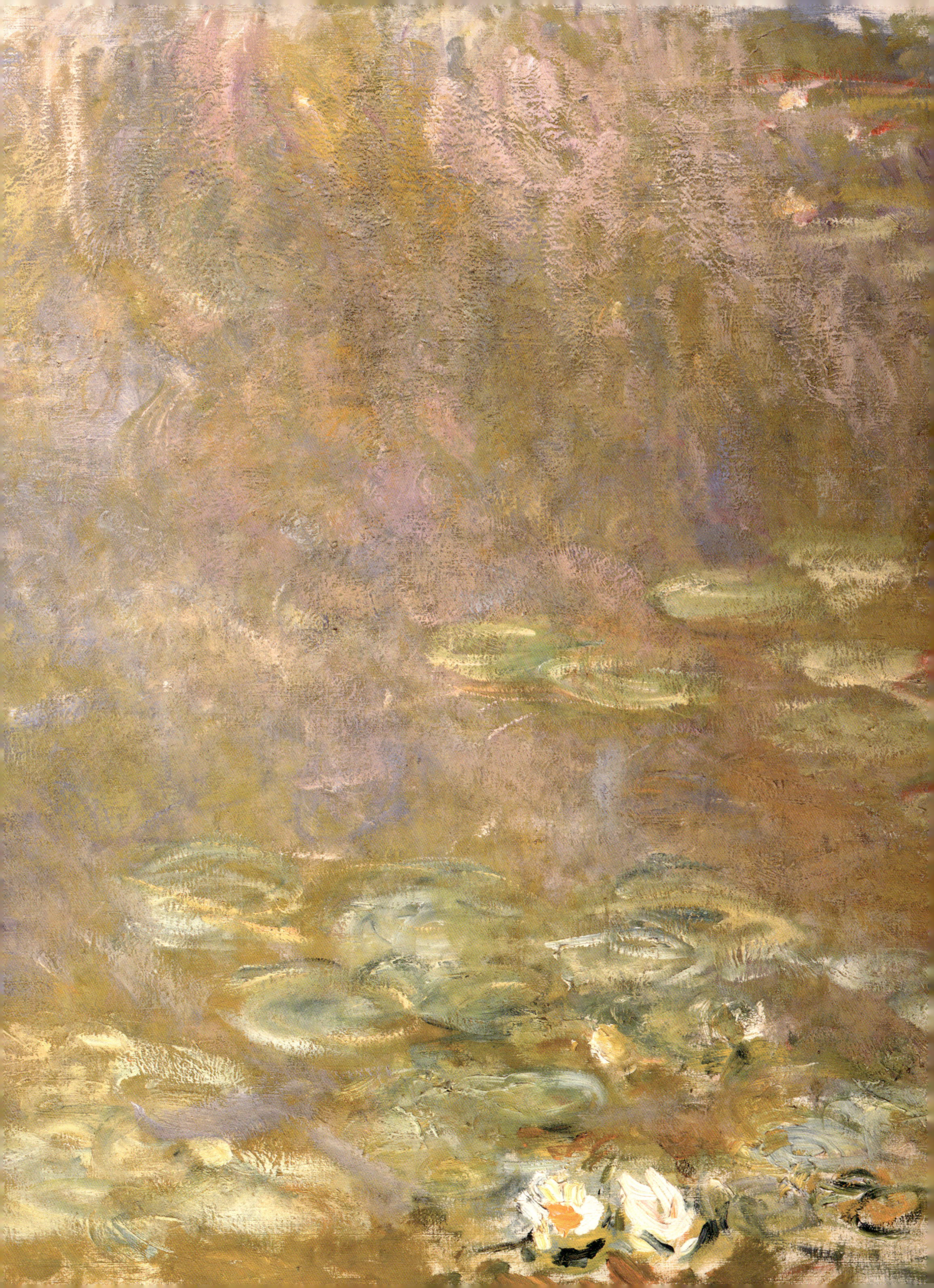

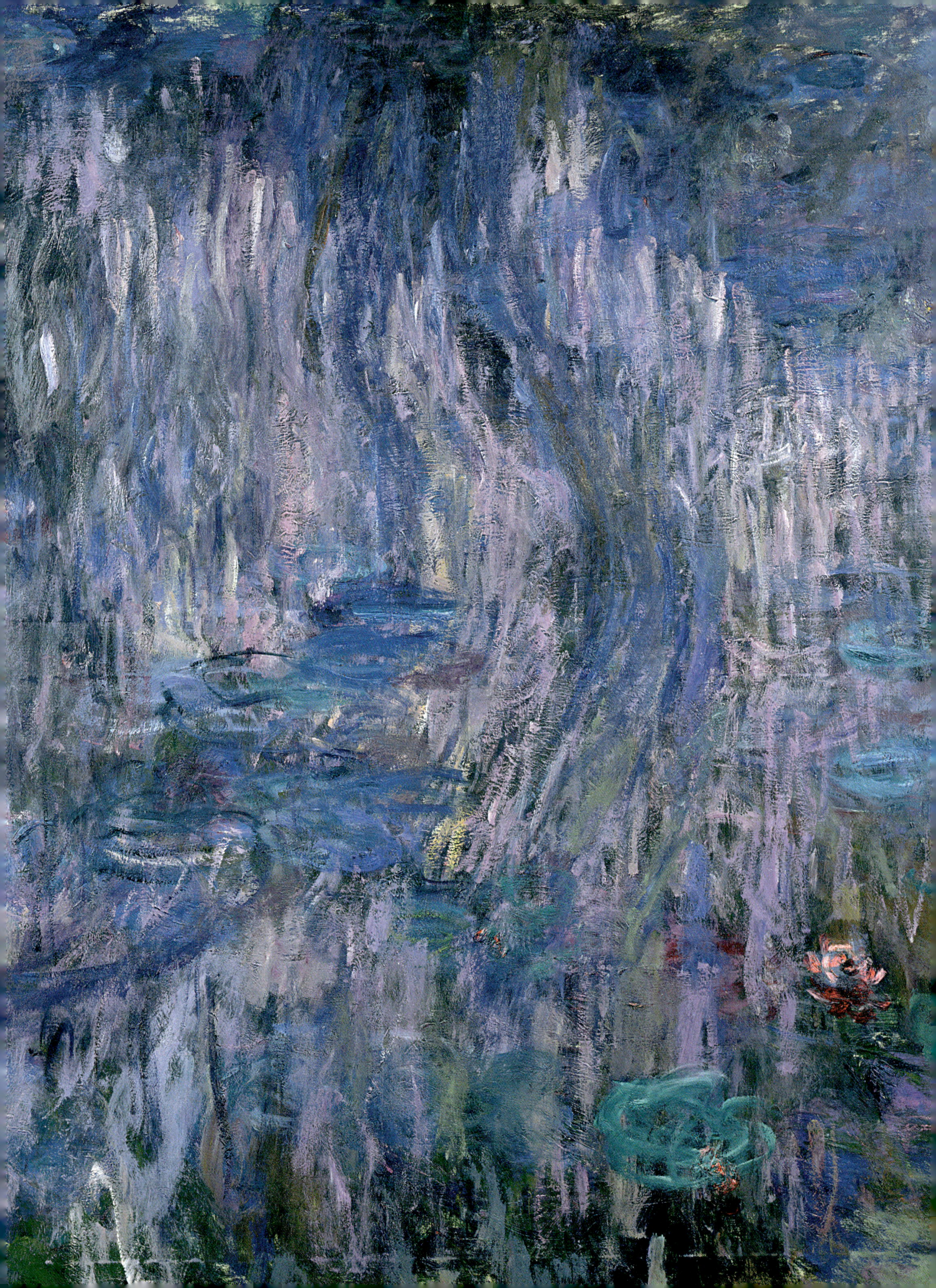

JEAN-DOMINIQUE REY

MIRRORS OF TIME

"The principal person
in a picture is light."
Édouard Manet

AN APPROACH TO MONET

Hinduism defines beings or objects by way of a dual approach, name and form, so it is perhaps tempting to think about our painter's name before going on to define the forms his art was to take. Names might well reveal something of the essence of their bearer, because they can never be entirely indifferent to them. In an idea taken up later by Goethe, the Ancients (and this will be practically the last reference made to them here) believed that each name has a special meaning for the one it belongs to. But only when a name earns a certain reputation is its true meaning brought forth, and only when its story comes to an end is it realized that a link had indeed been forged between person and name—and that that link was in truth simply a coincidence.

At first glance, it seems that the name Monet derives more or less directly from the Latin verb *moneo*, *monere*. Already the root announces something singular or, more exactly, unique. From our point of view, initially the most salient meaning of the verb is *to inform*, *to remind*. But one is still more struck when one reads that it also means *to inspire* and finally *to enlighten*. So, having been *informed* of a new path, Monet went on to *inspire* many painters. As for *enlighten*, it is hard not to be conscious of the fact that, from the very start, as by fate, Claude Monet was born under the sign of light—a light that his oeuvre was to make visible in the highest degree.

There we will leave off elementary semantics—though the implications might easily be further extended (Camille Bryen rightly noted that the first name Claude is already solar). But it was perhaps not entirely futile, before turning to the work, to show how it was symbolized—or even determined—by a name.

UNDER THE SIGN OF THE ELEMENTS

Monet was filled with an all-encompassing passion for painting. Of his other passions, we know only water, air, light, color. And, as he grew older, flowers. Generally then, complementary passions which shore up or overlap with the first: instruments or aids, media or expression, extension or result. And it was his life's work to make them join forces.

Water was the alpha and the omega as much of his existence as of his oeuvre. From Le Havre to Giverny, from his almost native sea to the unruffled ponds of his maturity, all his travels, his sojourns, all the places where he chose to live had as their common denominator the presence of this primal element. The list is endless: the Seine at Argenteuil and Vétheuil, the canals of Holland or Venice, the Thames at London, the sea at Le Havre and Bordighera, the open

PRECEDING PAGE
Water Lilies, Reflections of Willow
1916–19
78 ¾ × 78 ¾ in. (200 × 200 cm)
oil on canvas
Musée Marmottan
Paris, inv. 5122

FACING PAGE
Corner of the Pond at Giverny
1918–19
46 × 32 ¾ in. (117 × 83 cm)
oil on canvas
Musée des Beaux-Arts
Grenoble, inv. MG2168

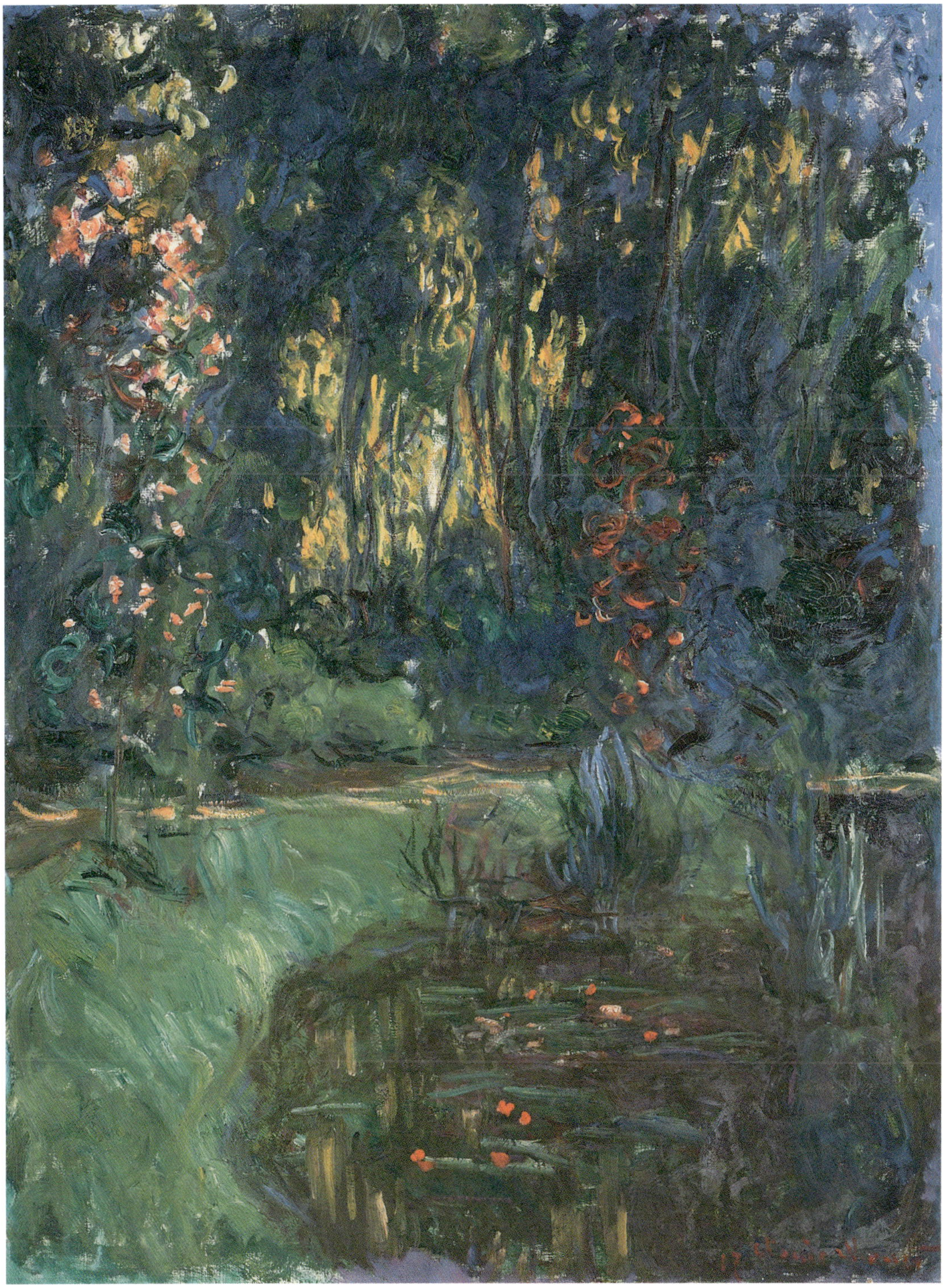

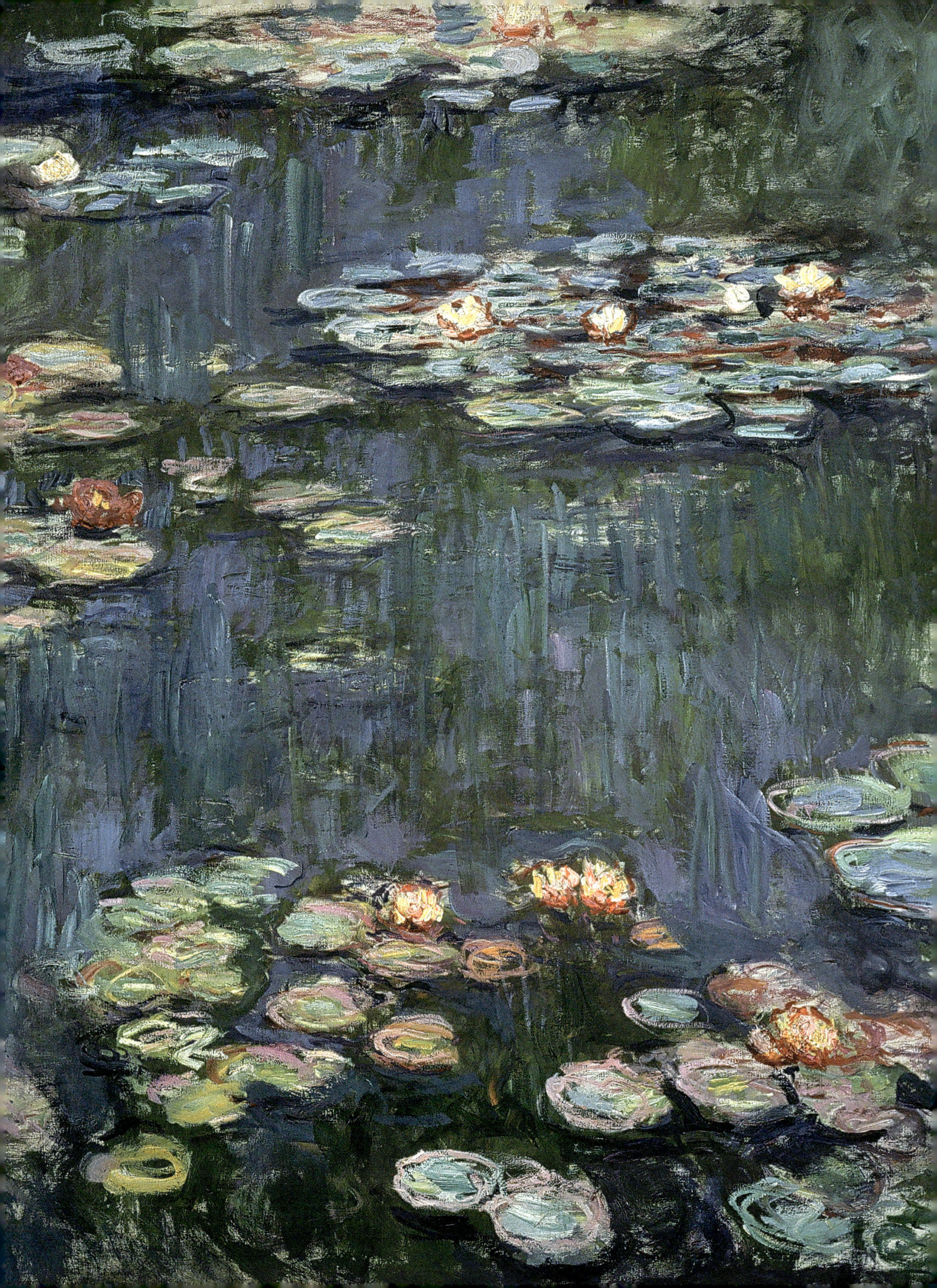

ocean at Belle-Île. The water he seldom excluded from any picture reigns supreme and runs through his work in every possible form: snow, river, canal, sea, rain, ice, fog. Not a single aspect of it, fluid, solid, or vapor, is neglected.

He was to be an attentive and tireless observer of the air. With no other painter, save his immediate forebears, Boudin and Jongkind, would the taste for the open air prove so essential, so fertile. Still lifes or cozy interior scenes form a negligible proportion of the oeuvre. Without going so far as to speak of claustrophobia, of which there is absolutely no sign, only outside did Monet seem to be able to live and create to the full. The opposite, then, of an intimist. His studio is open to the sky. No one was less of a townsman than him. He might go to a city every now and again, but he would soon feel alienated and would focus only on its most subtle and mobile elements: the smoke, the crowds, the trees, the basins—pretexts for movements of color, for dilution. His birth in Paris was mere happenstance, and already his departure for Le Havre aged five seems to encapsulate what he was to become.

The crucial adventure was to be light. Whipped up by the wind, glittering, and divided the better to invade the canvas, it is light that generates figures and forms, and light that he later uses to dilute them. Dappled in the sky over the English Channel, pinkish on the snows of March, transparent in Vétheuil, sulfurous through a London "pea-souper" fog, sourish in Venice, caressing or raw in the fleeting contrasts of the south, rough or vaporous. At the onset rejecting once and for all its negative counterpart, black, which he was to exclude from his palette, Monet tirelessly tracked down every variation in light.

And finally, color too represents a ceaseless search that has to be conquered afresh every day, a drug that will eventually distract him from other questions and finish by existing in and for itself, in its pure state, in the form of energy. Perceived from the subtlest nuance to the greatest intensity by the extraordinary acuity of his painter's eye, Monet succeeded in adding a supplementary octave, unparalleled in painting, thereby enlarging our sensibility. Once through the screen of the fog, where his outraged contemporaries saw only a white void, over time our experience has made it possible perceive a precise program: a new image beyond depiction.

As for flowers, which were present from very early on in their natural form, and later in their feminine form (one thinks of the open petal-shape of the gowns in *Déjeuner sur l'herbe*, the tremulous bouquets of *Women in the Garden*, the inverted corollas of the series of various *Woman with a Sunshade*; in the latter part of his life they will acquire such importance that they become the almost exclusive and soon unique theme of an extraordinary symphony in paint. But if—and in point of fact this is the real meaning of the work—we identify light with fire, then the flowers should represent a fourth element:

Water Lilies
1916
78 ¾ × 78 ¾ in. (200 × 200 cm)
oil on canvas
National Museum of Western Art, Tokyo, inv. P. 1959.151

the earth. Yet they are aquatic, luminous, airy, colorful, and therefore the quintessence of the preceding elements: their culmination, conjunction, and fusion. Thus, at the very last stage, Monet's diverse passions blossom into a spray of forces materialized by flowers.

AN ARTIST AGAINST THE GRAIN

But if these enthusiasms coincide so perfectly, it is only because for them everything had to be sacrificed, and for Monet there is no rupture between work and life, only concord and continuity. For him, the oeuvre is neither refuge nor negation nor rejection; it is instead the embodiment of an existence that he chose for himself, that he conquered against all odds, that he embraced with dynamism. This is why, even if there survive traces of the struggle, and if detritus and masterpiece, success and failure follow one another, as time goes by his body of work leaves such an impression of harmony, such an inalterable feeling of happiness—not happiness thrust upon one, but happiness earned, a sense of exceptional plenitude.

In the last analysis, this man has no history; the events of his life are those of his painting. One might as well forget—or almost—his biography, without this in the least affecting his work. His letters, with the exception of two or three phrases, are gloriously commonplace. He wove the threads of his life into the canvas of his painting; what was lived became color, vibration, light. This colossus (not so much in terms of physique as by dint of his stamina and capacity for work), a man nothing could hold back for long and who, like a rock, stood firm against foul weather and every ordeal or setback, possessed an incredible energy that he shared in equal measure between his creation and his life, passing from the one to the other in accordance with laws of an almost seamless osmosis, and this even—especially—at moments of crisis from which he always emerged victorious and enriched. Monet—or the opposite of schizophrenia. His doubts propelled him forward; he was at his best when he was at his most demanding.

He possessed none of the tempestuousness of that reluctant innovator, Manet, mortified by his lack of recognition; neither did he have the caustic misanthropy of Degas, the social concerns of Pissarro, the self-effacing timidity of Sisley. Nor did he possess the depressive rage of Gauguin, the dramatic "crises" of Van Gogh, or the aggressive self-absorption of Cézanne. Within the impressionist constellation, and in his period more generally, he occupies a unique place: at the head but apart, defined at the same time by an iron constitution, a prizefighter's temperament, and an intransigence that together make him singularly unsuited as a hero of a novel. From this viewpoint, his only peer might have been Renoir, if that artist, when about forty—an age when many choose to disavow their former achievements—had not made a U-turn to the museum, to Italy, to attachment to the past and social compromise.

In Monet on the other hand, no such backsliding is observed. He never retreated from his positions and followed his creative experiments to the limit of what was possible, in new ventures, never scurrying back to the fold of tradition. Even at the acme of his fame, he refused to be fobbed off with honors. He thought it as ignoble to accept medals (those markers of the social consecration of a celebrated artist) as to ask for them. It was a point on which he never yielded. As for the *Water Lilies*, he only agreed to hang them in the Orangerie because of Clemenceau's friendship, and it is symbolic that the show opened only after the painter's death. He had no truck with rhetoric, as contrary to his character as theory. His oeuvre reflects the doggedness of a man well qualified to fulfill the demands of his work. Thus, he did not only innovate in the field of painting, but also in his independent position with respect to social norms. This too is a fact worth insisting upon today.

A PAINTER IN THE PURE STATE

For Monet, painting must initially be understood in its most basic form: brushes of all kinds, instruments, pigments, and paints—elementary media reduced to their sole use.

In exploding the whole idea of "cuisine," of tricks of the trade, he was certainly aided by the invention of new, easier-to-handle chemical paints, which not only facilitated work in the open air, but also clarified the act of painting, entailing a more direct attack on the canvas and an accelerated execution, features that were to acquire increased importance in his search for fleeting light effects.

Following the exclusion of bitumen, another departure soon sees his pictures doing without varnish, which he rejected as an unwelcome expedient whose effects can prove detrimental. The unsullied paint, by turns thick for catching the light or else dilute to allow it to radiate all the more: such is Monet's domain. In an apparent paradox, it is dilution that allows a greater concentration of effect.

With Monet, all that is not painting in its pure state either does not exist or is gradually eliminated. Drawing? For no artist did it possess less importance, once—and this was relatively early—he had discovered his true path and privileged field of expression: color. After the brilliant, but only brilliant, arpeggios of adolescence had been put in a drawer, we do have a number of albums of drawings by his hand, and here or there a few works in charcoal or soft lead pencil, but they seldom amount to more than exercises or notations. Pastel? No more than a rare instant of preparation, that he almost never practiced as an end in itself, unlike Manet and especially Degas. And printmaking?

FOLLOWING PAGE
The Water-Lily Pond with Willows, Bright Morning with Willows
1914–18, triptych: each panel
78 ¾ × 167 ¼ in. (200 × 425 cm)
oil on canvas
Musée de l'Orangerie
Paris, inv. 20106

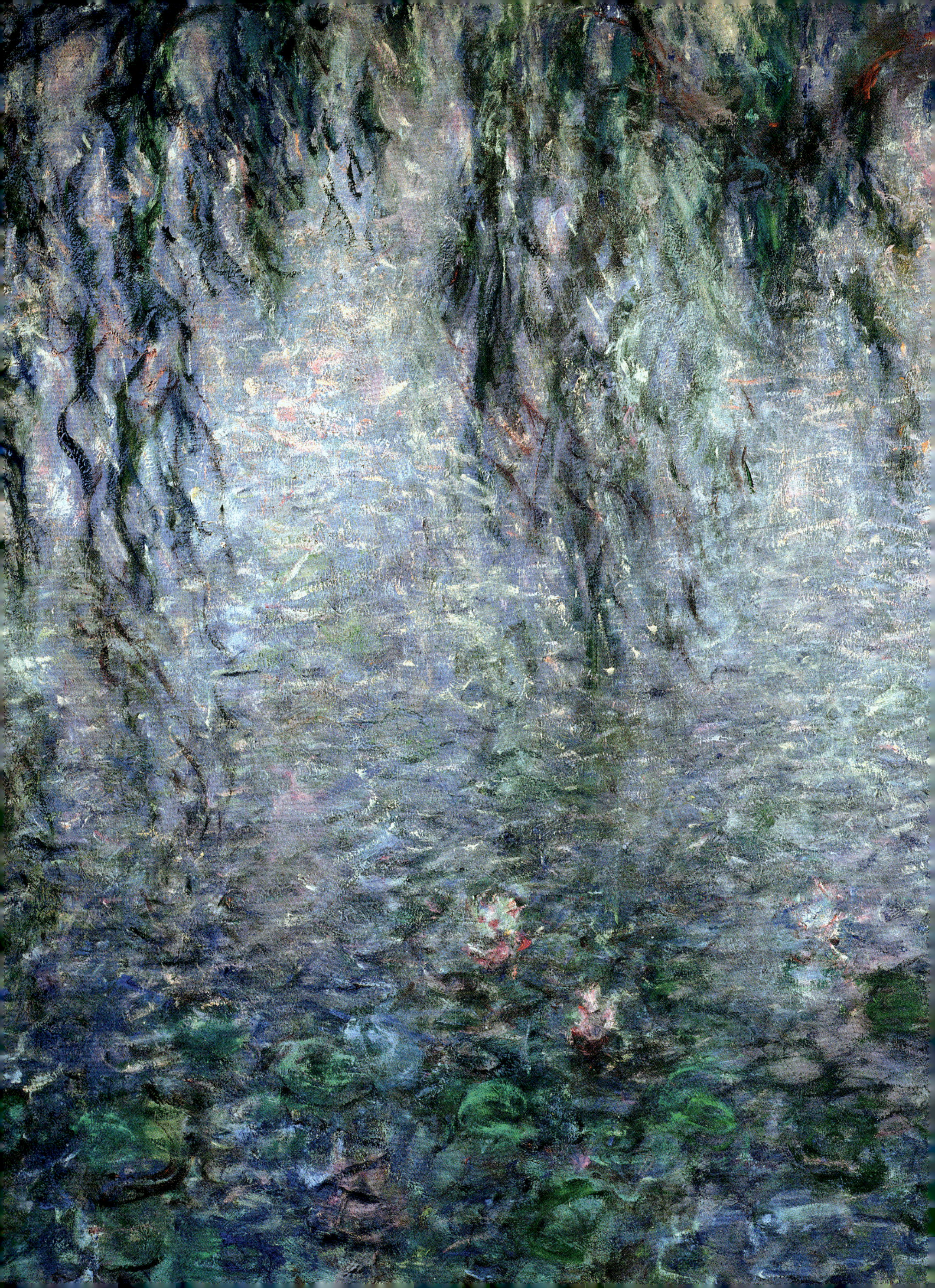

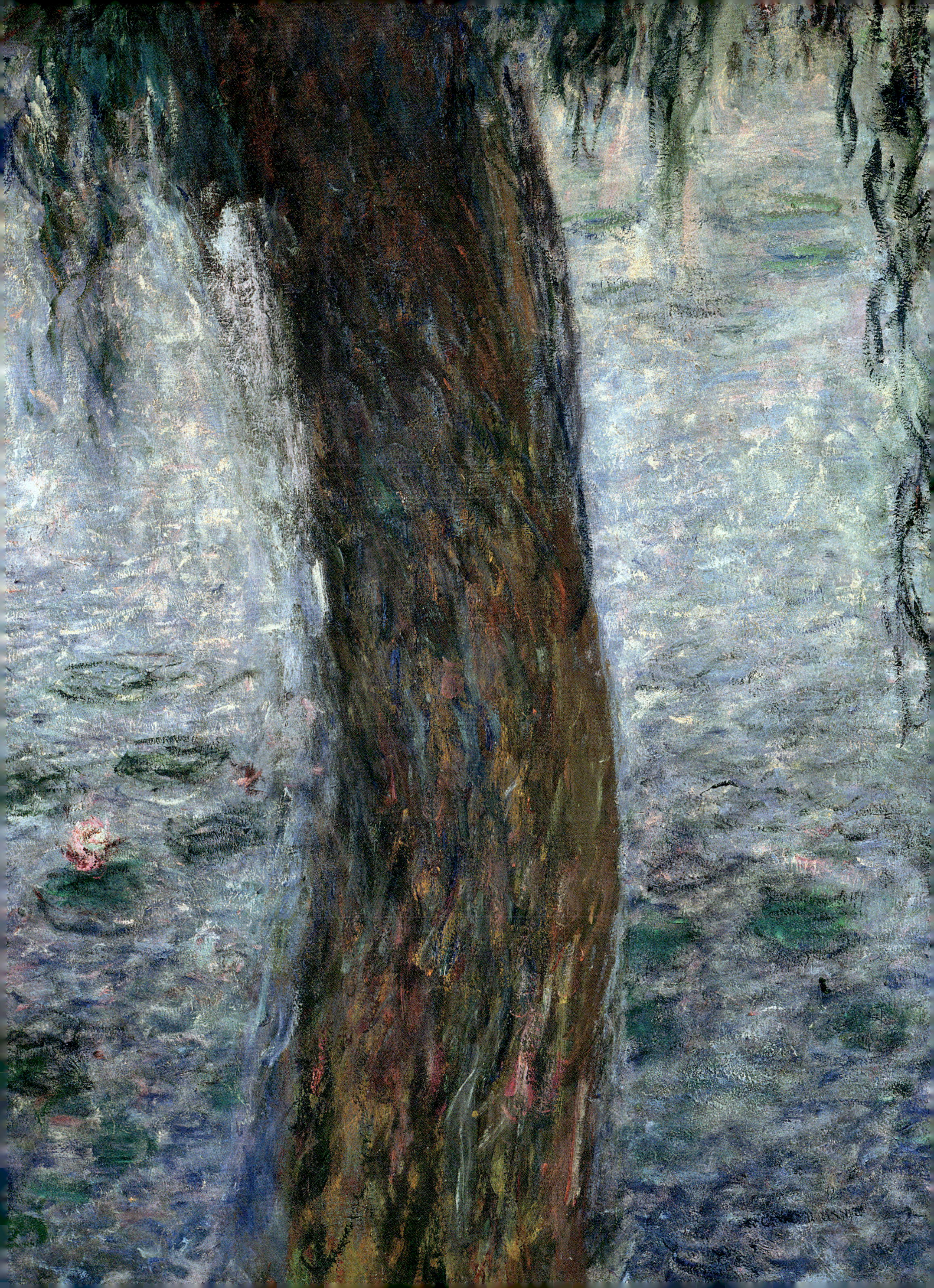

He is in all probability the only impressionist never to have meaningfully tried his hand at it, not as a research tool (Degas) nor in illustrations (Manet and again Degas) nor as the expression or an extension of drawing (Pissarro). Watercolor? No more than a handful of these readily come to mind, though this did not mean it was totally alien to him, because in certain canvases, and increasingly as he approaches the *Water Lilies*, he mastered the fluidity of this privileged medium of the moment, but it is integrated into the picture, transposed into the agile paint, the translucent brushstrokes.

Monet can thus be defined as a painter in a pure state, as an artist for whom painting remains the sole means of expression—an exclusive, or, more exactly, all-embracing passion. And he was to carry this purity, this means, this passion, to an extreme point, in gradually distilling an essence with which he gradually identified himself. He was to *become* painting: its act, its gestures, its spirit—the medium of pure painting.

The oddest thing in his case is that he started off with caricature, with cartoon portraits or sardonic drawings, that is, with anecdotes in line, graphic trivia. But the entire evolution of his work is made up of his surpassing an earlier position by seeing each experiment through to its end. He practiced drawing sufficiently and sufficiently early on for it never to become an obstacle for him and, though never incorporated into the canvas, it gradually melts away to the point that one day some were to carp about its defects or absence, unable to realize that, even invisible, it persists—an underlying but undeniable presence. With Monet, drawing is so well integrated into color that he was almost able to do without form, and, as color took on the primary function, it was to emit little more than an optical impression that imprinted itself on the retina or the memory. Just as, in keeping with the impressionist technique, he was simultaneously practicing the dissociation of tones (that is, not mixing the paints first) so that they might be recomposed "purely" by the viewer, the latter has to perform a dual reconstitution (starting out from the separate tones and submerged forms) as a rapid fusion, because the painter has succeeded in making the two stages coincide, reducing them to a single operation.

THE PATH OF ABNEGATION

This initial approach to Monet would not be complete without one further observation. If it is untrue to call him self-taught exactly, he nevertheless took little heed of the usual stages in an artist's training and never suffered from those lessons that might have held him in check, absorbing only what was to his purpose and fed into his research. Thus, in a further sign of his passion, he remained unburdened by over-explicit references to the past or by traditional methods. One might recall the oft-quoted quip of Gustave Courbet, who had been so intrigued to come across (in about 1865) a "young man who painted things other than angels."

It seems that from the very outset Monet was surprisingly free of the cultural hangover that demanded painting be religious, historical, and/or narrative. From the beginning then, he was resolutely modern. Not only is there not a single religious picture in the canon (a few appear in Manet's oeuvre), there are no historical ones (Degas tried his hand at these), nor anything with a social theme or purpose (Pissarro, as is well known, moved in this direction for a time), and even less so mythological subjects (Renoir, when over forty, returned to those pastures), or symbolic (Cézanne in his early days and Gauguin in his maturity). But for Monet these were more than just rejections, as they left him free to explore a world which, as we will see later, empowered him to venture beyond the object. As early as 1880, the paintings are no longer staged, portraiture becomes less frequent, the faces grow blurred and the figures diluted before evaporating entirely. Each of these characteristics of Monet's oeuvre announces modern painting, a painting which is alone both object and end.

However, before concerning ourselves with the final phase in a corpus that greatly exceeds the elements we have outlined here, and for which hastily advanced conclusions can scarcely do justice, it is necessary to go back to its foundations and reconsider for a moment the "crisis" of the 1880s from which the ultimate apotheosis of the *Water Lilies* was to arise.

MONET AS A PRECURSOR OF MONET

An inventive, creative, seminal body of work is never produced overnight; neither does it yield all facets of its meaning and implications after just a cursory glance. In painting, more even than elsewhere, spontaneous generation is an illusion. Innovation makes its mark in the world only at the cost of endless effort, groping, and guesswork. Manipulating both form and substance, a painter stumbles across what will one day be his future path without knowing exactly that it lies in that particular direction, since he remains as yet unable to view the breakthrough objectively or to make it bear fruit. And so, he turns away from what he has glimpsed since the time is not yet ripe. Maturity will come only when he can stand back and go beyond other less fundamental if necessary experiences, after time has had its way and he has made his slow and arduous conquest of freedom. Put another way, a painter is only able to integrate fully into his canvases his envisioned discoveries once he has acquired a means to give them external form. It is the job of the viewers to embrace the oeuvre in its totality once it is complete—this is, after all, the privilege of history; and so reconstitute the principles that guided it. It is in their eyes that there emerge at a precise date, at an exact point in time, those germs of the future whose importance can only be gauged in retrospective. With Monet, these seeds appear relatively early in canvases which, placed in the sequence of his development as an artist, today appear as heralds or forerunners.

One just has to think of the famous *Impression, Sunrise* (Musée Marmottan) of 1872, a canvas dating from when Monet was thirty, which, in circumstances familiar to all, spawned the term "impressionism." It is worth looking once more at its forms, drowned in fog, the ghostly masts, the docks and cranes brushed in a fugitive blue: the only thing the eye can hold on to is the orange disk of the sun. A comparison with other canvases by Monet or by his friends from the same period brings out the difference and shows just how innovative this *Impression* indeed was. The entire center and left foreground already display all the freedom of the *Water Lilies*, while the two or three boats bob about like flowers in the future *Water Gardens*, open-ended, mobile notations, leaking out from encircled forms in horizontal brushstrokes over a ground clarified with spirits of turpentine.

But there exists another, less famous canvas, equally important from the point of view of the present argument: *The Tuileries* of 1875 (Musée d'Orsay). The only identifiable feature of the garden is the great basin. But the trees on the right, a swirl of foliage, are possessed of a freedom of gesture, a lively, rapid, sinewy handling which, for the briefest of instants, and though at this stage of his oeuvre they lead to nothing, announce the supreme liberty of the *Water Lilies*. Comparing these trees with the right section of the panel entitled *Morning* in the first room of the *Water Lilies* in the Orangerie, we already have the same treatment—astonishingly modern, a lyrical ardor which was to blossom into the driving force behind the great canvases of his later years and from which Jean Messagier drew so much.

MONET IN 1880

An attentive examination of Monet's work might readily uncover further precursory signs of this type. Our contention, however, is not to accumulate materials from a history that has often been rehearsed, but instead to identify its consequences; to that purpose it is more important to identify the decisive moment when the painter was, as it were, reborn.

The year 1880 marked a turning-point in the existence of Claude Monet. With him, as with any groundbreaking creator, events are important only in so far as they resonate within, in how they affect the work and in the precise manner in which they modify it. A few months before the year we have taken as emblematic, his wife Camille died (September 1879). Leaving him distraught, this death drew down the curtain on the first half of his life. Temporarily he moved to Vétheuil, close by one of these watery landscapes without which he could neither live nor work. At the end of a particularly severe winter, Monet painted the ice breaking up on the Seine with an insistence that already prefigures the spirit of the "series" to come. Such a theme, at this precise juncture, possessed symbolic value. Monet was forty years old. The impressionist group, up to now so unified and whose heart-beat and leader he was, now, as was inevitable, began to fall out. Monet was distancing himself from the friends he had made early on during the first battles. These *Ice Floes* (*Débâcles*) signaled an explosion of form, a first "atomization," to be followed by many others. Theme, event, and necessity all coincided. Crucially, from this moment Monet abandoned—one might say expels—all figures, all human representation, in order to zero in solely on landscape elements. There appeared a sequence of convergences, a cluster of facts and decisions, whose unity today, from our perspective, is unmistakable. It was at this point that a second Monet was born and henceforth it is on him that we will focus.

Was this a clean break, then? Yes, but even more a kind of mutation. The change was a slow one. From now on Monet turned to a new program of research and his work entered an experimental phase whose evolution will be marked by the famous series of *Poplars*, *Haystacks*, *Cathedrals*, *Cliffs*, *London*, and *Venice*. This was the age of symphonies, where each movement followed the next, echoing and fitting in with its successor. There were new forms: the ascending spiral of the *Poplars* that deflects the perspective from its customary vanishing point and tends to create a two-dimensional space with the third hinted at only sporadically and as transparence; the appearance of water as a mirror (the *Poplars* again); a time-lapse approach to painting (the *Haystacks* at various times of the day, *Cathedrals* in every conceivable light); the dilution of the city into fog (*London*); iridescent towns (*Venice*)—all *proofs*[1] through which a new lyricism transpires and in which the painter allows due weight to whatever is in front of him, exhausting its possibilities. In the ten years between 1890 and 1900, Monet modified the dominant emphasis of painting, shifting it from space to time. Space, the customary responsibility of painting, is gradually corroded, frayed, diluted. Fleeting, mobile, imperceptible, time becomes a temptation, an obsession that soon seeps into the very stuff of the canvas.

1 It is understandable to pay heed to connotations from photography or printing in the term "proof," though it should also be taken as signifying something that permits a transition from one stage to the next. Some of these canvases however do seem to show reality as a negative.

A FRESH START

"At the heart of the physical lies the metaphysical."
Friedrich Nietzsche

The factor that distinguishes an ordinary painter from a great one lies in the latter's capacity, at a given moment of his life and usually at the end of a period of uncertainty and doubt, to start afresh and thereby avoid rehashing the same one or two good ideas that earned him attention, plaudits, and fame when he first began. Admittedly this severe but unforgiving criterion does not take account of artists who die prematurely, such as Raphael, Watteau, Seurat, and Toulouse-Lautrec; nor does not apply, it goes without saying, to the most gifted and long-lived painters like Titian, Picasso, and Monet.

In a modern context, this second lease of life is often achieved only at the cost of much soul-searching. On a more general level, it manifests itself in the discovery of an area of activity that was perhaps sensed before but which suddenly comes to fruition and renews an entire oeuvre by endowing it with a new-found lyricism or hitherto unsuspected forms. Degas' second career was made manifest in a double series of monotypes, in which form is completely uncoupled from the traditional manner, and in nervous sculptures impregnated by the carnal presence of the hand.

Long after the invention of cubism, in Picasso's case it followed the impasse of Ingresque neoclassicism, in a period haunted by monsters that runs from the preparatory pieces for *Guernica* to those still lifes of the 1940s shot through with a strong tinge of baroque style. In Matisse, it derives from the discovery of a new medium, *papiers découpés*, a source of rejuvenation that gave fresh impetus to his forms and colors through simplification and concentration.

The fresh start, then, amounts to a refusal to stand still, to repeat oneself. By eschewing the temptations of classicism and rhetoric, the artist regains his strength and, aided and abetted by new tools and the fruits of experience, he rises to a higher plane from which he can glimpse a previously unimagined Eldorado.

Water Lilies
1914–17
78 ¾ × 59 in. (200 × 150 cm);
now, 67 × 48 in. (170 × 122 cm)
oil on canvas
private collection

No painter better illustrates this idea than Claude Monet, and no work justifies it more assuredly than the *Water Lilies*. Intriguingly, the appearance of the earliest pictures with this title coincides with the advent of a new century. This feels like a sign, and, when one

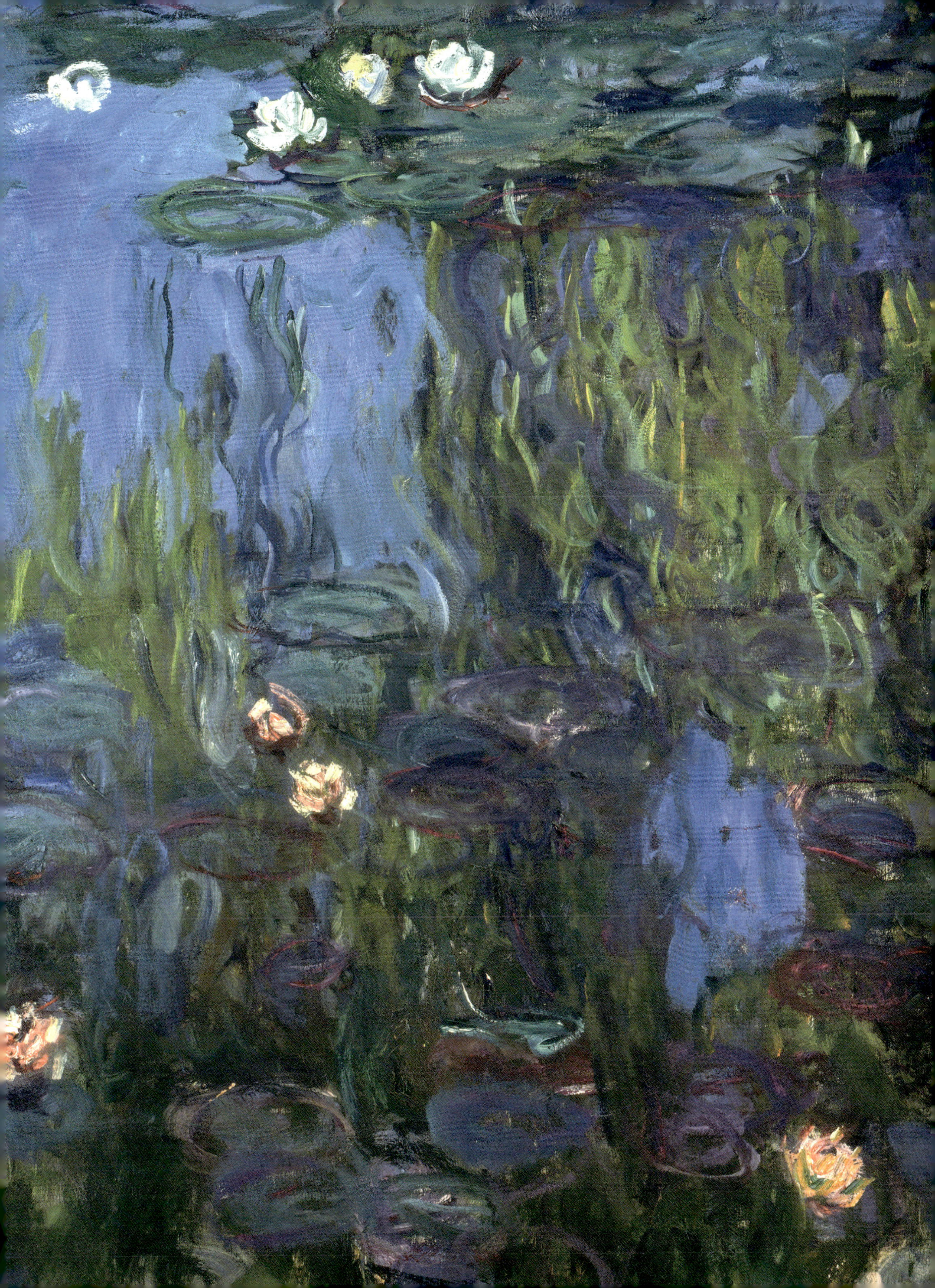

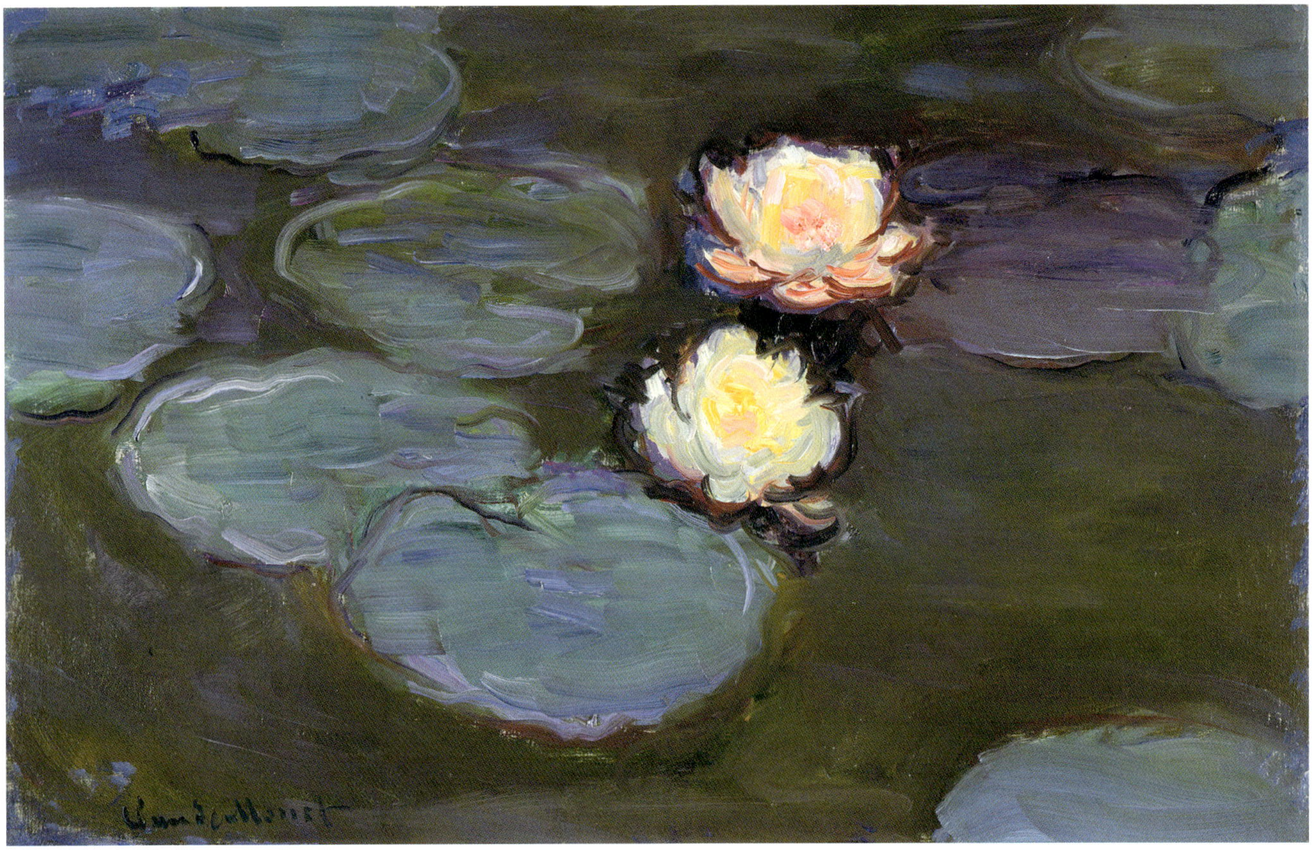

Water Lilies
1897–98
25 1/2 × 39 1/4 in. (65 × 100 cm)
oil on canvas
Los Angeles County Museum
inv. M.62.8.13

recalls what subsequently occurred, one is tempted to write "symbol." Between 1900 and 1926, between the pond and the studio in Giverny, there took place an extraordinary process, almost unnoticed—like everything far-reaching and too revolutionary to gain immediate favor—that transformed the art of Monet and painting generally forever. And this adventure will make Claude Monet, an artist of the nineteenth century, the painter responsible for the majority of the inventions of impressionism, into a genuine twentieth-century artist. Such a profound modification amounted to a veritable metamorphosis in the most literal sense of the term, since it allowed him, almost unwittingly, to overcome and go beyond all known forms. An artist can have no program, for otherwise it might founder; instead it is his acuter perceptions, his subtler intuitions and stronger impulses that usher him into the presence of the essence. Truly great art is almost always created once the necessary tools have been acquired: only then can the will be let go and the way be left open to invention.

Monet's discoveries led far beyond anything he might himself have had in mind. Indeed, it is characteristic of any path-finding work that it is freighted with a mass of factors of which the creator is quite unconscious and which develop much of their potential only after, sometimes a long time after, their author's death. At the same time as it impacts on other contemporary realities of which usually he would have been unaware, it conceals within it consequences for which he would be unlikely to claim credit were he to witness them. Yet he is their unarguable source, being the involuntary cause, a pioneer in the vast tracts of territory in which they take effect.

It is these latent possibilities, overlaps, and repercussions that we must now examine. They, more adequately than any description, will help us to edge towards a grasp of the true meaning of the *Water Lilies*, a work that is at once reality and impact, a work that contains its own analogies, modifications, and effects.

THE CLOSER VIEW

Considered from the viewpoint of nature, the whole history of painting could be boiled down to a single phenomenon: the progressive reduction of what was a vast and distant panorama (the horizon of the "primitives" and more generally that of landscapes that obey the laws of perspective) into close details that invade an entire canvas. From this stance, "pure" landscape between the seventeenth and nineteenth centuries represents a central phase in this evolution. In this sense, painting followed a course parallel to the evolution of science (physics, biology, etc.), where things start off from the general, from an overview, within a system still impregnated with a metaphysical and therefore synthetic spirit, to progress gradually towards a more local observation of a circumscribed, isolated domain where the analysis of the elements is made possible by the magnifying power of the microscope.

Monet sits at the fountainhead of this process of pictorial evolution. To a point he represents a culmination, beyond which the only possible path will be abstraction. He flirts with that abstraction, opening the door without actually passing through it.

The time then has come to stop seeing Monet as a mere landscape painter. What his efforts lead to, in the process begun in the second half of his life, is an unprecedented relationship with the components of nature, which are no longer treated as forms but intuited as forces, and where landscape, obliterated as perspective but recreated as perception, ceases to be an end in itself and becomes a vehicle for pure painting.

As Camille Bryen observed, what Monet forged was a kind of "space-time" of painting. To produce this "space-time," Monet collapsed the distances between the volumes, atomizing them so as to restore the continuity of nature, that fluid movement of the universe from which volume, a mental projection onto the space of the canvas, had estranged his art. Without ever venturing to theorize it—he was too energetic a spirit to wait for that—he had an intuition, expressed and visually demonstrated, of this continuum that scientists were shortly to define conceptually. In the context of painting, Monet represents a remarkable chapter in which the acuity of an eye—exceptional anyhow in his case—urged, even forced a man to hone his perceptions to perfection.

From this point he turned to the infinitesimal, to the infinitely fine, replacing phenomena organized in volumes, masses, and distances by an apprehension of corpuscles, to a photonic perception of light waves [2]. Cleansed of its habitual mental responses, the eye discovers an unmediated universe through a kind of knowledge that is neither pre-established nor schematic, but experiential and approximate. And with Monet, as one should never tire of repeating, this discovery arose solely from an intuition.

ART AND SCIENCE

At every seminal epoch in human history, art has a sense of scientific developments to come. This notion should be advanced prudently, because it can hardly be sufficiently stressed that art is neither the cause nor the result or consequence of science. The perceptions of a painter or a man of science might overlap, but they are nevertheless different and their methods mutually exclusive. But they are contemporary, they coexist, and creators and inventors work in the same climate, at the same period of time.

The artist, with his subtle antenna, intuits feelingly what science will later prove. He never expresses it objectively (that's not his field), nor does he rigorously define its concepts (not his role either), nor experimentally verify the laws governing it (he has neither the means nor the inclination). Nonetheless, between the two realms, an unspoken osmosis takes place that throws up far-reaching parallels and analogies. It is of record that at the beginning of impressionism painters found confirmation of their researches on color in the slightly earlier theories of the chemist, Chevreul. In the same way, the invention and marketing of chemical paints allowed them to leave the confines of the studio and work outside using material that was considerably less cumbersome.

Such phenomena concern the tools (pure colors) and technical matters (Chevreul's theory). But if we now turn to examining

2 Modern theories currently define light propagation as a synthesis of photon particles and waves.

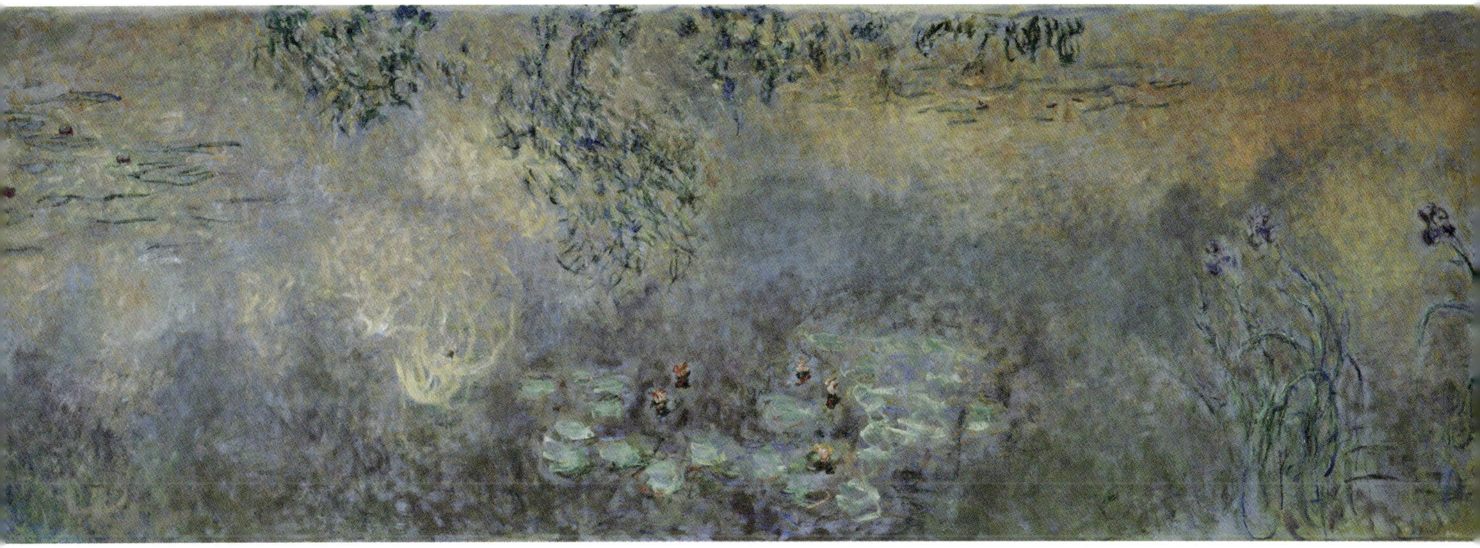

the evolution of some of the critical lines in science, let us say between the mid-nineteenth century and the first decades of the twentieth century, one is surprised to come across analogies in the work of Monet who, objectively, was quite unaware of them. We have already referred to the shift from overview to details that are enlarged and adopted as a value presently applicable to the totality, a process fostered in the area of science by observation under the microscope. With Monet, though part of an environment of which he was far from being the only representative, this change in direction might well have been facilitated by his exceptional visual acuity.

Furthermore in this context, one might mention the paradigm shift from form to energy. In Monet's case, this took place thanks to his intellectual freedom, untrammeled by the limits of visual culture, as we have already outlined, but also through the acquisition of new techniques, such as painting from nature and the penetrating observation of ever-changing light conditions. The move from form to energy occurred through the atomization of the given form into multiple particles (atoms, cells, photons) reorganized by the observer into energy fields and wave fronts.

From another perspective, what could be visually more evocative of the cellular system and its dynamic interplay than the discrete brushstrokes of impressionism that attract or repel one another, and split or join to form here a volume or a body and there an image? It would be a travesty to pursue the convergence of science and painting further, but the congruity is so extraordinary that it has to be brought out.

The Water-Lily Pond with Irises
c. 1914–22
78 ¾ × 236 ¼ in. (200 × 600 cm)
oil on canvas
Kunsthaus
Zurich, inv. 1952/10

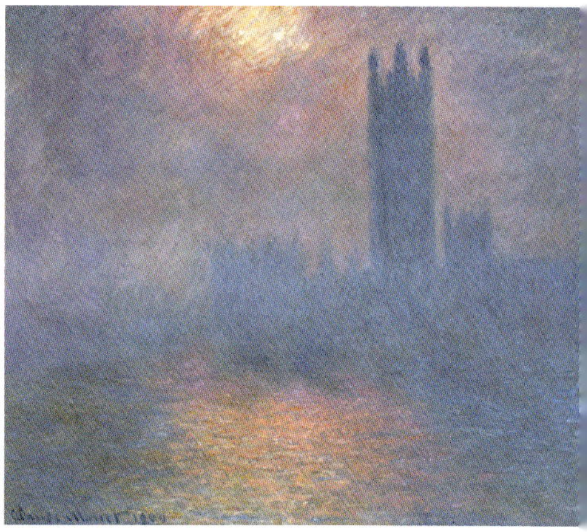

The Houses of Parliament, Seagulls
1903
32 × 36 ¼ in. (81 × 92 cm)
oil on canvas
Pushkin State Museum of Fine Arts
Moscow, inv. 3306

The Houses of Parliament (Sun Breaking through the Fog)
1904
32 × 36 ¼ in. (81 × 92 cm)
oil on canvas
Musée d'Orsay
Paris, inv. RF 2007

A CONTEMPORARY OF THE CINEMA

With hindsight—that singular advantage of the observer over the participant, and of the beholder over the painter—today we can place the unique, personal adventure of Claude Monet in the context of a more general history, and unearth implications of which he and, with more reason, his contemporaries, remained quite unaware. Remarkably, for example, Monet's striving to create through his "series" a time-painting appears at the same time as the earliest stirrings of the cinema.

In periods of transition, painting tends to maintain the same relationship of unspoken prophecy with technology as with science. Chronologically speaking, painting precedes technical innovation and opens new perspectives which, however, it does not seek to materialize. Remaining with the period that interests us, it has perhaps not been sufficiently observed that Georges Seurat's pointillism, the logical continuation and systematization of impressionism, was exactly contemporary with the introduction of the screen in printing photographic reproductions. This familiar process consists in reducing an illuminated image to rows of regularly spaced points which, once miniaturized and reproduced, are recomposed by the eye as a complete image. Today, it appears obvious that these two processes (painterly pointillism and photographic screen) must have been related in some way, even if it is hard at this distance and with the lack of documentation to establish direct links between them. It is in all probability advisable to speak of a climate rather than of

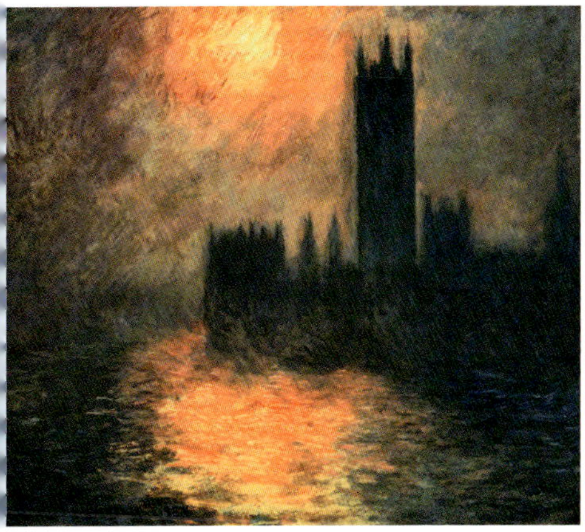

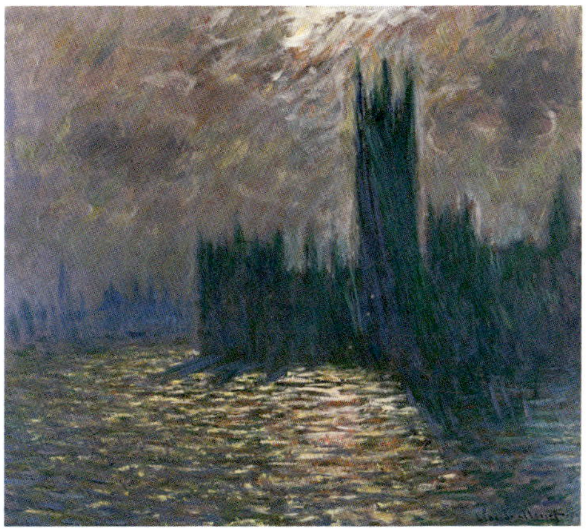

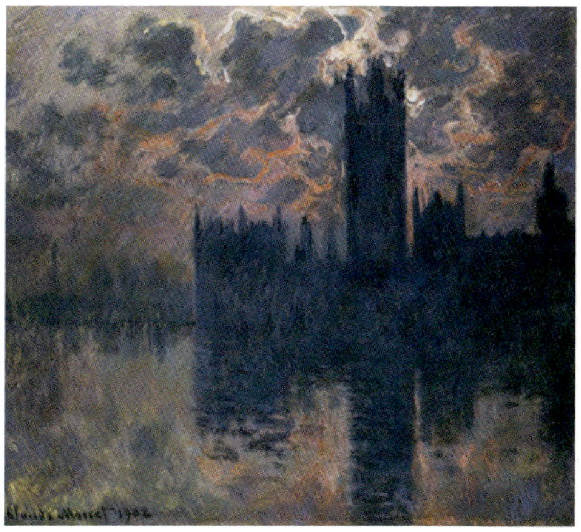

actual influence, of a shared environment, and revert to the concept of unconnected yet contemporary domains, whose outcomes converge, without the cognizance of the protagonists. A tendency exists, somewhere in the air, circulating beneath the radar, which is picked up by various intellects for different purposes and turned by some into the immediacy of an artwork or objectified by others in technology.

In the same connection, the convergence and analogy between the cinema (or the animation of the image by mechanical sequencing that captures the various stages of motion) and Monet's attempt to paint a monument (*Cathedral of Rouen*) in different light levels, or the same fragment of landscape at different times of the day (the *Haystacks*, which are in fact no more that a highly provisional "construction"), or the same view of a single garden under variable lighting conditions (the *Water Gardens*, from which monumentality recedes in favor of transitory reflection) have not attracted much attention. Here the painting, gropingly, uncertainly, through the use of different methods and however preordained to fail, precedes by a hair's breadth the cinematic process in the search for a technique which, if initially chaotic, soon created the illusion of perfectly synchronized movement.

Admittedly, there is something rather despairing in Monet's effort to grasp the various stages in the movement of light, to decompose its elements consecutively across various canvases on which he worked almost simultaneously and, as in the *Cathedrals*, to seek continuity in the juxtaposition of the results, pictures of the same size hung side by side. Indeed this period, which Camille Bryen

The Houses of Parliament, Sunset
1904
32 × 36¼ in. (81 × 92 cm)
oil on canvas
private collection

The Houses of Parliament, Reflections on the Thames
1905
32 × 36¼ in. (81 × 92 cm)
oil on canvas
Musée Marmottan
Paris, inv. 5007

The Houses of Parliament, Sunset
1902
32 × 36¼ in. (81 × 92 cm)
oil on canvas
private collection

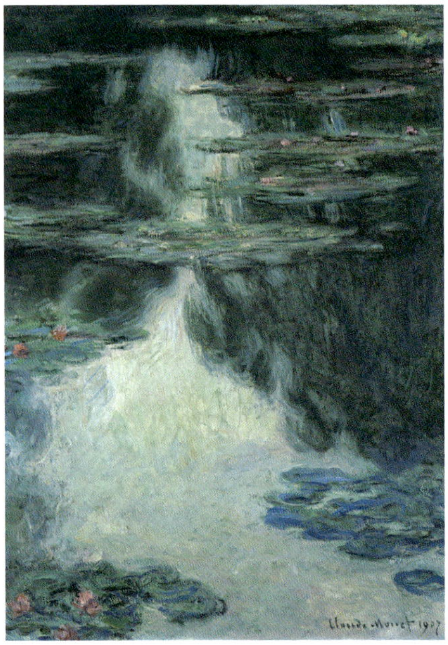

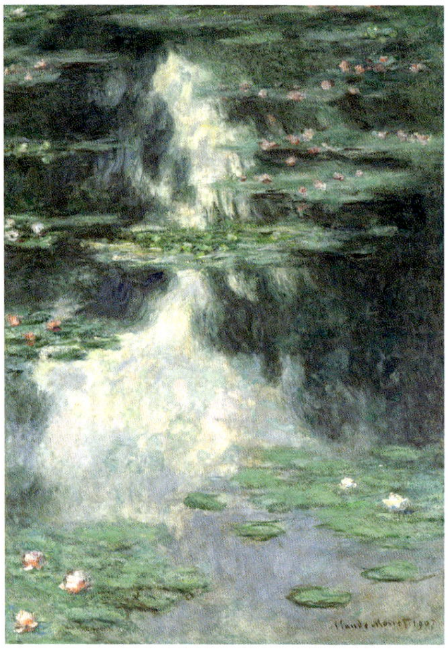

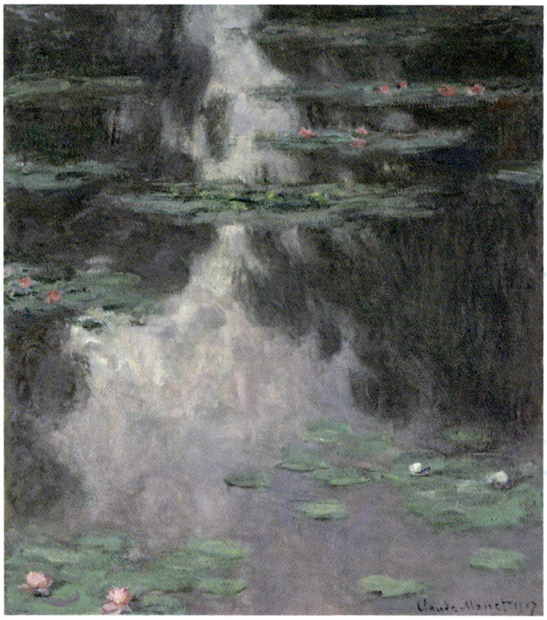

Water Lilies, Gray Day
1907
39 ¼ × 28 ¾ in. (100 × 73 cm)
oil on canvas
private collection

Water Lilies
1907
42 × 28 ¾ in. (107 × 73 cm)
oil on canvas
private collection

Water Lilies
1907
36 ¼ × 32 in. (92 × 81 cm)
oil on canvas
The Museum of Fine Arts
Houston, inv. 68-31

has prettily dubbed a "solar marathon," represents perhaps the only time when Monet's correspondence reflects a note of desperation concerning his art. Yet it seems to us that his efforts do amount to a genuine intuition of what the cinema was to bring. This is primarily the case since, in more than one respect, Monet's analysis tends solely towards synthesis, and film will be nothing other than the decomposition of the various moments of a changing image with a view to restoring continuity through accelerated motion.

Once again, such experiments, pushed by Monet to the limits of the possible, and which have been heretofore regarded as merely the reduction of painting to some extreme optical process, in fact radically transcended the historical period, as well as his own art. We replace his findings in context simply to bring out two implications, or more exactly two extrapolations, of this neglected facet of his painting which we can now proceed to examine.

First and foremost, and most probably for the first time in the history of painting, in Monet's "series," by way of an extraordinary step-change of which he seems to have been the unconscious initiator, *it is the process that becomes paramount, taking precedence over the result, i.e., the work created.* In addition, to explain the apparent puzzlement these "series" occasioned the critics and public when they were unveiled (reservations that lingered on well after the event), this fact also represents at the same time one of the aspects—though not the only one—by means of which young painters have more recently established a lineage between Monet and their own ambitions.

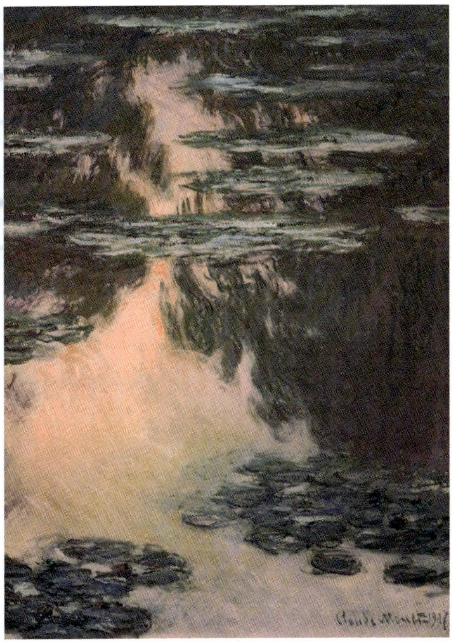

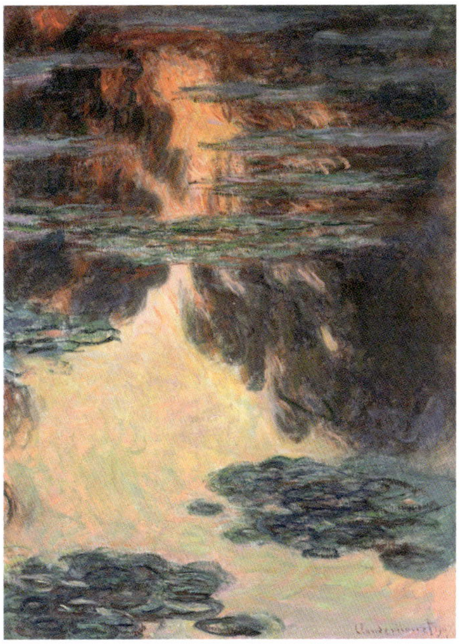

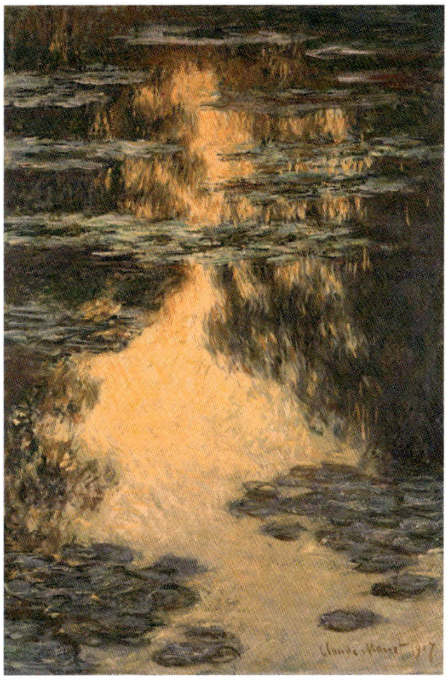

If inevitably gaining ground at the cost of an aesthetic quality that has to cede its preeminent position, this novel attitude continued to hold its own in terms of sensibility and life and was destined to become, if not universal, then at least widespread, and underpin not only art, but literature and even the new mathematics. (A famous mathematician recently declared that, in set theory such as it is currently taught, "The process is more significant than the result.") Here again, Monet, with the purely intuitive means at his disposal, appears as a precursor.

Moreover, the place of the "series" resurfaces, still more amplified, with a painter at a million miles from impressionism, who once joked that impressionist painting was "*toujours au beau fixe*" (both "always sunny and serene" and "with only beauty in mind")—that is Picasso, for whom a "picture" might be the result of a couple of dozen canvases. Of course, the fall of light harbored little interest for the genius from Malaga, but a multiplicity of possible visions or dual points of view did, to the degree that he turned painting into an art of alternatives. Here then, if only for an instant, opposites meet at what is an accidental but not insignificant asymptote.

But the analogy with the cinema would be little more than a key moment in Monet's oeuvre if thereafter, that is precisely in the *Water Lilies*, the painter had not actually solved the dilemma it poses. For us today, this is indeed their most important characteristic. For can anything more marvelous be imagined in film than these vast, elliptical panels, veritable panoramic shots ahead of time, in which, through a miracle of invention and technical innovation, Monet

Water Lilies
1907
39 ¼ × 28 ¾ in. (100 × 73 cm)
oil on canvas
Bridgestone Museum of Art
Tokyo, inv. F.P. 23

Water Lilies
1907
39 ¼ × 28 ¾ in. (100 × 73 cm),
oil on canvas
Musée Marmottan
Paris, inv. 5168

Water Lilies
1907
41 ¼ × 28 ¾ in. (105 × 73 cm)
oil on canvas
Konstmuseum
Göteborg, inv. GKM 2232

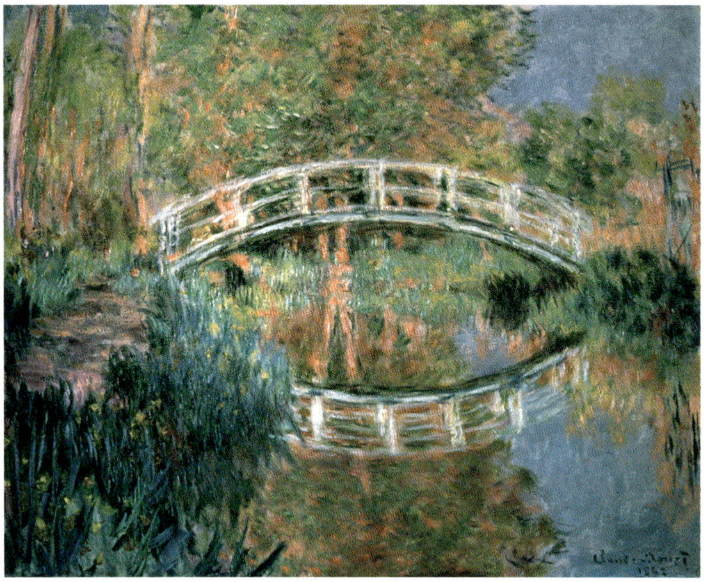

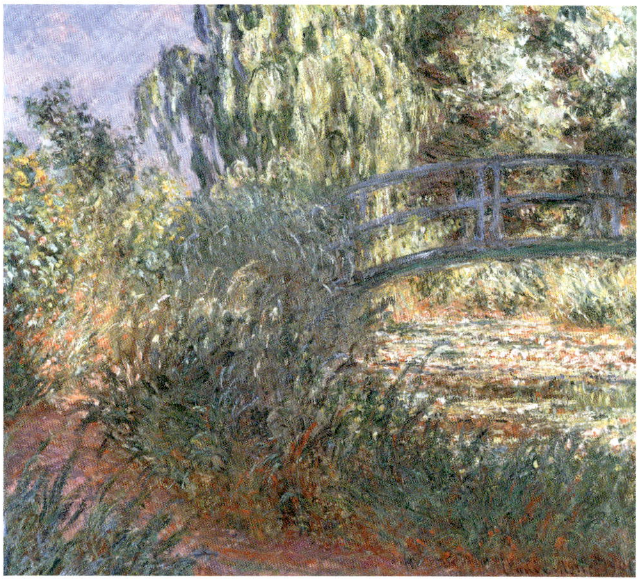

succeeds in inserting time into space, in weaving the weft of the one into the web of the other. With the *Water Lilies*, Monet succeeds in squaring the circle encountered with the juxtaposed, contiguous yet still separate *Cathedrals* by dissolving the successive episodes into a new continuity.

Naturally, these vast stretches of water dotted with flowers cannot move as they do in film, but they encourage the eye to shift from one side to the other and plunge into the canvas in an effort to grasp its overall continuity. This brings out the distinction with the cinema, which establishes its continuity upon a temporary support over a fleeting period of time. In this manner, once the movie has come to an end, its more or less fugitive impressions have to be conserved in the memory. Monet's canvases, on the other hand, remain present before us: ever-shifting time is thus fixed in a stabilized space.

FROM FRONTALITY TO DEPTH

As Frédéric Benrath once very pertinently observed in our hearing, Monet obtained such results by passing from frontality to depth—that is, by shifting dimensions. The shortcomings of the *Cathedrals* derive from their being depicted from the front, i.e., over a single, vertical plane resembling a wall, closed off, thereby preventing all extension in depth[3]. Perhaps it was

3 Still, some of the *Cathedrals* are depicted from below and off parallel. The oblique view offers a minor corrective to the overwhelming mass of the frontage, hinting at a solution which is never actually followed through.

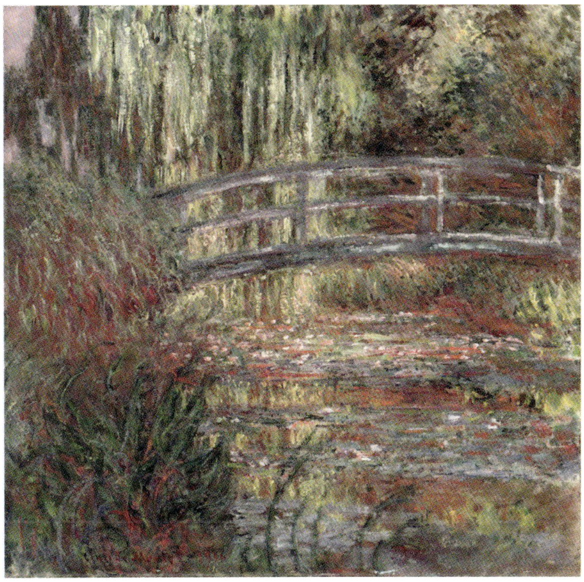

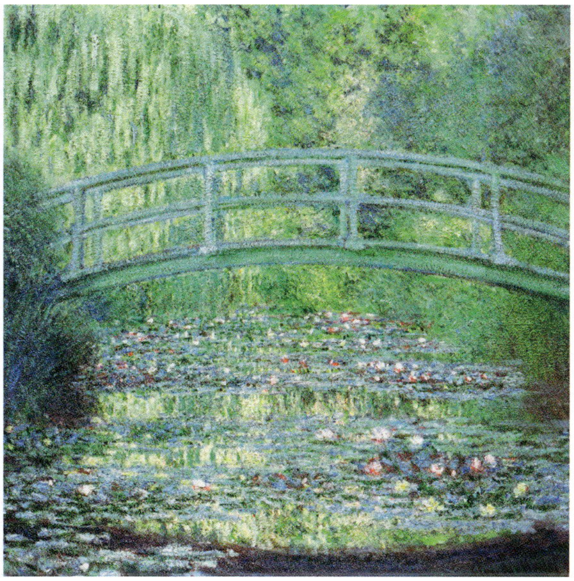

architecture itself, that is, forms organized into simple, opaque masses, that unsettled Monet, since it remains an object, and it was the object he was striving, unsuccessfully as it transpired here, to eliminate and dissolve into vibrations.

It seems that this relative but salutary failure was due to the absence of an element that seemed essential to Monet at every point in his life, the only thing that allowed him to give true expression to his freedom: water. Between the *Cathedrals* and the *Water Lilies* came the series of *London* and *Venice*, in both of which the aquatic element is paramount.

Later came the *Gardens at Giverny*, the *Japanese Footbridges*, and the first *Water Lilies*. Some of those still conform to frontality: a pond, a stretch of river remains vertical. Yet, on the one hand there is duplication—the water mirrors the sky or a tree; while, on the other, one notes the appearance of neutral zones, the presence of fog and some opaque reflections. Fundamentally, if shockingly to the eye, these neutral, opaque zones transcend both the object and its form, and gradually in a new departure that transported Monet to the other side of the mirror, depth is opened up. More exactly perhaps, absolute continuity is here established between a source and its reflection. (In certain canvases, such as *Water Lilies* no. 67, Musée Marmottan, the difference between source and reflection is completely abolished, with the circles of the water lilies persisting in the clouds by way of transparency, osmosis, and fusion.)

The Japanese Bridge
1892
32 × 39¼ in. (81 × 100 cm)
oil on canvas
private collection

The Path along the Water-Lily Pond
1900
35 × 39¼ in. (89 × 100 cm)
oil on canvas
private collection

The Water-Lily Pond
1900
35½ × 36¼ in. (90 × 92 cm)
oil on canvas
Museum of Fine Art
Boston, inv. 61.959

The Water-Lily Pond
1899
35 × 36¼ in. (89 × 92 cm)
oil on canvas
private collection

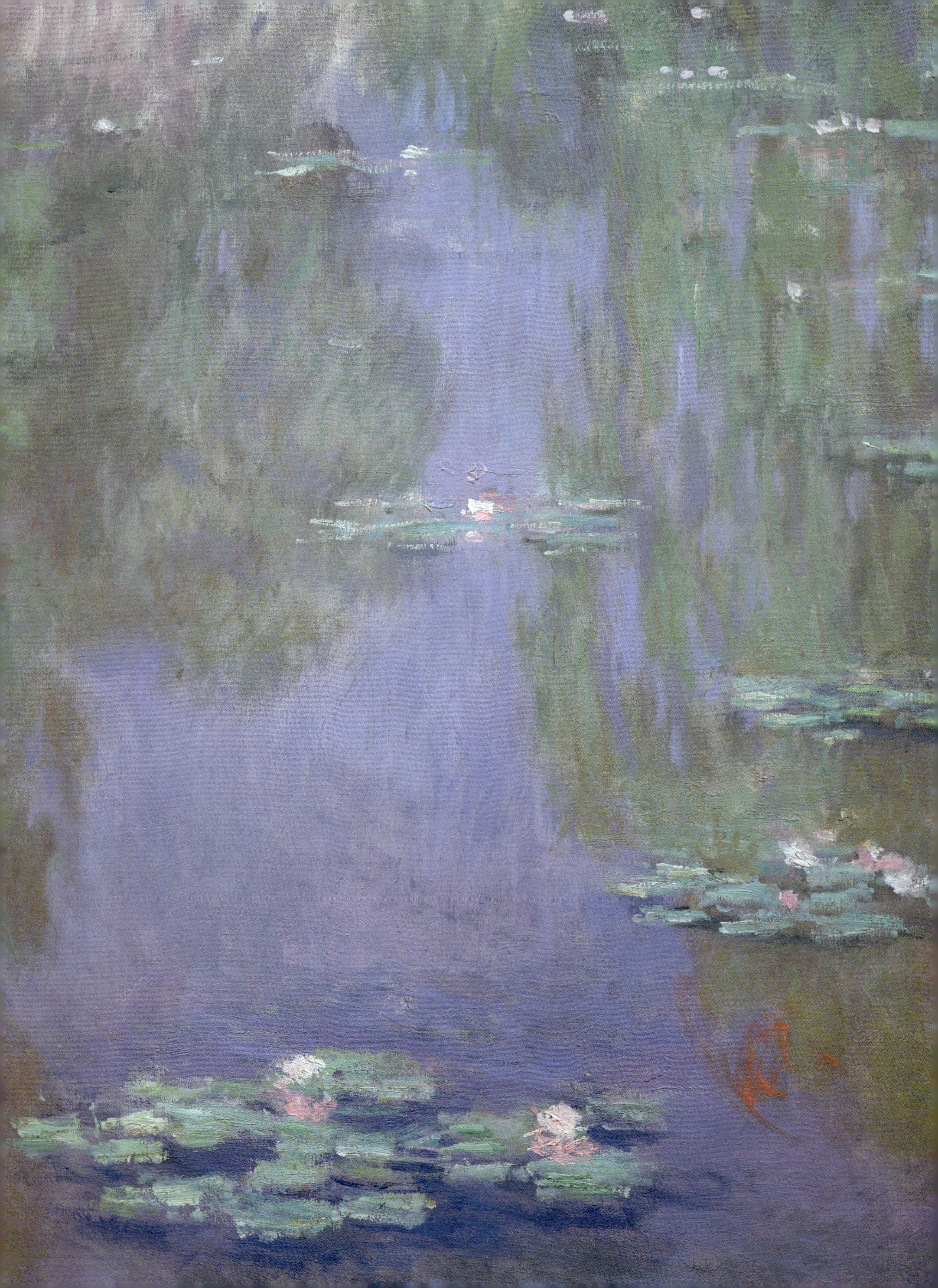

At this point, an experiment suggests itself: every one of the *Water Lilies*, *Water Gardens*, or aquatic landscapes of the period in which the water reflects trees, flowers, or the sky can be turned upside-down without affecting the balance of the canvas in any way. The signature is the only giveaway as to the orientation of the picture. For the first time to such a degree, one of the unwritten laws of modern painting is applied: "What is above is like what is below." Different worlds are no longer separate but fused, unified in their diversity and not simply reconstructed in the mind's eye. The last avatars of the Renaissance are swept away: painting ceases to be *cosa mentale* and rejoins the cosmic flux. The novelty and "scandal" of this reversible, invertible painting can be gauged from the words of Eugenio d'Ors, when, in the name of pictorial logic, he denied the *Water Lilies* any authentic existence: "Within the history of art, never could Monet's *Water Lilies* be taken as a normal product, nor ever will they: rather they are a caprice which, if it flatters our sensibilities for a moment, lacks the criteria to be accepted into the ennobling archives of our memory. The amusement of a quarter of an hour… a thing finally that one sees without looking at, which one takes in without thought, and which one forgets without regret."[4]

When it comes to stylistics, however, Cassandra-like prophecies often come up short: "never" is a dangerous word, sure to be contradicted in the long run. One day—admittedly after a quarter of century of oblivion "without regret"—for an entire generation of painters this "amusement of a quarter of an hour" was to become a seminal entity, one that underpinned, determined, and fertilized their own research. Yet, as an intellectual process, even such utter condemnation is worth a second look. Such misgivings, seen through the prism of a limited viewpoint, are aroused by a novel creation in the mind of a "thinker" who is totally assured of his own thought patterns, and as such they reveal with uncanny accuracy what was indeed new in the work. Innovation is never recognized immediately because it goes straight to the essential and disturbs the established order.

To return to the *Water Lilies*, such broad unfolding allows for the juxtaposition, this time skillfully orchestrated, of frontality and depth. Take as an example one of the most successful, the one which, in the first rotunda of the Orangerie, bears the title *Morning*. Elements indexing perspective, instead of receding towards a central point, veer off slightly towards the right. At the other end of the panel this redirection is echoed by a contrary movement, which, instead of retreating, surges up towards the viewer like a wind changing tack and plastering a sail over one's face. Meanwhile, at the extreme right, the grass, trees, and flowers are laid out frontally; that is, as a vertical plane, but this time as a diluted and simplified fragment of a whole. The whole piece—a genuine and indeed masterly "dissolve"—is thus conceived as the living

Water Lilies
1903
28¾ in. × 36¼ in. (73 × 92 cm)
oil on canvas
Musée Marmottan
Paris, inv. 51633

4 Eugenio d'Ors, *Vie de Goya* (Gallimard: Paris, 1929), 179 (after the French translation).

unity, subtle and varied, of the successive movements of a symphony. Instead of joining, these movements halt and collide, before passing one over the other, and finally, once the eye has adjusted and embraced the totality, melting into a new-found unity, which is no longer simply a given, but actually experienced and realized. Here, it is music that comes to mind. During the same period, Debussy (in *Jeux*) and soon Ravel (in *La Valse*) were heard introducing a similar process of rupture into the course of a melody by dint of counter movements designed to short-circuit the sentimental character of the sound flow (something to which Gabriel Fauré, for instance, remained wedded). The soundscape changes into a syncopated field, before ultimately folding into an envelope in which the harmony is resolved. Such a process also establishes a new form of continuity, which goes beyond the notion of opposing elements that alternate initially only to fuse in the final analysis. Soon the novel, too, was to take up the idea.

At critical periods of upheaval, painting usually precedes the other arts in terms of intuition and invention. This is due to the fact that it handles forms and forces that are physical rather than conceptual and that it can thus advance boldly into previously uncharted territory. And, though his place was long in being acknowledged, at this moment it is Monet who is in the vanguard.

PHYSIOLOGY AND CREATIVITY

We referred above to the opaque spots, the neutral zones which appeared at a crucial stage in the process that took Claude Monet from stalemate to solution. When we learn that the only accident that marred Monet's indomitable health was a failing of his sight due to the formation of a double cataract, which had to be operated on and which for a time resulted in a total incapacity to perceive color (a trauma for any painter, but particularly so for one blessed with such a subtle visual sense), one is inclined to think that these spots did not spring solely from changes in his art, but were in fact the initial telltale signs of his ailment.

Tempted to consider the relationship between these two phenomena as one of cause and effect, we consulted Doctor Jacques Mawas, who had examined Monet's eyes when, several months after the operation performed by Doctor Coutelas, the painter, impatient to get back to work, complained that he had not yet recovered his normal vision: "I can see blue," he told the physician, "I can't see red anymore, nor can I see yellow. That annoys me terribly because I know these colors exist and because I know that on my palette there's red, yellow, there's a special green, there's a certain violet. I can't see them as I once could and yet I remember clearly the colors as they used to look."

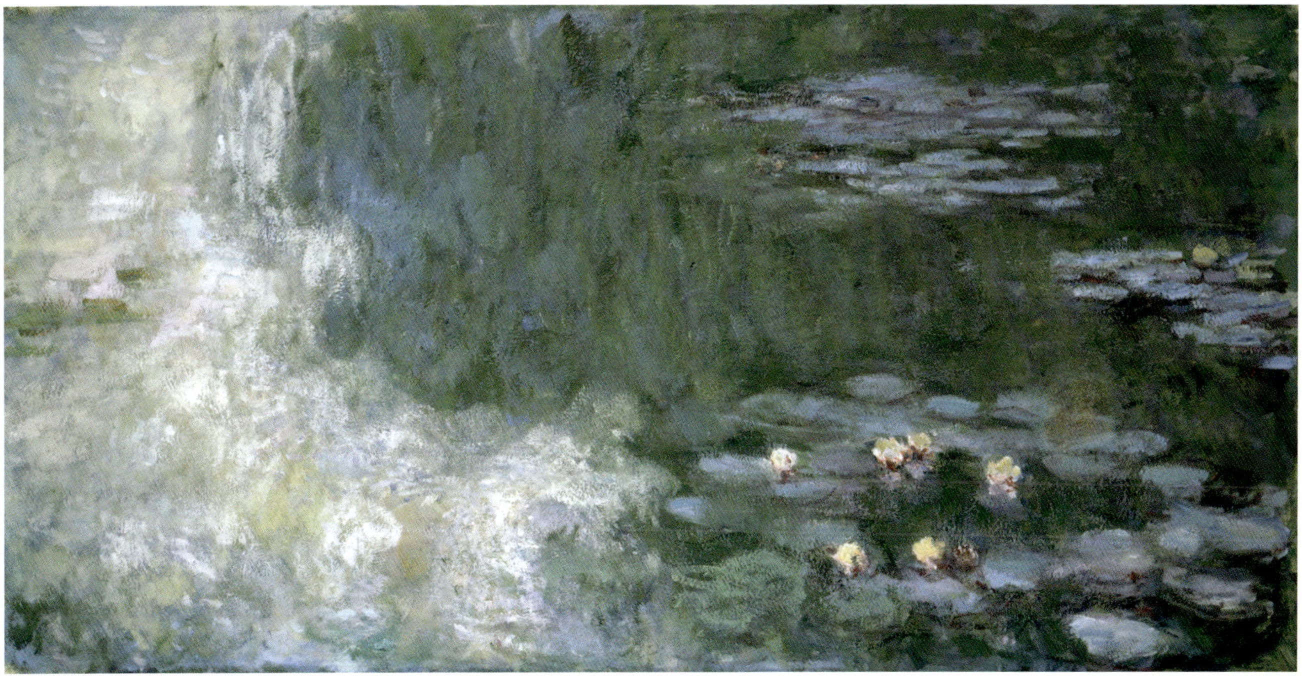

In point of fact, in a number of canvases from Giverny, some of which can be seen in the Musée Marmottan, a dominant blue can be observed which, little by little, invades the canvas almost to the point of monochrome, an effect that runs counter to Monet's entire art. An artist who had stared the sun in the face, and who, by observing its effects, had invented a new type of light, was suddenly struck with near-blindness; he who had banished black from his canvases was reduced to a kind of "night" vision. One might here indulge in allusions to myth and evoke a new Oedipus, a purblind old man guided by his daughter-in-law, whose first name was curiously a synthesis of all the colors, Blanche... but such facile temptations need to be resisted, especially as it is so at odds with an art that rejected all recourse to mythology. But in this connection, myth is just a brief interlude and the solar "passion" that gripped Monet, that pure Apollonian, soon reached a conclusion.

After examining the painter's eyes, Doctor Mawas managed to find some spectacles tinted yellow-green that absorbed the blue and part of the violet range, and so reestablish a balance that enabled the painter to gradually regain his color perception and begin working normally again. According to Doctor Mawas, the formation of a cataract—transparent lens, yellow pigment—while it upsets colors perception, does not usually occasion the appearance of blotches.

The Water-Lily Pond
1917–19
39 ¼ × 78 ¾ in. (100 × 200 cm)
oil on canvas
private collection

So the hypothesis above is to be abandoned, but the incident can still be interpreted symbolically. The canvases of Monet—a painter of the sun, of reflections, the untiring painter of light—were for an instant tarnished, misted even. In what is a highly revealing coincidence, just before his final victory, Monet passes through a "blind" phase, pictorially speaking, which precedes the physiological accident. These elements—where myth and reality for a moment intertwine—remain important in so far as Monet, in the later *Water Lilies*, as he extricates himself triumphantly from a pictorial dead end and is cured of his ailment, experiences one last apotheosis that crowns his oeuvre with a masterly finale: a celebration of recovered sight and regained use of color.

Once more, it was to water that Monet owed his triumph; to water, of which Paul Claudel was to write one day that it is, "*le regard de la terre, son appareil à regarder le temps*" ("the eye of the earth, its organ for gazing upon time"), a phrase that the philosopher Gaston Bachelard quotes in connection, interestingly, with Monet. Already water lilies themselves, by the shape of their leaves, have analogies with eyes. Even more striking in the two great rooms of the Orangerie (the arrangement and display for which was designed by the painter himself), is their elliptical, ocular form. To proclaim his newly recovered sight, the painter created two rooms like two immense eyes on curved surfaces over which unfolds a global vision, a Panic hymn to color, a celebration of cosmic light. Both by the structures containing the works that he rated most highly and by the very spirit of his painting, Monet allows us to enter *inside sight itself*.

THE ORIENT REGAINED

Referring back one last time to the opaque forms and neutral spots, in addition to their decisive importance at a juncture crucial to the painter's evolution, we can, without forcing the point, allot one further significance to them. Accidently or consciously, temporarily or instrumentally, inconclusively or incidentally, they introduce into painting—for the first time in so clear-cut a manner—the kind of abstract elements which, half a century later, tachism and abstract art were to make their own. There may have been some misunderstanding in the interpretation then made of them, and perhaps their impact was exaggerated; nonetheless, above and beyond the perhaps doubtful physiological causes and the fortuitous or unintended analogies with later abstraction, these "patches" do possess Far Eastern resonances that are hard not to perceive. As Émile Compard, a notable expert on Monet and a painter very close to the Chinese spirit, told us, they attain what Laozi called "a great form without outline, a square without corners," something which has no equivalent at all in earlier Western painting.

Study of Water Lilies
c. 1917
11 3/4 × 11 3/4 in. (30 × 30 cm)
oil on canvas
private collection

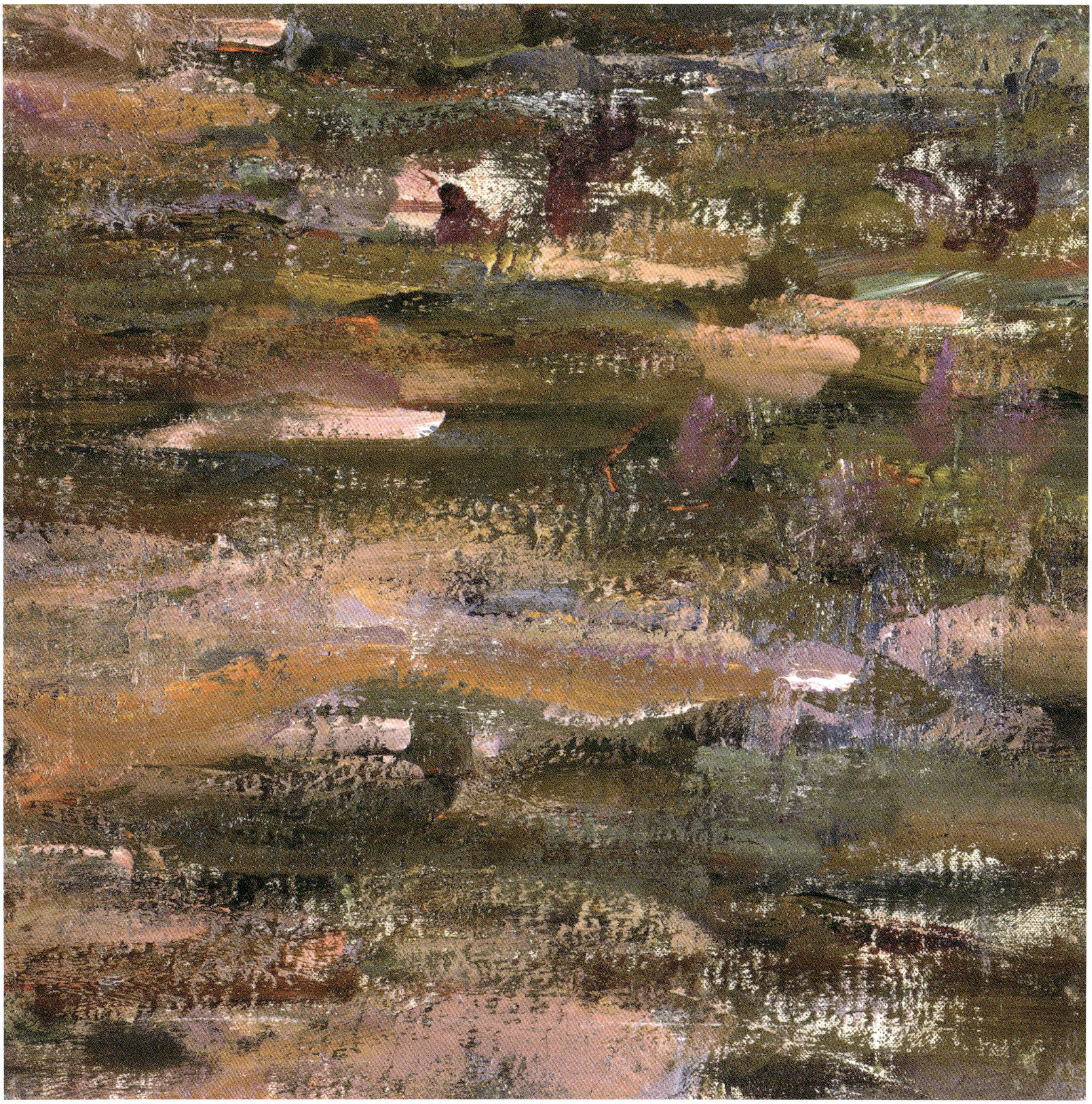

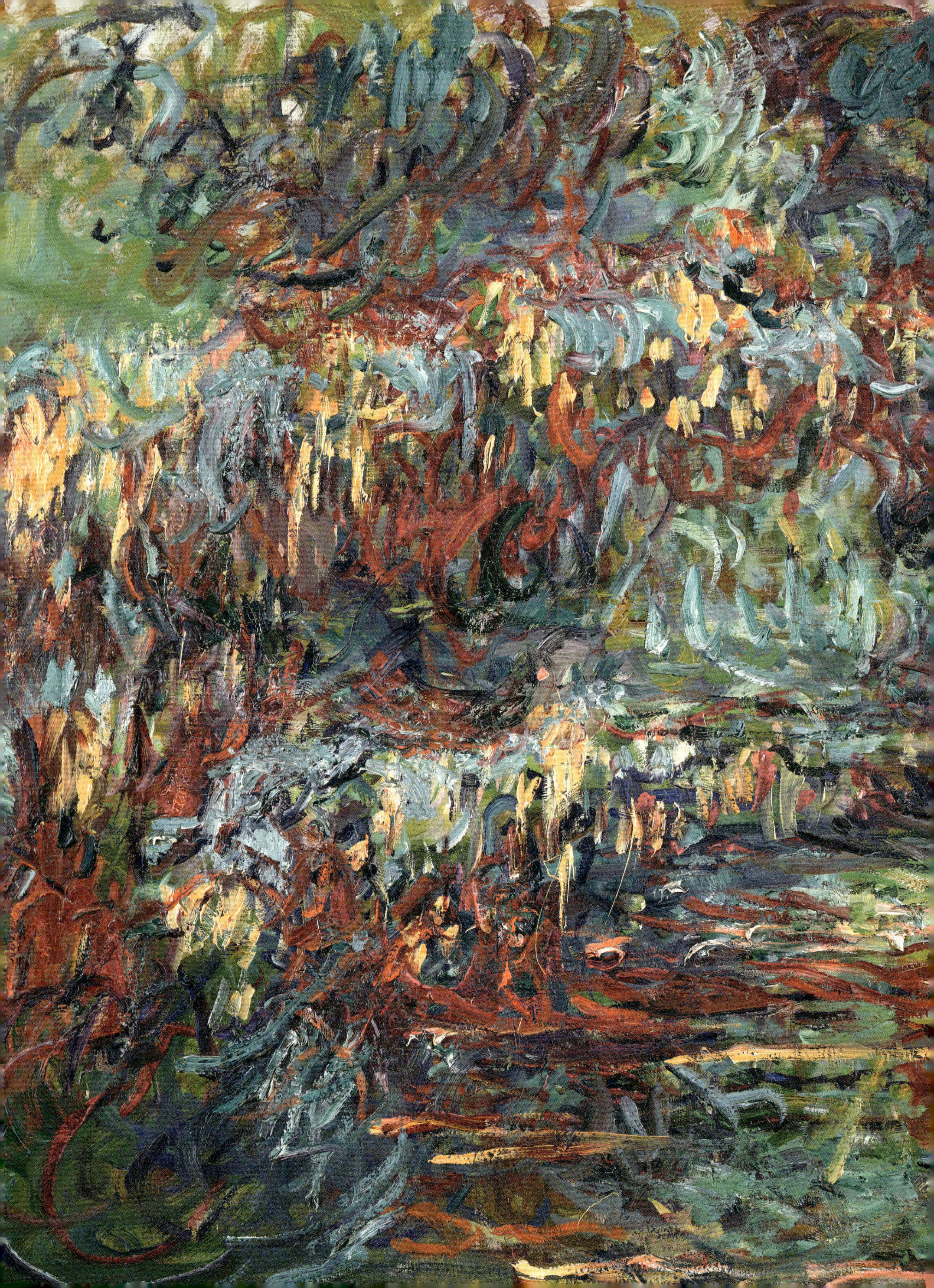

Of course, the notion that Monet's painting refers somehow to the Tao, to that fluid, to that current beyond all form that makes the world go round, can be dismissed out of hand. Once again (the point needs driving home even if this means repeating it) we are concerned here with intuition, with concordance. Monet, one feels safe in asserting, never read Laozi. Yet, instinctively, he could savor the same cosmic flow. Great painting is always a place for the discovery—or the rediscovery—of the fundamental, where the links with an arcane or long-forgotten essence are forged again.

This is perhaps an apt point at which to refer to the testimony of a contemporary Chinese painter who lives in France and whose art skirts the frontier between the two continents, Zao Wou-Ki: "In Monet's painting, the ambiance, the atmosphere is very Far Eastern, but there are no lines. It is the light, the way it plays that is crucial, while in Chinese painting lines are a more significant constructive basis than light. These are then two essentially differing facets, though the concept is almost the same. . . . The exercise takes place on two levels: Monet uses light while the Chinese painter uses space. With Monet, it is light that provides the space; in Chinese painting, it is the constructive line that provides the space. The departure point is not the same, but the result is."

THE EYE AND ITS CONSEQUENCES

Monet's painting has been hailed or condemned as an exclusively visual art. Cézanne's admiring remark, "Monet is just an eye, but what an eye!" has dogged his tracks and sticks to his work like a limpet. It is of course undeniable that Monet, with his exceptionally acute eye and subtle visual perception, did indeed inaugurate the primacy of the eye, the visual culture by which we are still governed (but for how long). He is its initiator and its prophet.

Yet, with the foresight typical of creative intuition, if he forms its culmination, he is also its resolution and even hints at its close. As his eye surveys the world and explodes its forms, as he rejoins the flux of nature and hearkens to the immediate, to the nearby, to the tangible, he also put an end to the tyranny of mental volume. The cataract that temporarily deprived him of his sight enabled him to divine a painting that began as impasto, and hence almost tactile and with at times almost expressionist accents (as in those practically suffocating *Gardens* through the arches), but which, once he regained his use of color, grew into an art that engulfs the beholder, a painting one enters and which therefore one is no longer merely looking at, but participating in. In shifting its dynamism from form to energy, Monet creates a painting "without discourse," as Camille Bryen has wonderfully expressed it,

The Japanese Bridge
1918–24
35 × 45¾ in. (89 × 116 cm)
oil on canvas
Musée Marmottan
Paris, inv. 5106

and so founded an art of communion. Patently, such an art was going to be ahead of its time and it first needed to fade into the background before it could reappear and be finally understood and triumphant.

Such eclipses are common in history, and geniuses such as El Greco, Georges de la Tour, Vermeer, and Alessandro Magnasco were all forgotten until sensibilities became attuned again to their work and it recovered its popularity. This might take two or even three centuries, depending. With our subject, the phenomenon of oblivion and rediscovery were accelerated, perhaps because our age is a faster one, or else because the succeeding generations for a time drive out the predecessors so that their inheritance is made clear only later. But above all there was in Monet's work a virtuality for which earlier audiences were not yet prepared. But that situation was about to change.

THE TWO CLAUDES

Monet shares this temporary obscurity with a composer. When one compares the character, work, and posthumous fate of Claude Monet and Claude Debussy, though they cannot be said to be identical in every respect, one is struck by their closeness. It seems amazing in fact that the parallel has not been drawn previously, save perhaps by the less scrupulous writers of their own time.

If the identity of their first name might whet the appetite, the two Claudes also possessed a similar taste for solitude and a certain ruggedness of character. This feature is hardly conclusive, since it is common to all true creators, the necessary condition of a passionate existence that elevates the development of a body of work above striving for success. The resemblance becomes closer, though, when one recalls their indomitable independence of mind, their shared contempt for all things official and similar tendency to overturn artistic conventions.

The similarity is further accentuated on moving to a deeper examination of their oeuvre. If the composer exalts sound to a point of incandescence at which it begins to exist in its pure state, the painter does the same for color. Beneath a fluidity that can seem ephemeral, both artists transpose structures that are no longer conceived on a descriptive (for music) or representational (for painting) level, but from a new, all-embracing approach that totally transcends the initial theme. Debussy's declaration, "I have sought music behind all the veils that cover it," could easily be countersigned by Monet just by replacing the word "music" by "painting." Monet and Debussy both founded a new freedom of gesture and composition—not in mere evanescence, as was long believed, but in going beyond form. Finally, the analogy resurfaces strikingly if one examines the impact of their respective oeuvres and the successive phases they both experienced

The Japanese Bridge
1918–24
34 ¼ × 35 ½ in. (87 × 90 cm)
oil on canvas
Museu de Arte
São Paulo, inv. 93/1948

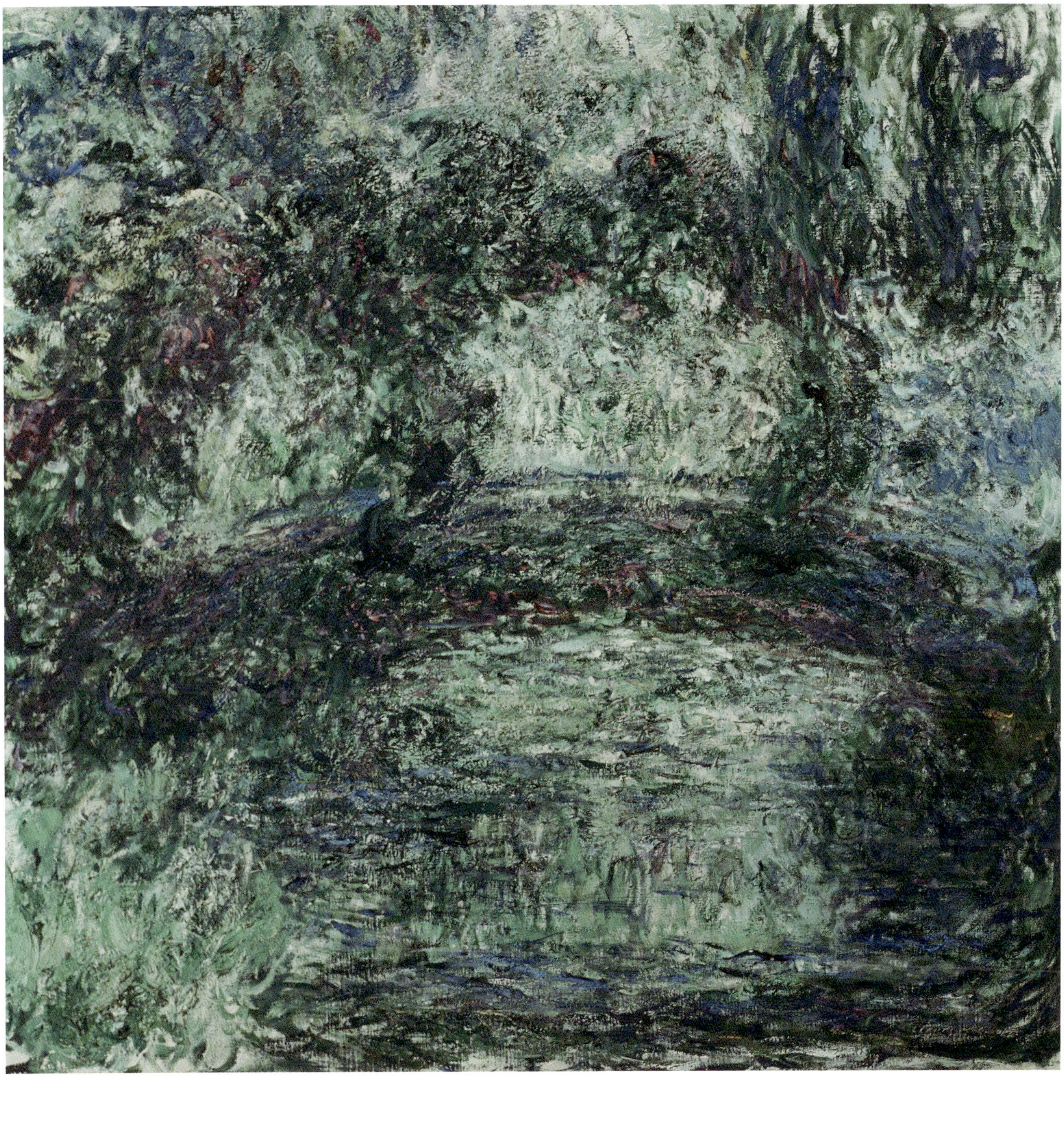

of rejection, acceptance, enthusiasm, and misunderstanding. In both instances, even in periods of relative success, their reception long obscured their true originality, afflicting their work with disregard and neglect. The objection could be raised that these are risks inherent in every work of significance. This one might concede were it not for the fact that both bodies of work, having been through the same misconstrued "success" and—its logical consequence—the same oblivion, underwent a sudden revival in popularity at the same time, going on to make a considerable impact on a single generation of painters and musicians. In this renewed interest of the 1950s, it was as if, all of a sudden, eyes had been opened and ears unclogged.

THE ERA OF CONTEMPT

A history of modern painting penned in about 1950 would have stressed the importance of Cézanne and practically passed over Monet. It was assumed by all that Cézanne had, albeit against his better judgment, generated cubism, and succeeding generations too were to derive new proofs and certainties from the solidity of his vision. Dominating the horizon and ordaining the future, Cézanne's position was universally assured.

As for Monet, he left no progeny. He had at most been an influence on Bonnard, but that painter, too, was to die without heirs. It was a time when Georges Braque could confide in Jean Bazaine, "Monet is a stupid fellow," and Fernand Léger could confess, also to Bazaine, that he was astonished to see that Bonnard's frescoes at the Palais de Chaillot had not yet been whitewashed. More or less at the same time, in 1949, Sir Kenneth Clark, in his *Landscape into Art*, having dismissed Monet's late canvases as "lacking rigor and sentimental," could perceive no link between contemporary painting and an irrelevant impressionism that "had run its course."

Already ten years earlier, a highly regarded historian of impressionism, Lionello Venturi, had proclaimed: "Monet wanted to go beyond painting, to make the invisible present: unfortunately, often all that subsists is a surface of indistinct nuances." These "indistinct nuances" had already shocked the baritone Faure when, in about 1880, he had refused to buy a painting of Vétheuil in "which there was nothing."

While the early Monet had earned an undisputed place in history as a central figure in impressionism, the second phase, that of the *Cathedrals* and *London*, the *Water Gardens* and the *Water Lilies*, was forgotten and despised. Just as they had been in the days of his youth, contemporary audiences, save for an odd exception[5], were once again blind to the magical world of this lyric visionary.

Water Lilies
1907
39 ¼ × 39 ¼ in. (100 × 100 cm)
oil on canvas
private collection

5 Among these exceptions, it would be unjust not to mention at least Louis Gillet, who in a study of 1924, wrote the following on the *Water Lilies*: "There would be one less masterpiece in the history of painting had the grand old man of Giverny not discovered a new way of identifying himself with the elements of the universe." Gillet went on in 1927 to characterize these pictures as an "astonishing painting, without drawing, without edges, a canticle without words, pictures in which the painter's only subject is himself," before wondering point blank: "Will this oeuvre, one of boldest ever attempted in painting, ever be understood?" (*Trois variations sur Claude Monet* [Paris: Plon, 1927] 83, 110–11).

Following generations, however, turned a blind eye to this extraordinary exploration of an as yet unseen world. However, while the naysayers were in the majority, opinions were slowly being revised and this hitherto neglected oeuvre was soon to explode on to the scene. Suddenly, in conditions that could never have been foreseen, it regained its topicality, and the time was ripe to discover within it previously unsuspected dimensions that coincided with new ideas. Monet's work had been biding its time. The great reservoir had been long neglected, but now it was to become a wellspring once again. Painfully slowly, eyes were opening to the untapped riches it contained.

EXTREMES MEET

The most extraordinary thing about this turn of events is that two generations—one for long committed to painting, the other just starting out—more or less simultaneously rediscovered and embraced late Monet as their own. All of a sudden his name was being hailed from all sides.

In the first case, Claude Monet was a source of rejuvenation, a catalyst for a new departure or total metamorphosis. From very different horizons, but hitherto favoring poetic content and the shock of bizarre imagery rather than pure painting, these painters experienced a revelation, and soon their art undertook a radical change in direction. One was Marc Chagall, the second André Masson, and the third Camille Bryen. Looking back to this period, Chagall confided in Pierre Schneider: "I couldn't bear to look at Monet. I discovered him after the war on the steamer bringing me back from America. There on the ocean I asked myself the following question: from whom does color flow as from a fountainhead? And I replied: Monet. Today, for me, Monet is the Michelangelo of our time from the chemical point of view."[6]

What Chagall was discovering at this time, that is, around 1949–50, was color—no longer confined by form, no longer layered into flat zones, but as the very pigment of sensation, as a halo of hitherto unfathomable dimensions, one which reinforced in his eyes the poetic element. One has just to visit the new rooms of the Musée Marmottan to see *The House at Giverny Seen from the Rose Garden* (*Maison de Giverny sous les roses*) of 1922 (no. 39) to understand how Chagall, without even having seen the picture, might have been touched by the spectrum of the painter of Giverny.

As for André Masson, whose acute intelligence made him a perceptive observer of major artistic currents throughout his stormy relations with surrealism, in about 1951 he staggered out of the double rotunda of the *Water Lilies* in a daze: "The Orangerie is the

6 In Pierre Schneider, *Les dialogues du Louvre*, (Paris: Denoël, 1972) 42.

7 This remark echoes Emile Compard's observation: "*The Water Lilies* are the Altamira of painting."

Sistine Chapel of impressionism"[7], adding: "Monet's oeuvre: one of the great turning-points in painting. Such turmoil." To this work, which had been ignored for twenty years or more, he even devoted a text entitled *Monet le fondateur*[8], that advances the first definition of the *Water Lilies* in modern terms: "His solar passion sees the light in all things, even in shadow, and in the festival he opened nothing is black… A new way of seeing, of feeling, of loving nature… The enveloping of the atmosphere is recreated at the artist's behest. He does not abandon himself to the passivity of sight; nature thrusts upon him a profusion of connections that he encapsulates in a few main chords. Here imagination reasserts its rights. There is no form a priori. Based on the power of light, the exaltation of color leads to the negation of all contour, all limit. The finished work achieves its point of balance in the fusion of elements. The absence of formal delimitation allows for extraordinary inventiveness in brushwork. It is this that gives rise to the diverse bodies composing the picture (the principal one being the atmosphere). The brushstrokes are accented very differently: intersecting, disheveled, oscillating. You have to look at it close to: what fury!"

The same year, a poet who had reached a dead end in language, gradually edged towards painting. Camille Bryen, in dialogue with Audiberti, wrote: "Painting passes beneath humanizing tunnels and through dehumanized interludes of brightness. At this moment it is the light-giving tendency that prevails… The tsunami begins its march with the impressionists. Man is an eye, Monet says. The eye is already no longer a man, but a pretext for forms and colors. Yes, in the innocent-looking motifs of *Cathedral at Rouen* or *Gare Saint-Lazare,* it is humanism in painting that is dissolving. Painting strives to depict the beautiful, but untrammeled by the delectation the human presents to the human. Since the beginning of historical time, no European artist had ever dared to do that."[9]

Rereading these three exactly contemporary testimonies, by Marc Chagall, André Masson, and Camille Bryen, one is forcibly struck by the fact that the first three painters of our age to speak about Claude Monet as a relevant force, relate him to present-day problems; all had, in differing degrees, some relationship to surrealism. Fellow travelers rather than card-carrying members they may have been for the most part, but the phenomenon itself is still remarkable.

What strikes André Masson the most in the *Water Lilies* is the frenzy of a painter drunk with color, his furious brushwork. What delights Marc Chagall is the baroque appearance of the coloring, the zest of a "chemistry" freed from all constraint. What interests Camille Bryen above all is how the painter liberates himself from form and discourse. All three positions are worth dwelling on since they all provided fresh impetus to the reception of Monet's oeuvre.

FOLLOWING PAGES
Water Lilies, Reflections of Willow
1916–19
39 ¼ × 78 ¾ in. (100 × 200 cm)
oil on canvas
private collection

8 Published in *Verve*, 27–28, Paris: Tériade, 1952.

9 Jacques Audiberti and Camille Bryen: *L'Ouvre-boîte, Colloque abbhumaniste*, (Paris: Gallimard, 1952) 88–89.

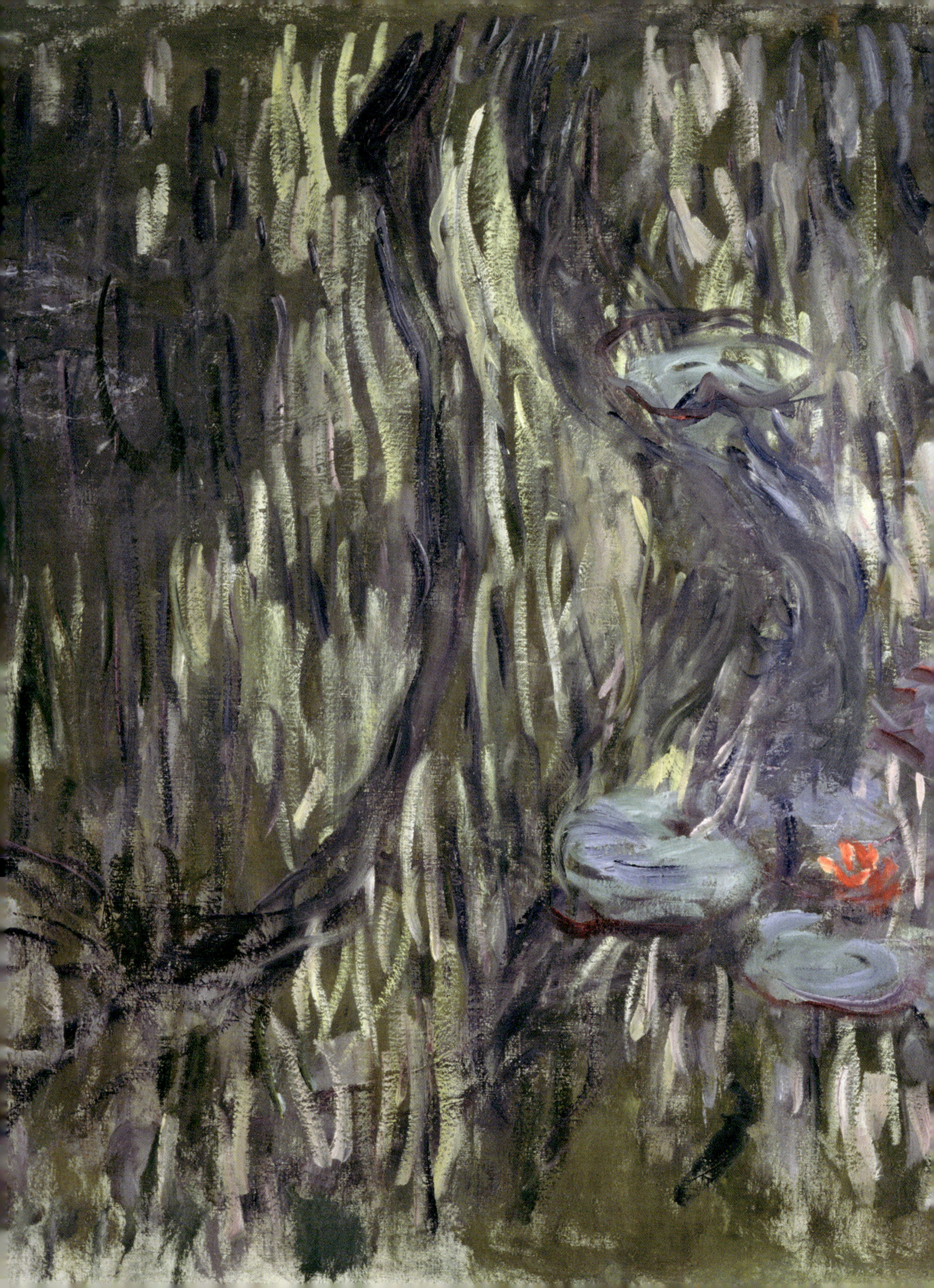

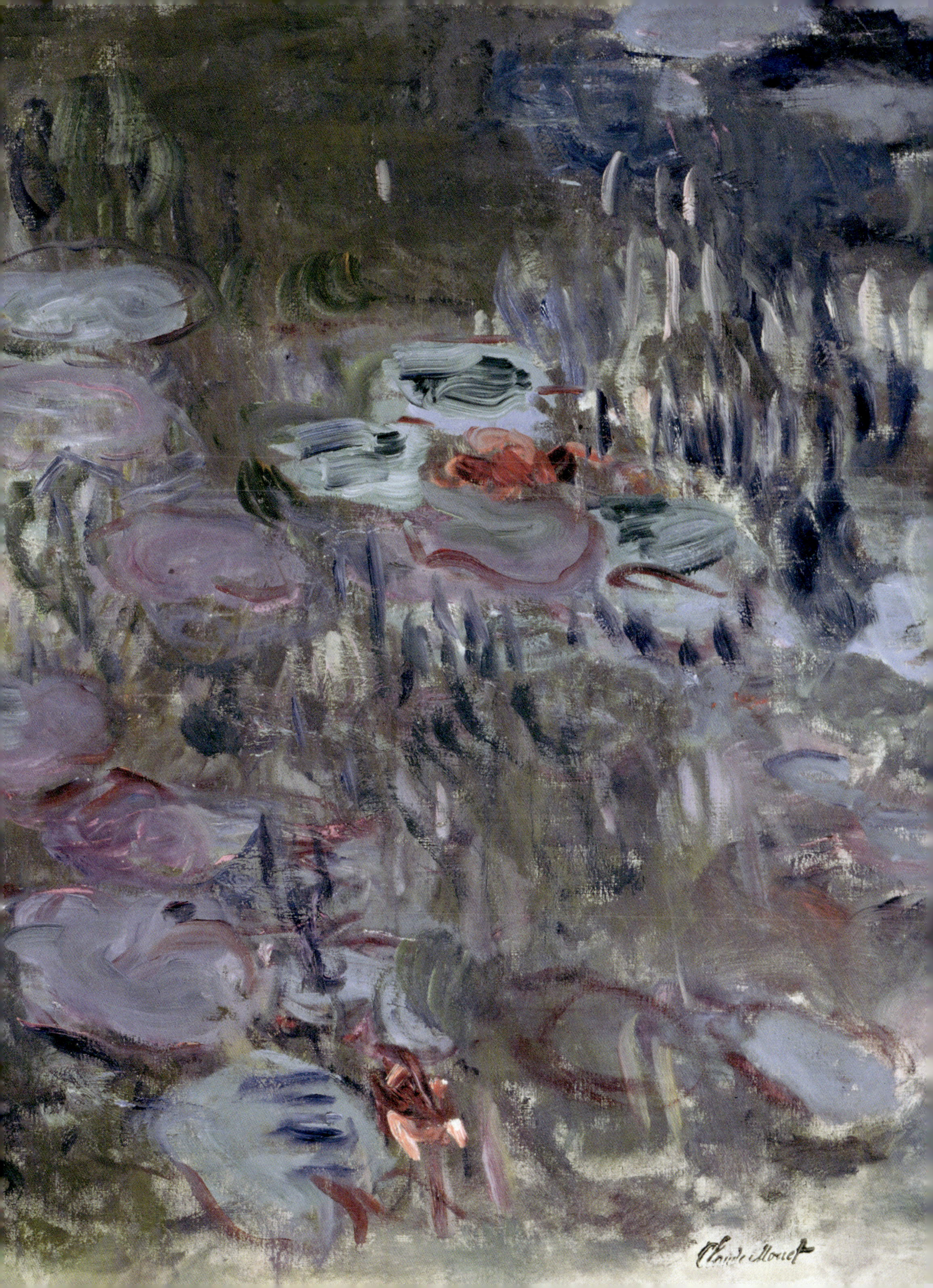
Claude Monet

THE NEW GENERATION

Monet rediscovered by the frontiersmen of surrealism is a paradox that turns the usual laws of historical affiliation on their head to the point that not even the most lateral-thinking commentator could have believed it possible. But later happenings were to confirm the paradox.

North America was to play an essential role in the rediscovery of Monet, since in 1972—that is to say twenty years later than the event we have just described—the phenomenon repeated itself in New York. If Masson and Chagall had opened their eyes to Monet on their return from America, at the same time America was becoming more receptive to Monet. A painter, on whom moreover André Masson exerted a certain influence and who by his technique of "dripping" was to extend the bounds of painting and picture-making, Jackson Pollock offered a tribute to Monet in the shape of one of his most vehement canvases entitled *Cathedral*. Some time later, a Canadian no less imbued with surrealism, Jean-Paul Riopelle, could think of no better name for a series of canvases than *Water Lilies*, a title on which, as he told us, everyone concurred. Not that there was the least strand of an aquatic plant in his pictures—no more, as one can readily believe, than a Gothic façade appears in the Pollock. Borrowing and coexistence here concern the processes, the freedom, the lyricism. Lastly, and at the same time, another American, Sam Francis, asked by his friend Bernard Schultze about his work, had no hesitation in answering: "I'm doing pure late Monets."

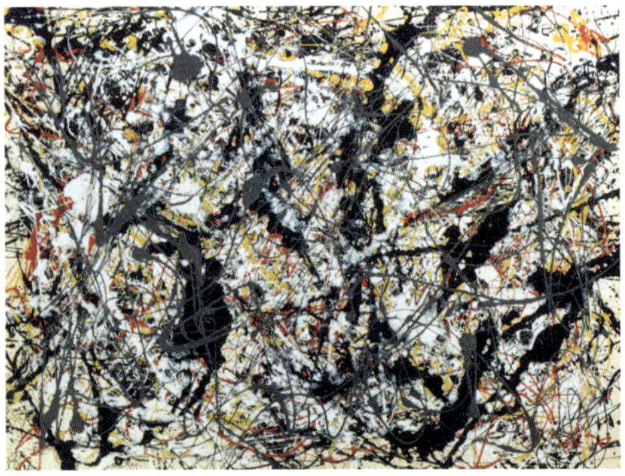

Jackson Pollock,
Painting (Silver on Black, White, Yellow, and Red)
1948
24 × 31½ in. (61 × 80 cm)
oil paint, glue-mounted
Musée National d'Art Moderne, Centre Georges Pompidou
Paris, inv. AM 1972-29

There is in these three painters a kind of cultural innocence that allowed them to look at late Monet as at a sun whose glare did not blind them. Admittedly the only link between Monet and Pollock lies in freedom of gesture and in a common intention to explode the traditional limits of the picture. Yet today, if one looks at a sketch such as *Water Lilies* (no. 53) at the Musée Marmottan, it can be seen as prefiguring aspects of Pollock, an effect even more noticeable in a canvas in the Smeets Collection. Perhaps this intuitive overlap derived from a shared Far Eastern sense for unbounded space. Both painters, though, certainly possessed a vehemence that strives to break out from anything and everything that might limit their space and thus to enter the very heart of painting.

The same interest in the unconfined seems to have motivated Sam Francis. As Pierre Schneider rightly noted: "Francis no more looked to works from the past than he drew drawings. At most there was the Monet of the *Water Lilies*, less for the pictures themselves than because of the attitude of their creator, due to a pantheist position that induced him to expand his canvas indefinitely in the madcap hope of making the limited means of painting express his experience of the boundless."[10]

10 Pierre Schneider, *Les dialogues du Louvre*, (Paris: Denoël, 1972) 72.

As for Jean-Paul Riopelle, Monet became instrumental in his work on two occasions. In about 1950, in large canvases where areas of blue, green, and red are juxtaposed like luminous shards to create a dense, strikingly impressionistic and almost magnetic vibration, which should be compared to certain of Monet's less explicit and more dynamic ponds. And then more recently in brighter pictures, where the ease of gesture harks back to the Giverny painter's pantheism. To get an idea of what Monet represents for Riopelle, here follow some observations on space he made to Pierre Schneider: "'As I am of Canadian origin, people always refer to the great Canadian forests in connection with my pictures. I remember going on a journey to Montreal with a Frenchman who was visiting for the first time. We travelled by train to Halifax. It was full of little woods. Forty hours later, we were in Montreal in front of the same little woods. That's the Canadian forest I know' 'So when people speak about your feeling for space, they're wrong?' 'No, but it has nothing to do with the nature of Canada. I am not a painter of virgin forests, of boundless prairies.' 'OK. But you find the feeling of space in... ' 'A leaf on a tree.' 'A leaf?' 'That's enough, isn't it? It has the whole forest. The point is to be able to see it. My idea is not abstraction, it is to go towards it, with free gestures... to try and understand what nature is, to start not from the destruction of nature, but toward the world.... You know, if we could go now and visit Giverny, the place where Monet painted his *Water Lilies*, we'd see it's the size of a basin. It's unimaginable: such vast, such disproportionately large pictures were made in front of a tiny, insignificant pond'."[11]

These last words remind one of an expression James Joyce was fond of: "A world in a nutshell." For a creator, nature is a pretext, a springboard—a pond, a pool, a leaf are enough to allow him to dream of the world, to recreate it. This is the thousand-year-old conception of the microcosm as the image of the macrocosm, no longer boiled down to a minute sphere, but expanded to the dimensions of a whole wall. Of course, it is necessary to underline that it was Monet who discovered this new conception, while the "abstracts" took it up later, stimulated by his example. And one awaits the day when it will be accepted that even the most "abstract" painting was but the rediscovery of the world on the level of the elements, at the heart of creation.

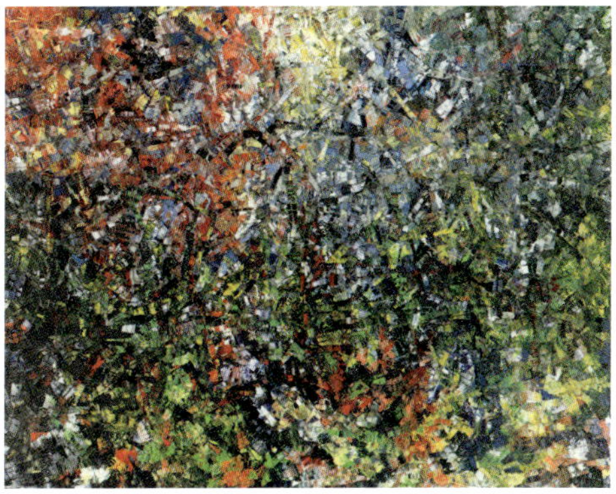

Jean-Paul Riopelle,
Chevreuse
1954
118 ½ × 154 in. (301 × 391 cm),
oil on canvas,
Musée National d'Art Moderne,
Centre Georges Pompidou
Paris, inv. AM 3881 P

It would be wrong to pass over the much neglected work of Joan Mitchell, a grandiose hymn to pure painting in abstracts that seem impregnated by the echo of Monet's discoveries. And finally it is hard not be struck by the fact that Jean-Paul Riopelle and Joan Mitchell long worked in the same house at Vétheuil where, as we saw above, Monet's work was transformed. In this case, the present flows into the symbolic.

11 Pierre Schneider, *Riopelle*, (Paris: Maeght) 1972.

But we should not leave North America without at least quoting the testimony of another American who settled in France, Shirley Goldfarb, who readily confessed to the role Monet played in her evolution: "Monet went beyond impressionism because he was not at all thinking about what he was doing. It came from within him. Monet invented Monet. He was something of a magician. When I came to France in 1954, I was impressed solely by Monet. Not by contemporaries, save a few Americans. Exclusively by Monet. Monet for me was Paris. The light. I had never seen a Monet in New York. Here, it came as a revelation for me. When I saw the light of Paris and when I saw Monet, I thought finally, it was the same thing. The same idea of space. Monet modified my way of seeing, as is testified by the large canvases I exhibited with Joan Mitchell in 1957 at the show organized on rue de Grenelle by John Ashbery, *Americans in Paris*. At this time, I learned much from Monet."

In yet another of those boomerang phenomena so common in the history of art, it thus seems that at the turn of the 1950s Monet became for some North American painters and for others coming from North America a catalyst that enabled them to release energies that transmogrified their painting and greatly widened their horizons.

THE 1950S PHENOMENON

Fragmentary in form, recent history is difficult to reconstitute. If some materials simply fail to emerge, other transitory documents disappear in due course. But, in history, the painstaking accumulation of details often masks other perspectives, or force fields, which are in fact far more pertinent. The salient point here is that between 1950 and 1959, the gradual revelation of Monet's *Water Lilies*, previously forgotten or unnoticed, sparked in a great number of painters a chain reaction, a wave of exultation that will result in their more general acceptance.

Though nothing is ever purely the result of chance, suddenly there arose a coincidence, an acknowledged, conscious crossover between Monet's work and the sensibility of certain contemporary painters: the late vision of the sage of Giverny developed and amplified the new vision of these young artists. Without demur, all the overhasty, bitter critical judgments, which for twenty or thirty years had ordained that the art of Monet would have no future, were swept away. It was realized on the contrary that art, like everything else in the world, does not progress linearly, like a neat perspective drawing, but in cycles which unroll in response to some unpredictable factors. Soon on the case, historians began ferreting through the archives.

Water Lilies
1914–17
51¼ × 35½ in. (130 × 90 cm)
oil on canvas
private collection

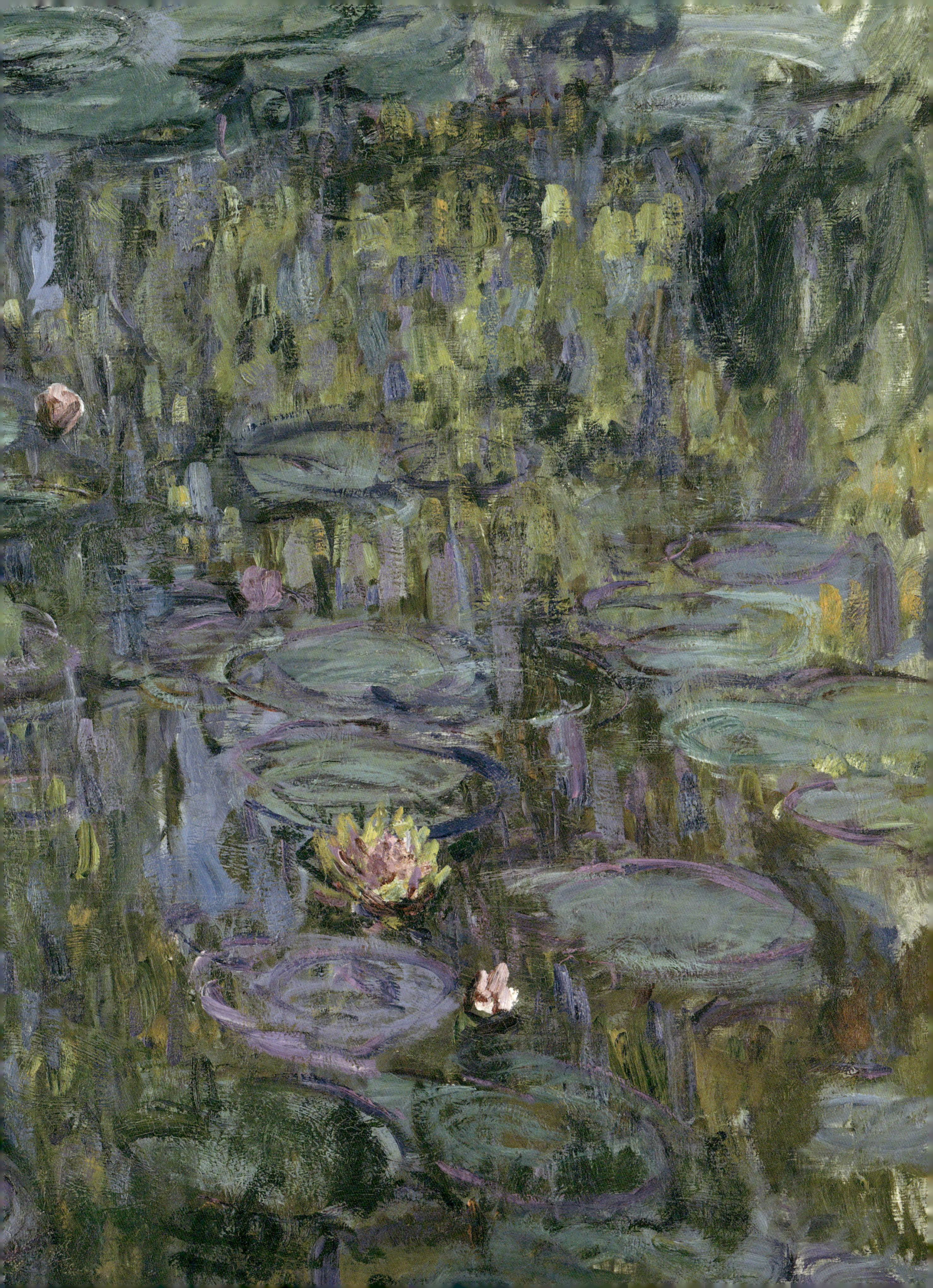

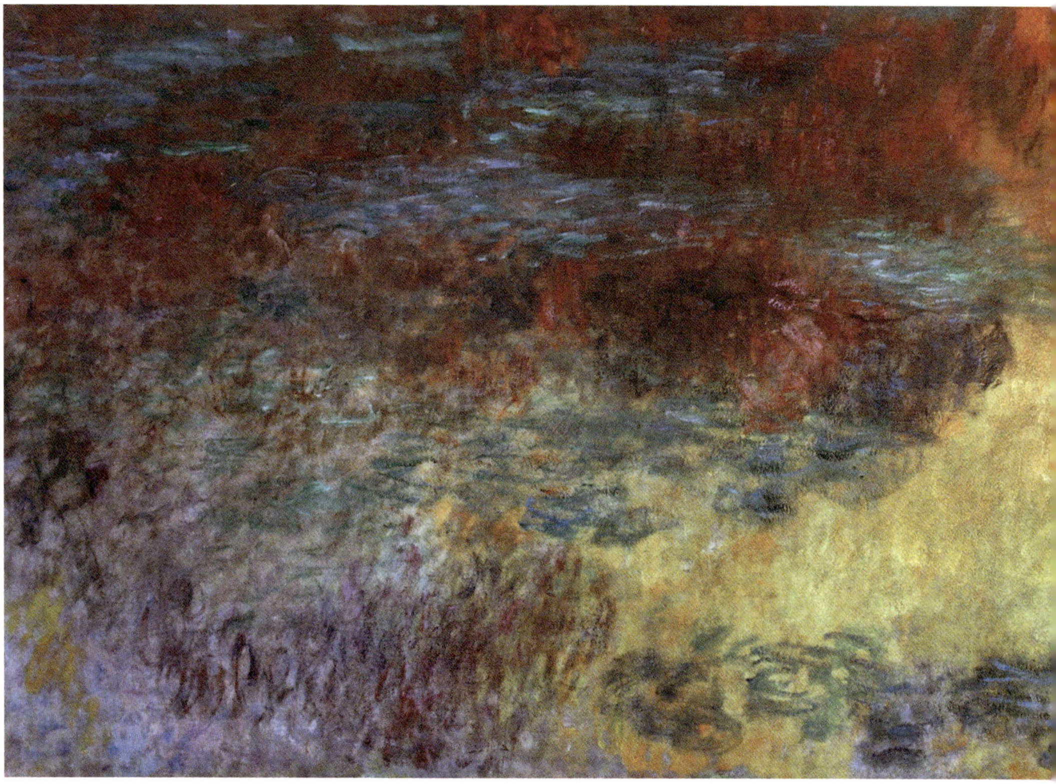

The Water-Lily Pond, Evening
c. 1922
diptych: each panel 78¾ × 118 in.
(200 × 300 cm)
oil on canvas
Kunsthaus
Zurich, inv. 1952/64

They soon discovered that Kandinsky, the unchallenged father of turn-of-the-century free abstraction, had discovered his true path one day on seeing one of Monet's *Haystacks* for the first time. He noted: "What was however quite clear to me was the unsuspected power of the palette, previously concealed from me, which exceeded all my dreams. Painting appeared with a fairy-tale splendor and power. And, albeit unconsciously, the object becomes discredited as an essential element within the picture."

The merit of having unearthed this text so opportunely devolves to Léon Degand, who was also the first to observe: "In truth, Monet has become an involuntary prophet for today's younger generation, just as Cézanne was the involuntary prophet of cubism."[12]

It's noticeable that, at the same time, Mondrian, the sire of a more geometric abstraction, pored over the *Cathedrals* and took direct inspiration from them in an early stage in the series' maturing. Thus it was that the story was slowly reconstituted. Monet, before exerting his influence by ricochets, had direct heirs other than Bonnard. His eclipsing was only apparent; his reemergence was mysterious, but relentless. The light was beginning to shine through.

12 Léon Degand, "Vicissitudes de Claude Monet," in Léon Degand and Denis Rouart, *Monet*, (Geneva: Skira, 1958) 111ff.

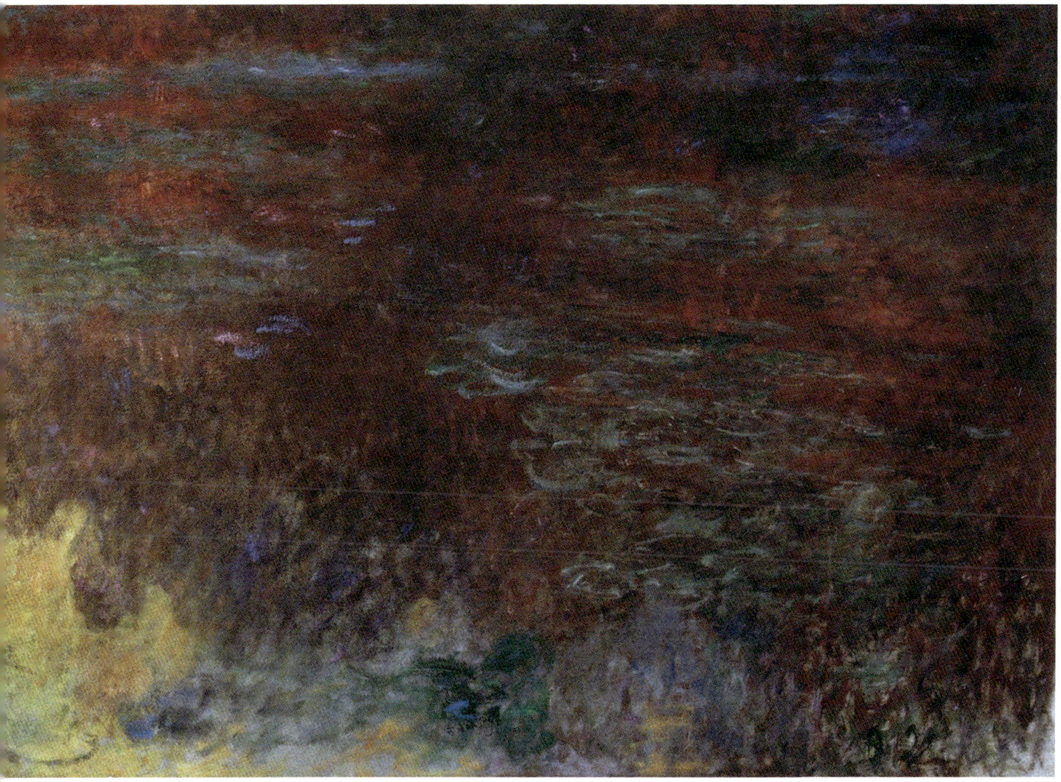

Soon, between 1957 and 1958, the Galerie Katia Granoff was staging a series of exhibitions showing groups of *Water Lilies*, then unknown since they had been left behind in the studio at Giverny. Post facto, we have interviewed a number of painters from different generations, but all closely involved with a certain abstraction, be it non-figuration, lyrical abstraction, nuagism, or tachism. All acknowledged unanimously that at this juncture these then previously unrecognized paintings played a role for them.

As Arpad Szenès told me, "Between 1924 and 1957, for thirty-four years, I lived in Paris without troubling myself about Monet. Who touched me more at the time was Degas for his drawing, Cézanne for his structure, and Odilon Redon for his poetry. In 1958, everything changed. At that point I went almost every day to see Monet at Katia Granoff's. It gave me a real shock, which I tried a bit to forget, but for days on end I was filled with wonder.... Such an encounter is an extraordinary chance in life. And it's rare. A little like the blond, golden light over Lake Balaton. Or that of the sea in Portugal. Meeting Monet in my maturity changed my painting. Monet is the greatest precursor of modern painting. He is the most modern

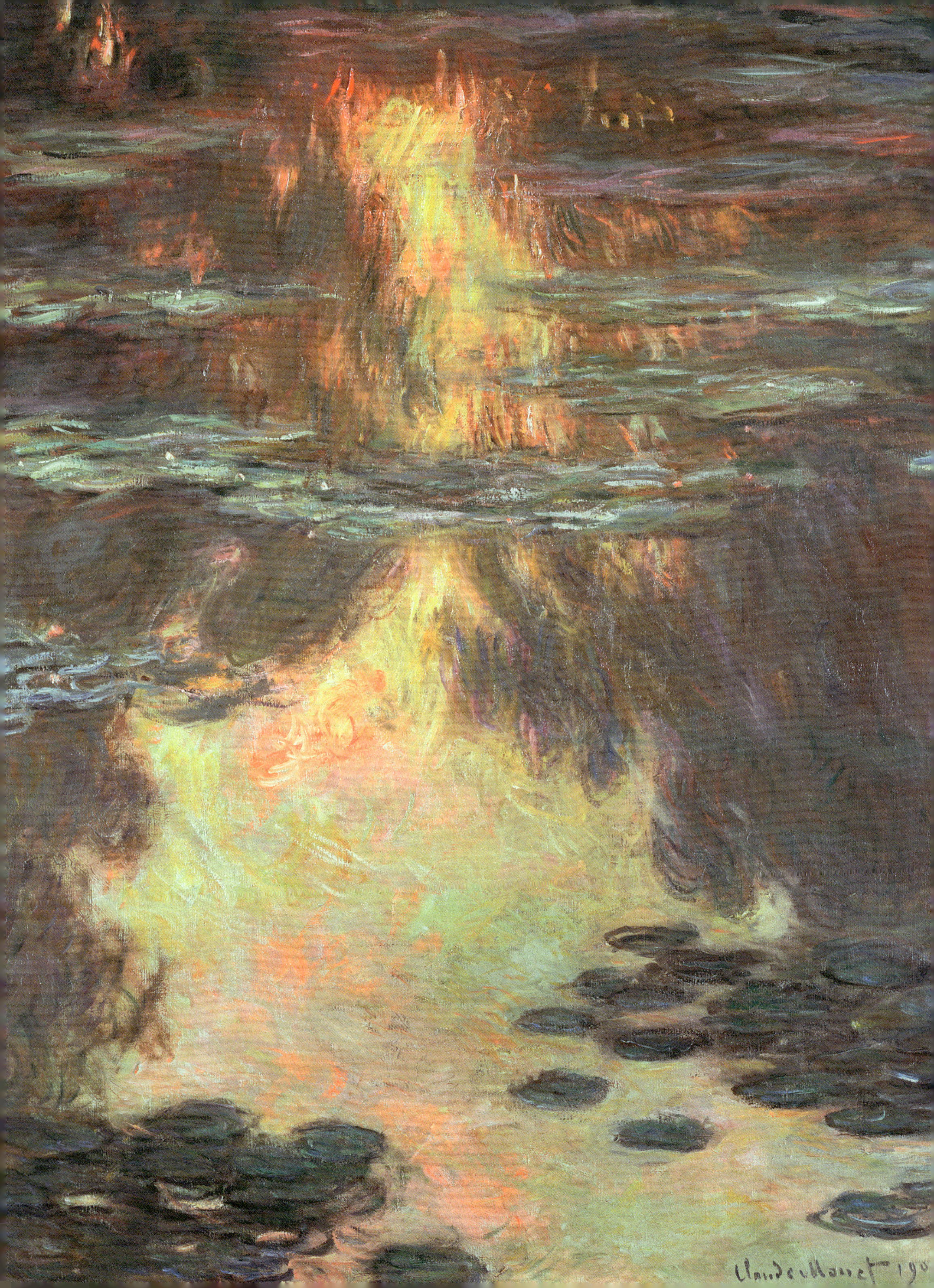
Claude Monet 190

of painters. The '*informel*' existed with him, but nobody could see it." Informels, tachists, nuagists would bump into one another at the *Water Lilies*. Some, though, had not even waited for the 1958 show. A few years earlier, Frédéric Benrath arrived in Paris and made his way to the practically deserted Orangerie: "What struck me the most the first time I saw the *Water Lilies* is that I was leaving the domain of figuration and was nearing abstraction. I could think of no contemporary painter, except Wols perhaps, able to incite me to go beyond myself to such this extent. It was on seeing the *Water Lilies* that I said to myself: something is going on there that concerns me intensely. I had the feeling that Monet had put his finger on a problem that had haunted me and which I had not yet been able to define. I would go back there every day."

The testimony of these two generations overlaps. If we now turn to the example of Jean Messagier, nowhere does the trace, the impact of Monet, appear more seminal. When this painter states he "wants to attain form... to the point where it is hacked to pieces in the light," one might be listening to Claude Monet. Both oeuvres are shot through with the same lyricism, the same drive to capture pure sensation through the annihilation of form and contour, the same fullness of color. In retrospect, we can say that Messagier's work could not been created without Monet's far-reaching experiments. In a letter to us, Jean Messagier offers confirmation of the significance of this encounter, how it marked him and how he subsequently had to shake himself free of it: "I let myself plunge in his ponds for only a very short time. I really wanted to see the *Water Lilies* as a fairyland chasm. I needed them as therapy, as a machine that let me breathe the oxygen for which Piero della Francesca had given me a taste in Tuscany... but the *Water Lilies* always reappeared through the impressionist performance. I just had to kill them. It helped me to treat Monet as the 'superior lyric' that Clemenceau mentions, but I also had to flee his methods and eliminate every conventional trap of nature so as to attend more closely to the advancing hoarfrost, to the tufts of grass, to find once more the triggers for a tree, breaths, rose-ology, the Palaces of frost, the Palaces of buzzing, and all the Pneumatism of Franche Comté."

Let us return for a moment to the story of this rediscovery. Once the double exhibition at Katia Granoff's closed, it became obvious that there were so many analogies between Monet and contemporary painting that it seemed the time was ripe for a confrontation. As early as 1959 and no more than a month apart, two critics as diverse as Pierre Restany and Waldemar George (this agreement between two generations of critics equates to that between the artists mentioned above) organized shows in which canvases by Monet were hung harmoniously next to recent contemporary works full of immediacy.

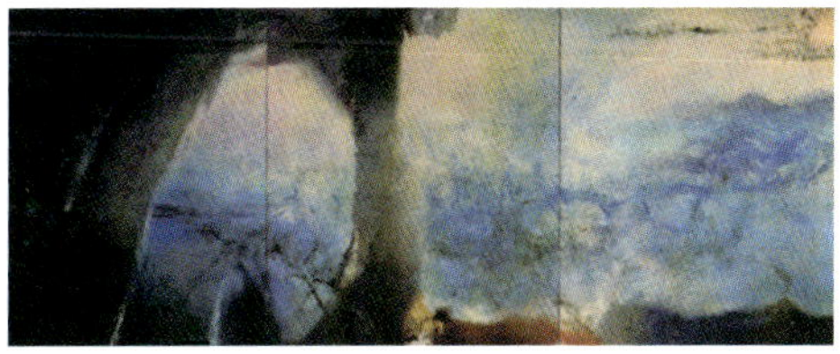

Zao Wou-Ki,
Homage to Claude Monet
1991
triptych, 78¾ × 191¼ in. (200 × 486 cm)
oil on canvas

FACING PAGE
Water Lilies
1907
39¼ in. × 32 in. (100 × 81 cm)
oil on canvas
private collection

At the Galerie Art Vivant, Waldemar George placed several *Water Lilies* at the center of a series of works by Camille Bryen, Alexandre Garbell, André Masson, Arpad Szenès, and Vulliamy. In the catalog foreword he wrote: "Those artists today who head off to conquer the brightness of the sun are rehabilitating Monet.... Here we place a few limpid pages from Monet's artistic will and testament next to a choice of canvases by painters who, without wanting to take up his torch, are wedded, like him, to the rhythm of the universe. The Paris School... turns once more to the external world, imploring it to reveal its secrets. Post-abstract painting, spatial painting is born.... It is an art whose signs conserve their independence with respect to the motifs and to the themes that convey them. Schemas with plant-like structures emerge from a magma of disembodied hues before being absorbed into a chaos of scratches and interwoven waves. If the images governed by the laws of optics can only be detected with great difficulty, the harmony between man and the natural environment that surrounds him is here endorsed. Such a lyrical concord was, however, announced, if not prefigured, by the worthy hermit on the banks of the Epte. Monet is a Lar, the guardian god of a pantheistic painting that gives soul back to an art of a century without one and permeates an elixir of life through inert matter."

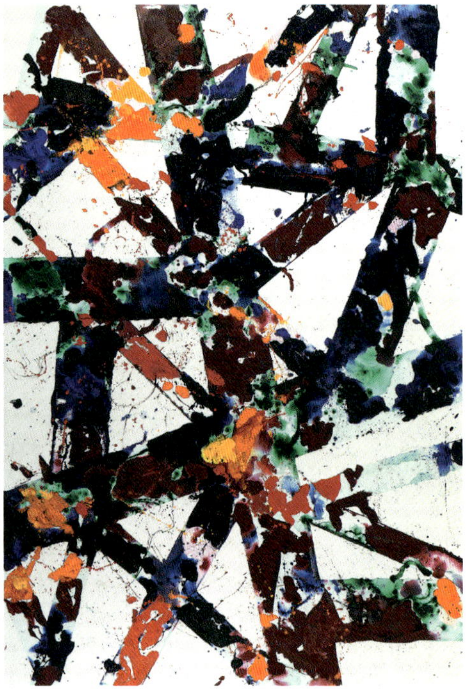

Sam Francis,
Untitled
1977
218 ¾ × 153 ½ in. (556 x 390 cm)
acrylic on canvas
Musée National d'Art Moderne
Centre Georges Pompidou
Paris, inv. AM 1980-480

Pierre Restany's selection stresses other artists: Sam Francis, whom we have already mentioned, Tal Coat, whose art—underpinned until then by encircled forms—at this time underwent a certain dilution, an allusive lyricism that recalled rather closely Monet's evolution. The foreword is worth quoting at length, because it remains the most precise and most decisive document relating to the encounter between Monet and the modern: "The tribute to Claude Monet is at once a reference and a pretext. Since 1954, I pointed out in the *Water Lilies* a visual effect of the first order: the coming into being of a new pictorial spatiality, a lyrical pantheism, an art of effusion and of total participation. The lyric and cosmic vision of the master of Giverny led him to break with... architectonic rationalism. The abandonment of the logical structures of pictorial space correctly translates the conscience of this communion of the Creator Being and the Universal.... The painter takes on board a dual osmosis that absorbs the universe into him and dissolves him into it in turn. [In] this exhibition... a space bounded by no perspective, that no structure assigns, that is only light and motion... All the endeavors presented here aim at synthesis, at a chromatic order able through plastic resonances to intimately and immediately designate extension.... The presence of space as it flees is incorporated into the quivering canvas." And lastly, in conclusion: "One has to climb into these canvases as one breathes."

In a few years then, the earlier state of affairs was stood on its head. In 1960, at the Stedeljik Museum, Amsterdam, W. Sandberg devoted a show to the ten artists who had most marked recent modern art. Monet came at the head of the list, designated as the "father of action painting." We shall go on to quote several of the statements we collected from painters who knew best how to explain the role played by Monet, if not always directly on their own art, then at least on modern painting generally. From a lengthy interview with Camille Bryen, the following lines stand out: "Claude Monet attempted a revolution in perception which was terrifically in advance of his time. When he said that man was an eye, he had attained an extraordinary state of clarity with respect to the photonic side of painting, and therefore to a completely new continuum that no longer had anything to do with discourse and which was thus completely freed from the word.... With the *Water Lilies* we arrive at a moment of extraordinary solar rapture whose only corollary is Einstein's space-time. One might say that Monet discovered a pictorial space-time that after him could never be excised from painting.... Today Monet can teach us how to attain a liberated nonfigurative painting... because he introduced a vision of light into painting of such violence that it dissolves, traumatizes its forms.... There is a pantheistic side to Monet, because he carried out a revolution in perception, that is, a desacralization which turned to transforming the world through action, through the apprehension of the world and not at all through explaining the world."

Visiting the Musée Marmottan, Philippe Hosiasson, even if he is for his part more receptive to the *Cathedrals* than to the *Water Lilies*, agrees that one can see in the latter a forerunner of modern painting: "First of all, this is a very good point for modern painting. It would mean that it did not come about fortuitously or gratuitously. Modern painting is given ample justification by this man, Claude Monet, who is regarded as visual perfection, as the extraordinary eye, and who, actually, by delving further into his art, became a kind of *vates*, a prophet. But even more valuable is that he became one without wanting to and without trying. Monet was a real Christopher Columbus who sought a country like the Indies and who instead discovered something quite different that threw open the sluice-gates of Dionysian painting.... Urged on by his will to be true, he forged a conception of nature fundamentally different from that of his time, and by this alone he is certainly one of the forefathers, one of the pioneers of the more valid elements in current research."

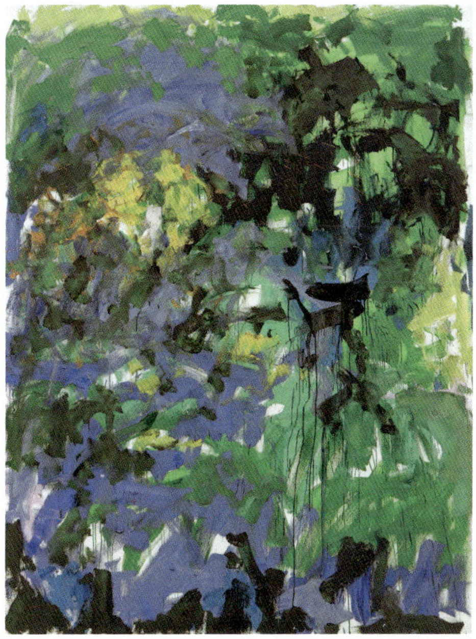

Joan Mitchell,
The Great Valley IV
1983
102 ¼ × 78 ¾ in. (260 × 200 cm)
oil on canvas
H. Lebrun Collection

THE PATRIARCH OF MODERN PAINTING

The movements, the passions of today will perhaps all too quickly exhaust their potential. After 1965, with the appearance of new fashions, different solutions, with a certain retreat from abstraction, it seemed that Monet had once again been sidelined. Until, in 1971, there appeared in America a new school of singular and dynamic vitality. With these young painters—let's mention John Seery, Ronnie Landfield, and Philip Wofford for a start—who united a certain technique (that of acrylic resin) to the same lyrical zest, the path opened by Monet to a painting without form or edge once again came to the forefront. At the same time new rooms were inaugurated in the Musée Marmottan that revealed, thanks to the Michel Monet donation, a prestigious series of unknown Monets. At the head of the staircase that will carry them "close to the heart of creation," visitors are greeted by an enlarged photograph of the patriarch of Giverny. Of considerable stature, with the white beard of God the Father. This image is less a document than a symbol. Twenty-five years earlier, the opening of this museum had gone unnoticed. Today it teems with visitors and painters.

When one enters the basement rotunda, one is plunged into a series of pictures carried out at the beginning of the twentieth century whose topicality and presence hits one in the eye. Here, an interplay of forms and mix of colors announce Chagall. There, we have hints at André Masson and his fugitive silhouettes soaked up by color. Opposite, there is "dripping," some thirty years before Pollock. Elsewhere is a density that recalls the name of Jean-Paul Riopelle. Further on, the great open spaces of Joan Mitchell. Another sports a Sam Francis.... Over there, some gardens look fauvist. One canvas is brushed with the lyric dash of a Messagier. Nasser Assar and Frédéric Benrath come forth. Jean Bazaine is not far off. Each of these painters, with whom we have been able to see these canvases time and time again, has sanctioned our impression, confirmed the debt, acknowledged the analogies.

Late Monet is a mirror in which the future can be read. The generation that, in about 1950, rediscovered it, also taught us how to see it for ourselves. And it was Monet who allowed us to recognize this generation. Osmosis occurred between them. The old man, mad about color, drunk with sensation, fighting with time so as to abolish it and place it in the space that it sets free, atomizing it into a sumptuous bouquet and creating a complete film of a "beyond painting," remains of consequential relevance today.

The Water-Lily Pond with Willows, Reflections of Trees
1914–18
triptych: each panel 78 ¾ × 334 ¾ in
(200 × 850 cm)
oil on canvas
Musée de l'Orangerie
Paris, inv. 20107

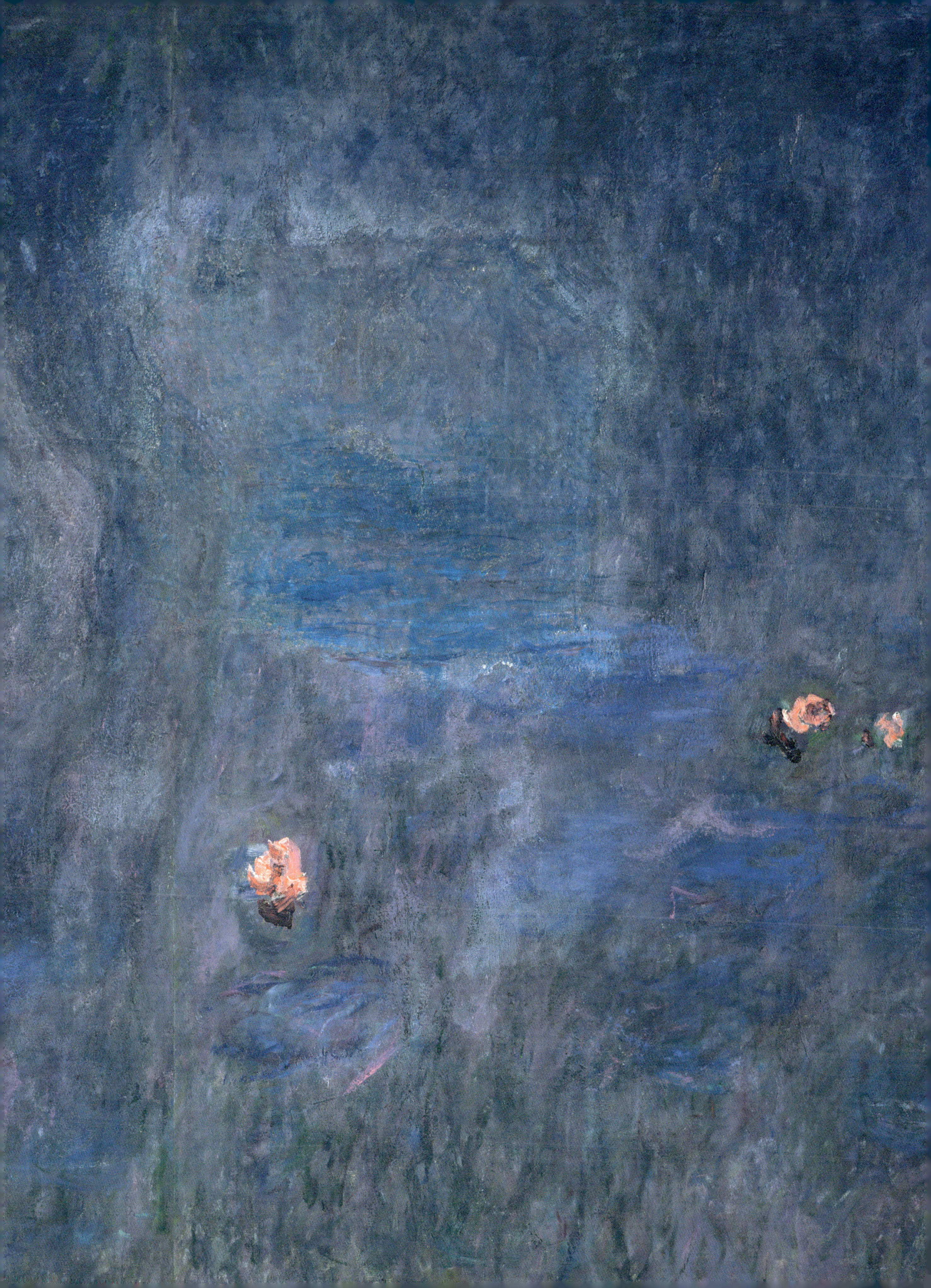

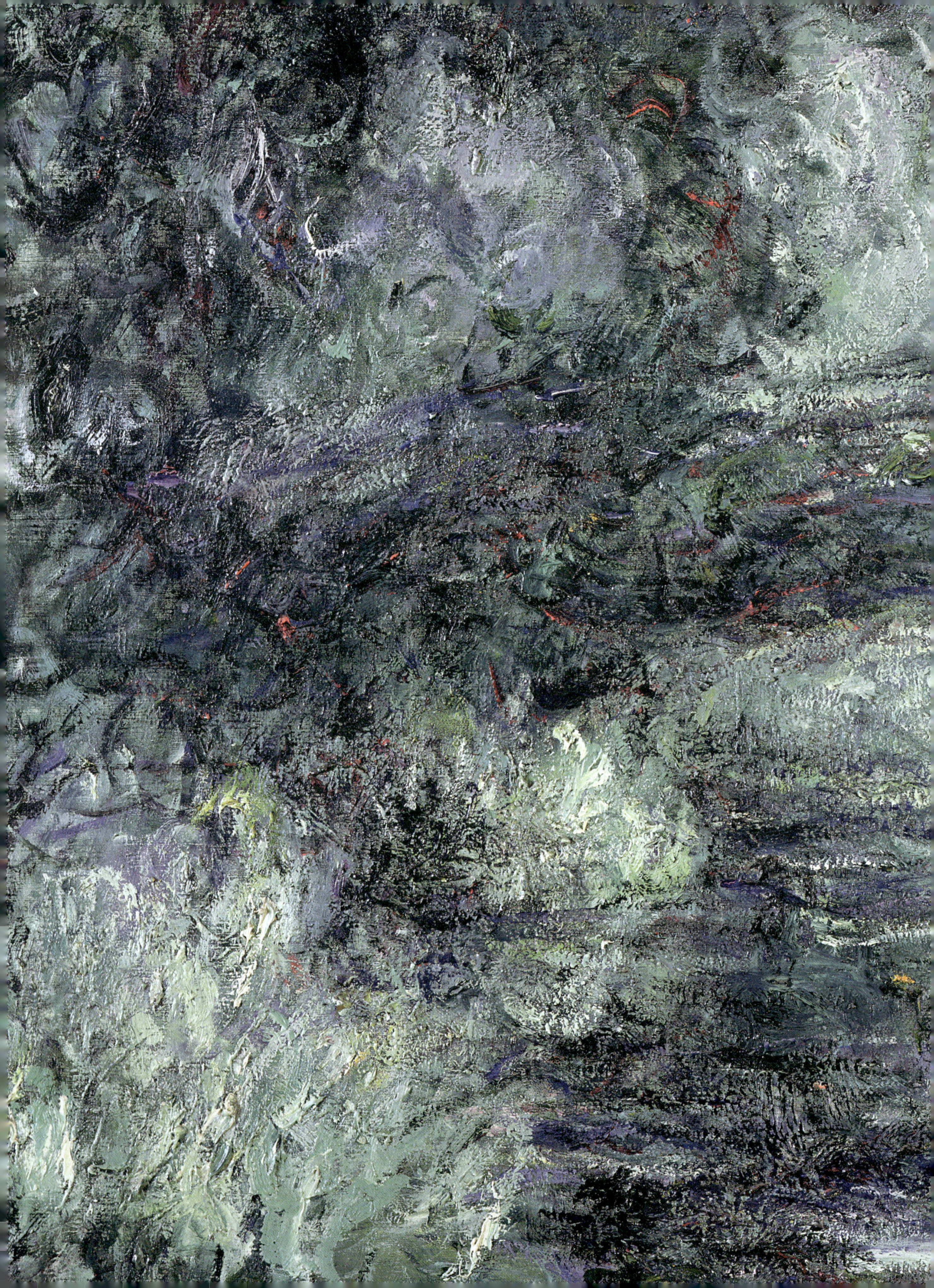

JULIE ROUART

WITH CAMILLE SOURISSE

CATALOGUE RAISONNÉ

The catalogue presented here features works from the series known as the *Water Lilies (Nymphéas)*, painted between 1892 and 1926, which remains the largest series ever composed by Claude Monet. It includes all the paintings of the "water garden" at Giverny, as well as those with direct links to it, such as the *Japanese Bridges*, the *Weeping Willows*, the *Wisterias*, and on occasion even the *Irises*.

A first catalogue raisonné, drawn up by Robert Maillard and published by Fernand Hazan in 1972, ran to 236 numbers. Thanks to the publication in 1985 of volume four of the Monet catalogue raisonné by Wildenstein, our catalog is able to include some 254 pictures. We have placed the emphasis on bringing together works by series, all the while respecting chronological order for dated works.

All works are oil on canvas.

The Japanese Bridge
1918–24, 29 1/4 × 36 1/4 in.
(74 × 92 cm),
oil on canvas,
Musée Marmottan,
Paris, inv. 5177

The Japanese Bridge
1892, 32 × 39 ¼ in. (81 × 100 cm)
private collection

The Water-Lily Pond, Water Irises
1900, 35 × 36 ¼ in. (89 × 92 cm)
private collection

The Water-Lily Pond
1899, 35 ½ × 35 ½ in. (90 × 90 cm)
The Art Museum, Princeton University, inv. 72-15

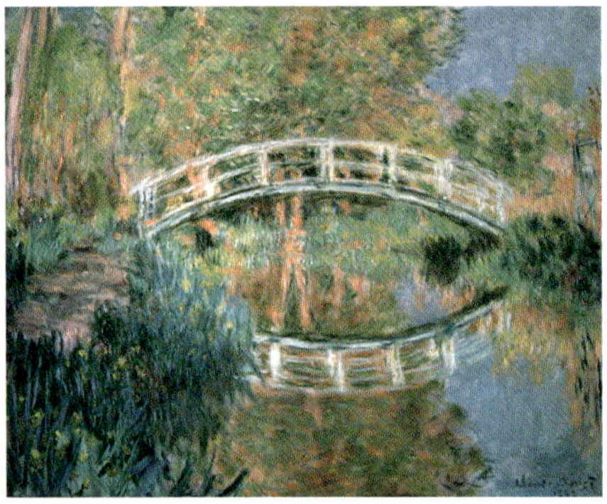

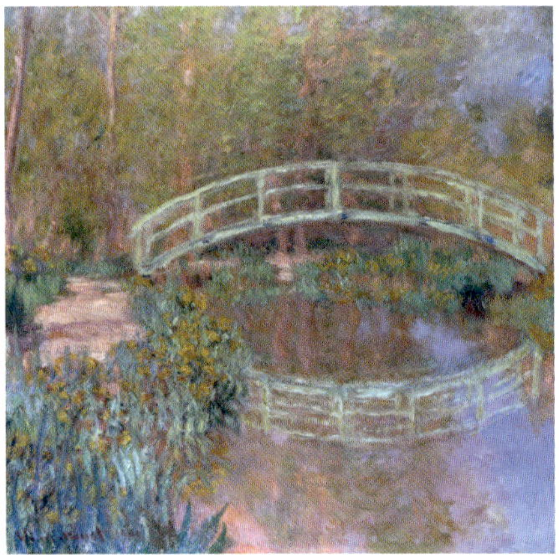

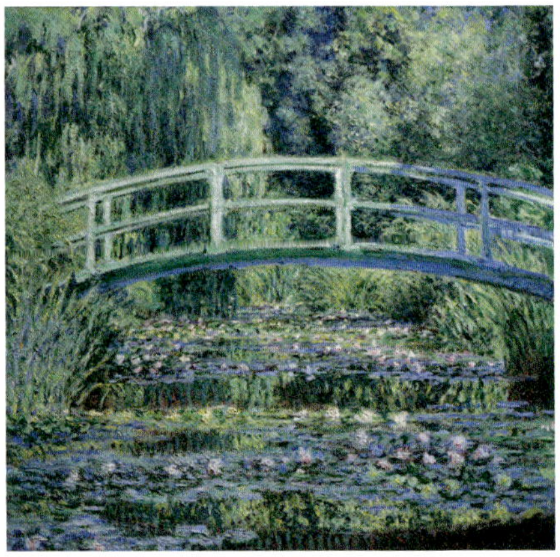

The Water-Lily Pond
1899, 35 × 36 ¼ in. (89 × 92 cm)
private collection

The Water-Lily Pond
1899, 35 × 36 ½ in. (89 × 93 cm)
Philadelphia Museum of Art, inv. 63-116-11

The Water-Lily Pond
1899, 35 × 36 ½ in. (89 × 92 cm)
Pushkin Museum, Moscow, inv. 3309

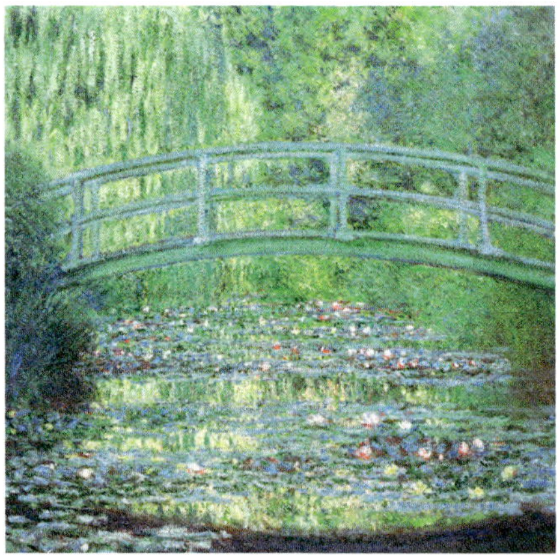

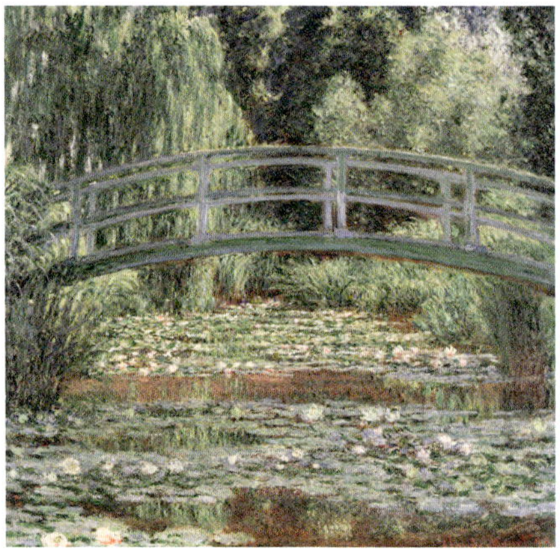

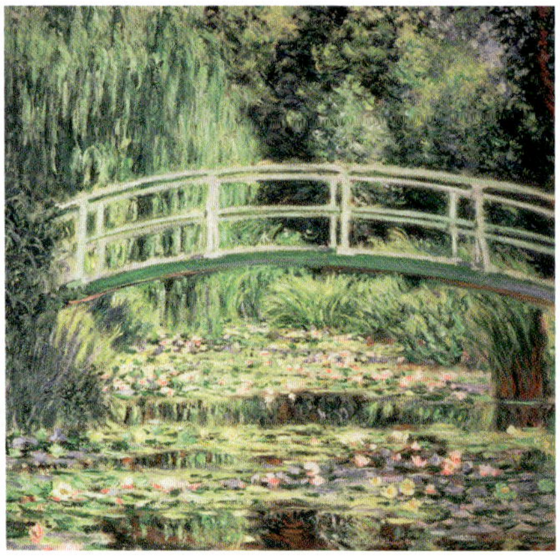

The Water-Lily Pond, Green Harmony
1899, 35 × 36 ½ in. (89 × 93 cm)
Musée d'Orsay, Paris, inv. RF 2004

The Water-Lily Pond
1899, 32 × 39 ¼ in. (81 × 100 cm)
private collection

The Water-Lily Pond
1899, 35 × 36 ¼ in. (89 × 92 cm),
National Gallery, London, inv. 4240

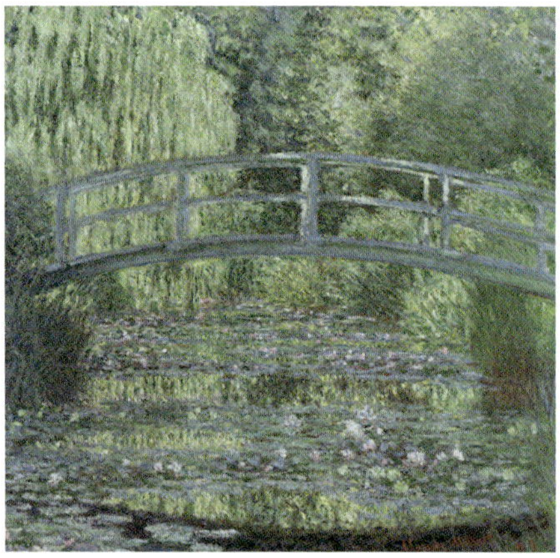

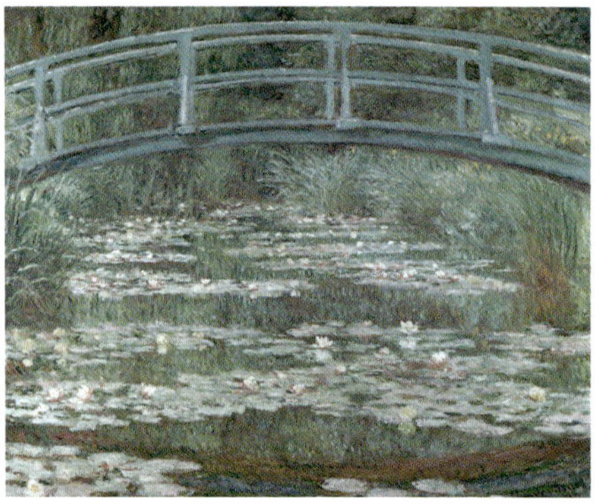

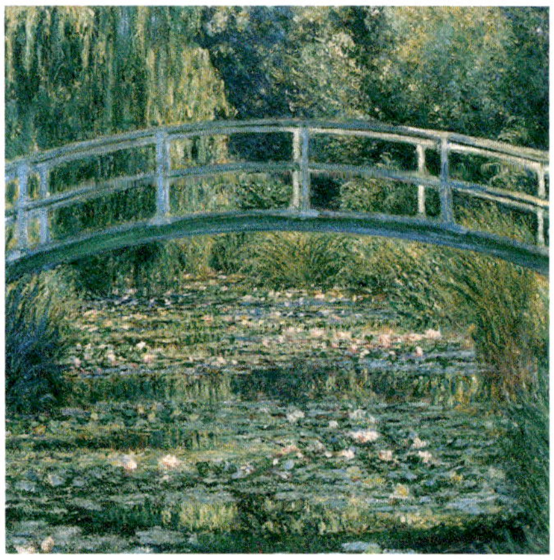

Water-Lily Pond, the Bridge
1905, 37 ½ × 39 ¼ in. (95 × 100 cm),
private collection

Water-Lily Pond, the Bridge
1905, 32 × 39 ¼ in. (81 × 100 cm),
private collection

Water-Lily Pond, the Bridge
1905, 35 ½ × 39 ¼ in. (90 × 100 cm),
private collection

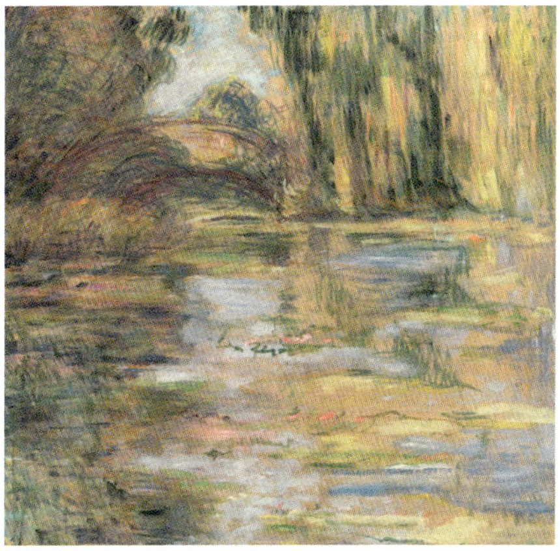

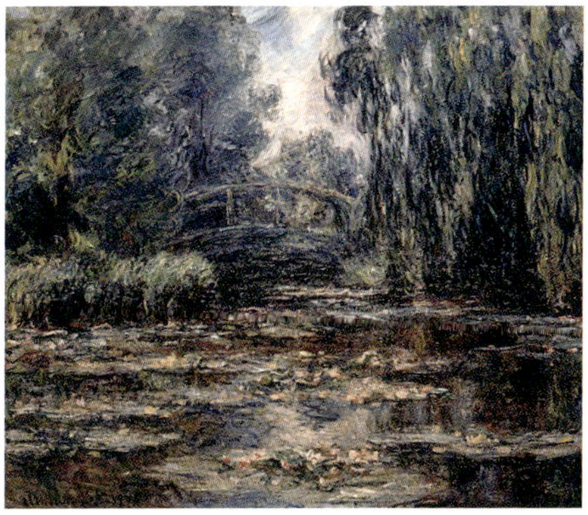

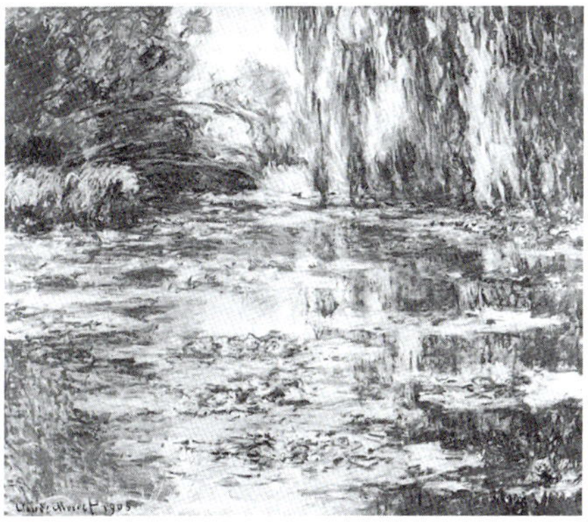

The Water-Lily Pond
1899, 36 ½ × 29 ¼ in. (93 × 74 cm), Metropolitan Museum of Art, New York, inv. 29.100.113

The Water-Lily Pond, Pink Harmony
1900, 35 ½ × 39 ¼ in. (90 × 100 cm)
Musée d'Orsay, Paris, inv. RF 2005

The Bridge over the Water-Lily Pond, Giverny
1900, 35 × 39 ¼ in. (89 × 100 cm),
Art Institute of Chicago, inv. 1933.441

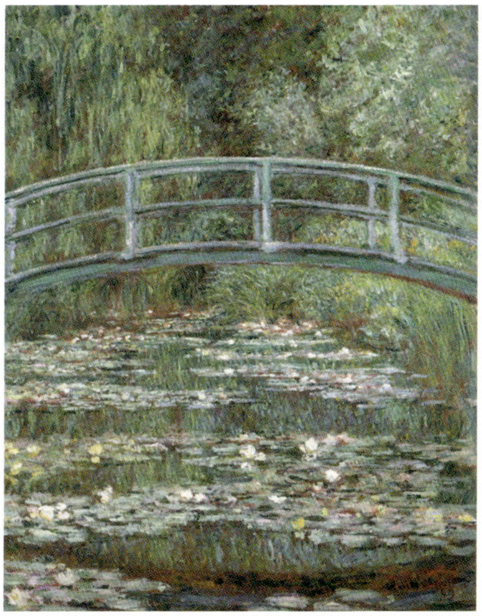

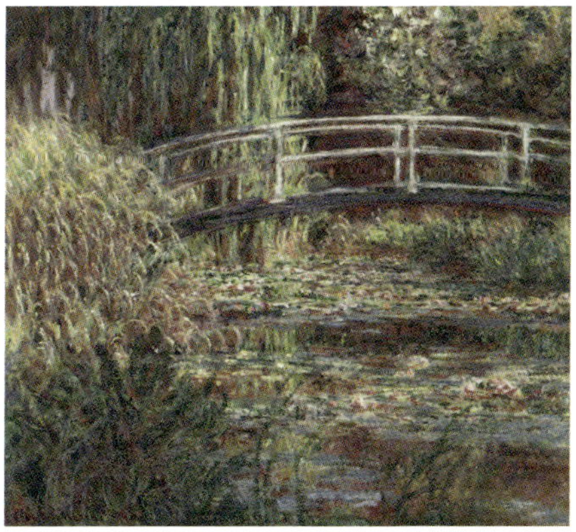

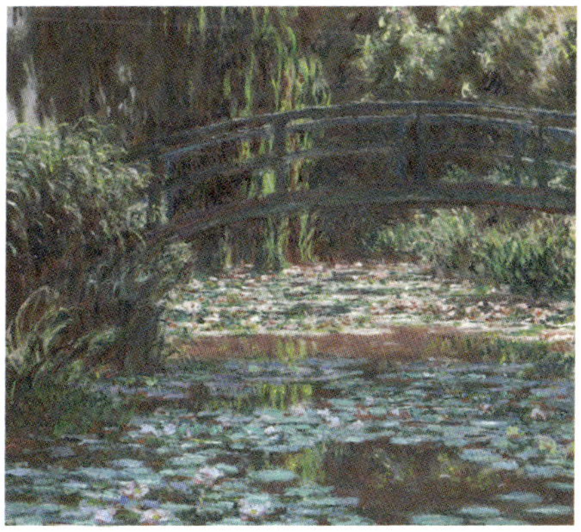

The Water-Lily Pond
1900, 35 ½ × 36 ¼ in. (90 × 92 cm)
Museum of Fine Art, Boston, inv. 61.959

The Water-Lily Pond, Water Irises
1900, 35 × 36 ¼ in. (89 × 92 cm),
private collection

The Water-Lily Pond and Path by the Water
1900, 35 × 39 ¼ in. (89 × 100 cm)
private collection

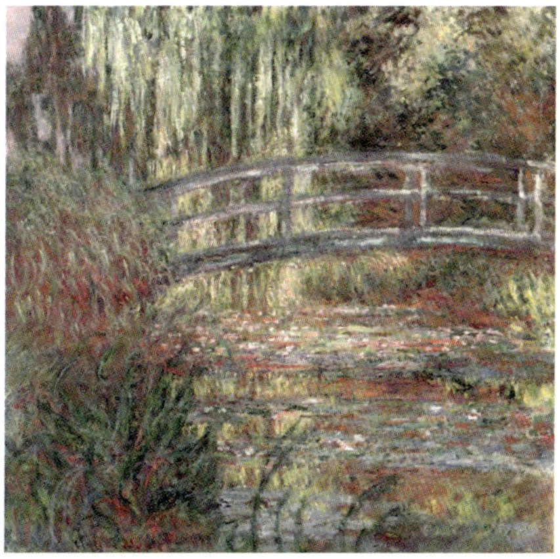

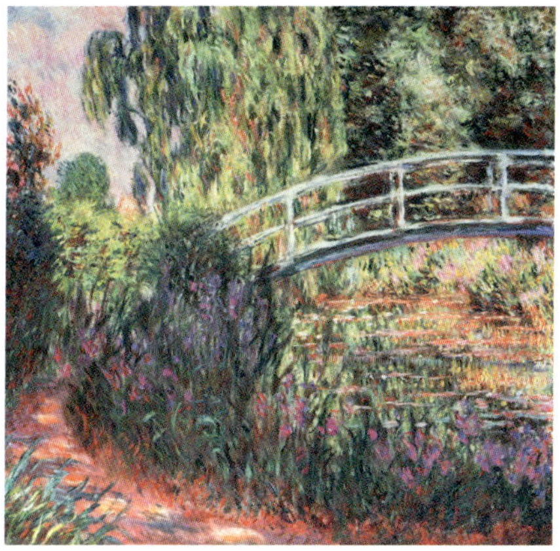

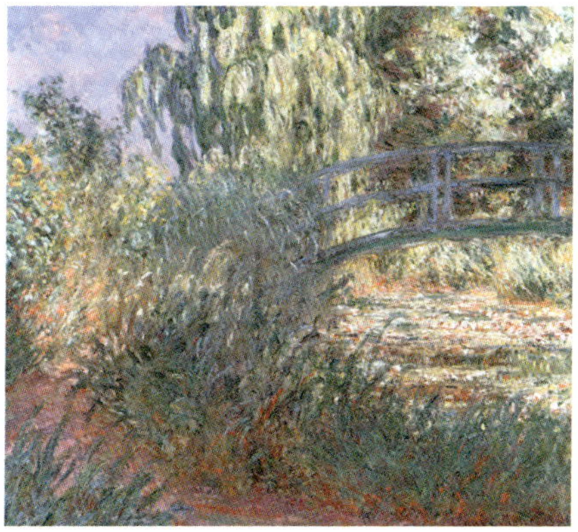

The Water-Lily Pond
1899, 36½ × 35½ in. (93 × 90 cm)
private collection

The Water-Lily Pond
1899, 35 × 36¼ in. (89 × 92 cm)
private collection

The Water-Lily Pond, Water Irises
1900, 35 × 39¼ in. (89 × 100 cm)
private collection

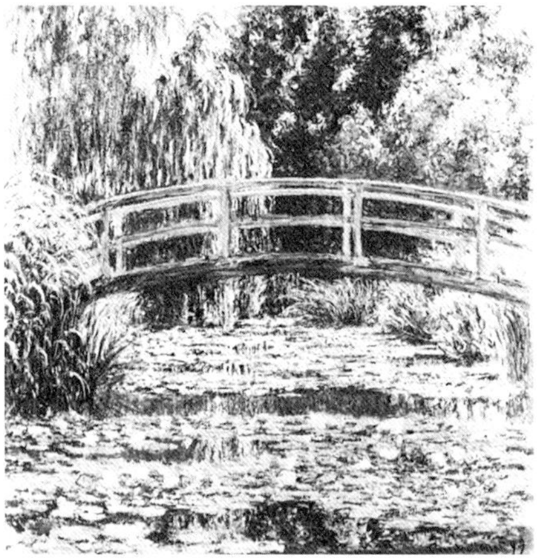

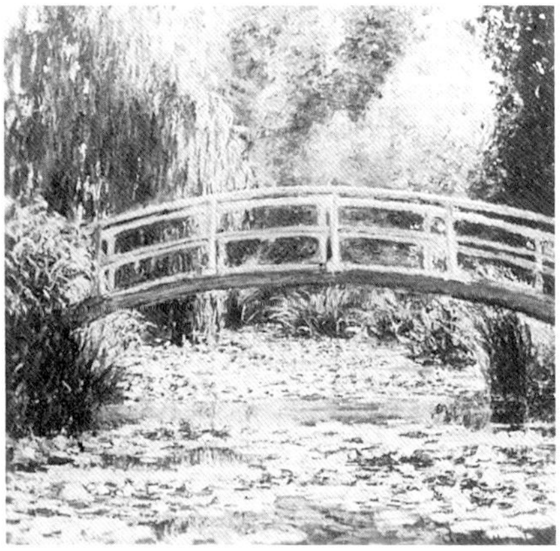

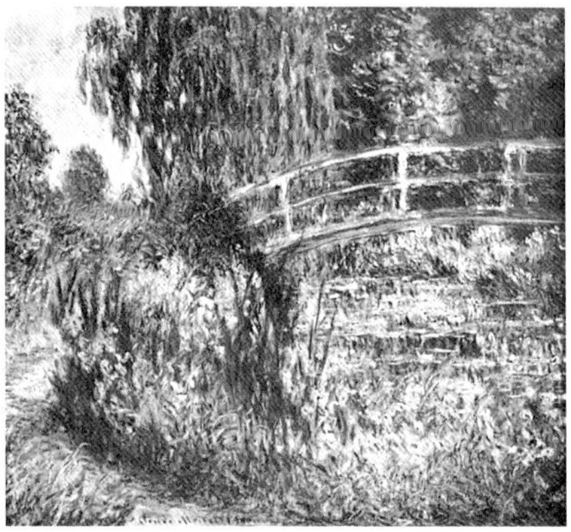

The Bridge with the Water Lilies
1899, 45¾ × 35 in. (116 × 89 cm)
Mahmoud Khalil Museum, Cairo

Water Lilies
1906, 35 × 36¼ in. (89 × 92 cm)
private collection

Water Lilies
1905, 32 × 39¼ in. (81 × 100 cm)
private collection

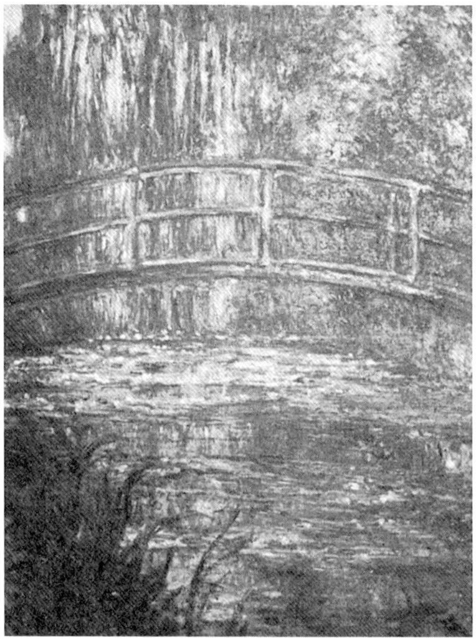

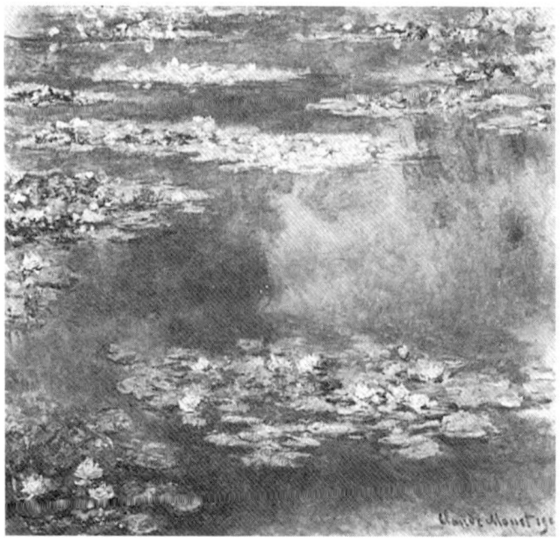

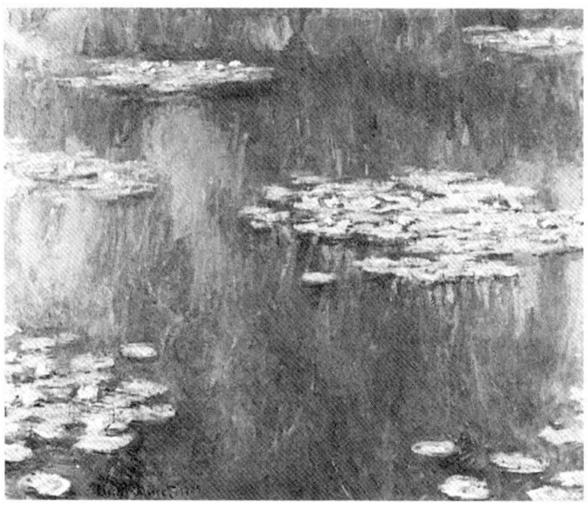

Water Lilies
1905, 35½ × 39¼ in. (90 × 100 cm)
private collection

Water Lilies
1905, 35½ × 39¼ in. (90 × 100 cm)
private collection

Water Lilies
1905, 35½ × 39¼ in. (90 × 100 cm)
private collection

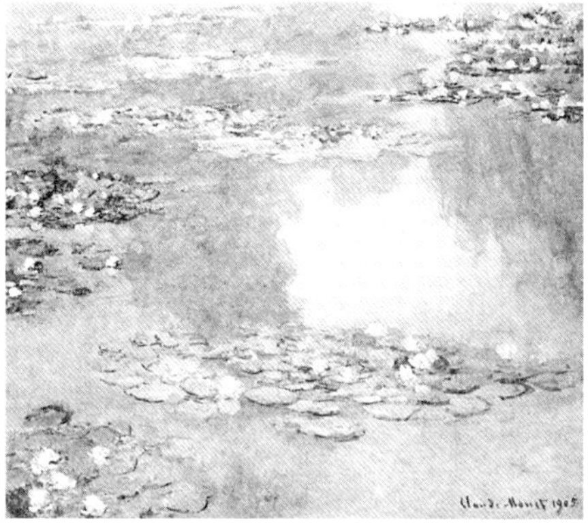

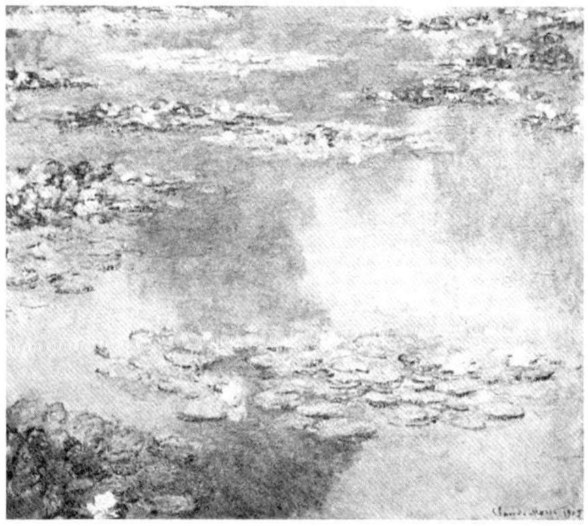

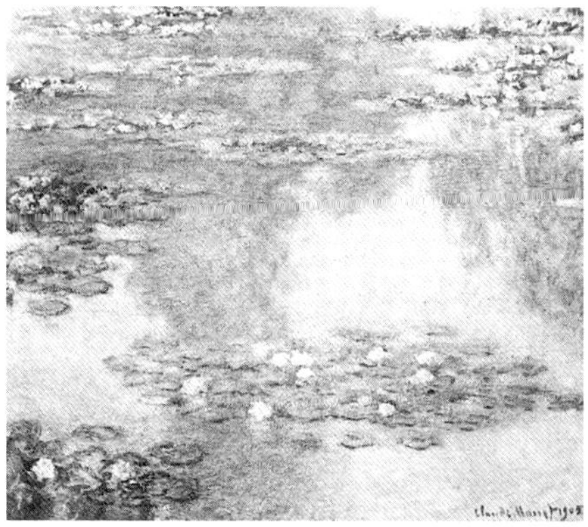

Water Lilies
1905, 28 ¾ in. × 41 ¼ in. (73 × 105 cm)
private collection

Water Lilies
1897–98, 39 ¼ × 39 ¼ in. (100 × 100 cm)
private collection

Water Lilies
1897–99, 35 × 51 ¼ in. (89 × 130 cm)
private collection

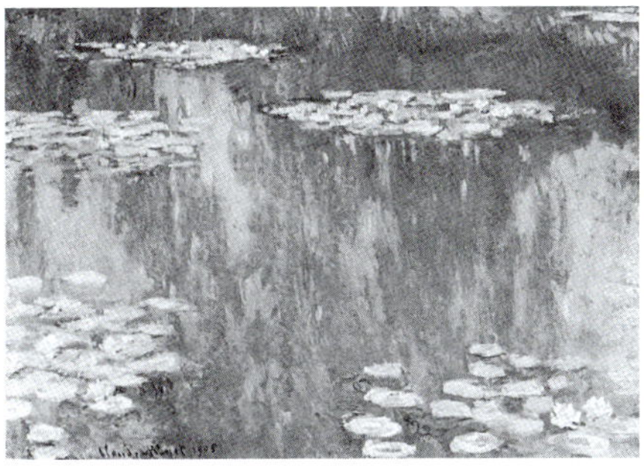

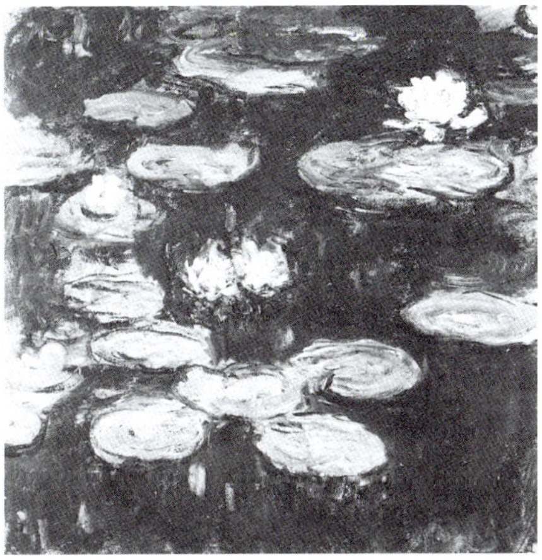

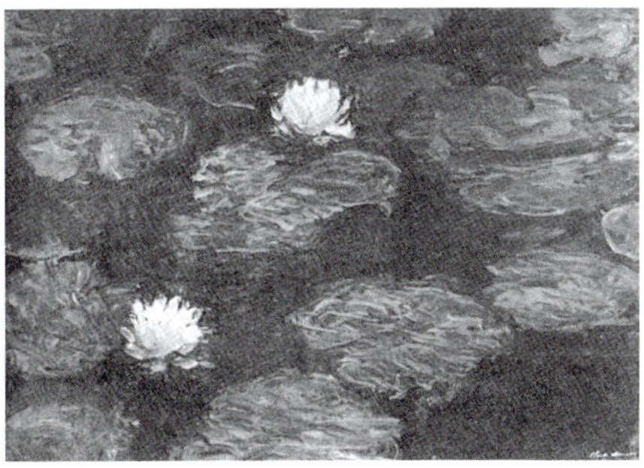

Water Lilies
1897–98, 25 ½ × 39 ¼ in. (65 × 100 cm)
Los Angeles County Museum, inv. M.62.8.13

Water Lilies, Evening Effect
1897–98, 28 ¾ × 39 ¼ in. (73 × 100 cm)
Musée Marmottan, Paris, inv. 5167

Pink Water Lilies
1897–99, 32 × 39 ¼ in. (81 × 100 cm), Galleria Nazionale di Arte Moderna, Rome, inv. 5163

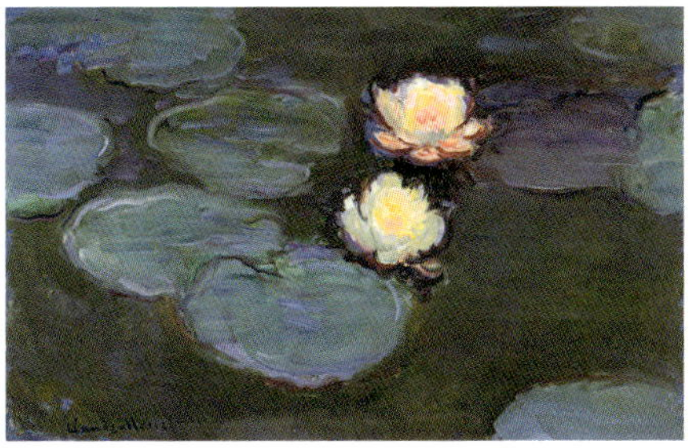

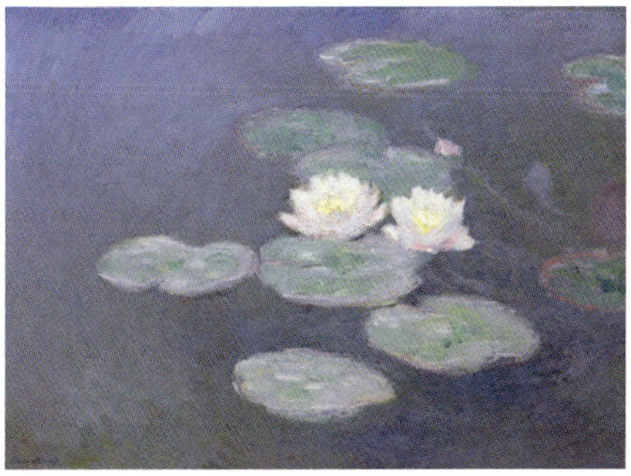

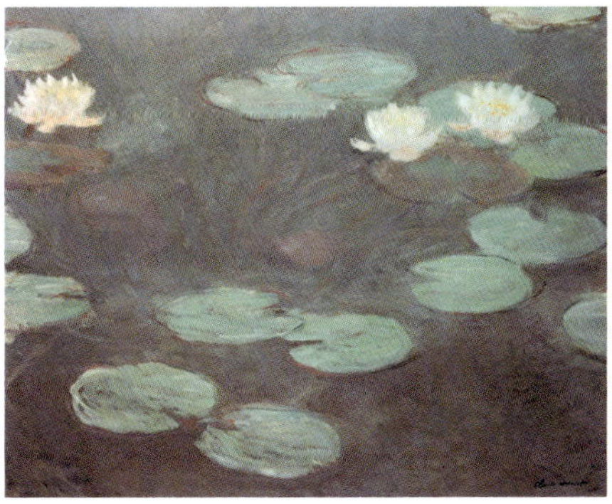

Water Lilies
1897–98, 28 ¾ × 36 ¼ in. (73 × 92 cm)
private collection

Water Lilies
1897–99, 51 ¼ × 59 ¾ in. (130 × 152 cm)
private collection

Water Lilies
1897–98, 29 ½ × 39 ¼ in. (75 × 100 cm)
private collection

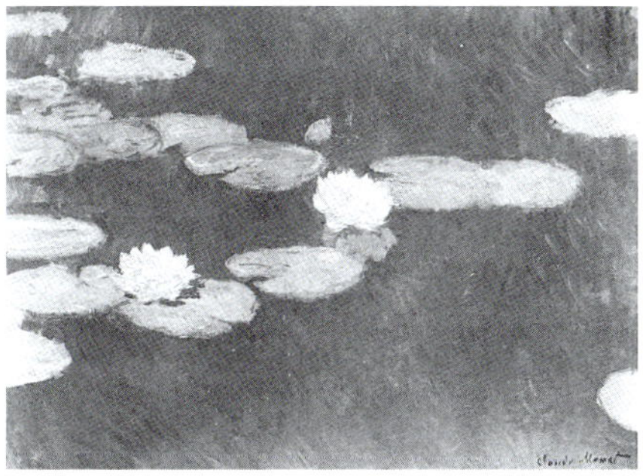

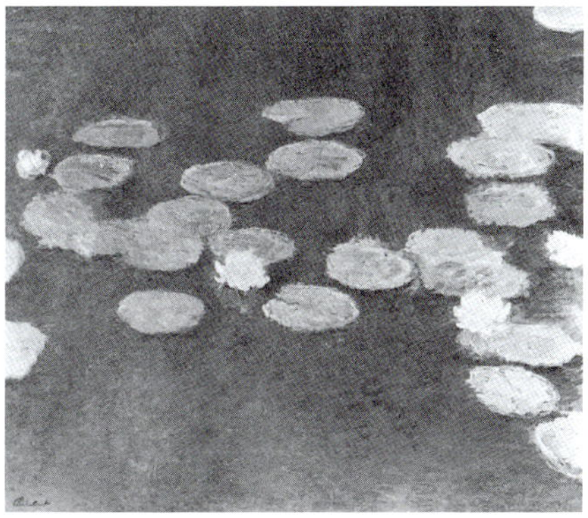

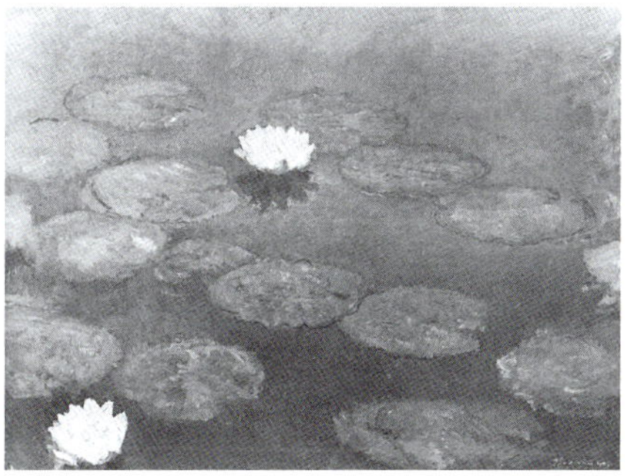

Water Lilies
1903, 32 × 39 ¼ in. (81 × 100 cm)
Dayton Art Institute, Ohio, inv. 53.11

Water Lilies
1903, 32 × 39 ¼ in. (81 × 100 cm),
Bridgestone Museum of Art, Tokyo, inv. F.P. 22

Water Lilies, Water Landscape, the Clouds
1903, 28 ¾ in. × 39 ¼ in. (73 × 100 cm)
private collection

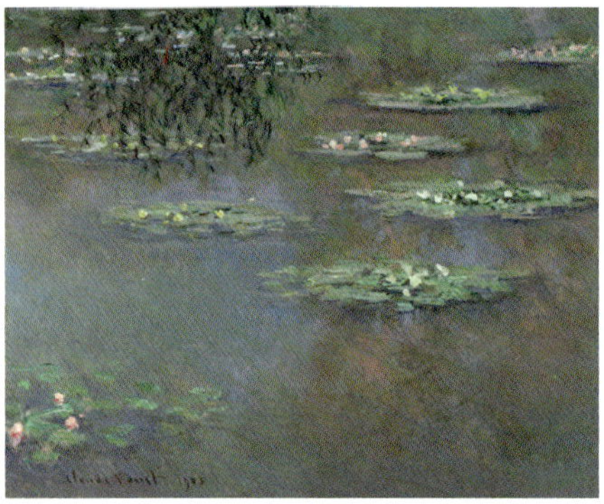

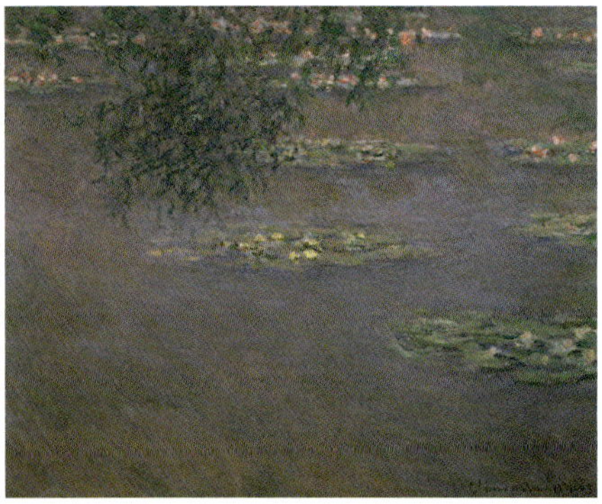

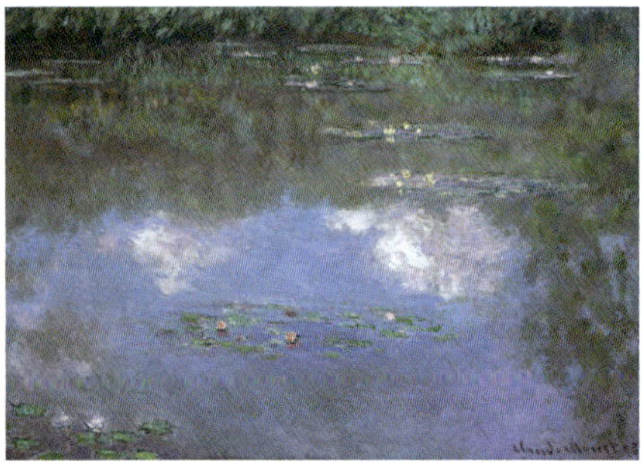

Water Lilies
1905, 32 ¼ × 39 ¼ in. (82 × 100 cm), National Museum of Wales, Cardiff, inv. NMW A 2484

Water Lilies
1906, 35 ½ × 36 ½ in. (90 × 93 cm)
Art Institute of Chicago, inv. 33.1157

Water Lilies
1905, 35 × 39 ¼ in. (89 × 100 cm)
private collection

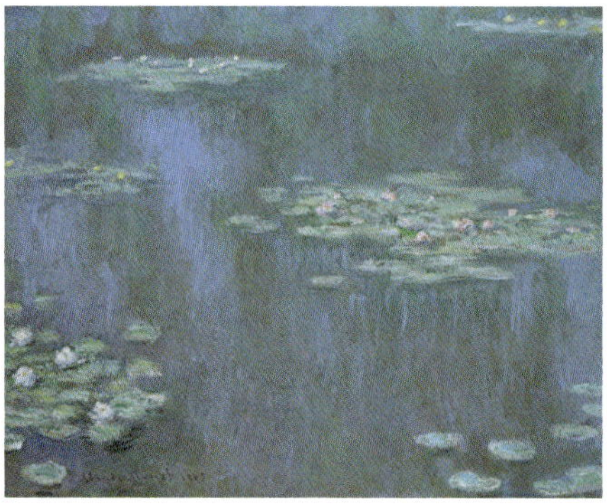

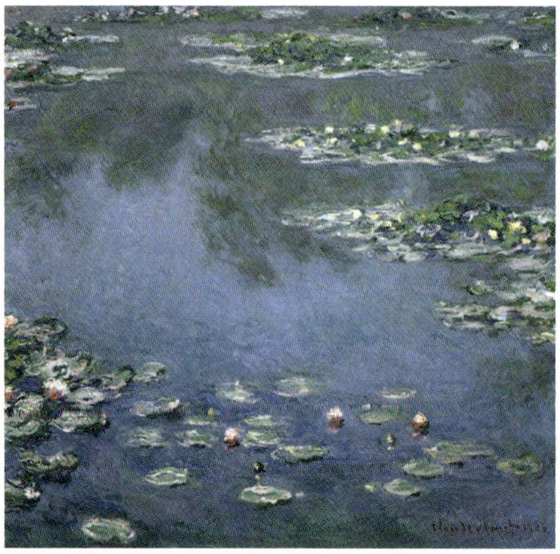

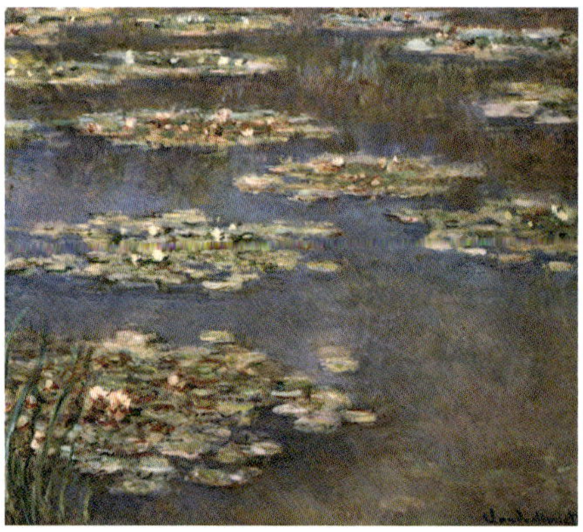

Water Lilies
1905, 28 ¾ in. × 41 ¼ in. (73 × 105 cm)
private collection

Water Lilies
1907, 28 ¾ in. × 39 ¼ in. (73 × 100 cm)
private collection

Water Lilies
1906, 32 × 36 ¼ in. (81 × 92 cm)
private collection

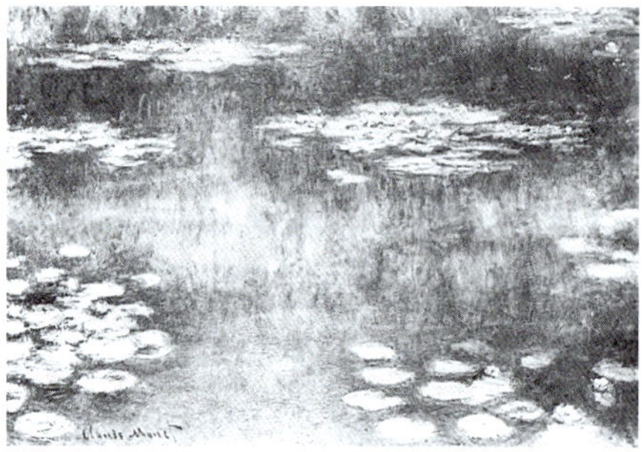

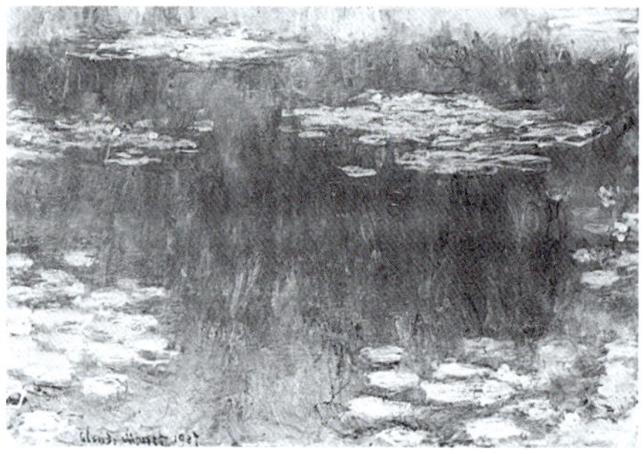

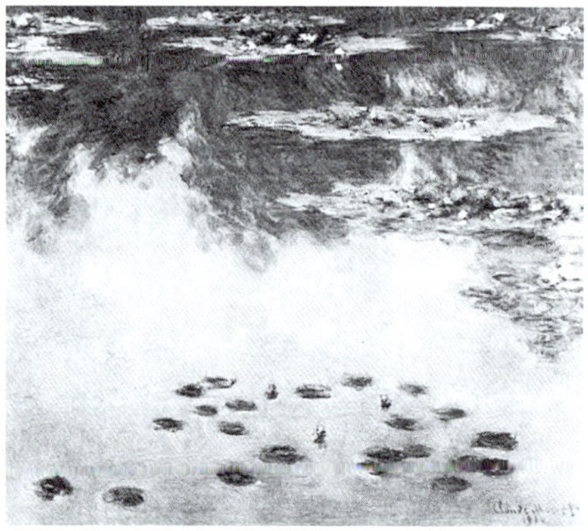

Water Lilies
1907, 36½ × 35 in. (93 × 89 cm)
private collection

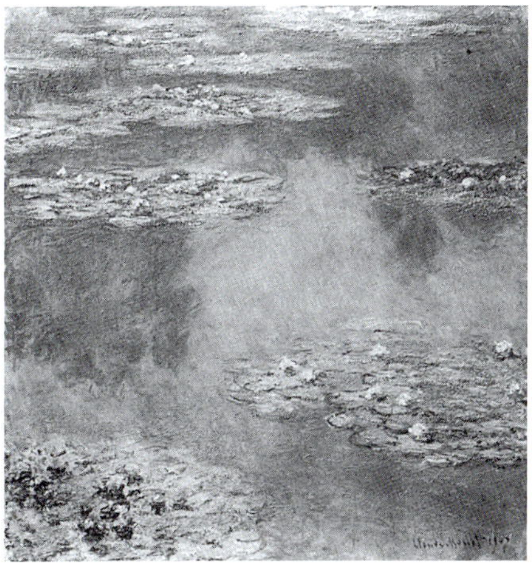

Water Lilies
1907, 39¼ × 35½ in. (100 × 90 cm)
private collection

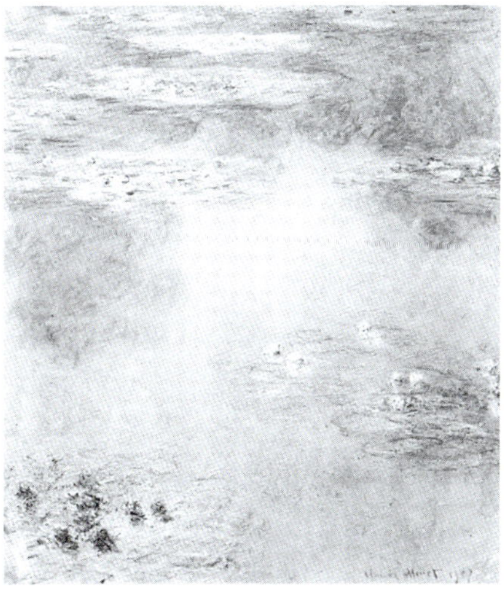

Water Lilies
1907, 35 × 51¼ in. (89 × 130 cm)
private collection

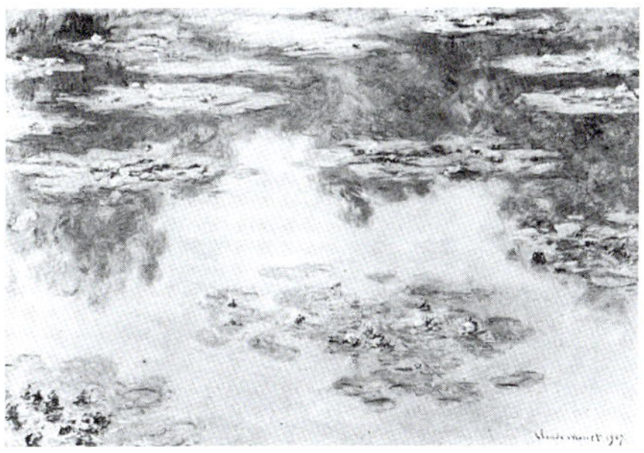

Water Lilies
1903, 28¾ × 36¼ in. (73 × 92 cm)
Musée Marmottan, Paris, inv. 5163

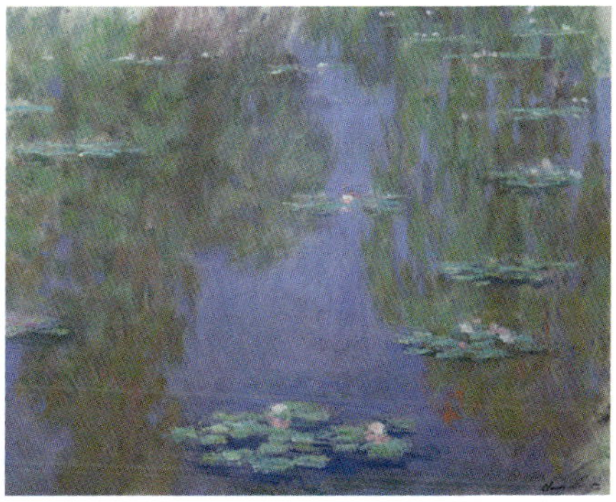

Water Lilies
1908, 36¼ × 32 in. (92 × 81 cm)
private collection

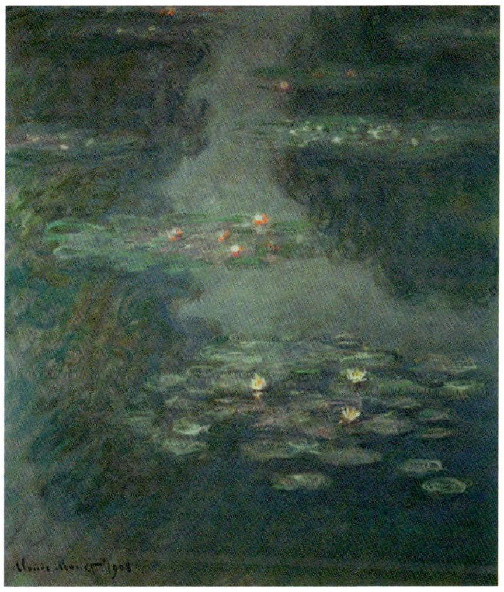

Water Lilies
1908, 39¼ × 32 in. (100 × 81 cm)
National Museum of Wales, Cardiff, inv. 798

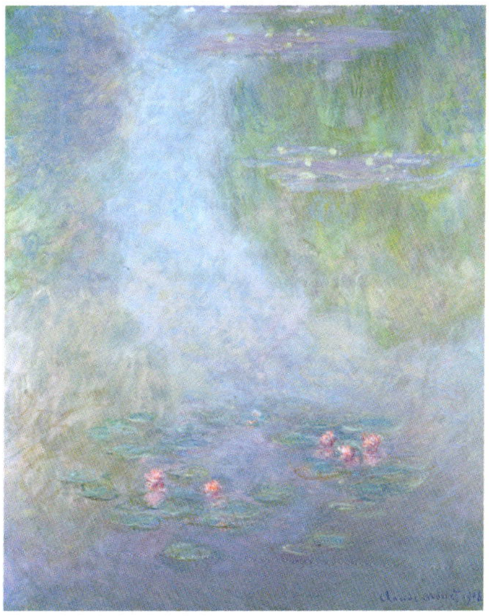

Water Lilies
1903–04, 35 × 39¼ in. (89 × 100 cm)
Musée Marmottan, Paris, inv. 5166

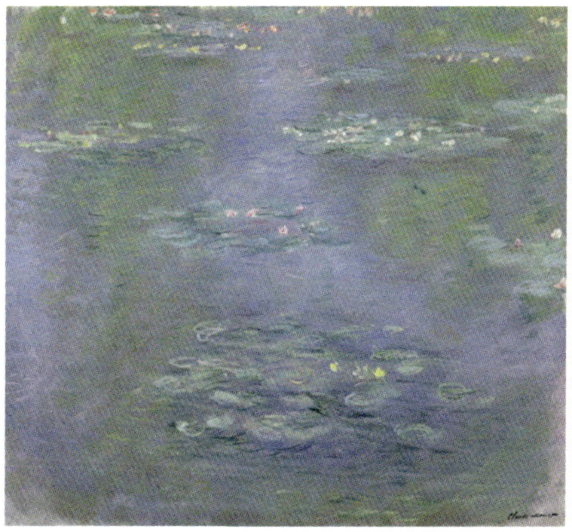

Water Lilies
1908, 39¼ × 39¼ in. (100 × 100 cm)
private collection

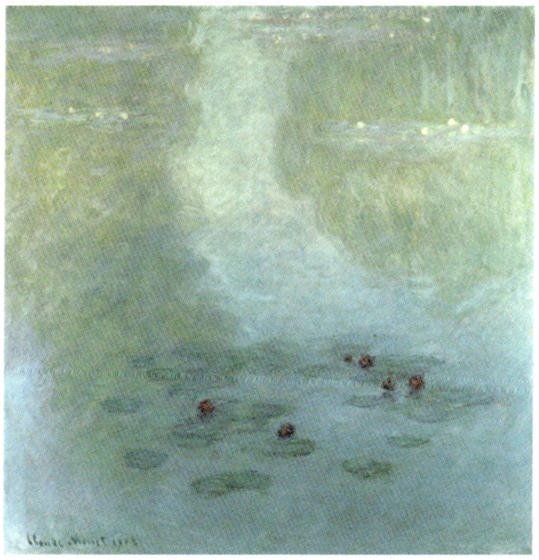

Water Lilies
1908, 39¼ × 35½ in. (100 × 90 cm)
private collection

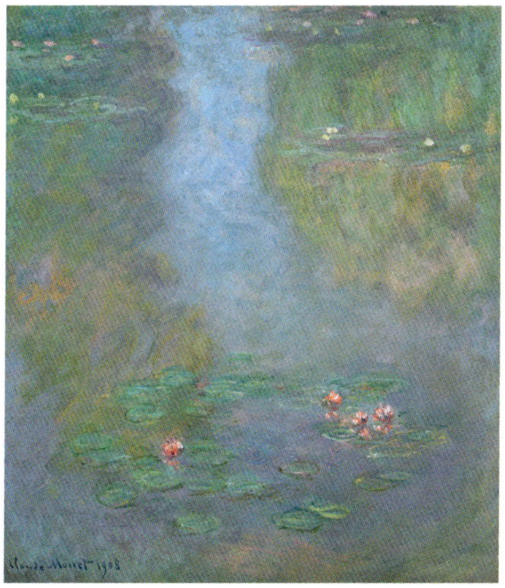

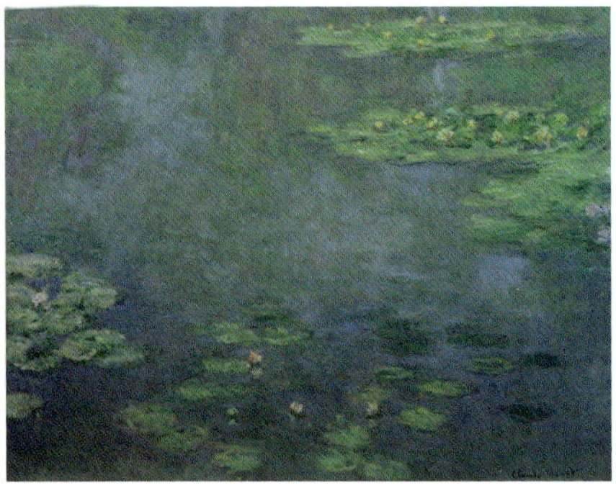

Water Lilies
1906, 28 ¾ × 36 ¼ in. (73 × 92 cm), The Ohara Museum of Art, Kurashiki (Japan), inv. 8

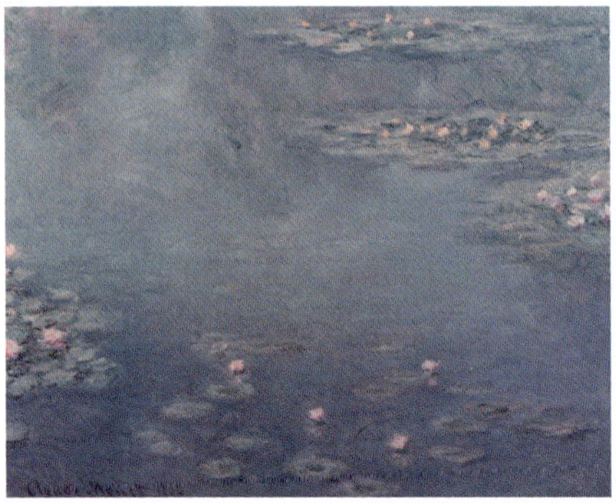

Water Lilies
1906, 32 × 39 ¼ in. (81 × 100 cm)
private collection

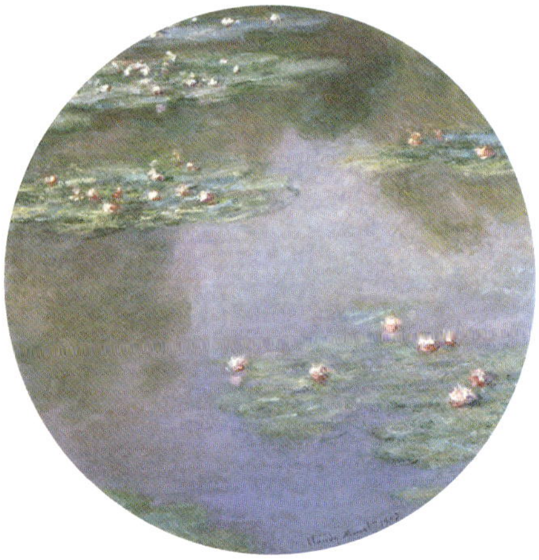

Water Lilies
1907, diameter 32 in. (81 cm)
private collection

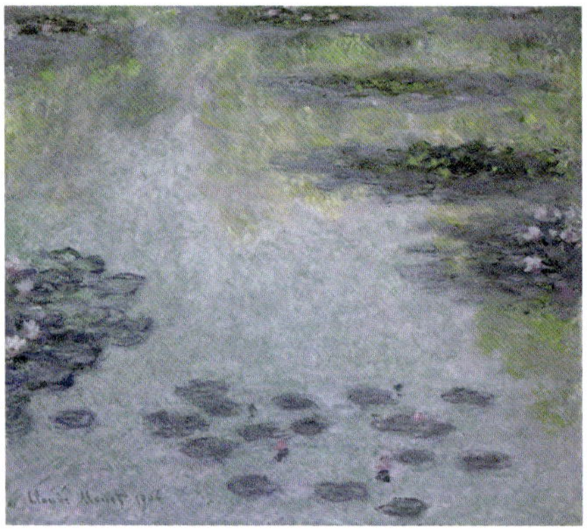

Water Lilies
1906, 32 × 36 ¼ in. (81 × 92 cm),
National Museum of Wales, Cardiff, inv. 797

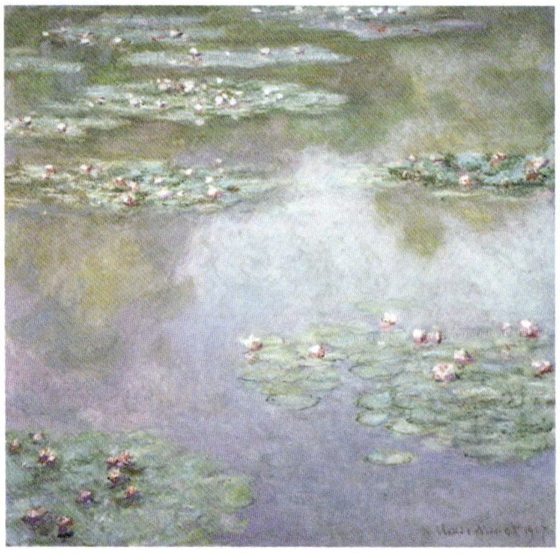

Water Lilies
1907, 35 ½ × 36 ½ in. (90 × 93 cm)
Museum of Fine Art, Boston, inv. 19.170

Water Lilies
1907, diameter 32 in. (81 cm), Musée Municipal d'Art et d'Industrie, Saint-Étienne, inv. 924

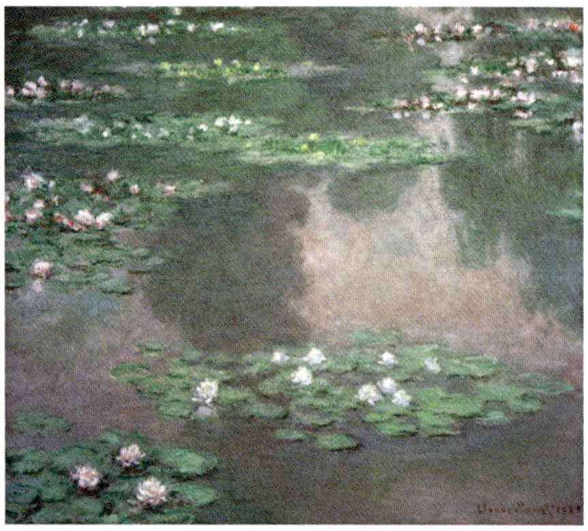

Water Lilies
1905, 35 ½ × 39 ¼ in. (90 × 100 cm)
Museum of Fine Art, Boston, inv. 39.804

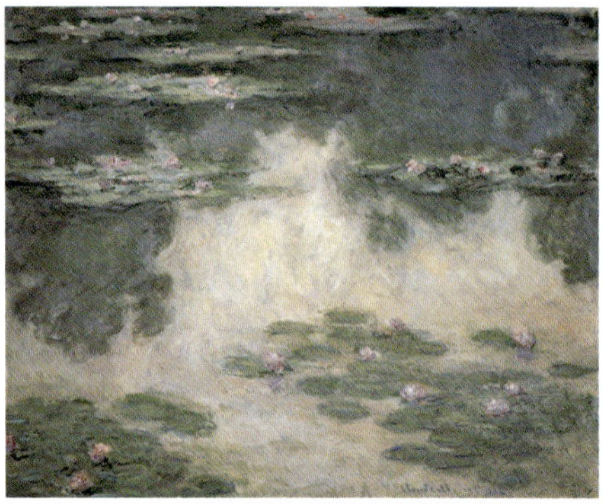

Water Lilies
1906, 32 × 39 ¼ in. (81 × 100 cm)
Mahmoud Khalil Museum, Cairo

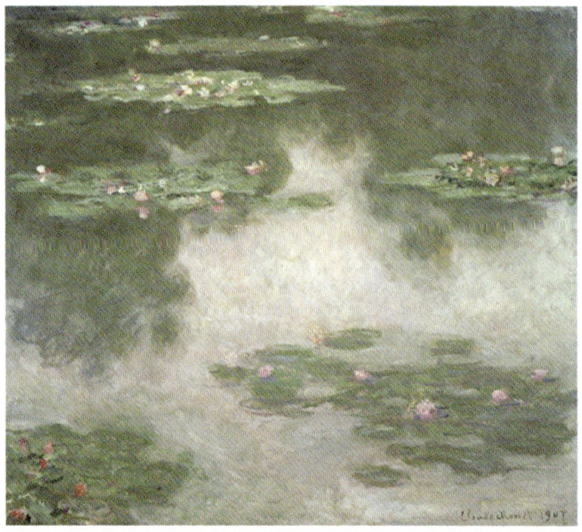

Water Lilies
1907, 32 × 36 ¼ in. (81 × 92 cm), Wadsworth Atheneum, Hartford, CT, inv. 1957.622

Water Lilies
1904, 32 × 39 ¼ in. (81 × 100 cm)
private collection

Water Lilies
1904, 35 ½ × 36 ¼ in. (90 × 92 cm)
private collection

Water Lilies
1907, 35 ½ × 36 ½ in. (90 × 93 cm)
private collection

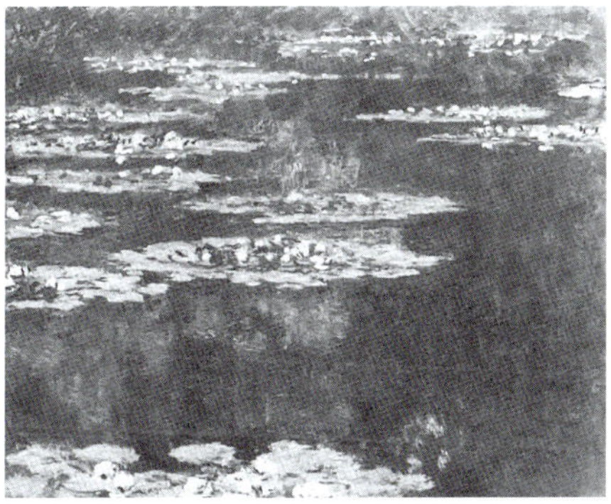

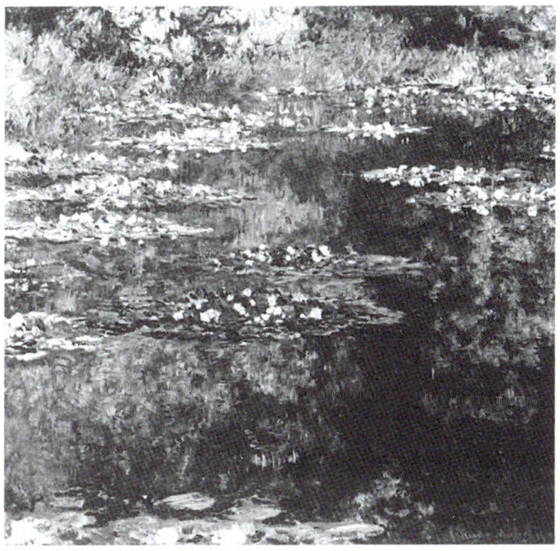

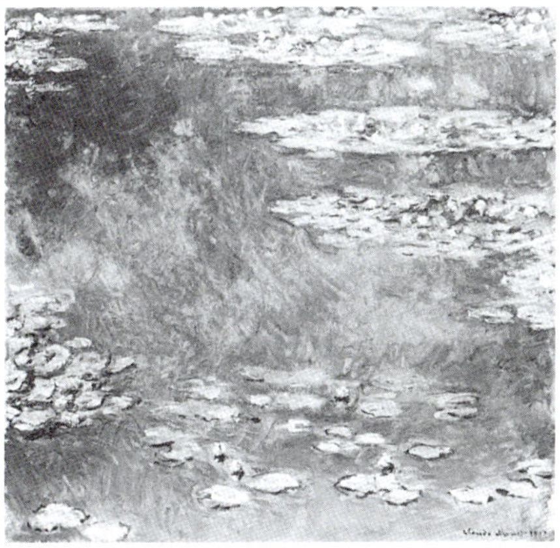

Water Lilies
1904, 35 × 36 ¼ in. (89 × 92 cm)
The Denver Art Museum, inv. 4/1935.14

Water Lilies
1904, 35 ½ × 36 ¼ in. (90 × 92 cm),
Musée des Beaux-Arts, Caen, inv. MNR 214

Water Lilies
1904, 35 ½ × 36 ½ in. (90 × 93 cm), Nouveau Musée des Beaux-Arts, Le Havre, inv. 486

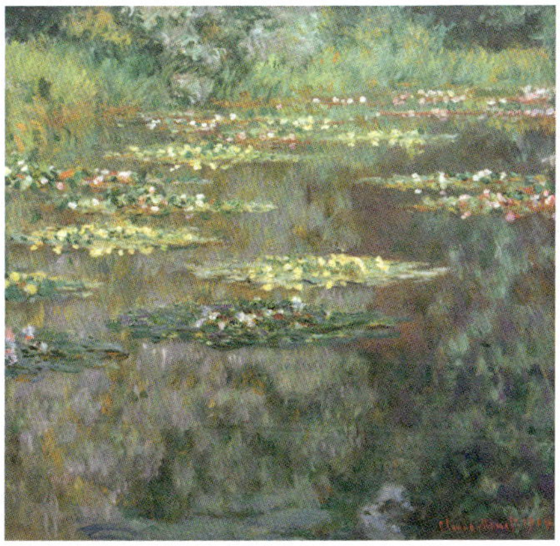

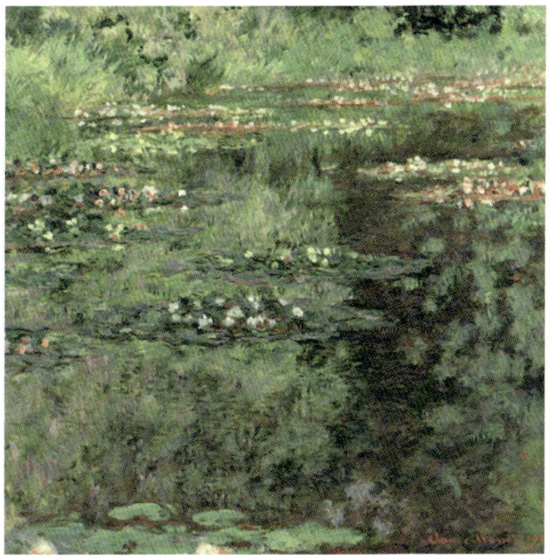

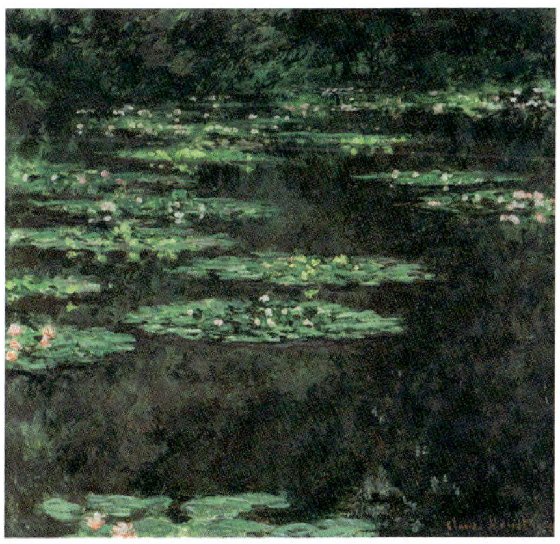

Water Lilies
1906, 32 × 36 ¼ in. (81 × 92 cm)
private collection

Water Lilies
1906, 35 ½ × 39 ¼ in. (90 × 100 cm)
private collection

Water Lilies
1906, 35 ½ × 36 ½ in. (90 × 93 cm)
private collection

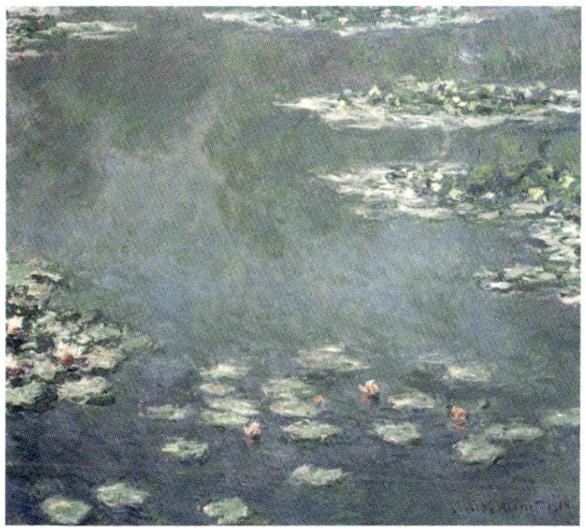

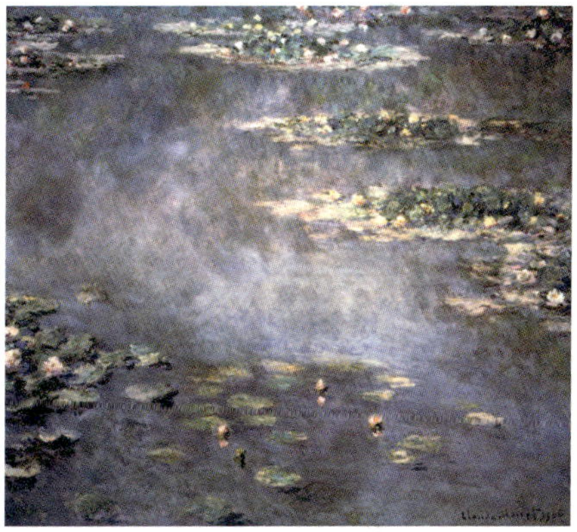

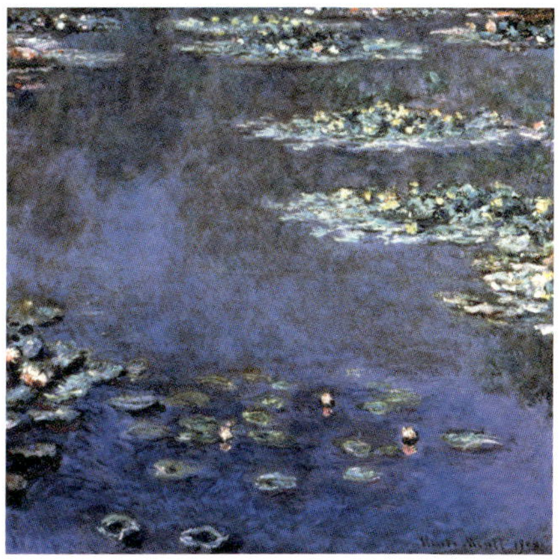

Water Lilies
1907, 39 ¼ × 32 in. (100 × 81 cm)
private collection

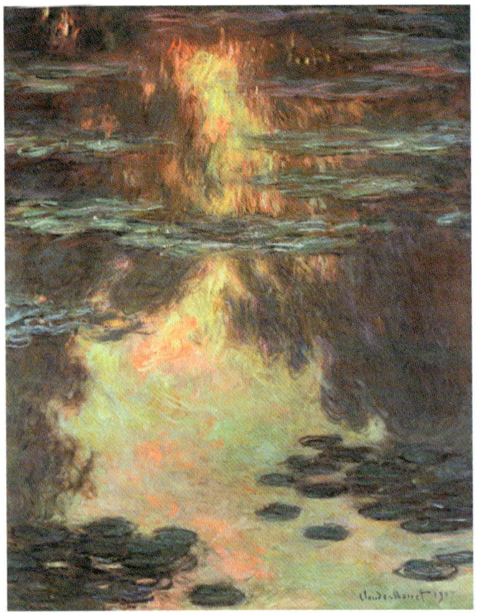

Water Lilies
1907, 41 ¼ × 28 ¾ in. (107 × 73 cm)
private collection

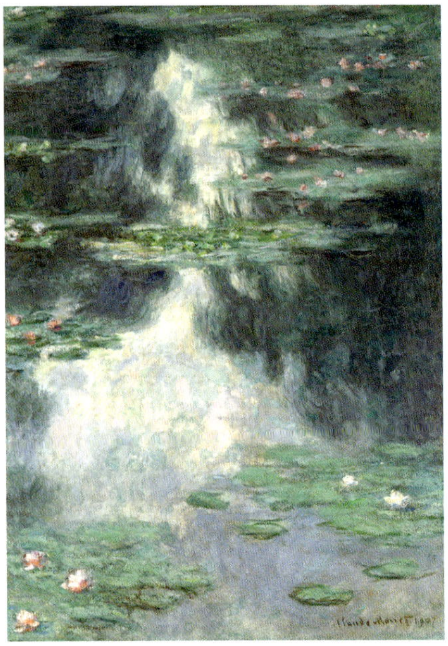

Water Lilies
1907, 41 ¼ × 28 ¾ in. (105 × 73 cm)
Konstmuseum, Göteborg, inv. GKM 2232

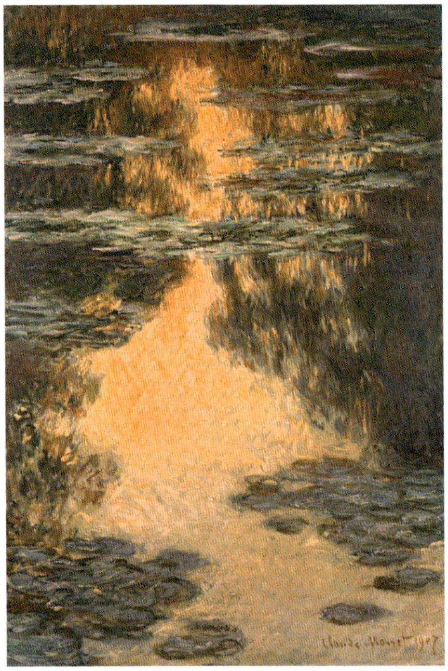

Water Lilies
1907, 39 ¼ × 28 ¾ in. (100 × 73 cm)
Musée Marmottan, Paris, inv. 5168

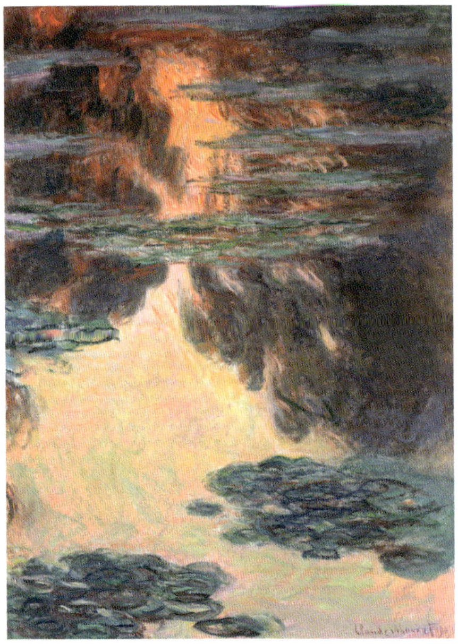

Water Lilies
1907, 36 ½ × 28 ¾ in. (93 × 73 cm)
private collection

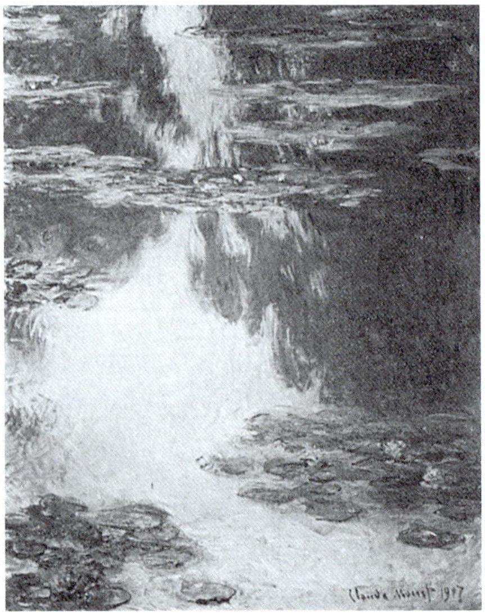

Water Lilies
1907, 36 ¼ × 28 ¾ in. (92 × 73 cm)
private collection

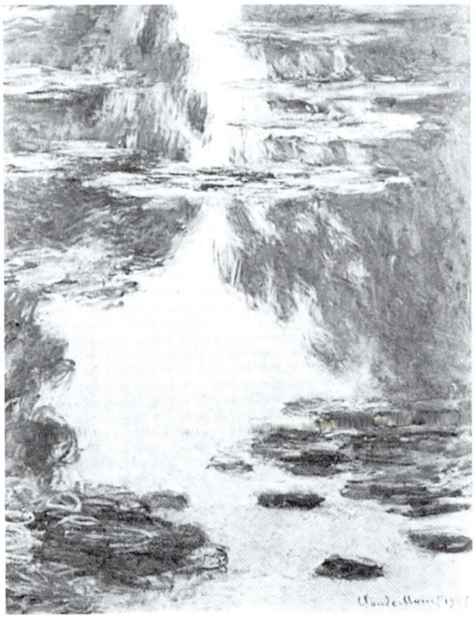

Water Lilies
1907, 36 ¼ × 32 in. (92 × 81 cm)
Museum of Fine Arts, Houston, inv. 68-31

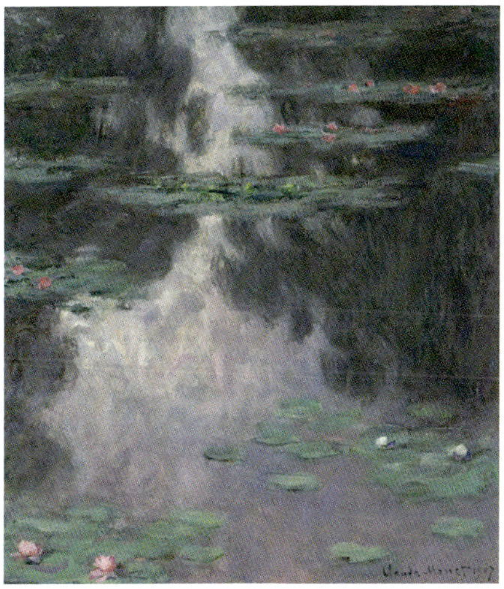

Water Lilies
1907, 36 ¼ × 28 ¾ in. (92 × 73 cm),
private collection

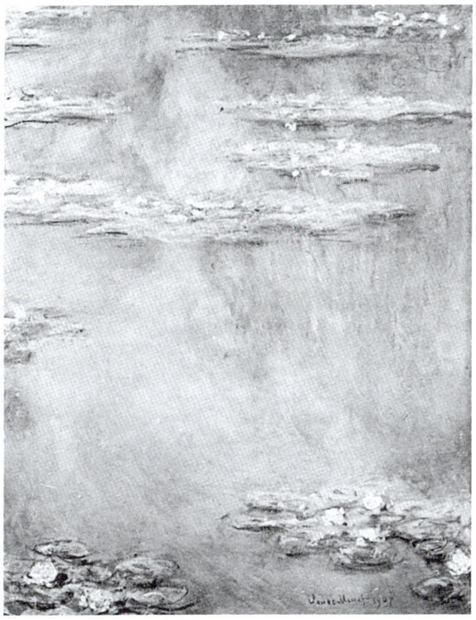

Water Lilies
1907, 41 ¼ × 28 ¾ in. (105 × 73 cm)
Musée Marmottan, Paris, 5109

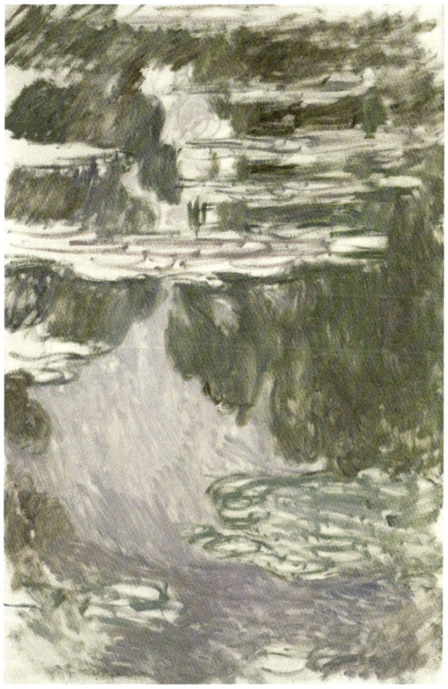

Water Lilies
1907, 39 ¼ × 28 ¾ in. (100 × 73 cm)
Bridgestone Museum of Art, Tokyo, inv. F.P. 23

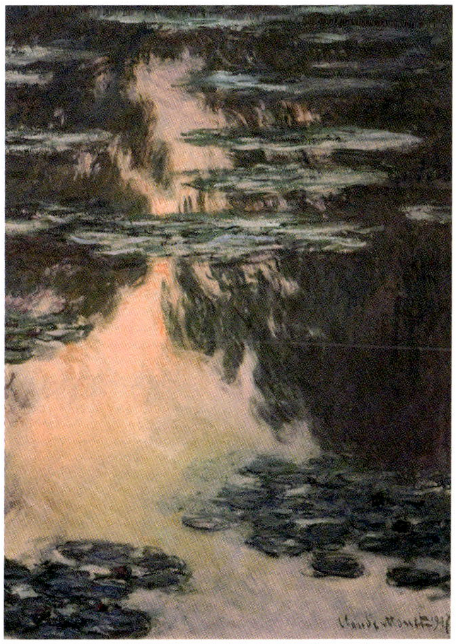

Water Lilies
1907, 36 ¼ × 28 ¾ in. (92 × 73 cm)
private collection

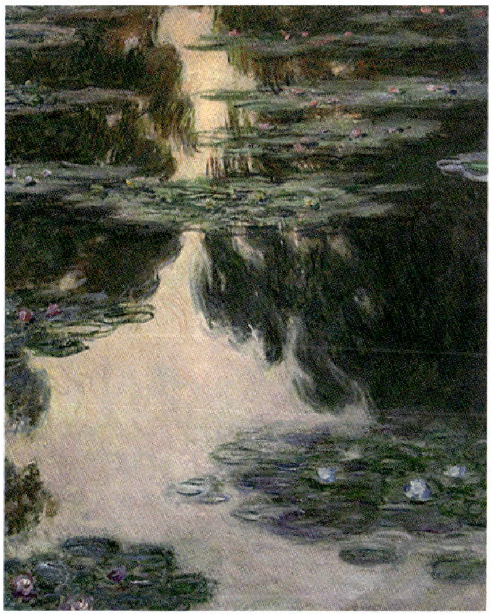

Water Lilies, Gray Day
1907, 39 ¼ × 28 ¾ in. (100 × 73 cm)
private collection

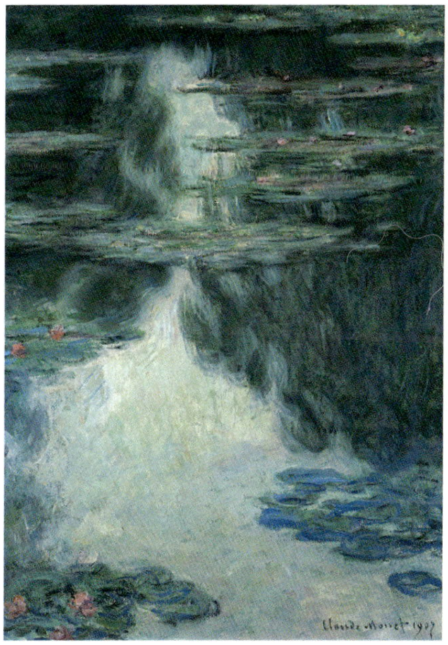

Water Lilies
1907, 41¾ × 28¾ in. (106 × 73 cm)
private collection

Water Lilies
1907, 36½ × 32¼ in. (93 × 82 cm)
private collection

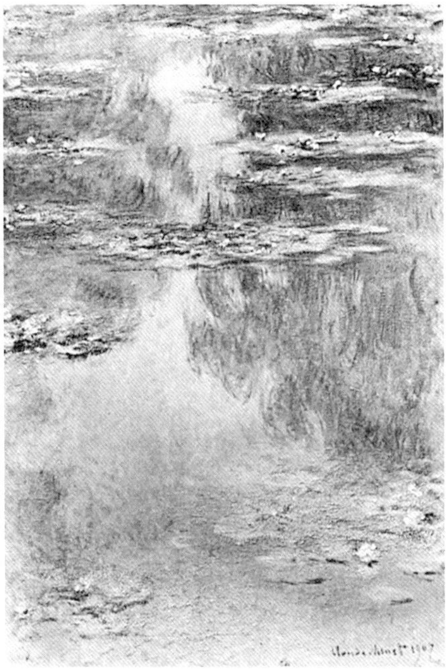

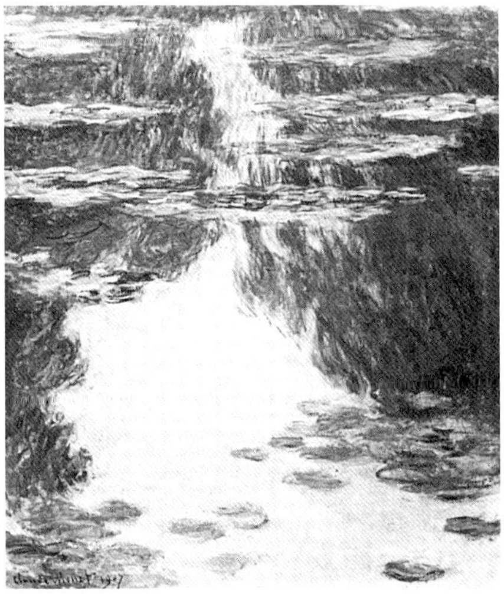

Water Lilies
1907, 39¼ × 32 in. (100 × 81 cm)
private collection

Water Lilies, Sunset
1907–08, 28¾ × 36¼ in. (73 × 92 cm)
private collection

Water-Lily Pond
sketch, 1907–08, 28¾ × 42 in. (73 × 107 cm)
private collection

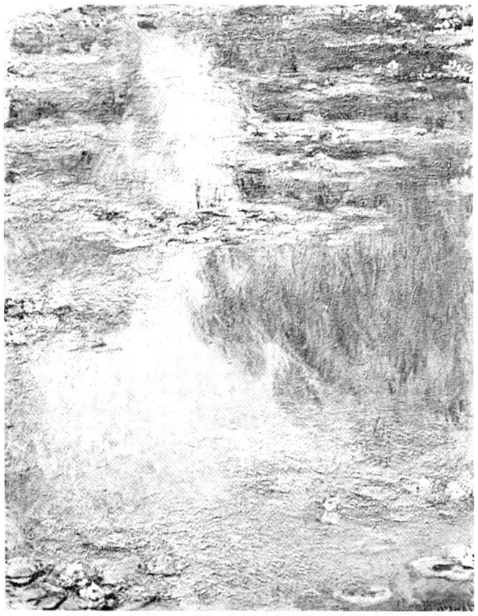

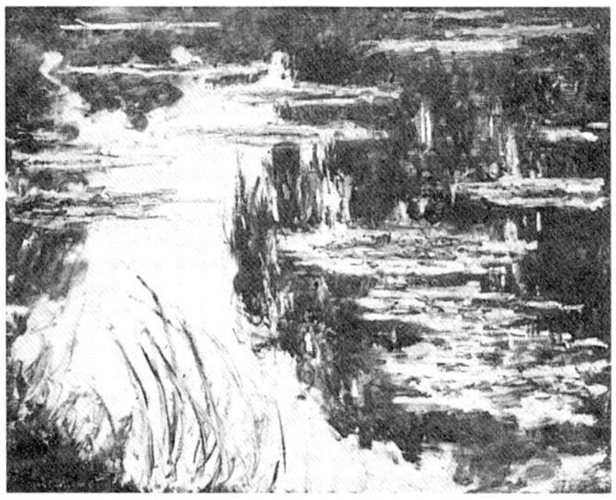

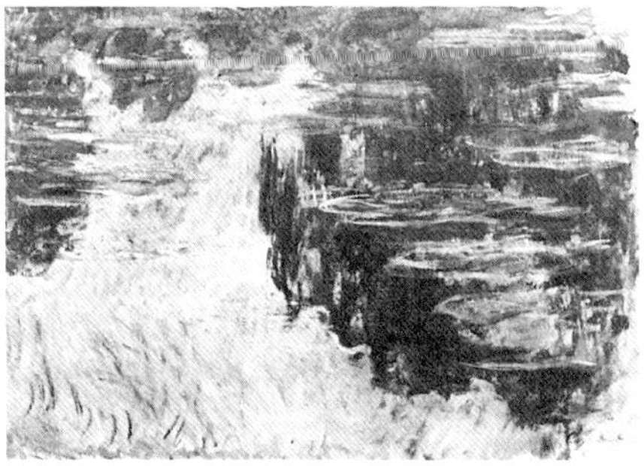

Water Lilies
1908, 35½ × 36¼ in. (90 × 92 cm)
private collection

Water Lilies
1908, 39¼ × 39¼ in. (100 × 100 cm)
private collection

Water Lilies
1908, 39¼ × 32 in. (100 × 81 cm)
private collection

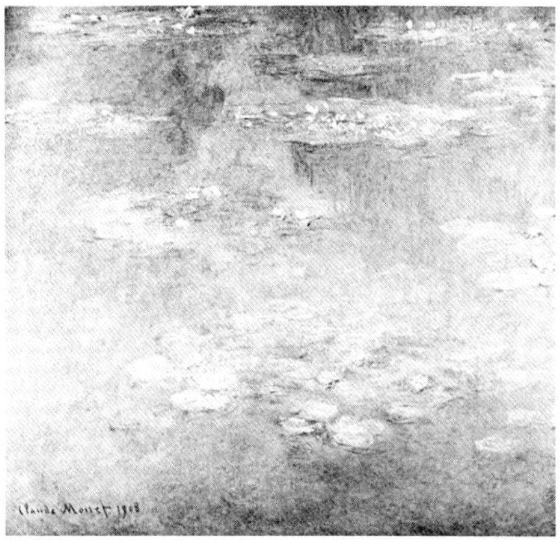

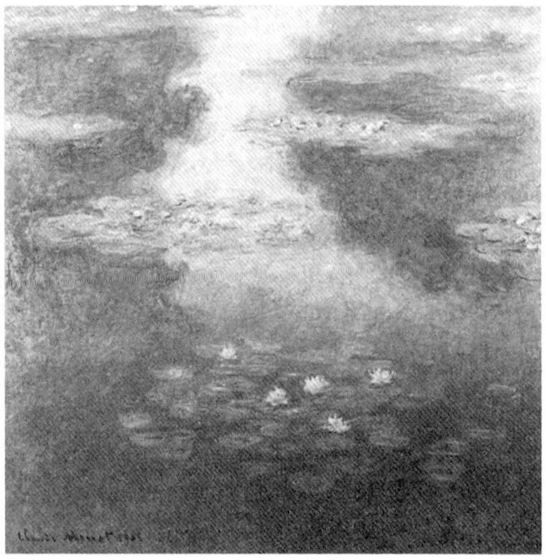

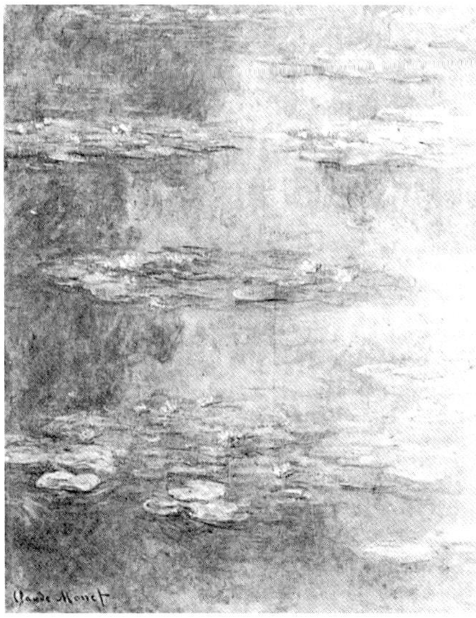

Water Lilies
1908, 39 ¼ × 32 in. (100 × 81 cm)
private collection

Water Lilies
1907, 36 ½ × 35 in. (93 × 89 cm)
private collection

Water Lilies
1908, 35 ½ × 34 ¼ in. (90 × 87 cm)
private collection

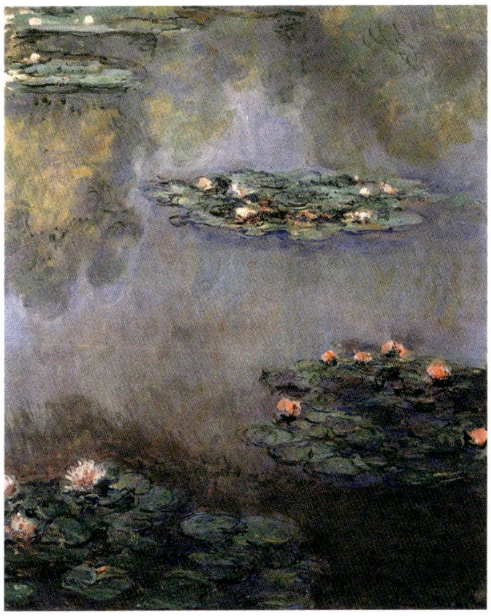

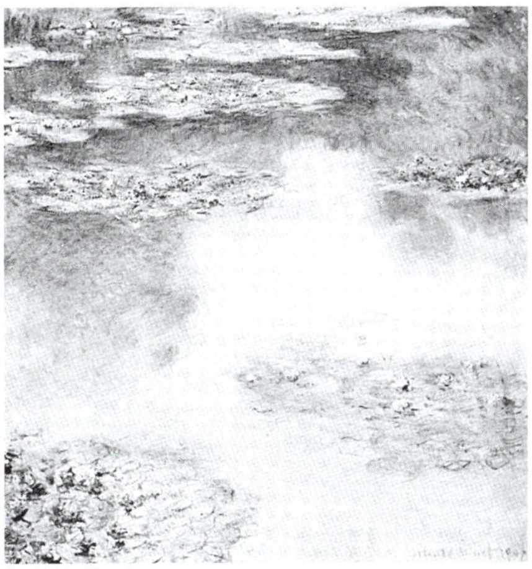

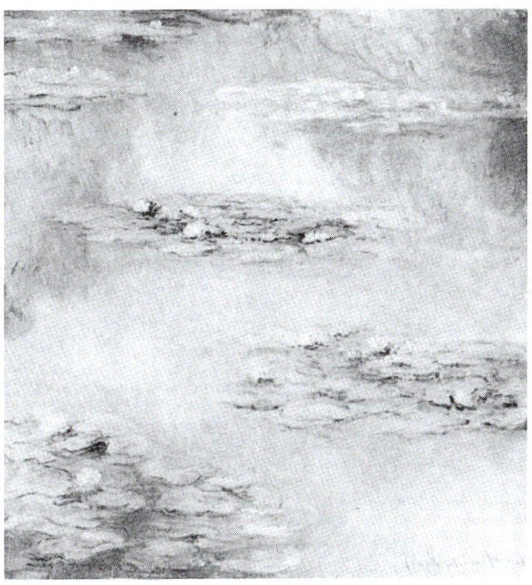

Water Lilies
1914–17, 70 ¾ × 57 ½ in. (180 × 146 cm), The Fine Arts Museums of San Francisco Legion of Honor, inv. 1973.3

Water Lilies
1908, 36 ¼ × 35 ½ in. (92 × 90 cm), Worcester Art Museum, MA, inv. 1910-26

Water Lilies
1908, diameter 35 ½ in. (90 cm), Musée Municipal Alphonse-Georges Poulain, Vernon, inv. 25.4.1

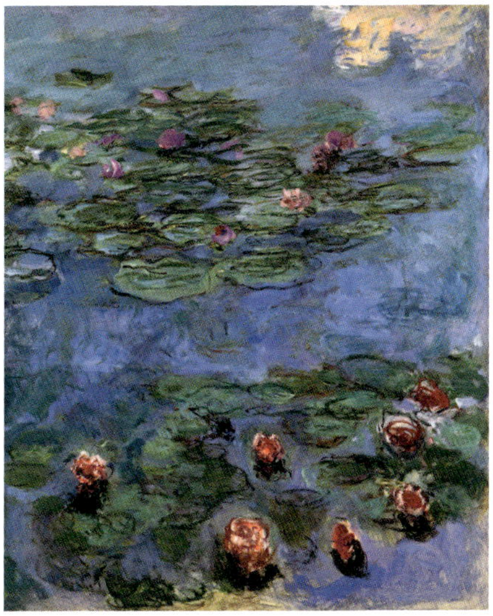

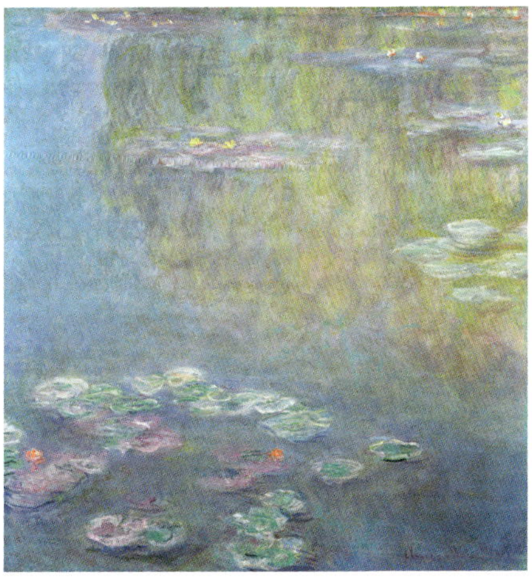

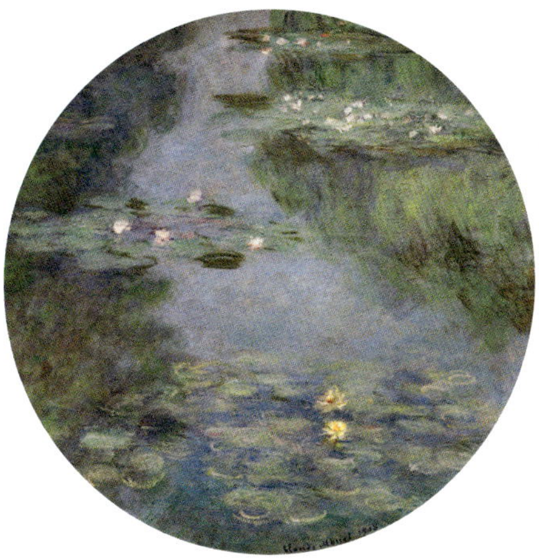

Water Lilies
1907, 39 ¼ × 39 ¼ in. (100 × 100 cm)
private collection

Water Lilies
1908, 36 ¼ × 35 in. (92 × 89 cm)
private collection

Water Lilies
1908, diameter 32 in. (81 cm)
Dallas Museum of Fine Arts, inv. 1981.128

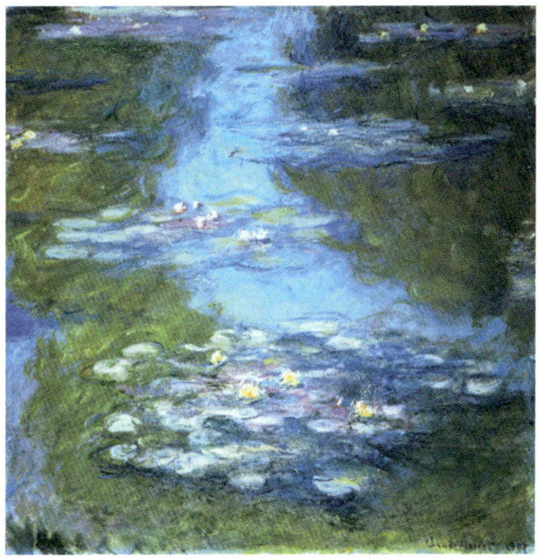

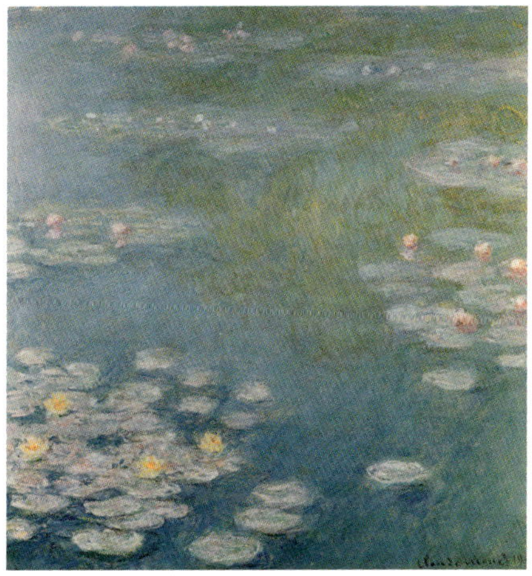

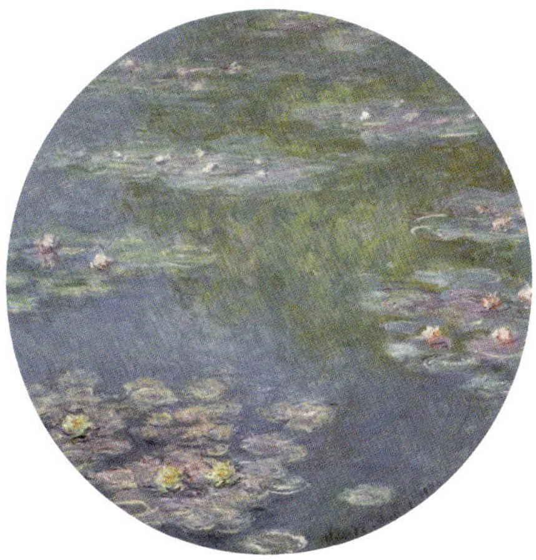

Water Lilies
1914–17, 53¼ × 57 in. (135 × 145 cm)
private collection

Water Lilies
1914–17, 51¼ × 78¾ in. (130 × 200 cm)
private collection

Water Lilies
1914–17, 53¼ × 57 in. (135 × 145 cm)
private collection

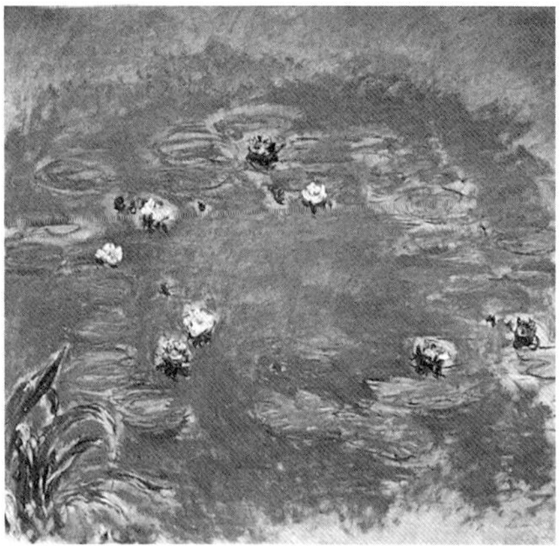

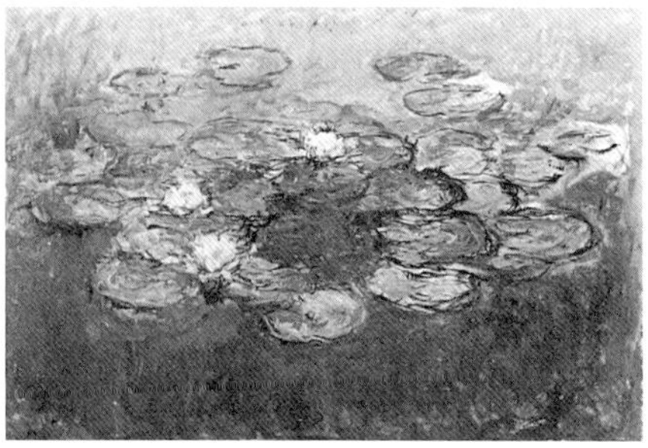

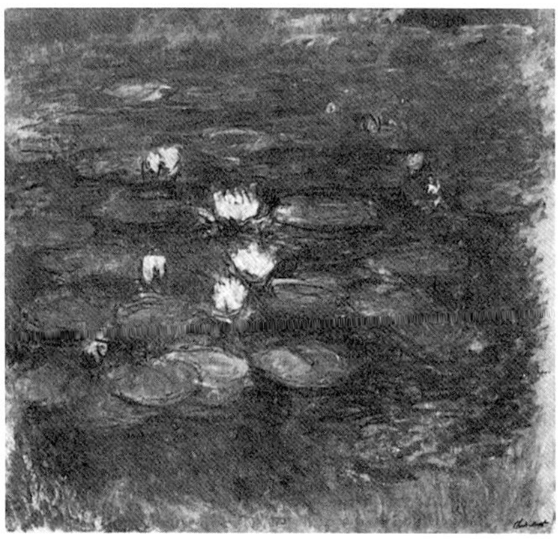

Water Lilies
1914–17, 59¾ × 78¾ in. (152 × 200 cm)
private collection

Water Lilies
1914–17, 78¾ × 78¾ in. (200 × 200 cm)
private collection

Water Lilies
1914–17, 63 × 70¾ in. (160 × 180 cm)
private collection

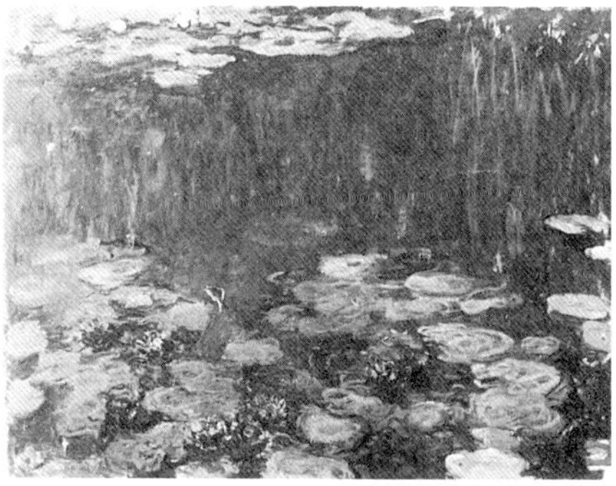

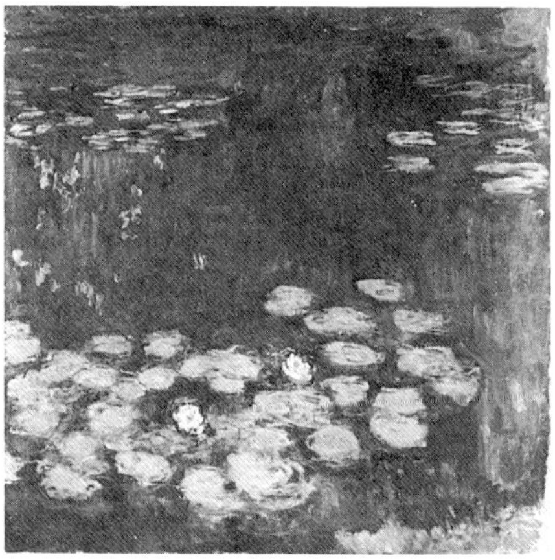

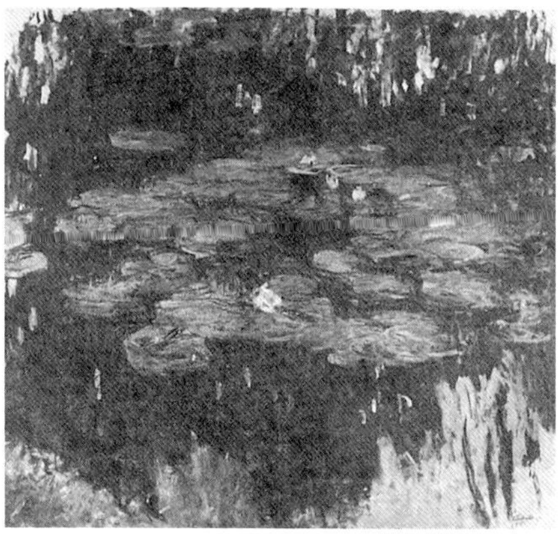

Water Lilies
1914–17, 70¾ × 78¾ in. (180 × 200 cm)
private collection

Irises and Water Lilies
1914–17, 51¼ × 78¾ in. (130 × 200 cm)
private collection

Water Lilies
1914–17, 63 × 70¾ in. (160 × 180 cm)
private collection

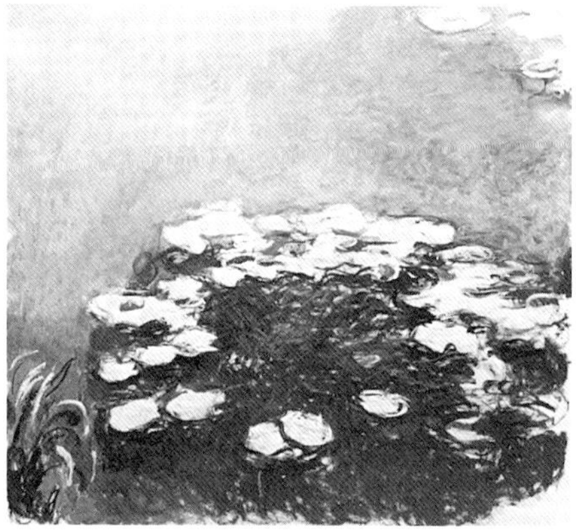

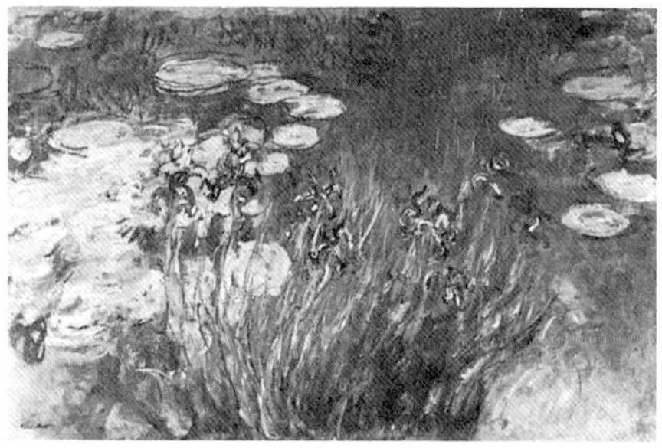

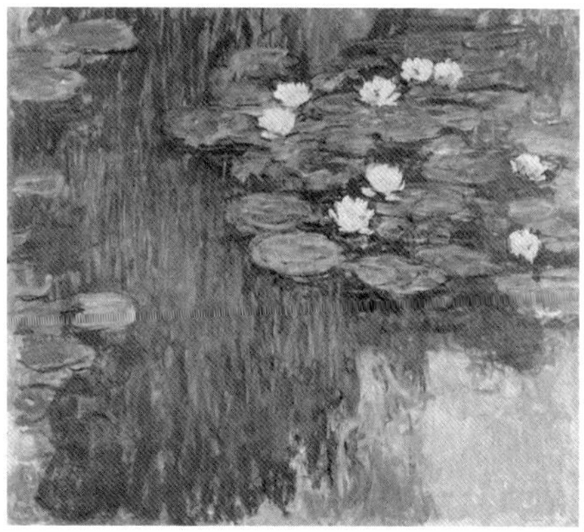

Water Lilies
1908, 33 ¼ × 35 ½ in. (86 × 90 cm)
private collection

Water Lilies with Reflection of Tall Grass
1914–17, 51 ¼ × 78 ¾ in. (130 × 200 cm)
private collection

Water Lilies
1914–17, 59 × 78 ¾ in. (150 × 200 cm)
private collection

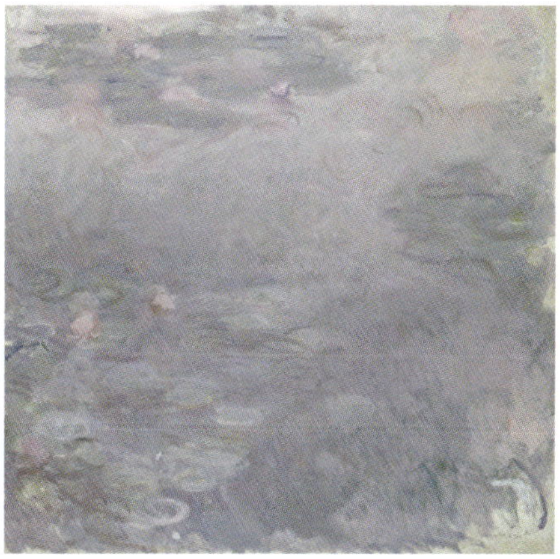

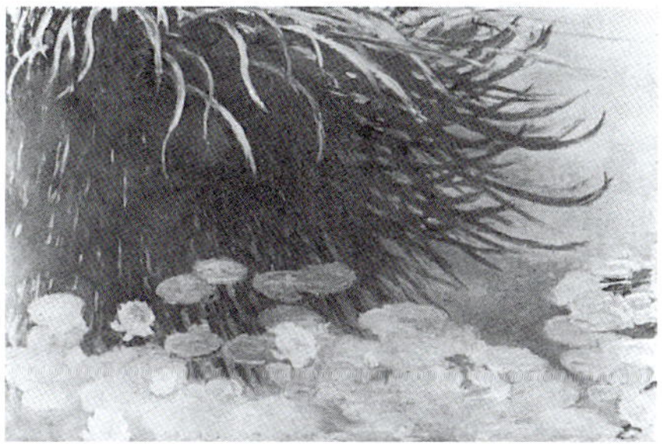

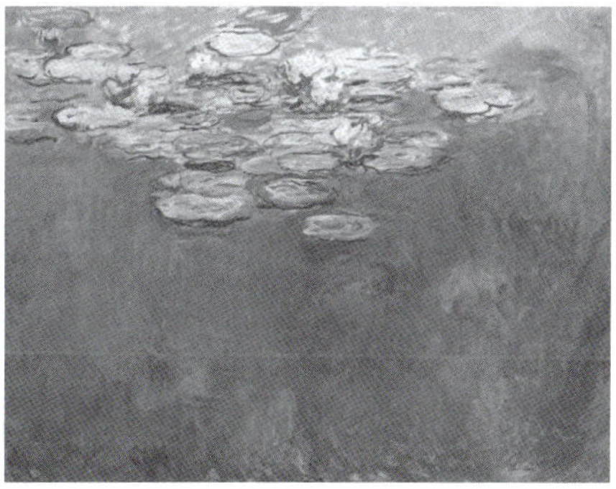

Water Lilies
1914–17, 51 ¼ × 59 in. (130 × 150 cm)
Musée Marmottan, Paris, inv. 5085

Water Lilies
1914–17, 59 × 78 ¾ in. (150 × 200 cm)
Museum of Fine Arts, Boston

Water Lilies
1914–17, 51 ¼ × 35 ½ in. (130 × 90 cm)
private collection

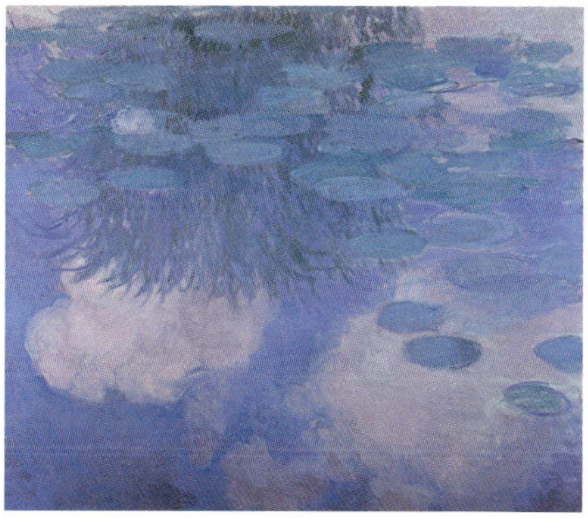

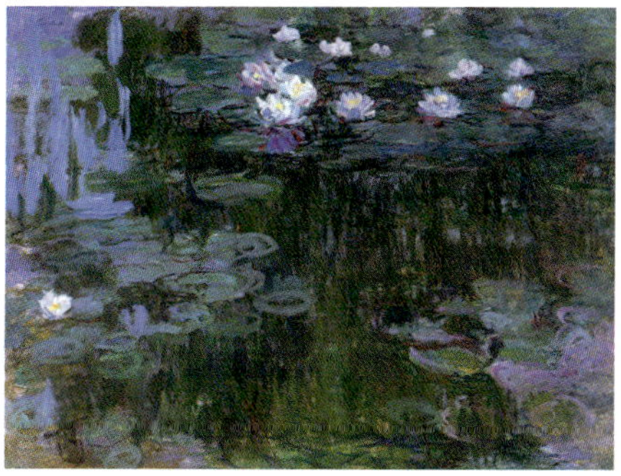

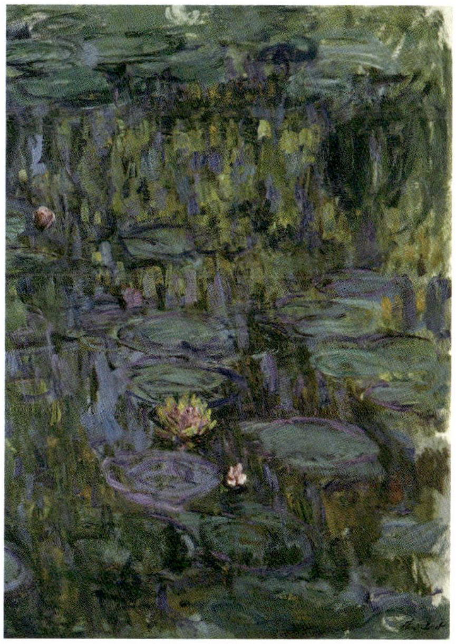

Water Lilies
1914–17, 51 ¼ × 59 in. (130 × 150 cm)
Art Institute of Chicago, inv. 64-201

Water Lilies
1914–17, 69 × 53 ¼ in. (175 × 135 cm)
private collection

Water Lilies
1914–17, 59 × 78 ¾ in. (150 × 200 cm)
Musée Marmottan, Paris, inv. 5116

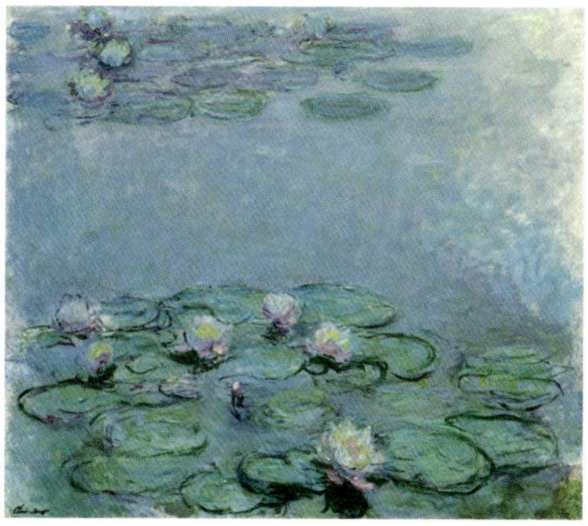

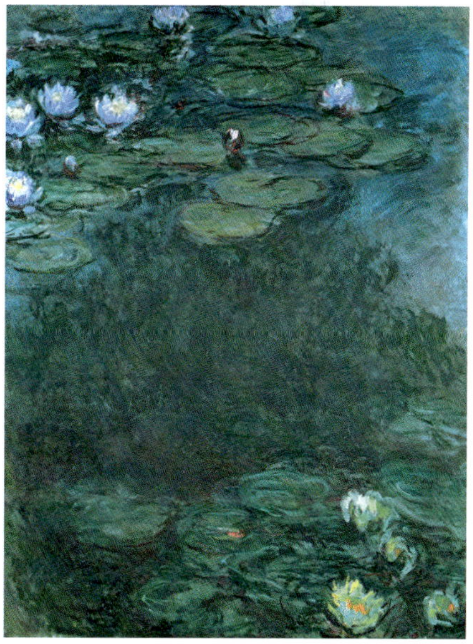

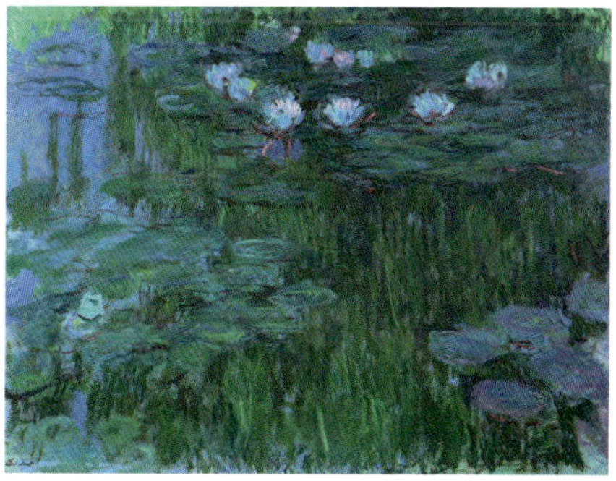

Water Lilies
1914–17, 63 × 70 ¾ in. (160 × 180 cm)
Portland Art Museum, Oregon, inv. 59.16

Water Lilies
1914–17, 51 ¼ × 32 ¼ in. (132 × 84 cm)
private collection

Water Lilies
1914–17, 51 ¼ × 60 ¼ in. (130 × 153 cm)
private collection

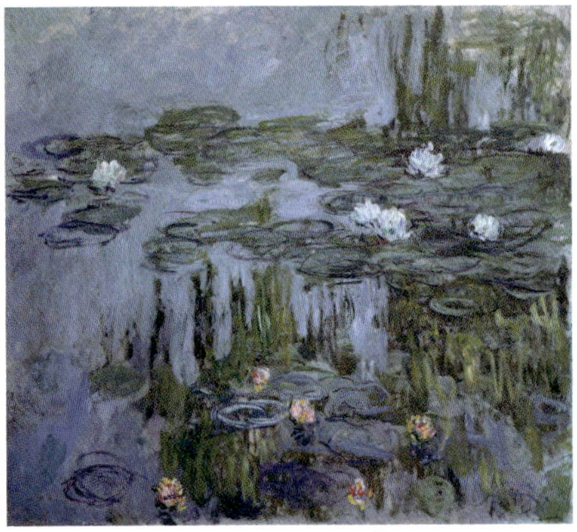

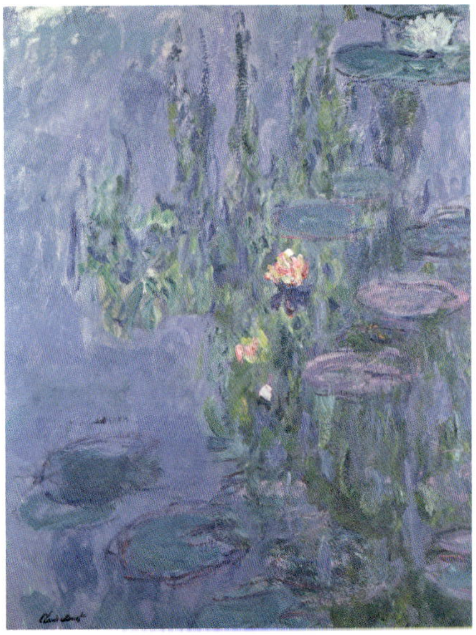

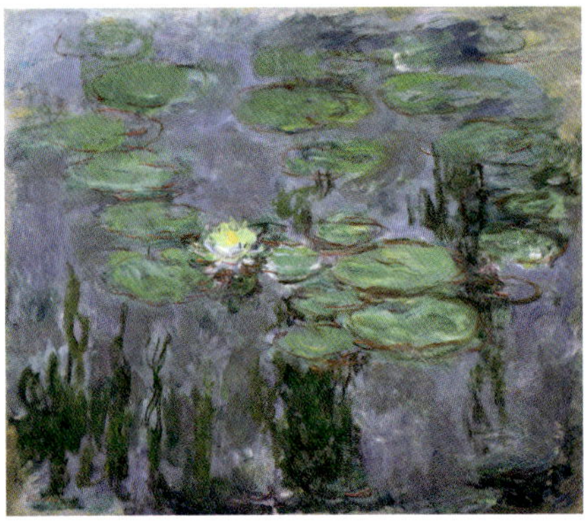

Water Lilies
1914–17, 78 ¾ × 59 in. (200 × 150 cm)
now 67 × 48 in. (170 x 122 cm), private collection

Water Lilies
1914–17, 59 × 78 ¾ in. (150 × 200 cm), Neue Pinakothek
Staatsgalerie Moderner Kunst, Munich, inv. 14562

Water Lilies
1914–17, 59 × 78 ¾ in. (150 × 200 cm)
Fondation Beyeler, Riehen/Basel

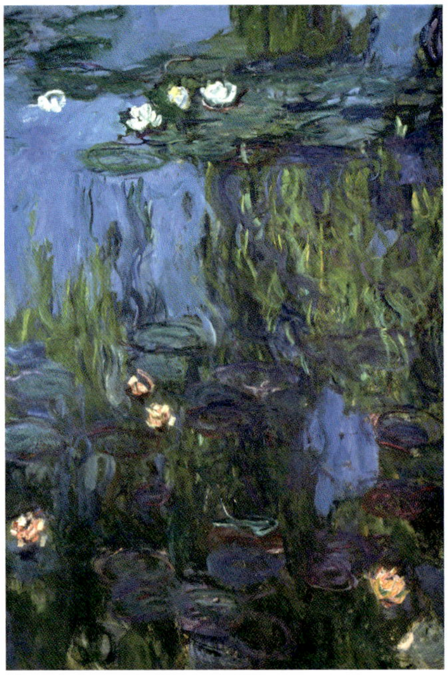

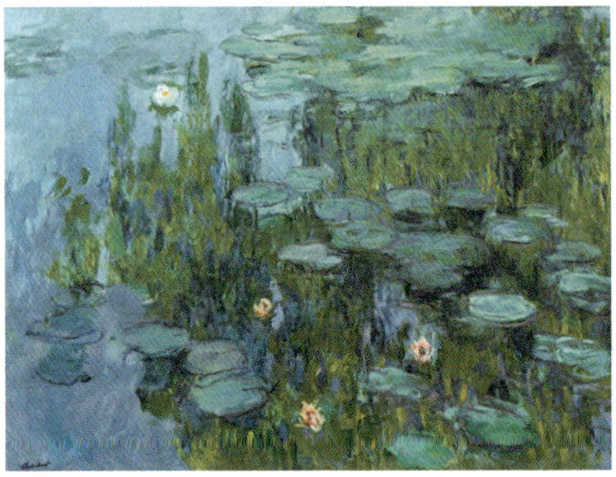

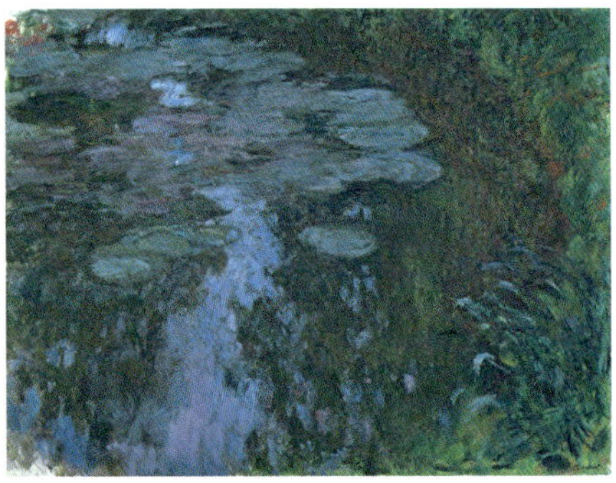

Water Lilies
1914–17, 78 ¾ × 78 ¾ in. (200 × 200 cm)
private collection

Water Lilies, Bouquet of Grasses
1914–17, 78 ¾ × 83 ¾ in. (200 × 213 cm)
private collection

Water Lilies
1914–17, 70 ¾ × 78 ¾ in. (180 × 200 cm)
The Museum of Modern Art, New York (destroyed in a fire at the museum on April 15, 1958, inv. 291–56)

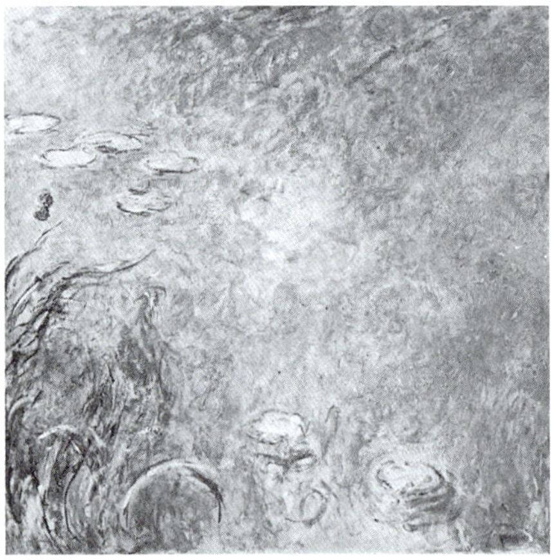

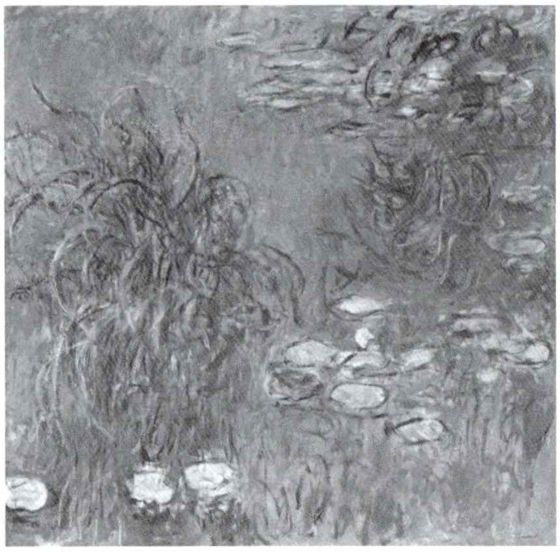

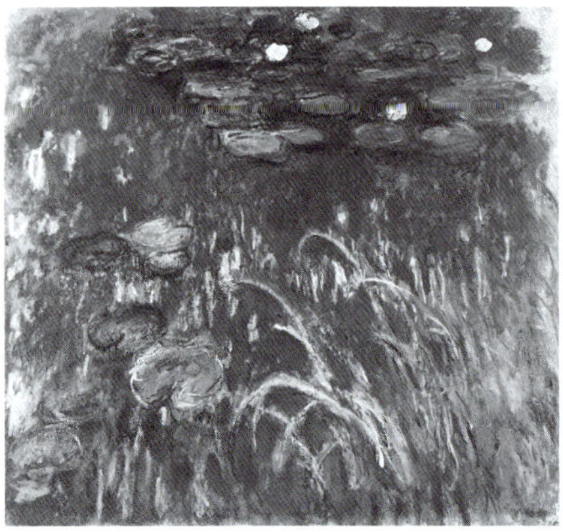

Water Lilies
1914–17, 51 ¼ × 59 in. (130 × 150 cm)
private collection

Water Lilies, Reflections on the Water
[1907], 28 ¾ × 36 ¼ in. (73 × 92 cm)
Musée Léon Alègre, Bagnols-sur-Cèze, inv. 98

Water Lilies
1914–17, 70 ¾ × 78 ¾ in. (180 × 200 cm)
Musée Marmottan, Paris, inv. 5120

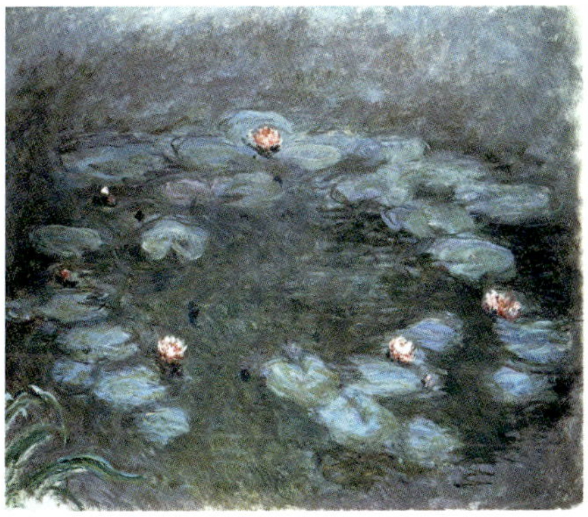

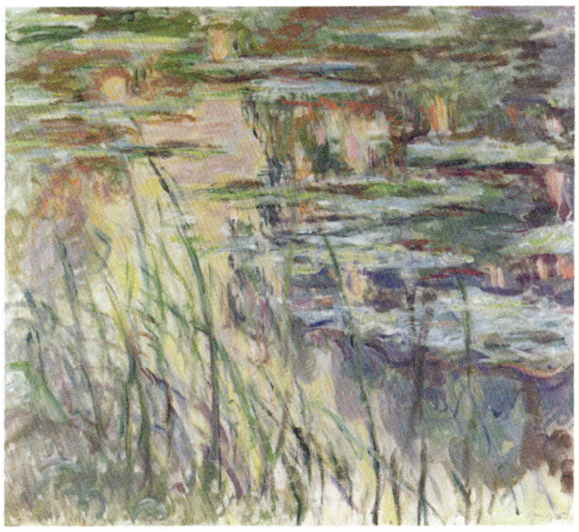

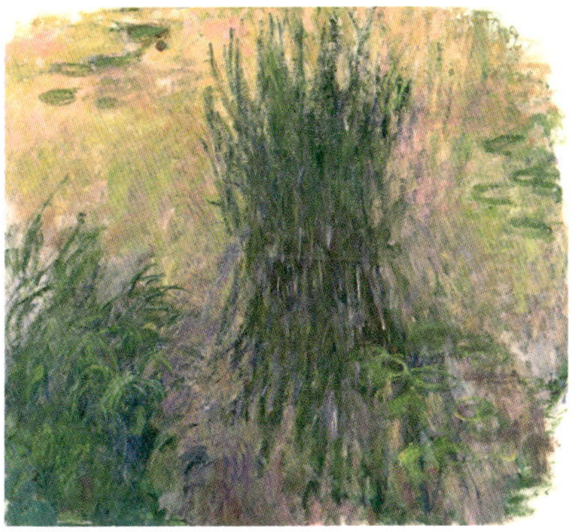

White and Yellow Water Lilies
1914–17, 78 ¾ × 78 ¾ in. (200 × 200 cm)
Kunstmuseum, Winterthur, inv. 813

Water Lilies
1916, 78 ¾ × 78 ¾ in. (200 × 200 cm), National Museum of Western Art, Tokyo, inv. P. 1959.151

Water Lilies
1914–17, 78 ¾ × 78 ¾ in. (200 × 200 cm)
private collection

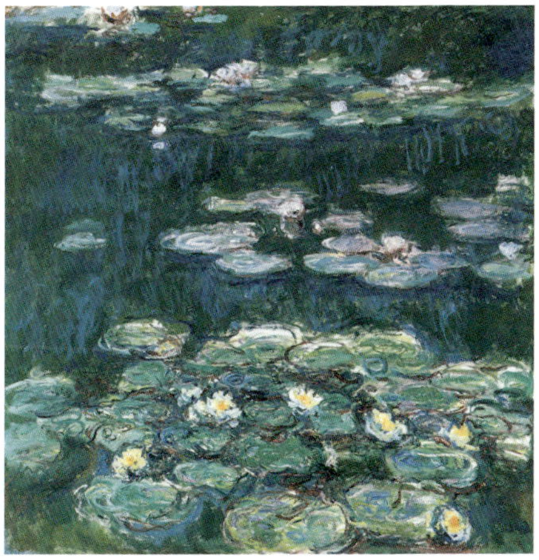

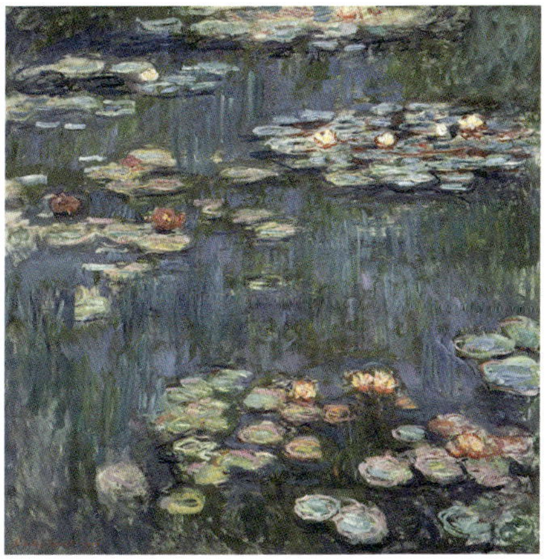

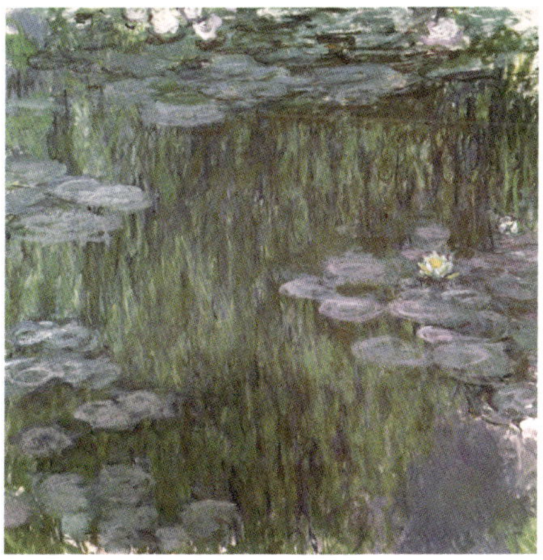

Water Lilies
1914–17, 70 ¾ × 78 ¾ in. (180 × 200 cm), National Gallery of Australia, Canberra, inv. 1979.2858

Water Lilies
1914–17, 70 ¾ × 78 ¾ in. (180 × 200 cm)
Wallraf-Richartz-Museum, Cologne, inv. WRM 3266

Yellow and Lilac Water Lilies
1914–17, 78 ¾ × 84 ½ in. (200 × 215 cm)
The Toledo Museum of Art, Toledo, OH, inv. 81-54

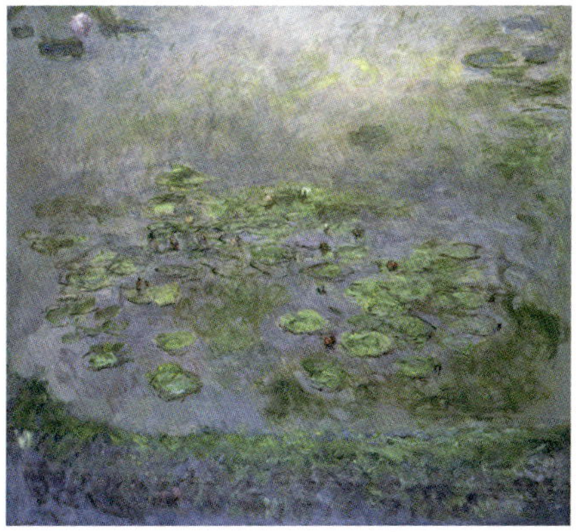

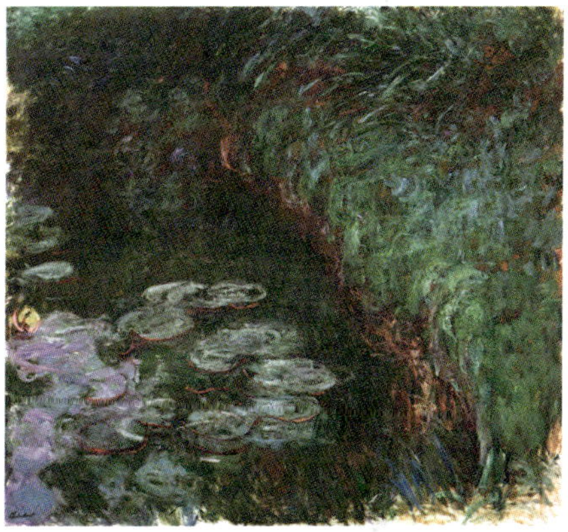

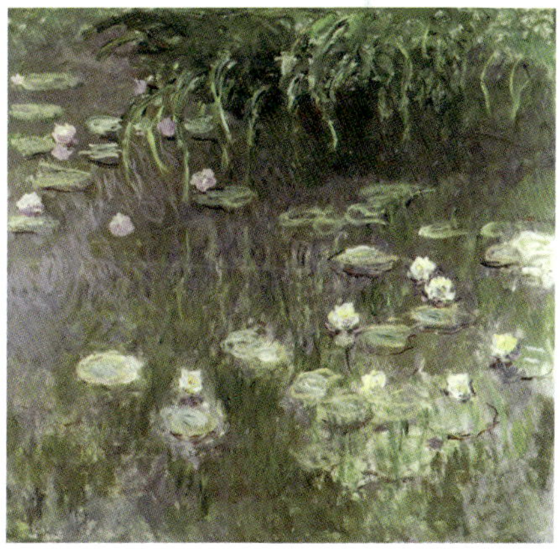

Agapanthus
1914–17, 78¾ × 59 in. (200 × 150 cm)
Musée Marmottan, Paris, inv. 5121

Water Lilies and Agapanthus
1914–17, 55 × 47¼ in. (140 × 120 cm) (damaged picture: former state, 78¾ × 51¼ in./200 × 130 cm)
Musée Marmottan, Paris, inv. 5084

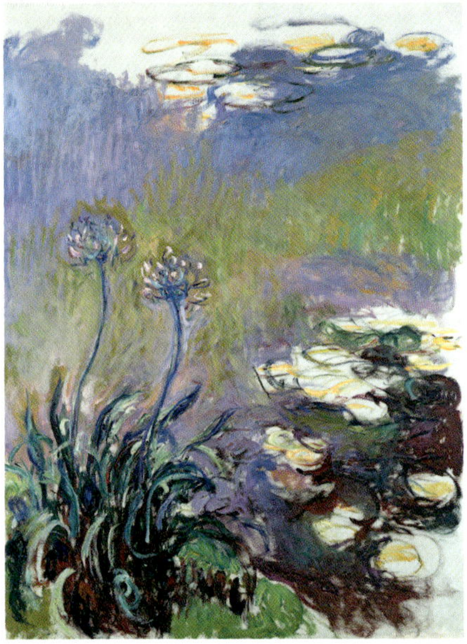

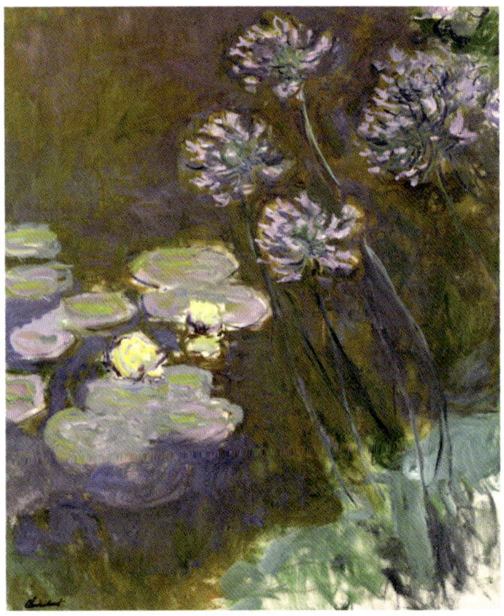

Water Lilies
1914–17, 78¾ × 78¾ in. (200 × 200 cm)
Musée Marmottan, Paris, inv. 5115

Weeping Willow and Water-Lily Pond
1916–19, 78¾ × 70¾ in. (200 × 180 cm)
Musée Marmottan, Paris, inv. 5125

Water Lilies
1914–17, 59 × 78¾ in. (150 × 200 cm); now, 59 × 65 in. (150 × 165 cm), private collection

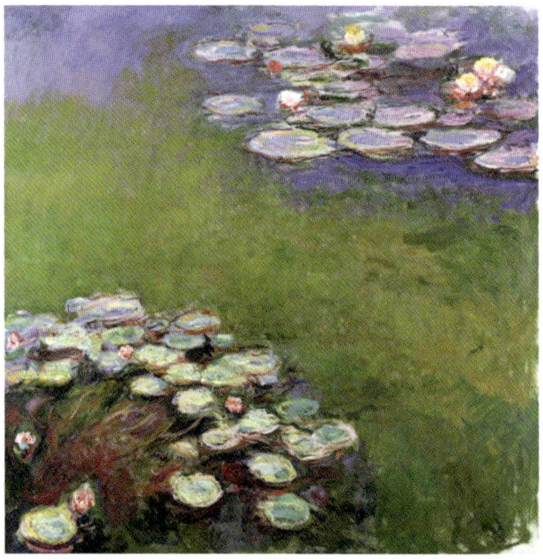

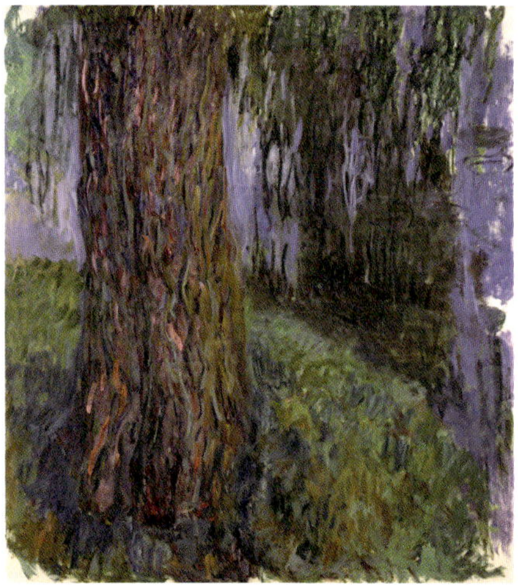

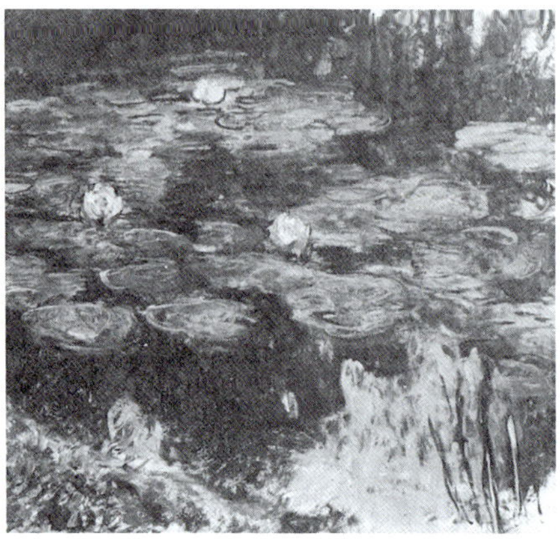

Water Lilies
1916–19, 78¾ × 70¾ in. (200 × 180 cm)
Musée Marmottan, Paris, inv. 5117

Weeping Willow and Water-Lily Pond
1916–19, 78¾ × 70¾ in. (200 × 180 cm)
private collection

Water Lilies, Reflections of Willow
1916–19, 51¼ × 78¾ in. (130 × 200 cm)
private collection

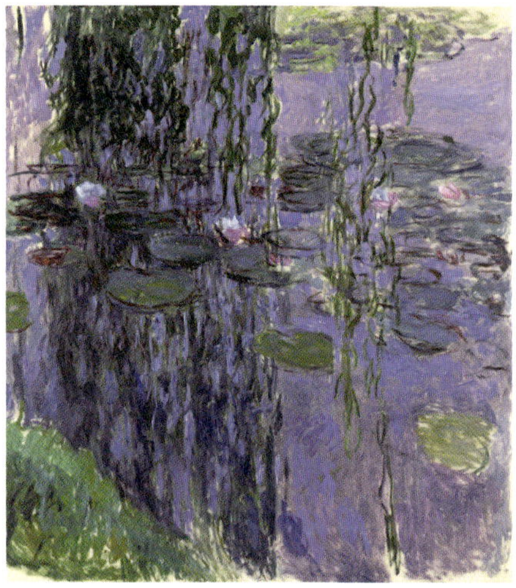

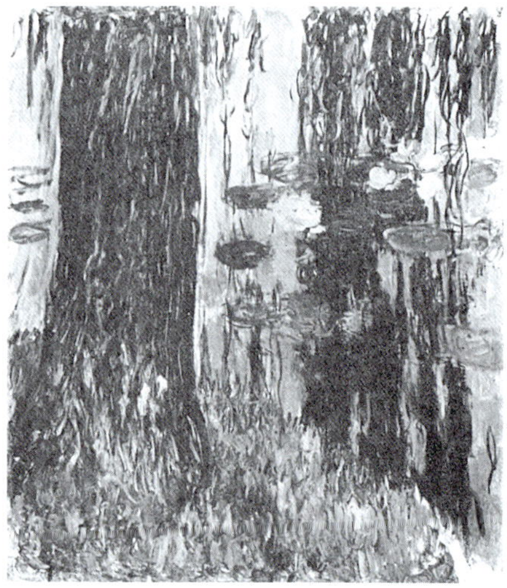

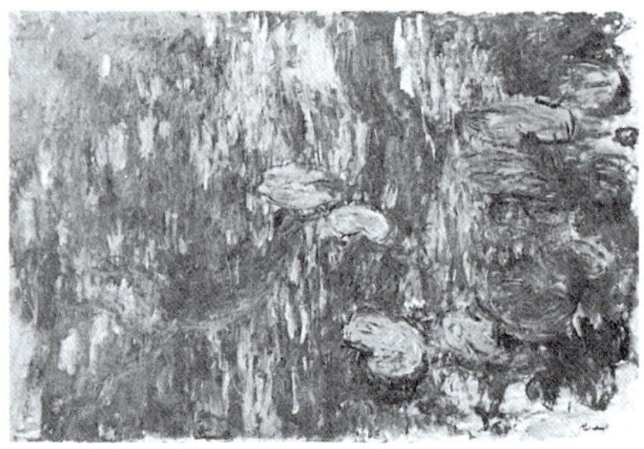

Water Lilies
1916–19, 51¼×78¾ in. (130×200 cm)
private collection

Water Lilies
1916–19, 35×51¼ in. (89×130 cm)
private collection

Water Lilies,
1916–19, 51¼×78¾ in. (130×200 cm)
private collection

Water Lilies, Reflections of Willow
1916–19, 51¼×78¾ in. (130×200 cm), The Metropolitan Museum of Art, New York, inv. 1983.532

Water Lilies, Reflections of Willow
1916–19, 52×78¾ in. (132×200 cm)
Musée Marmottan, Paris, inv. 5099

Water Lilies, Reflections of Willow
1916–19, 78¾×78¾ in. (200×200 cm)
Musée Marmottan, Paris, inv. 5122

Water Lilies
1916–19, 78¾×70¾ in. (200×180 cm)
Musée Marmottan, Paris, inv. 5119

Water Lilies
1916–19, 78¾×70¾ in. (200×180 cm)
Fondation Beyeler, Riehen/Basel, Beyeler Collection

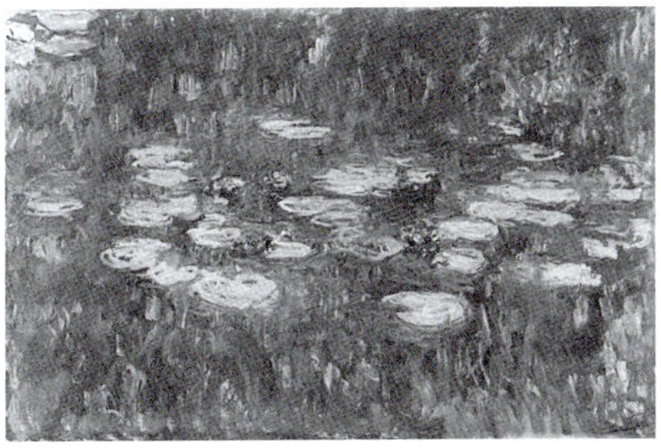

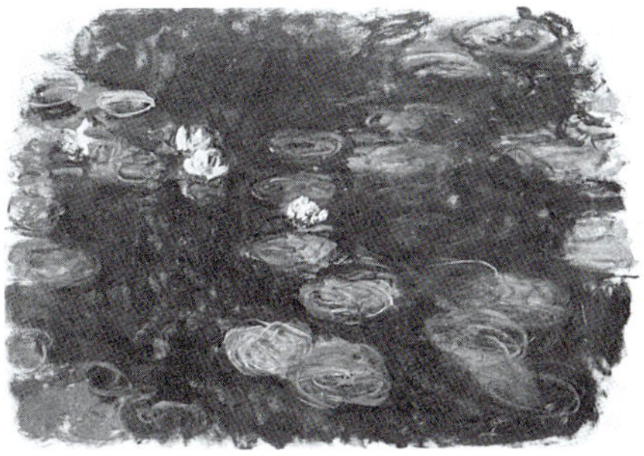

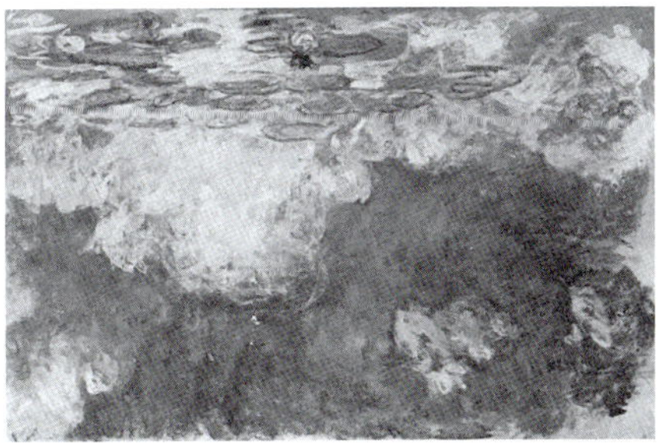

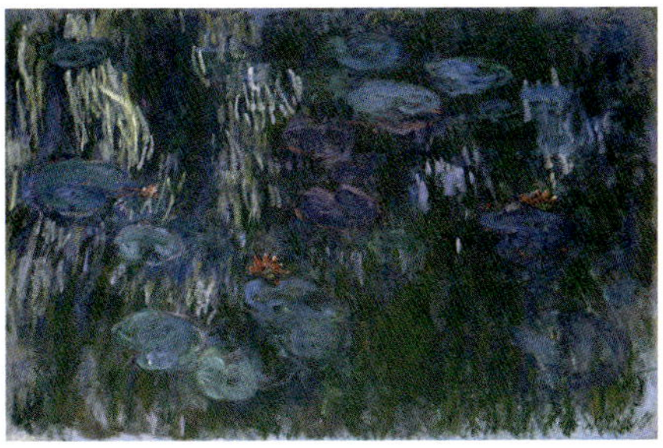

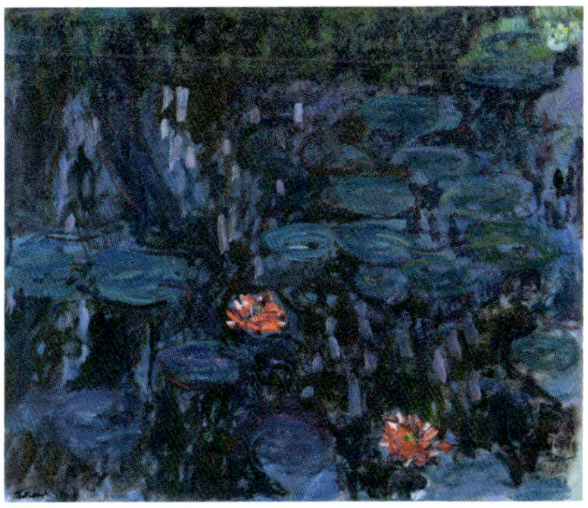

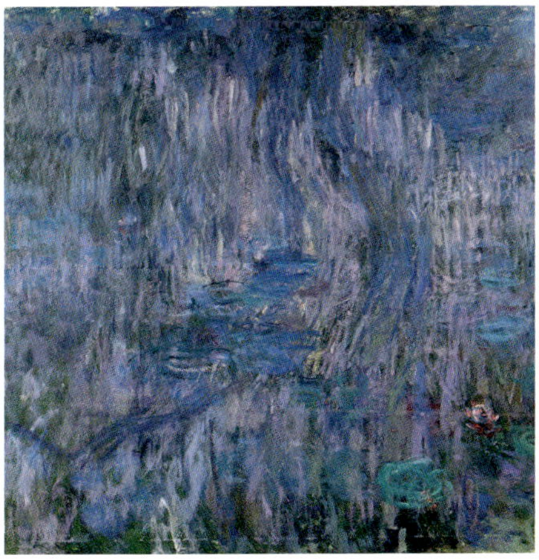

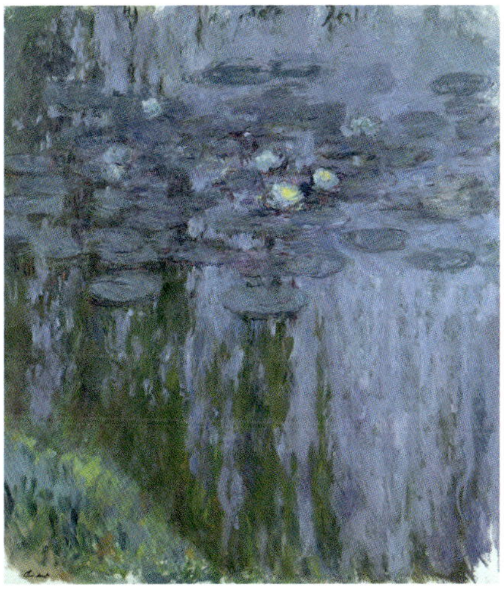

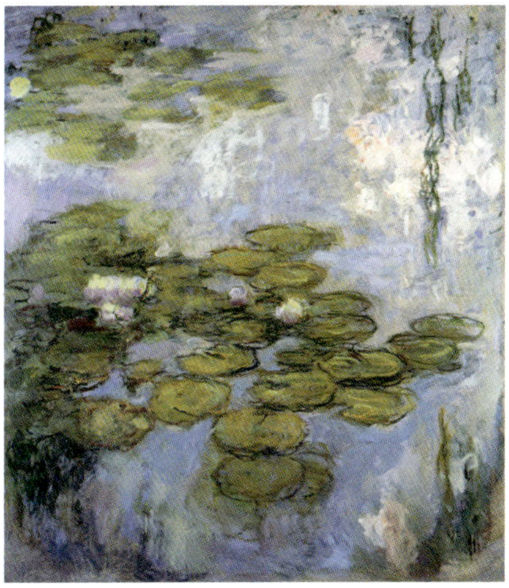

Water Lilies
1916–19, 59 × 78 ½ in. (150 × 197 cm)
Musée Marmottan, Paris, inv. 5164

Water Lilies, Willow Branches
1916–19, 41 × 70 ¾ in. (104 × 180 cm)
private collection

Blue Water Lilies
1916–19, 78 ¾ × 78 ¾ in. (200 × 200 cm)
Musée d'Orsay, Paris, inv. RF 1981-40

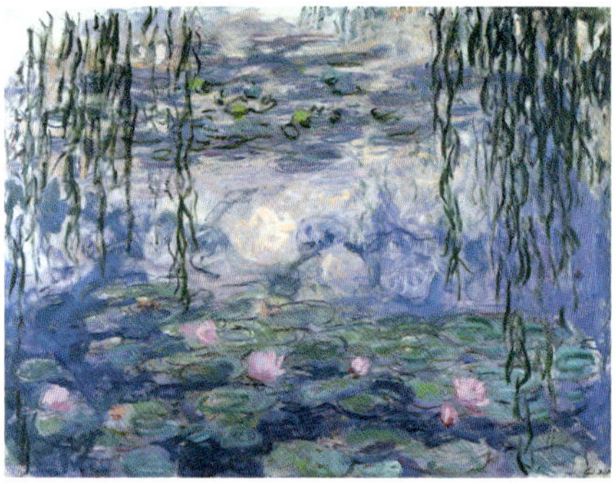

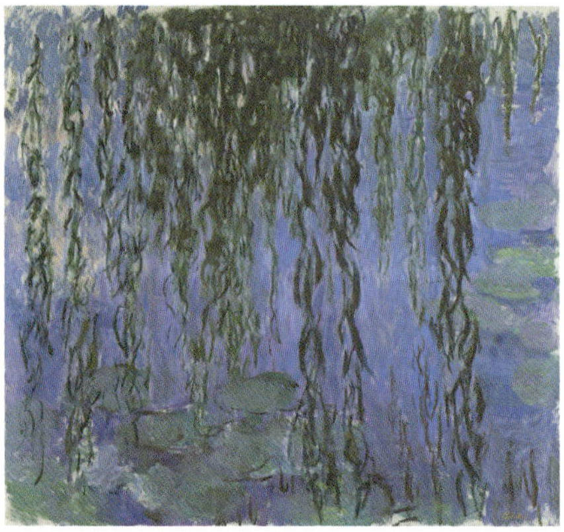

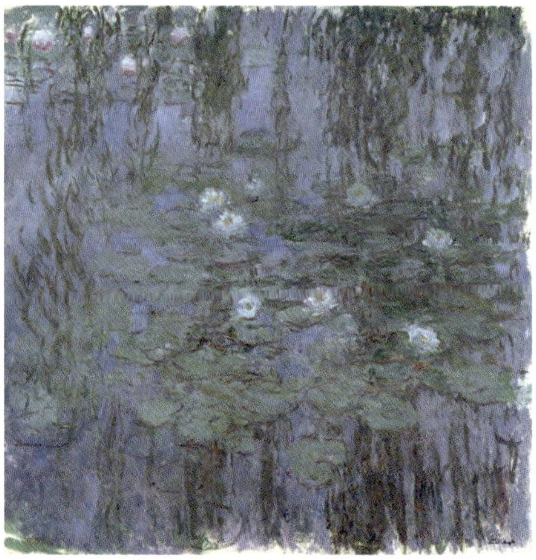

Water Lilies, Reflections of Willow
1916–19, 51 ¼ × 78 ¾ in. (130 × 200 cm)
private collection

Water Lilies, Reflections of Willow
1916–19, 39 ¼ × 78 ¾ in. (100 × 200 cm)
private collection

Water Lilies
1916–19, 51 ¼ × 59 ¾ in. (130 × 152 cm)
Musée Marmottan, Paris, inv. 5098

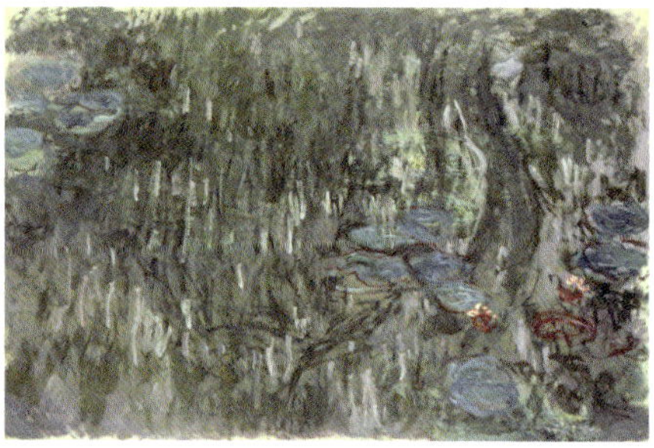

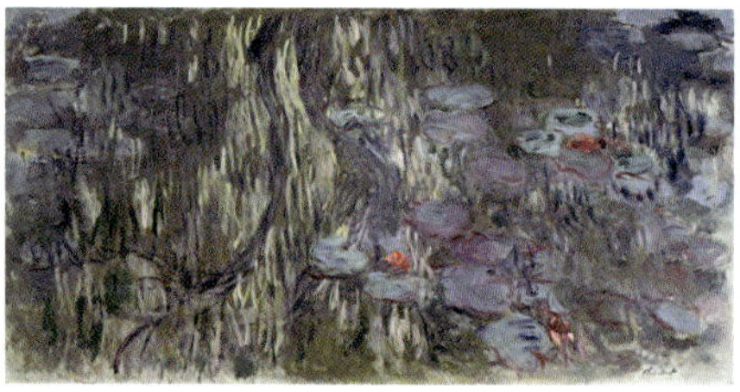

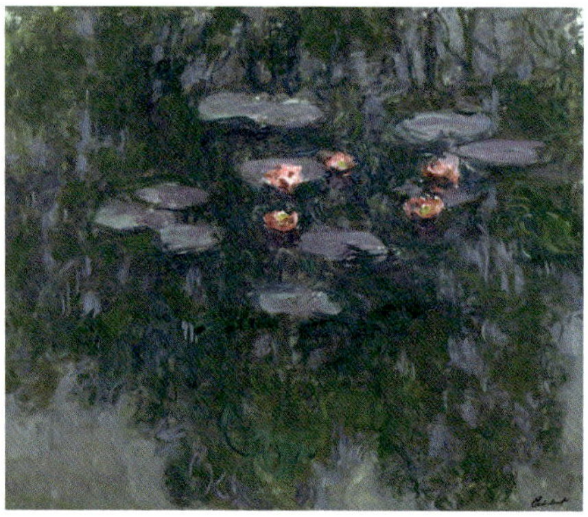

Corner of the Pond at Giverny
1918–19, 46 × 32 ¾ in. (117 × 83 cm)
Musée des Beaux-Arts, Grenoble, inv. MG2168

View of the Water-Lily Pond with Willow
1918–19, 59 × 51 ¼ in. (150 × 130 cm)
private collection

Water Lilies
c. 1917, 19 ¾ × 37 ½ in. (50 × 95 cm)
private collection

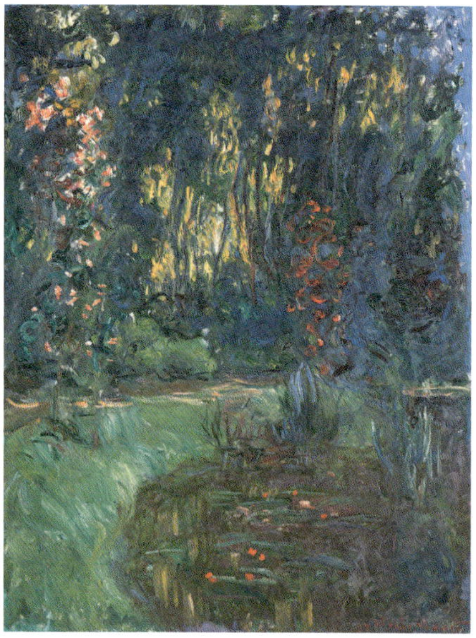

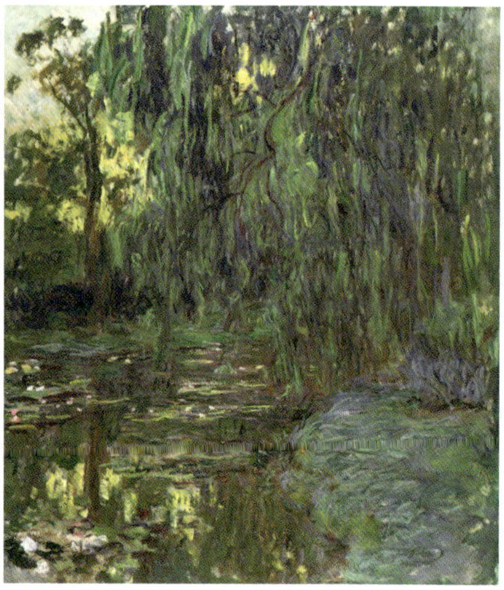

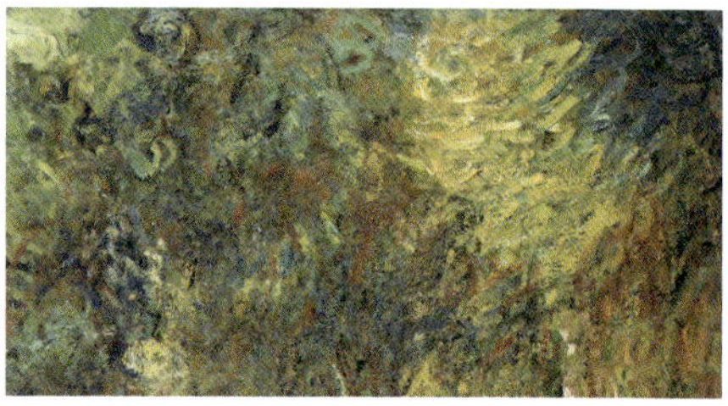

Corner of the Water-Lily Pond
1918–19, 47¼ × 35 in. (120 × 89 cm)
private collection

Corner of the Water-Lily Pond
1918–19, 50¾ × 35 in. (129 × 89 cm)
private collection

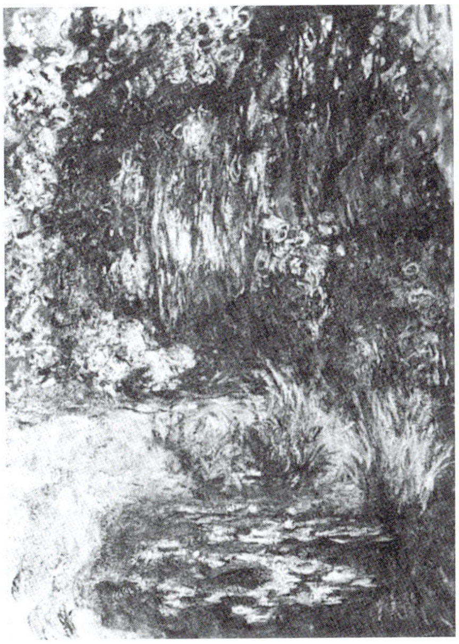

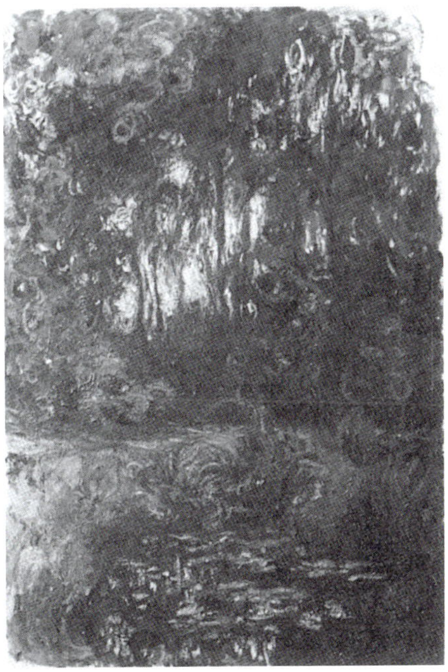

View of the Water-Lily Pond with Willow
1918–19, 55 × 59 in. (140 × 150 cm)
private collection

Corner of the Water-Lily Pond
[1918], 51¼ × 34¾ in. (130 × 88 cm)
private collection

Water-Lily Pond
1918–19, 28¾ × 41¼ in. (73 × 105 cm)
Musée Marmottan, Paris, inv. 5105

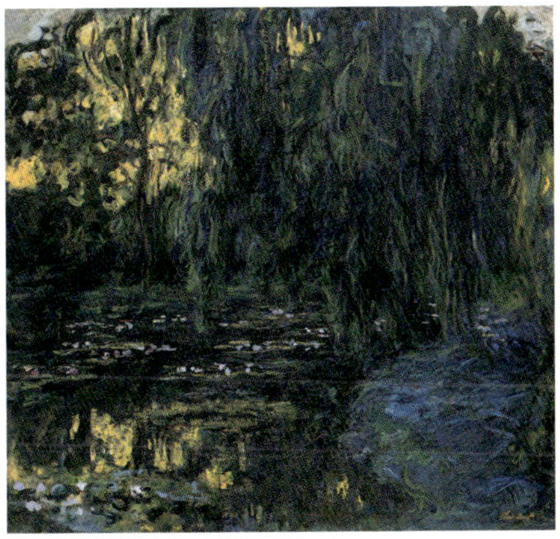

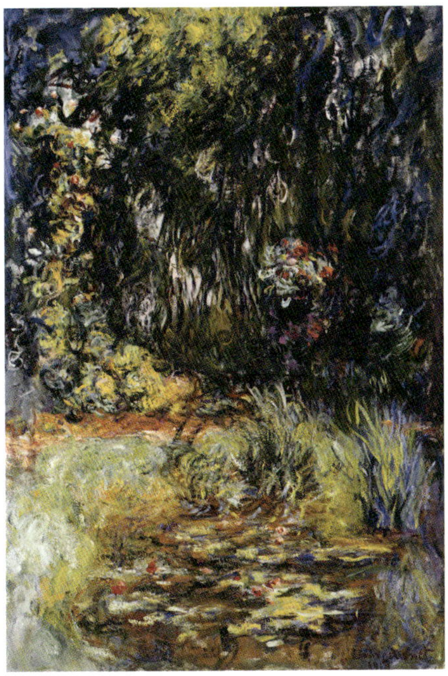

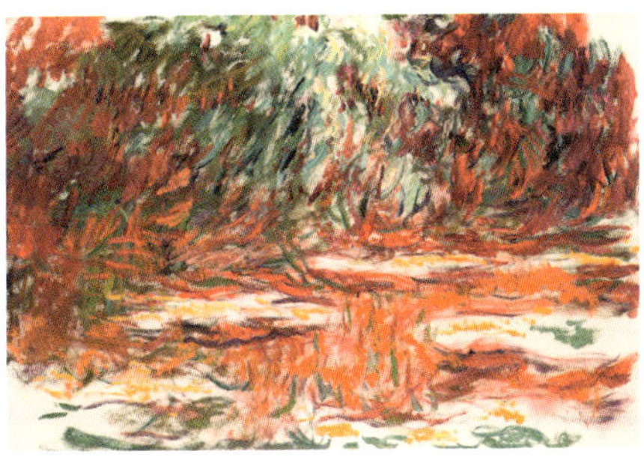

Water-Lily Pond
1917–19, 39¼ × 78¾ in. (100 × 200 cm)
private collection

Water-Lily Pond
1917–19, 51¼ × 78¾ in. (130 × 200 cm)
Museum Folkwang, Essen, inv. 343

Study of the Water Lilies
c. 1917 11¾ × 11¾ in. (1917, 30 × 30 cm)
private collection

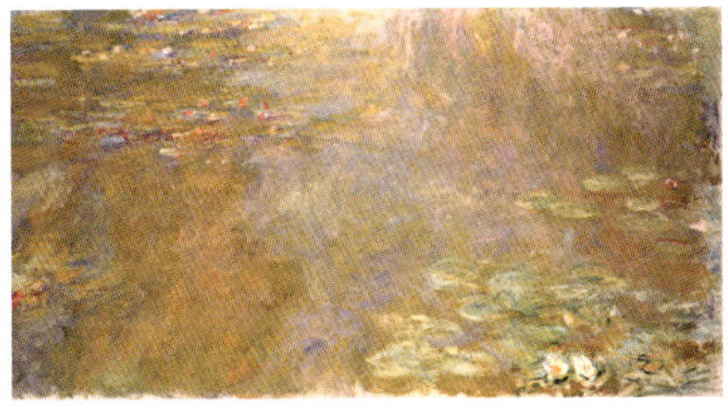

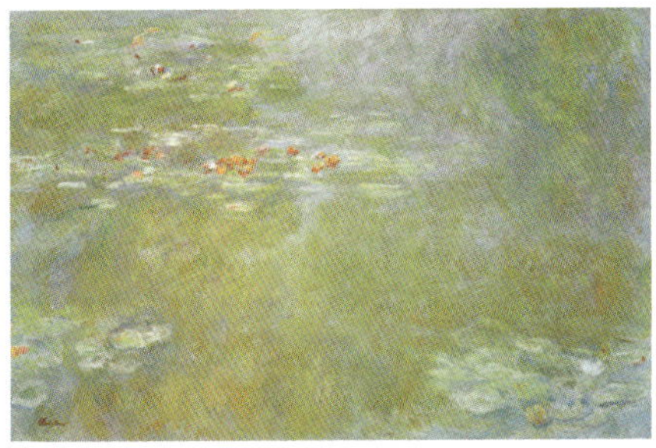

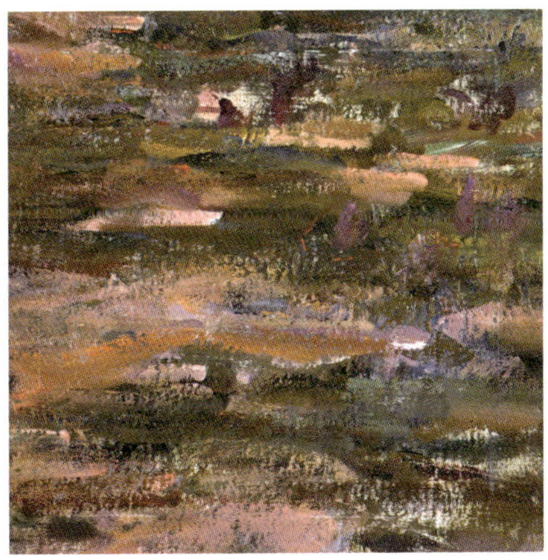

The Water-Lily Pond
1917–19, 51 ¼ × 78 ¾ in. (130 × 200 cm)
Museum of Art, Atami

The Water-Lily Pond
1919, 39 ¼ × 78 ¾ in. (100 × 200 cm)
private collection

The Water-Lily Pond
1917–19, 39 ¼ × 78 ¾ in. (100 × 200 cm)
private collection

The Water-Lily Pond
c. 1917–20, triptych: each panel 78 ¾ × 118 in. (200 × 300 cm), Fondation Beyeler, Riehen/Basel, Beyeler Collection

The Water-Lily Pond, the Evening
c. 1922, diptych: each panel 78 ¾ × 118 in. (200 × 300 cm), Kunsthaus, Zurich, inv. 1952/64

The Water-Lily Pond
c. 1918–24, diptych: each panel 78 ¾ × 118 in. (200 × 300 cm), private collection

The Water-Lily Pond, Reflections of the Willow
c. 1918–24, 78 ¾ × 167 ¼ in. (200 × 425 cm)
private collection

The Water-Lily Pond
1917–19, 39 ¼ × 78 ¾ in. (100 × 200 cm)
private collection

The Water-Lily Pond
1919, 39 ¼ × 78 ¾ in. (100 × 200 cm) (painting split into two parts), private collections (two separate)

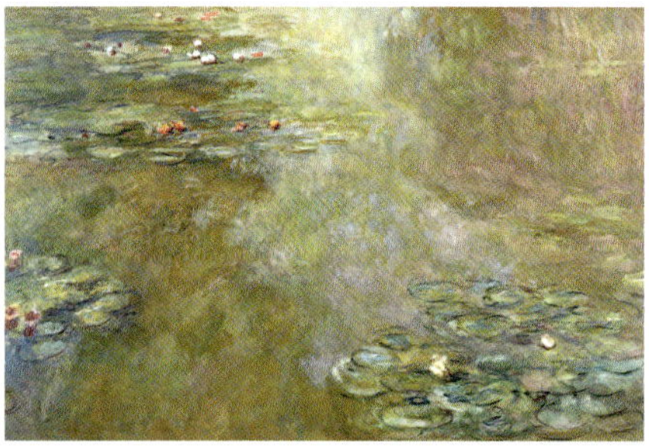

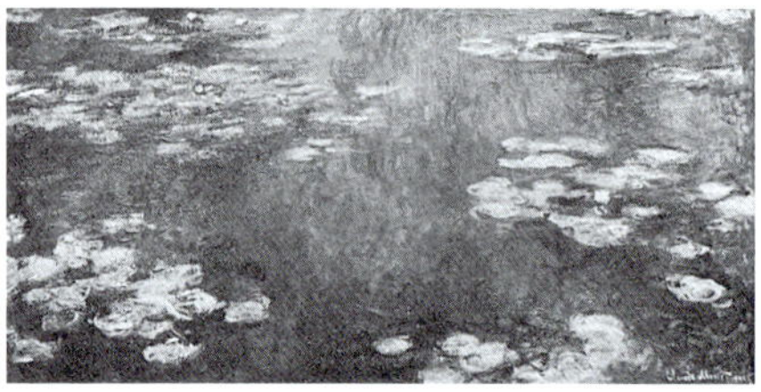

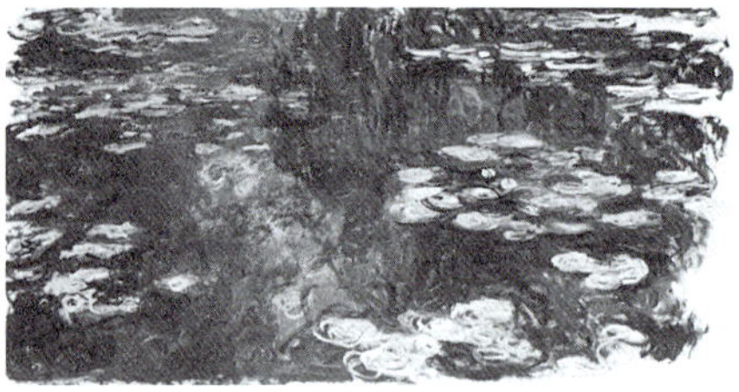

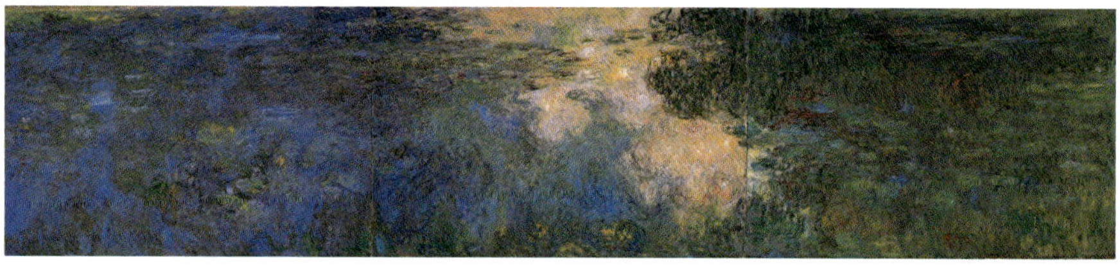

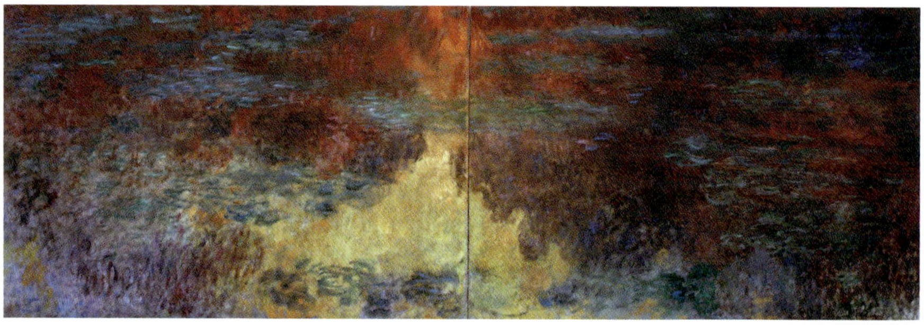

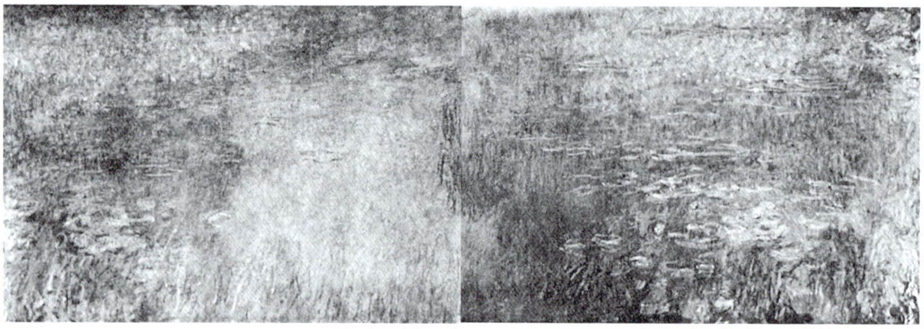

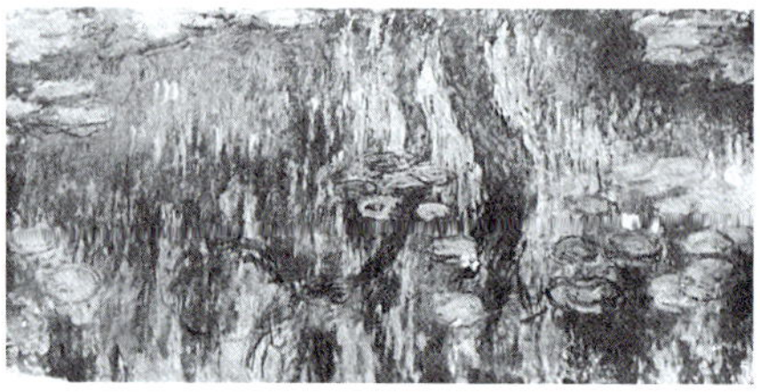

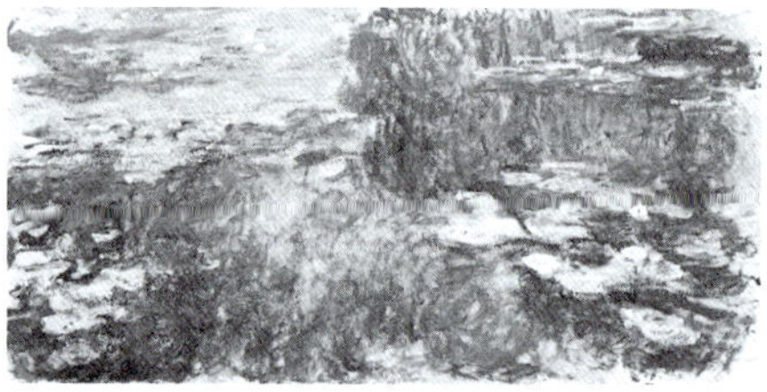

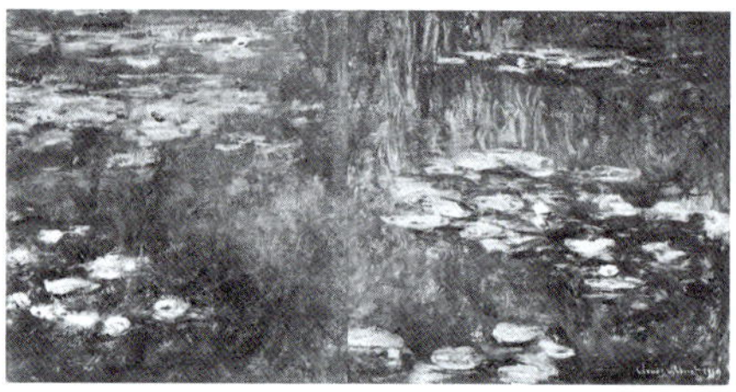

The Water-Lily Pond
1917–19, 51¼ × 78¾ in. (130 × 200 cm)
private collection

The Water-Lily Pond
1917, 39¼ × 78¾ in. (100 × 200 cm)
Musée des Beaux-Arts, Nantes, inv. 2233

The Water-Lily Pond
1917–19, 51¼ × 47¼ in. (130 × 120 cm) (partially destroyed: originally 51¼ × 78¾ in. [130 × 200 cm]. Right-hand part: unknown), Musée Marmottan, Paris, inv. 5165

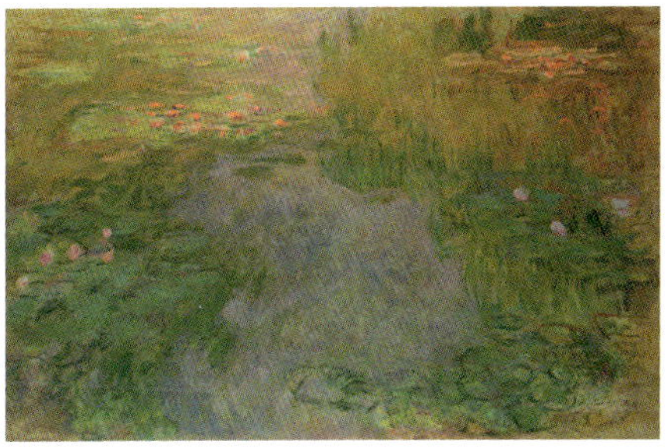

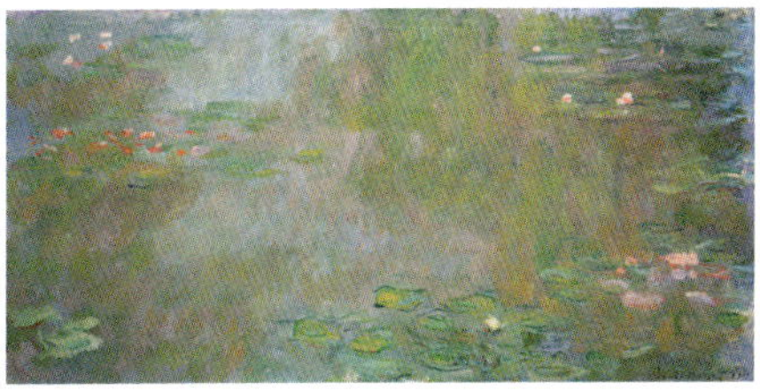

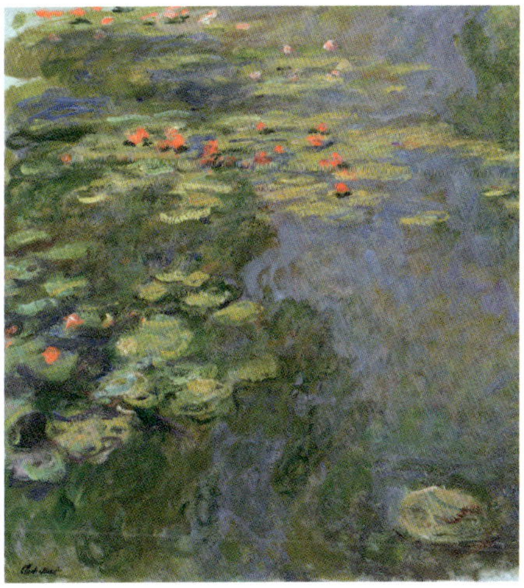

The Water-Lily Pond
1919, 39¼ × 78¾ in. (100 × 200 cm)
private collection

The Water-Lily Pond
1919, 39¼ × 78¾ in. (100 × 200 cm)
private collection

The Water-Lily Pond
1917–19, 51¼ × 78¾ in. (130 × 200 cm)
The Art Institute of Chicago, inv. 1982.825

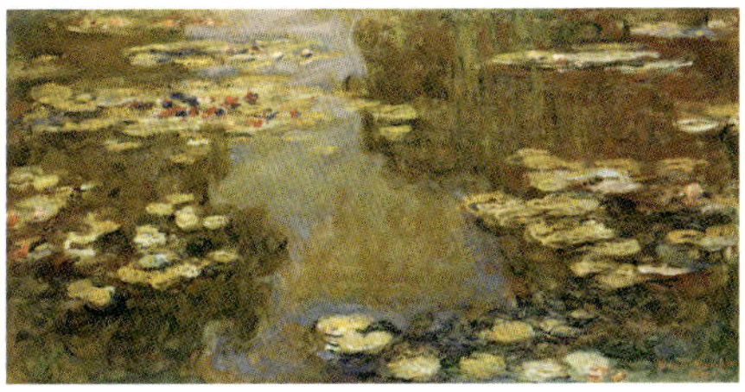

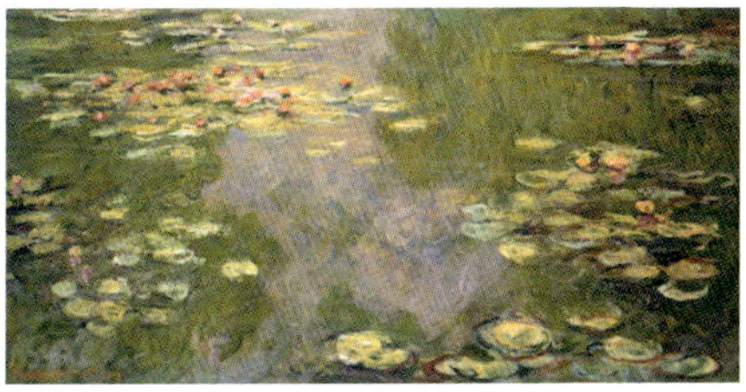

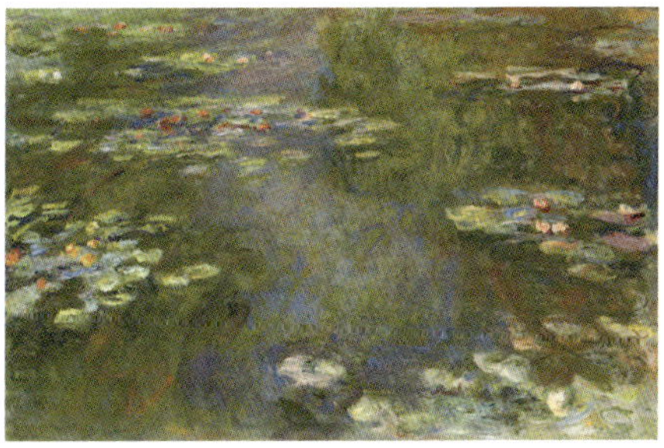

The Water-Lily Pond
1917–19, 39¼ × 78¾ in. (100 × 200 cm)
private collection

The Water-Lily Pond
1917–19, 39¼ × 78¾ in. (100 × 200 cm)
private collection

The Water-Lily Pond
1917–19, 39¼ × 78¾ in. (100 × 200 cm)
Honolulu Academy of Arts, HI, inv. 3385.1

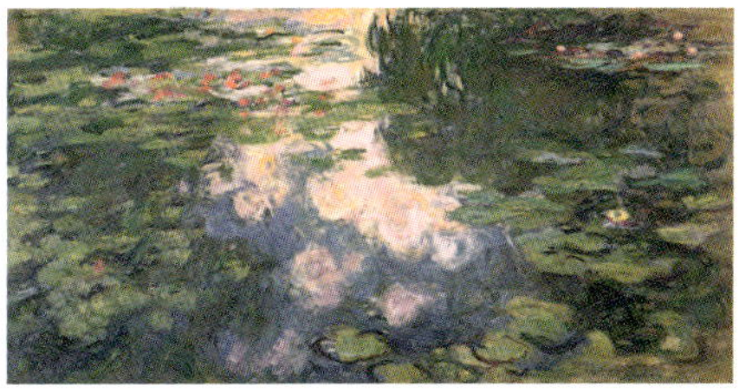

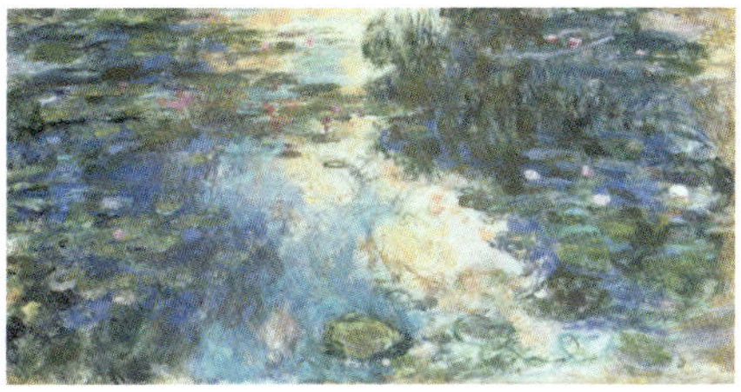

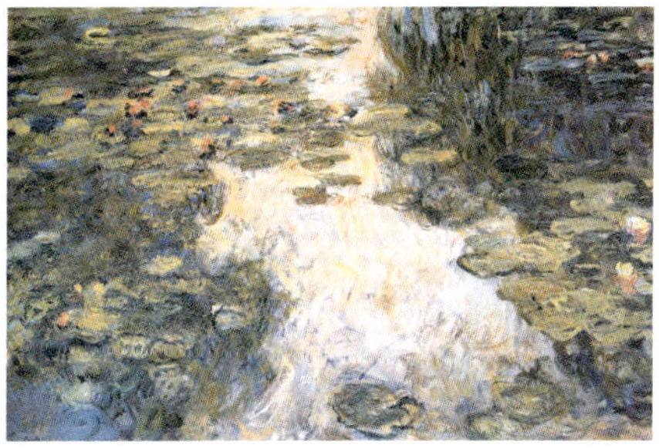

The Water-Lily Pond
1917–19, 39 ¼ × 78 ¾ in. (100 × 200 cm)
private collection

The Water-Lily Pond
1917–19, 39 ¼ × 78 ¾ in. (100 × 200 cm)
private collection

The Water-Lily Pond
1917–19, 39 ¼ × 78 ¾ in. (100 × 200 cm) (today in two parts),
private collections (two separate)

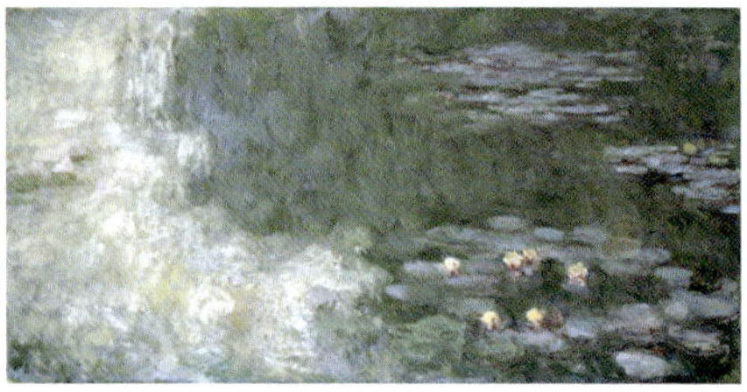

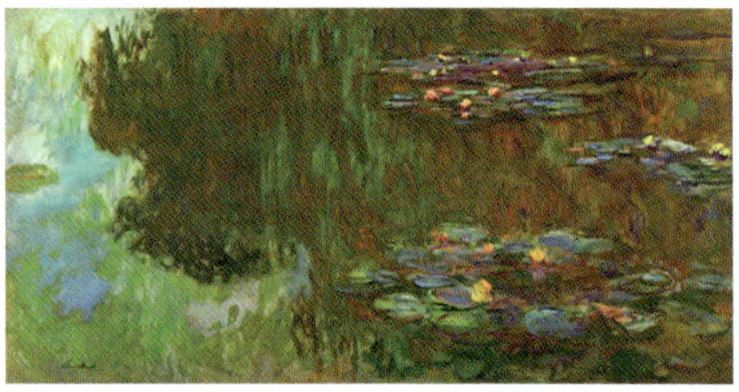

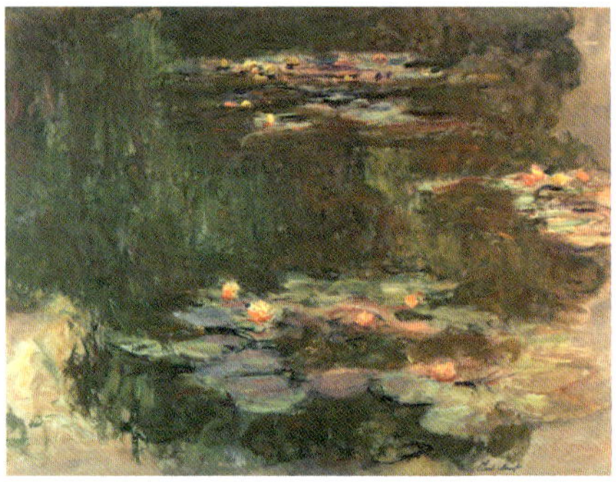

Water Lilies
1919–20, 39 ¼ × 118 in. (100 × 300 cm)
Musée Marmottan, Paris, inv. 5118

The Japanese Bridge
1918–24, 31 ½ × 36 ¼ in. (80 × 92 cm)
private collection

The Japanese Bridge
1918–24, 34 ¼ × 35 ½ in. (87 × 90 cm)
Museu de Arte, São Paulo, inv. 93/1948

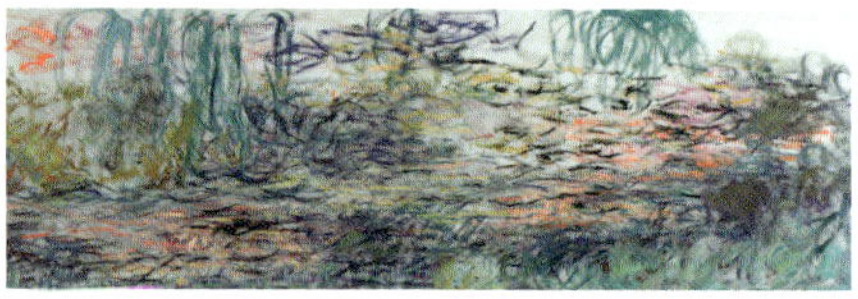

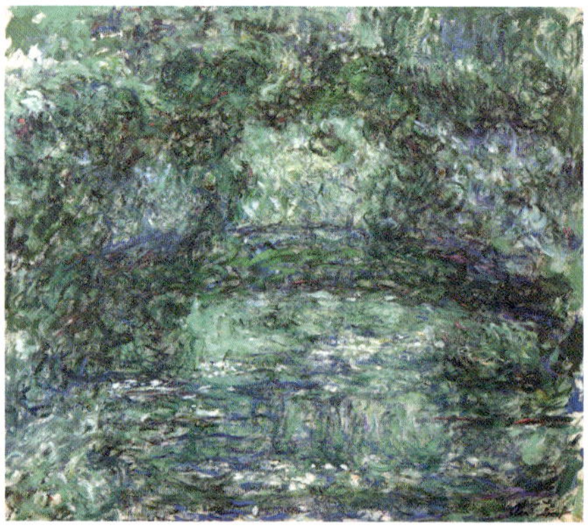

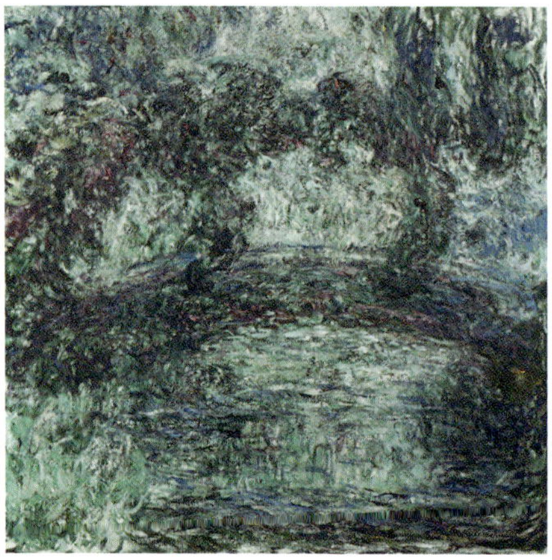

The Japanese Bridge
1918–24, 24 ¼ × 36 ¼ in. (74 × 92 cm)
Musée Marmottan, Paris, inv. 5177

The Japanese Bridge
1918–24, dimensions unknown
private collection

The Japanese Bridge
1918–24, 35 × 45 ½ in. (89 × 116 cm)
Fondation Beyeler, Riehen/Basel, Beyeler Collection

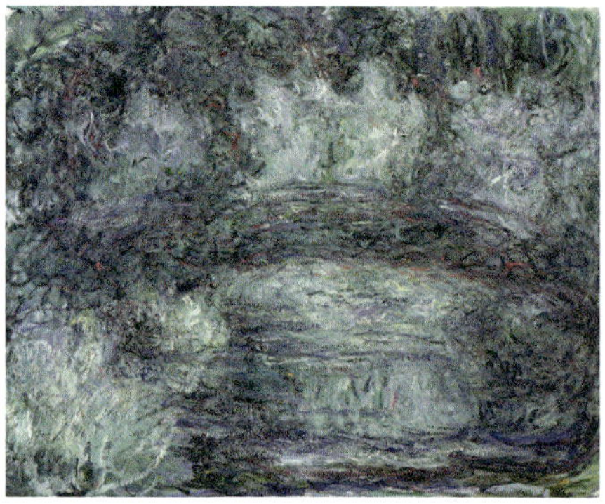

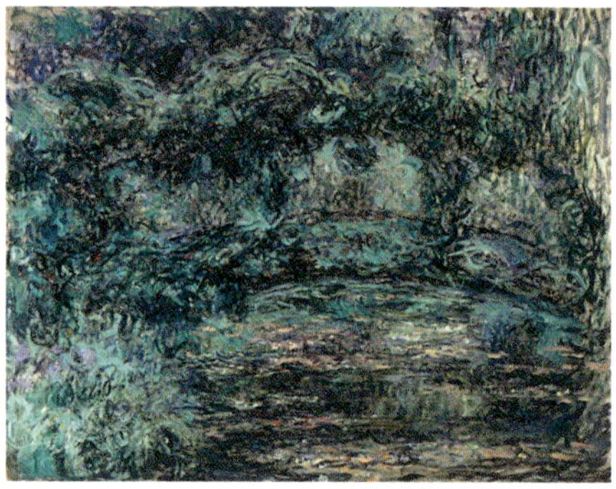

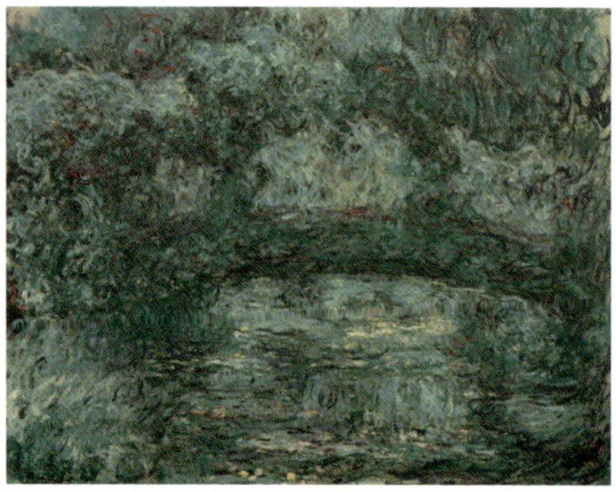

The Japanese Bridge
1918–24, 28¾ × 42¼ in. (73 × 107 cm)
private collection

The Japanese Bridge
1918–24, 35 × 45½ in. (89 × 116 cm)
Musée Marmottan, Paris, inv. 5106

The Japanese Bridge
1918–24, 35 × 36½ in. (89 × 93 cm)
Museum of Fine Arts, Houston, John A. and Audrey Jones Beck Collection, inv. 76.198

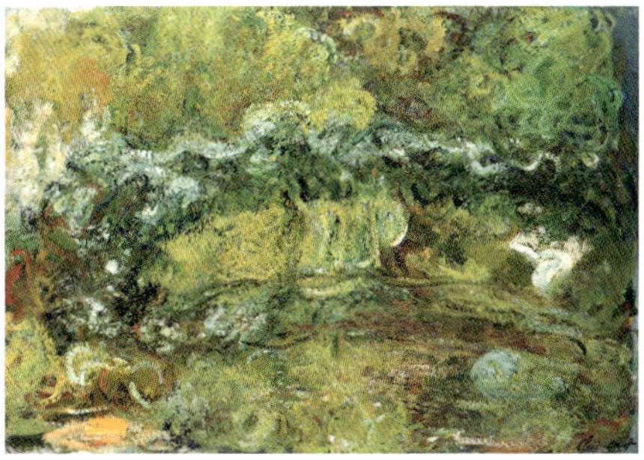

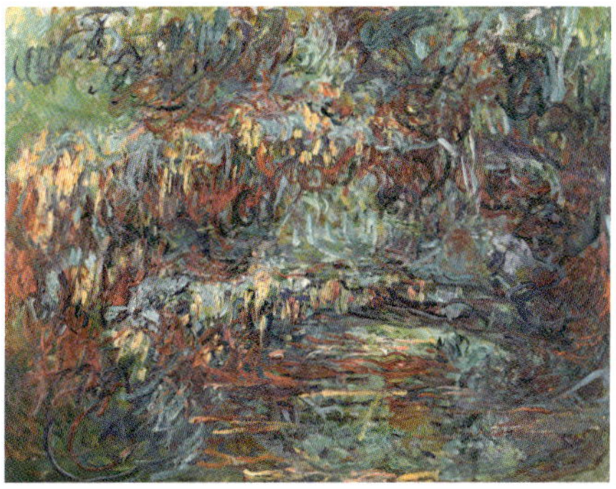

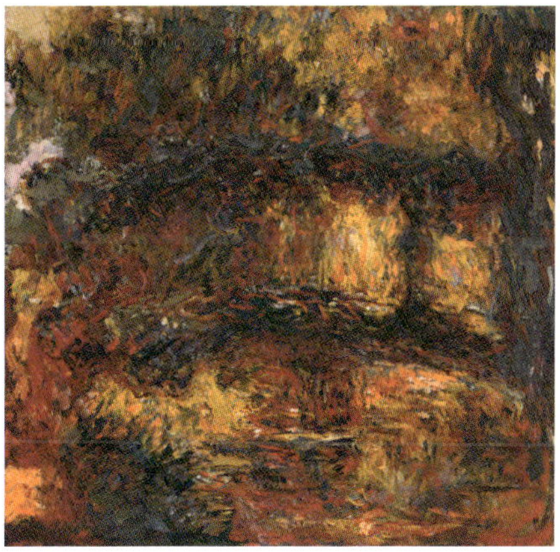

The Japanese Bridge
1918, 39¼ × 78¾ in. (100 × 200 cm)
Musée Marmottan, Paris, inv. 5079

The Footbridge over the Water-Lily Pond
1919, 25½ × 42¼ in. (65 × 107 cm)
private collection

The Japanese Bridge
1918–24, 35 × 35¾ in. (89 × 91 cm), Philadelphia Museum of Art, The Albert M. Greenfield and Elizabeth M. Greenfield Collection, inv. 1974.178.38

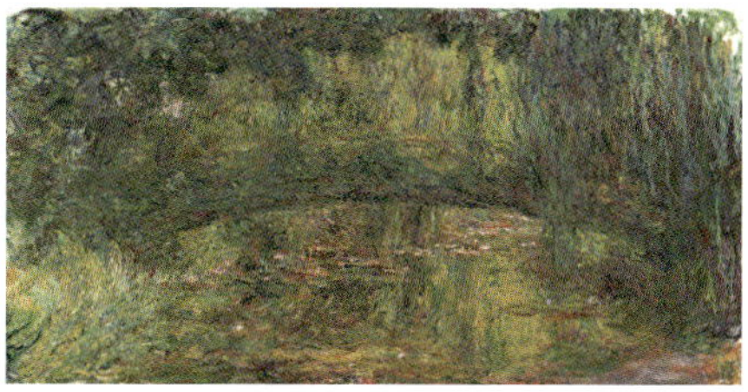

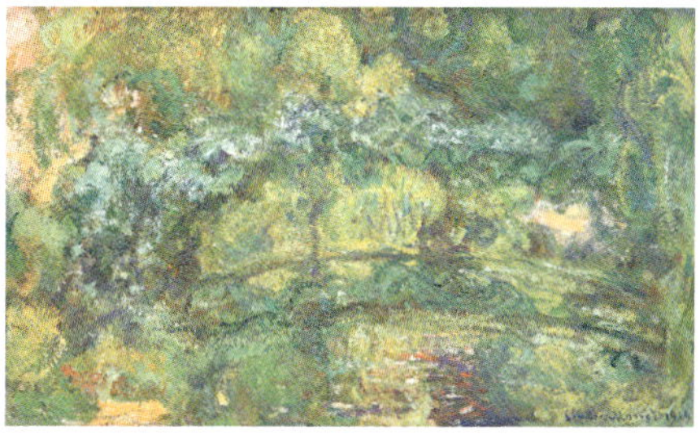

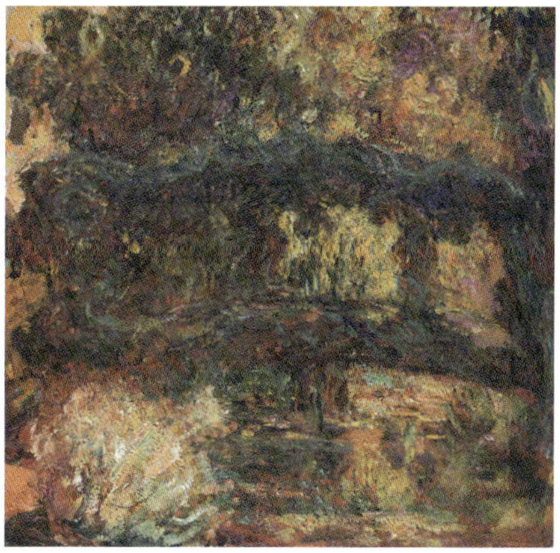

The Japanese Bridge
1918, 39¼ × 78¾ in. (100 × 200 cm)
Musée Marmottan, Paris, inv. 5077

The Japanese Bridge
1918–24, 35 × 39¼ in. (89 × 100 cm)
Musée Marmottan, Paris, inv. 5091

The Japanese Bridge
1918–24, 35 × 39¼ in. (89 × 100 cm)
Musée Marmottan, Paris, inv. 5094

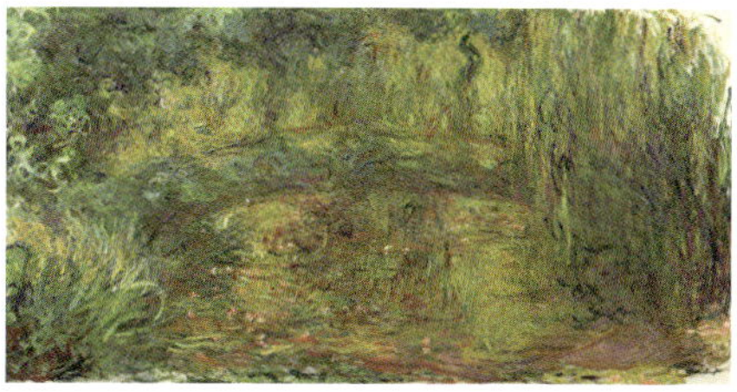

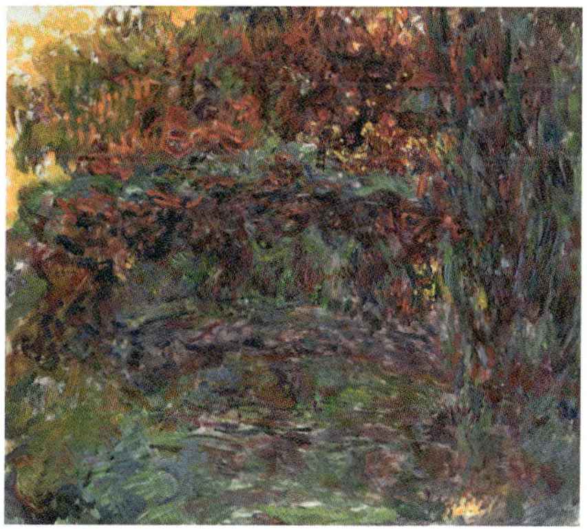

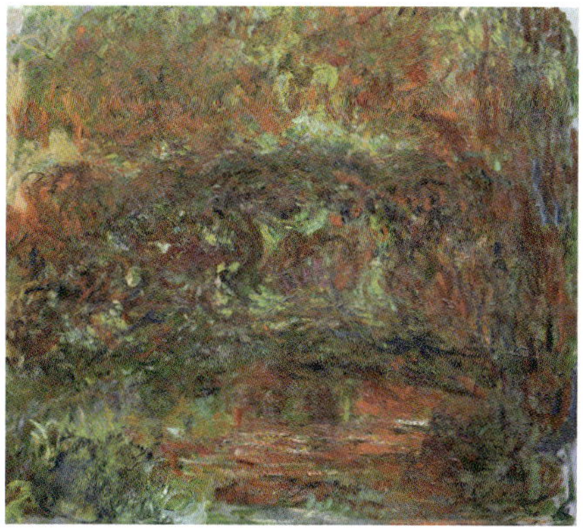

The Japanese Bridge
1918–24, 35 × 45 ¾ in. (89 × 116 cm)
The Minneapolis Institute of Art, inv. 61.36.15

The Japanese Bridge
1918–24, 35 × 45 ¾ in. (89 × 116 cm),
Museum of Modern Art, New York, inv. 242.56

The Japanese Bridge
1918–24, 35 × 39 ¼ in. (89 × 100 cm)
Musée Marmottan, Paris, inv. 5093

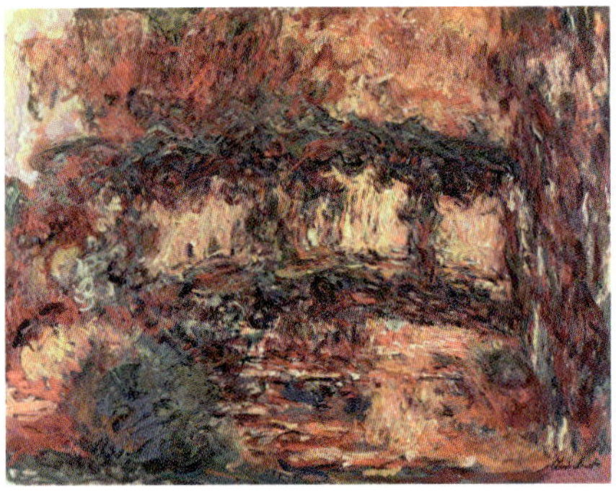

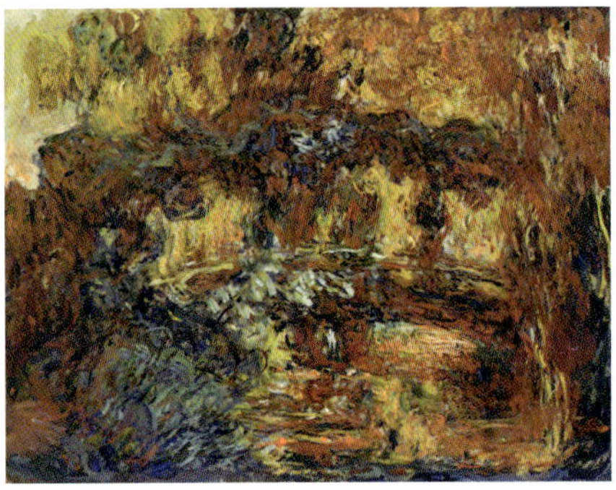

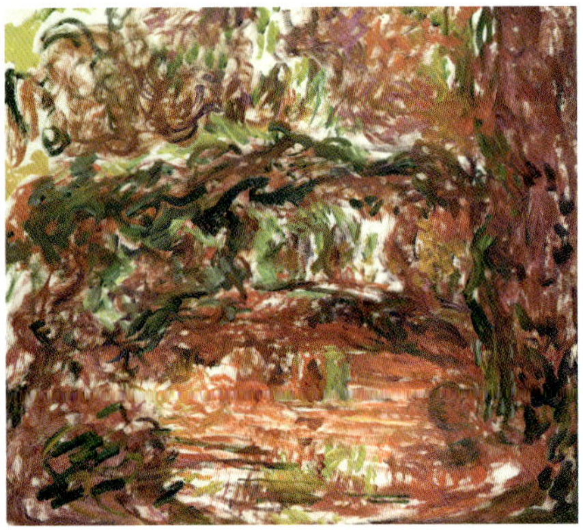

The Japanese Bridge
1918–24, 35 × 39 ¼ in. (89 × 100 cm)
Musée Marmottan, Paris, inv. 5092

The Japanese Bridge
1918–24, 35 × 36 ½ in. (89 × 93 cm)
Galerie Daniel Malingue, Paris

The Japanese Bridge
1918–24, 35 × 36 ½ in. (89 × 93 cm)
private collection

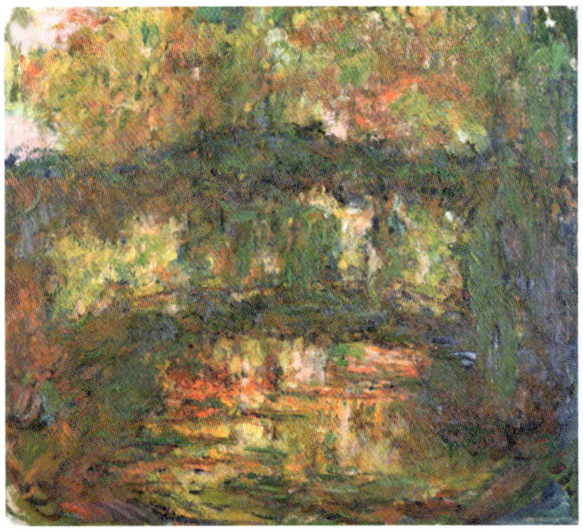

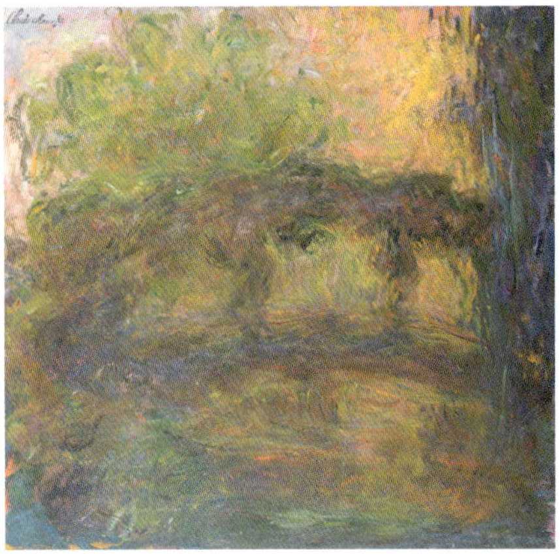

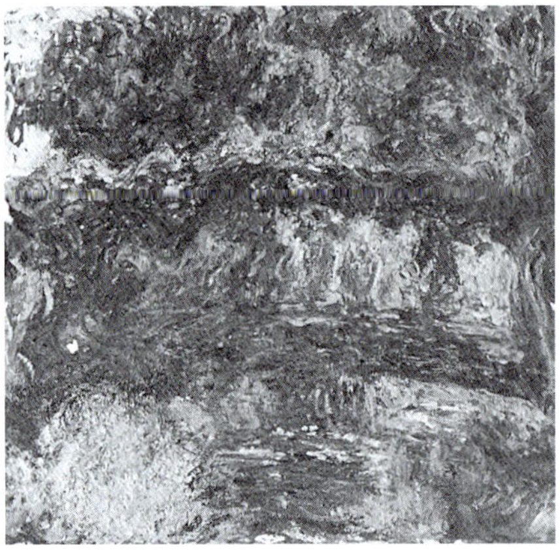

The Japanese Bridge
1918, 39 ¼ × 78 ¾ in. (100 × 200 cm)
private collection

The Japanese Bridge
1918–24, 28 ¾ × 39 ¼ in. (73 × 100 cm)
private collection

The Japanese Bridge
1918–24, 35 × 36 1/4 in. (89 × 92 cm)
private collection

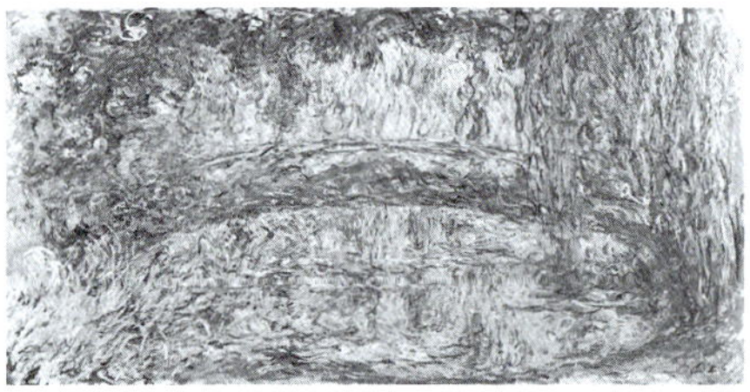

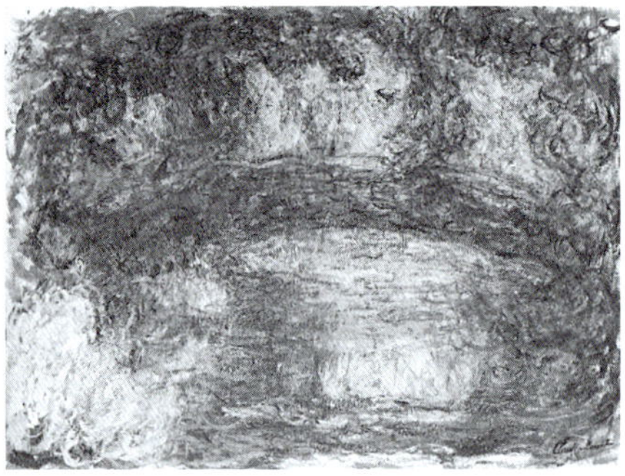

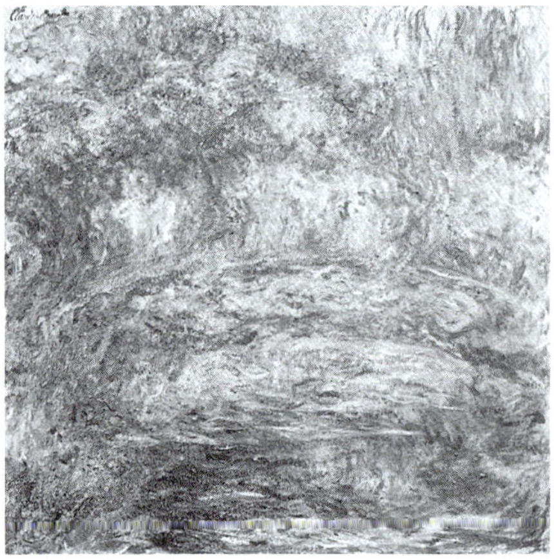

Water Lilies, Agapanthus
c. 1915–26, triptych, each panel 78¾ × 167¼ in. (200 × 425 cm), Part 1: Cleveland Museum of Art, inv. 60.81; part 2: Saint Louis Art Museum, The Steinberg Charitable Fund, inv. 134.1956; part 3: William Rockhill Nelson Gallery of Art, Atkins Museum of Fine Arts, Kansas City, inv. 57.26 (Gallery P 31)

Reflections of Clouds on the Water-Lily Pond
c. 1920, triptych: each panel 78¾ × 167¼ in. (200 × 425 cm), Museum of Modern Art New York, inv. 666-59-1/2/3

The Water-Lily Pond
c. 1916, 78¾ × 167¼ in. (200 × 425 cm) National Gallery, London, inv. NG 6343

The Water-Lily Pond, Green Reflections
c. 1910, 78¾ × 167¼ in. (200 × 425 cm) Foundation E. G. Bührle Collection, Zurich

The Water-Lily Pond
c. 1925, 78¾ × 221¼ in. (200 × 562 cm), Museum of Modern Art, New York, inv. 155.55 (destroyed in a fire at the museum on April 15, 1958)

The Water-Lily Pond
c. 1920, 78¾ × 236¼ in. (200 × 600 cm) Museum of Modern Art, New York, inv. 712.59

The Water-Lily Pond with Irises
c. 1914–22, 78¾ × 236¼ in. (200 × 600 cm) Kunsthaus, Zurich, inv. 1952/10

The Water-Lily Pond
c. 1915–26, 78¾ × 236¼ in. (200 × 600 cm) Carnegie Institute, Pittsburgh, inv. 62-19-1

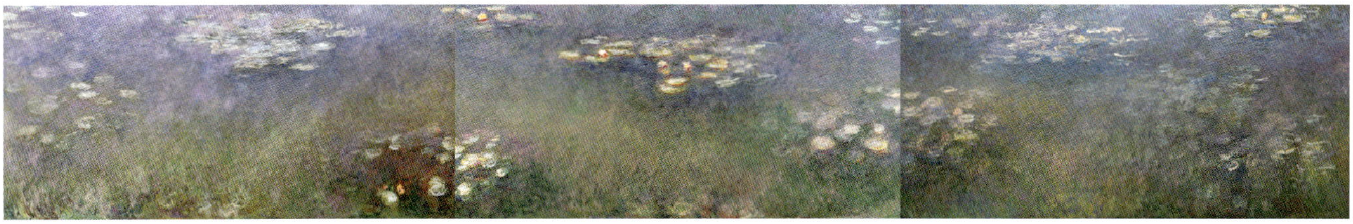

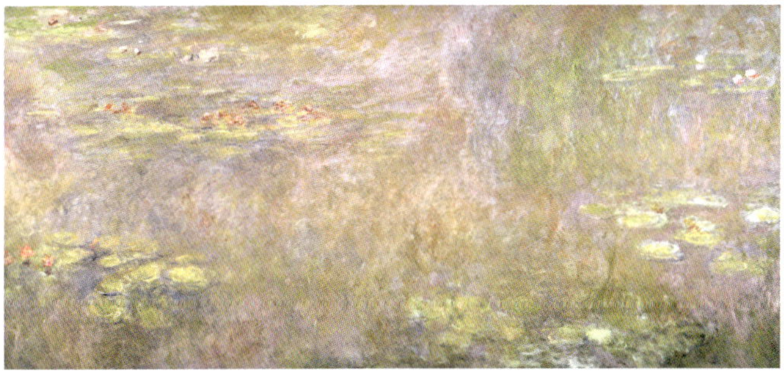

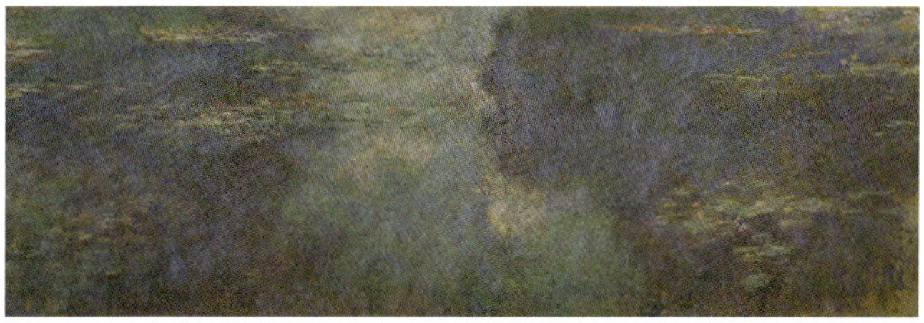

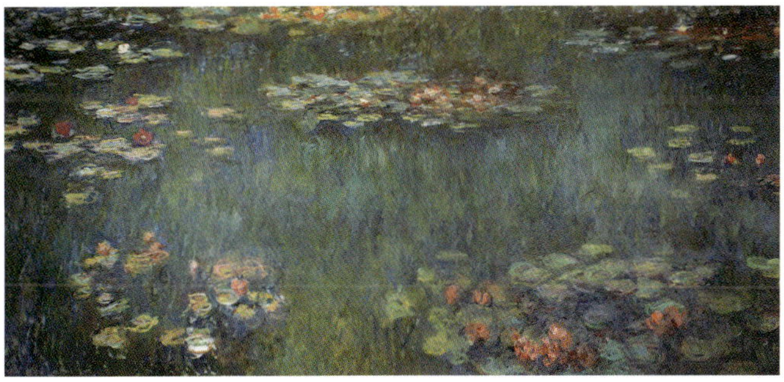

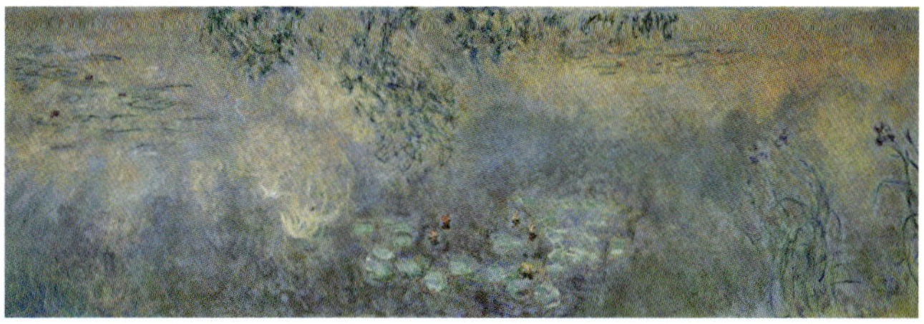

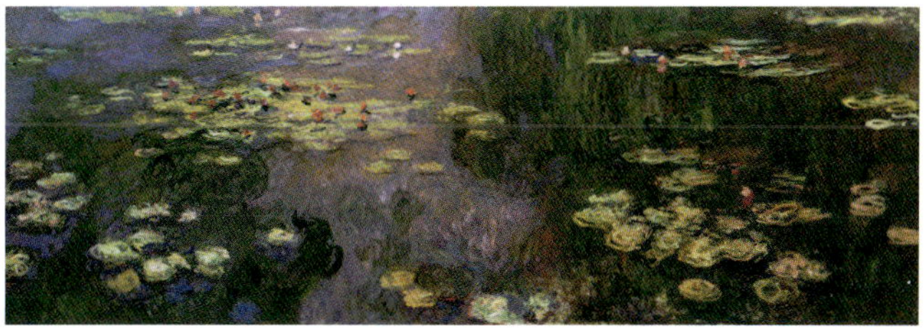

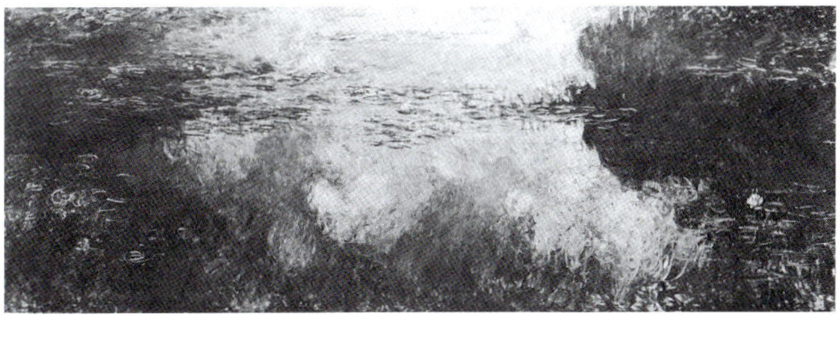

Groups without Willows at the Orangerie

The Water-Lily Pond, the Clouds
1915–26, triptych: each panel 78 ¾ × 167 ¼ in. (200 × 425 cm)
Musée de l'Orangerie, Paris, inv. 20100

The Water-Lily Pond, Green Reflections
1914–18, diptych: each panel 78 ¾ × 167 ¼ in. (200 × 425 cm)
Musée de l'Orangerie, Paris, inv. 20102

The Water-Lily Pond, Morning
1914–18, four panels 78 ¾ × 83 ¾ in. (200 × 212.5 cm), 78 ¾ × 167 ¼ in. (200 × 425 cm), 78 ¾ × 167 ¼ in. (200 × 425 cm), 78 ¾ × 83 ¾ in. (200 × 212.5 cm), Musée de l'Orangerie, Paris, inv. 20101

The Water-Lily Pond, Sunset
1914–18, 78 ¾ × 236 ¼ in. (200 × 600 cm)
Musée de l'Orangerie, Paris inv. 20103

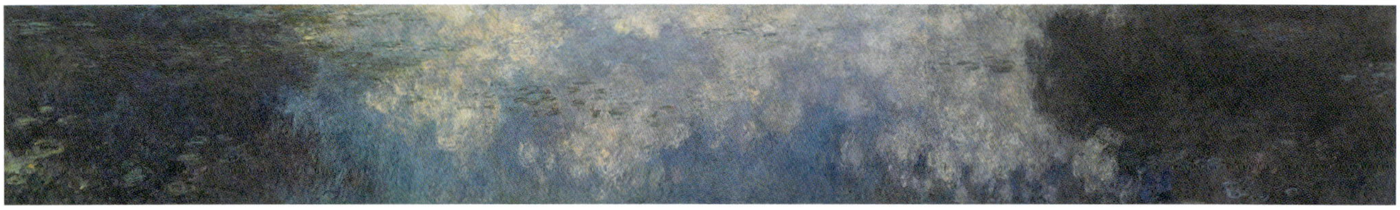

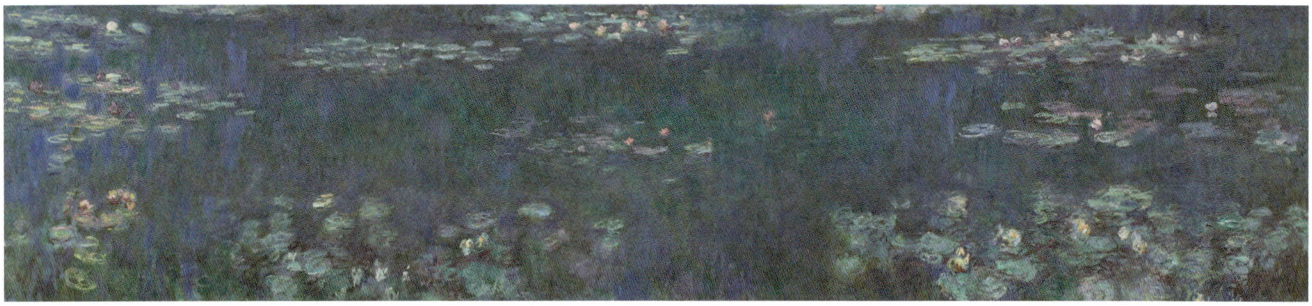

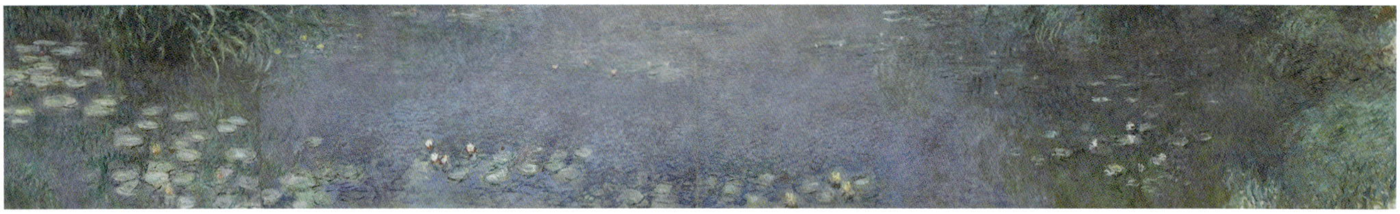

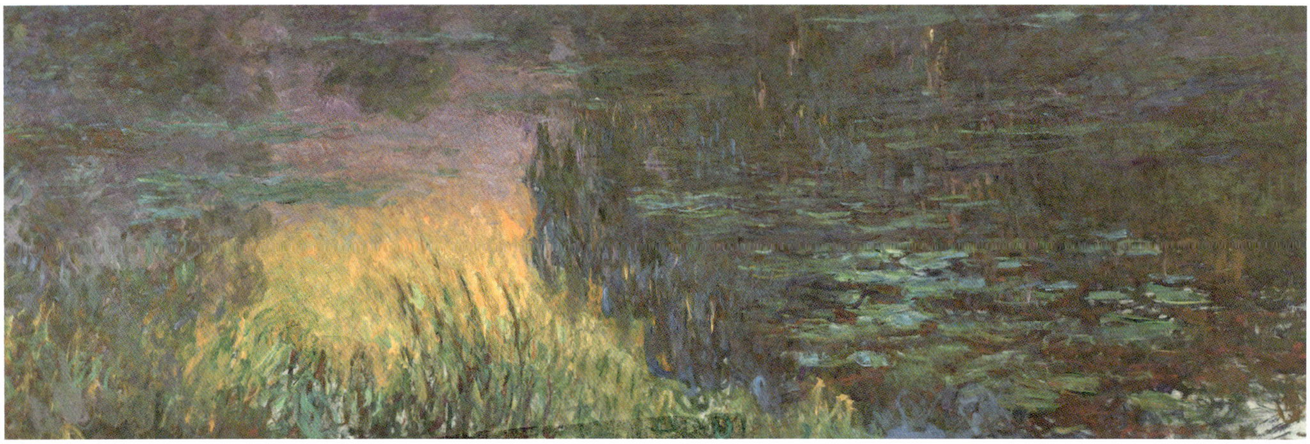

Groups with Willows at the Orangerie

The Water-Lily Pond with Willows, Morning with Willows
1914–18, triptych: each panel 78¾ × 167¼ in. (200 × 425 cm)
Musée de l'Orangerie, Paris, inv. 20105

The Water-Lily Pond with Willows, the Two Willows
1914–18, four panels, each 78¾ × 167¼ in. (200 × 425 cm)
Musée de l'Orangerie, Paris, inv. 20104

The Water-Lily Pond with Willows, Bright Morning with Willows
1914–18, triptych: each panel 78¾ × 167¼ in. (200 × 425 cm)
Musée de l'Orangerie, Paris, inv. 20106

The Water-Lily Pond with Willows, Reflections of Trees
1914–18, triptych: each panel 78¾ × 167¼ in. (200 × 425 cm)
Musée de l'Orangerie, Paris, inv. 20107

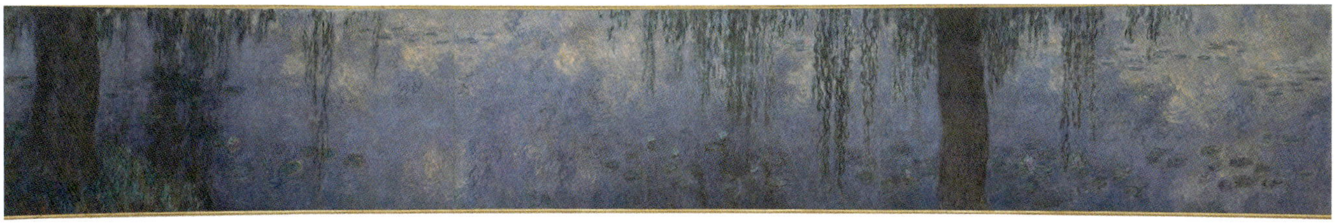

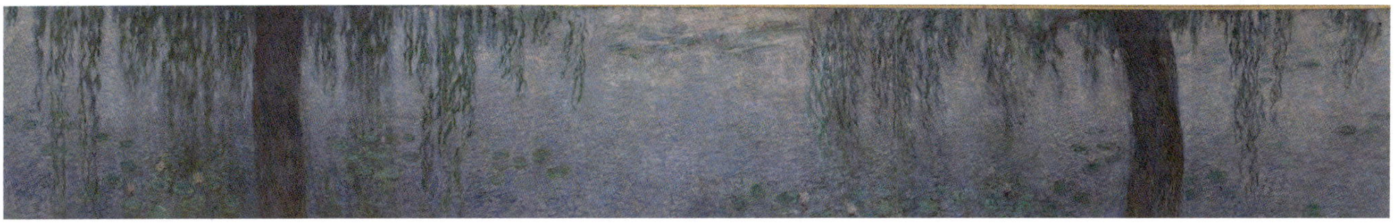

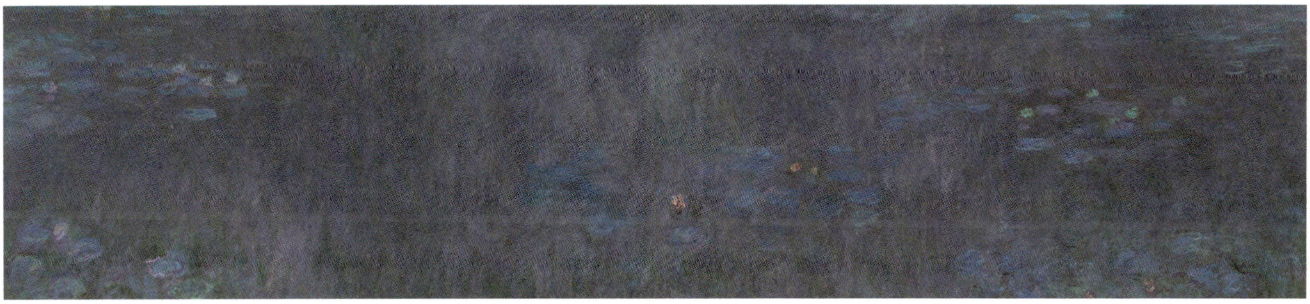

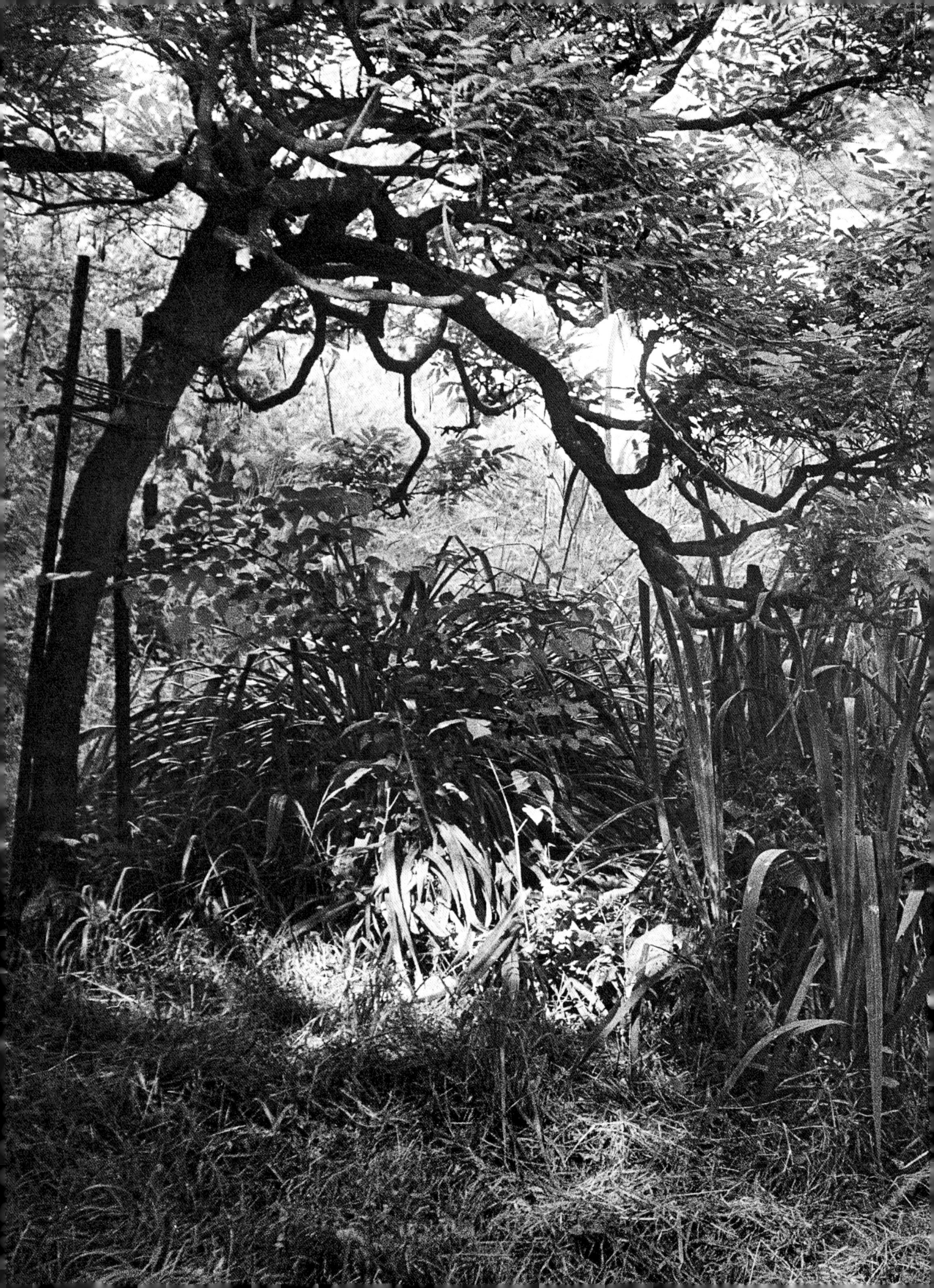

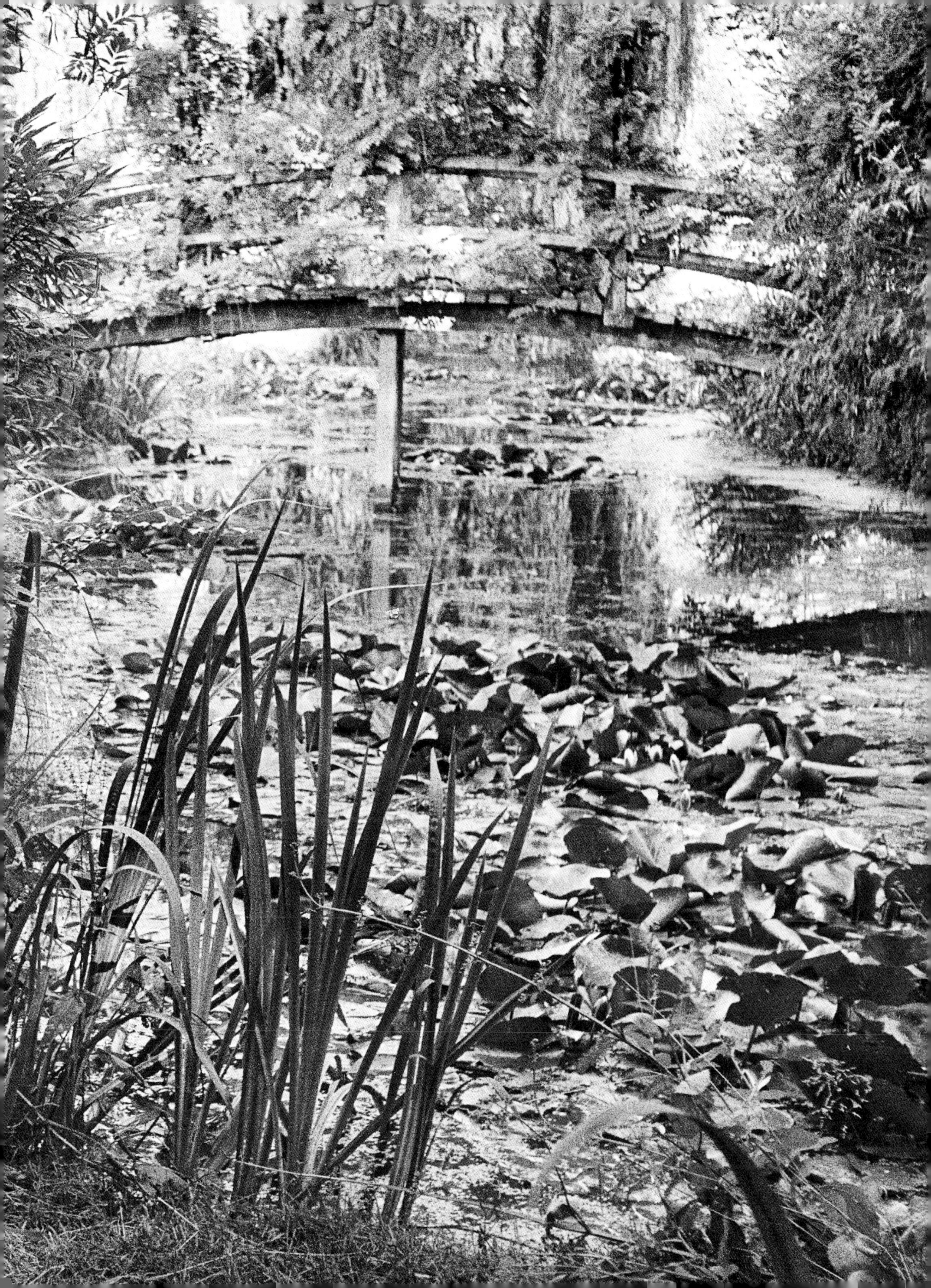

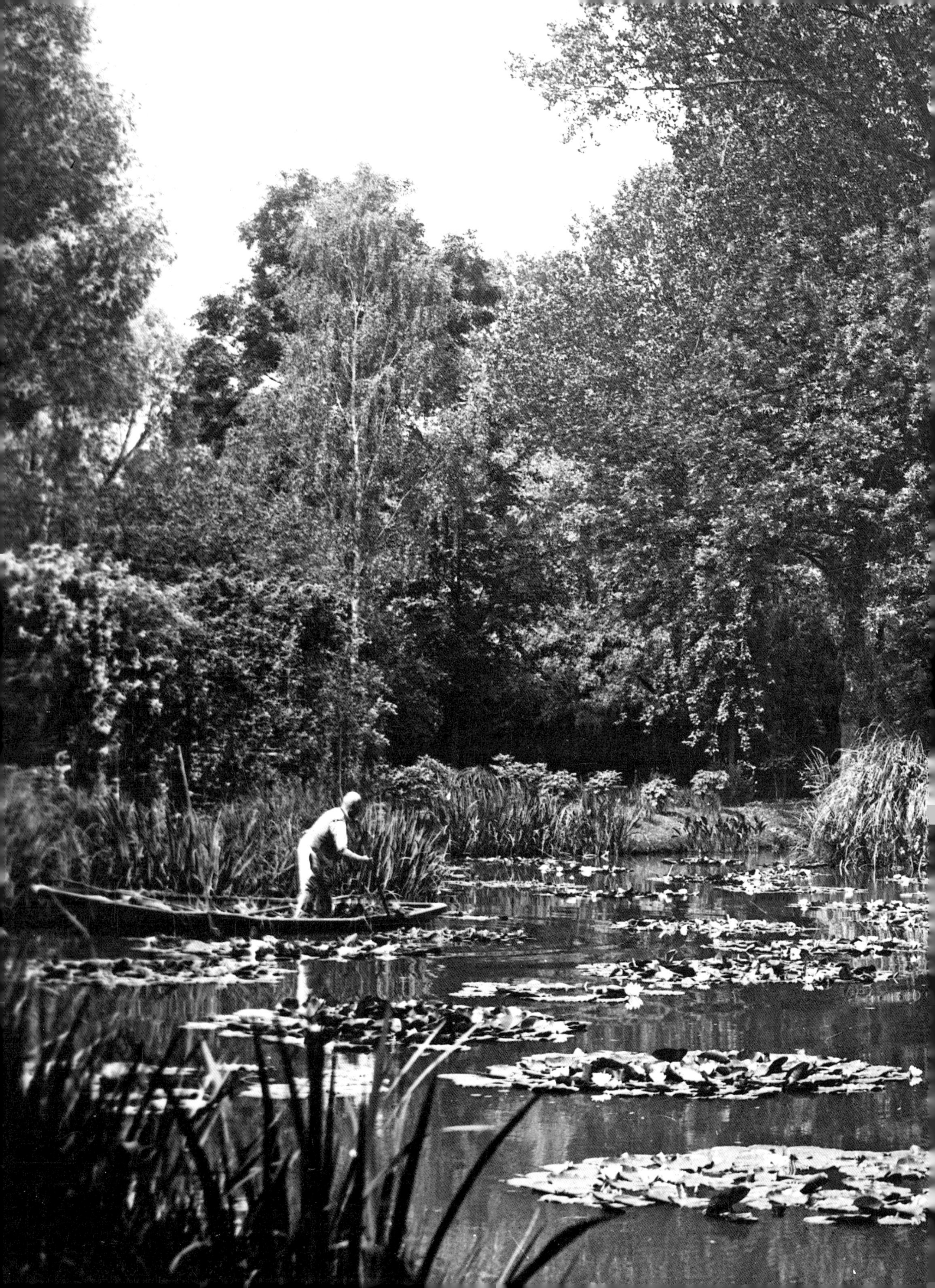

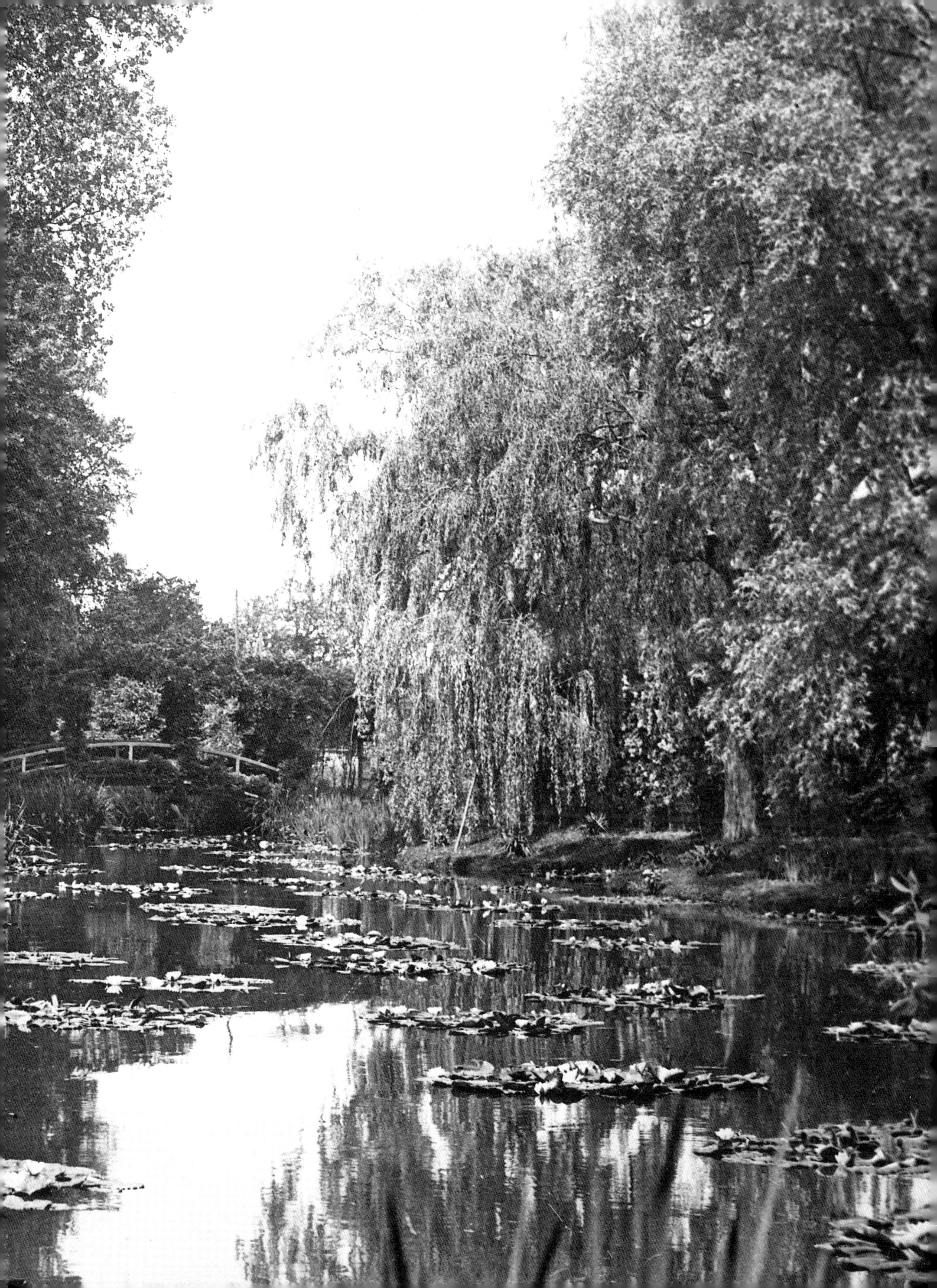

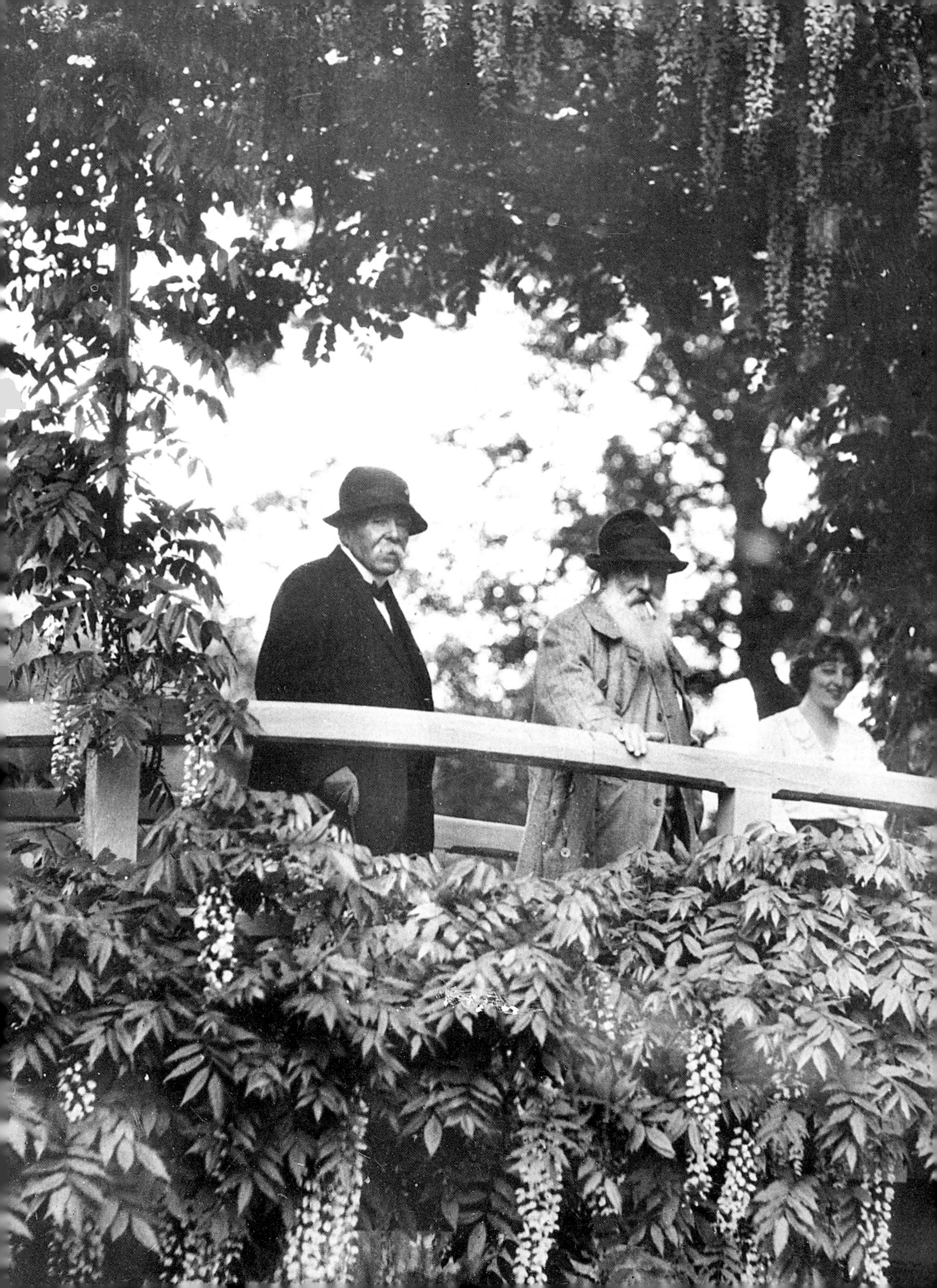

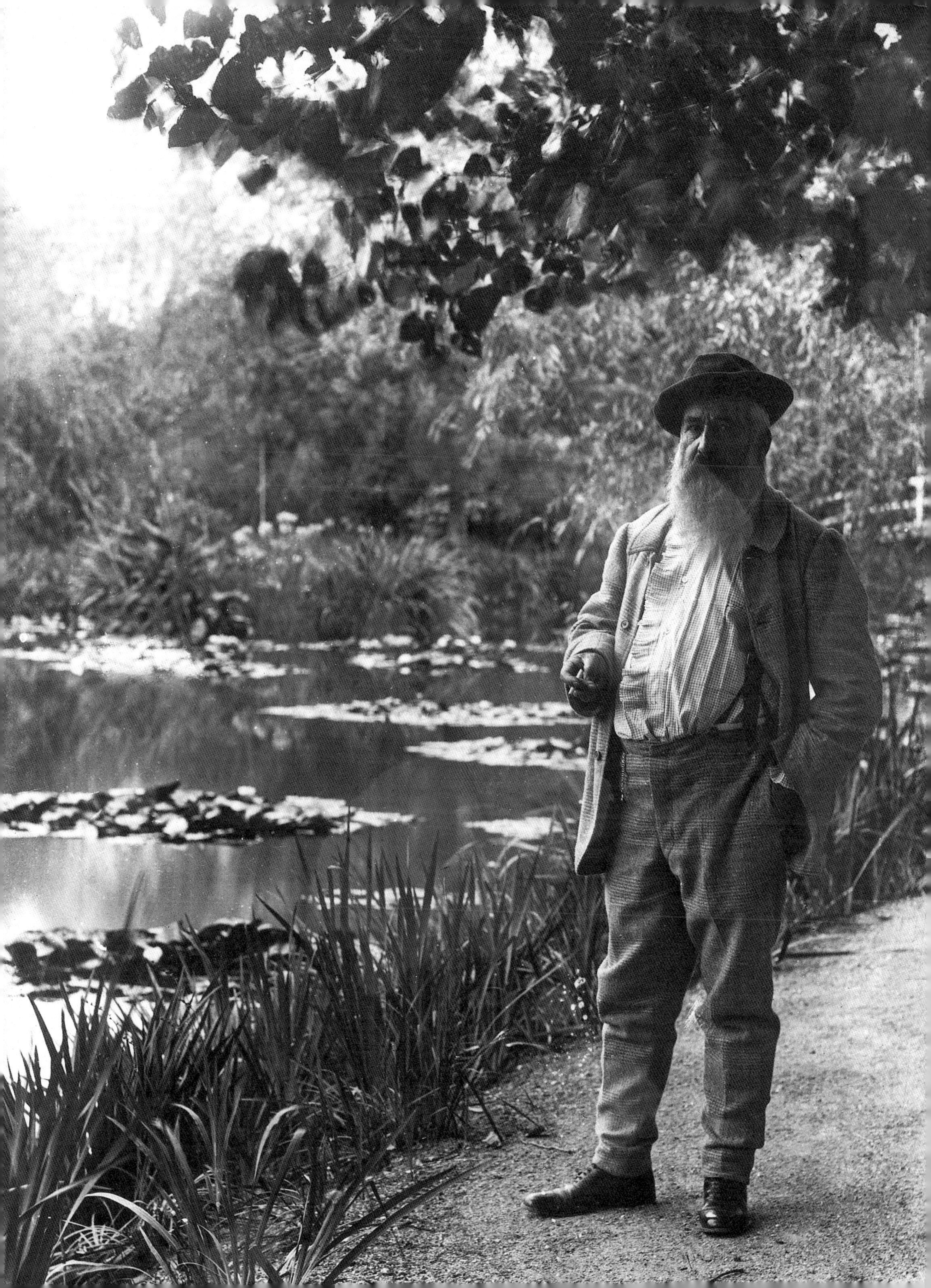

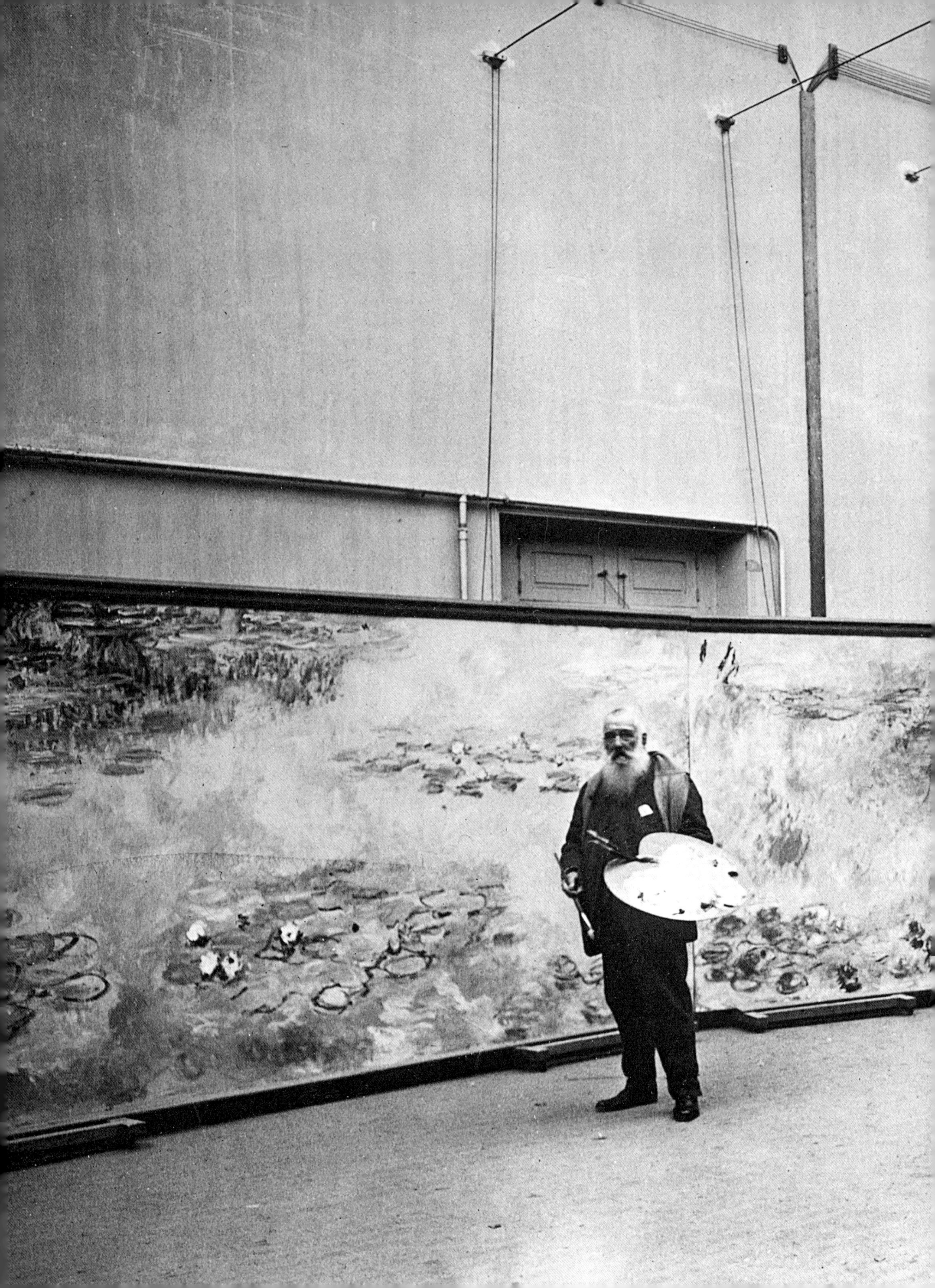

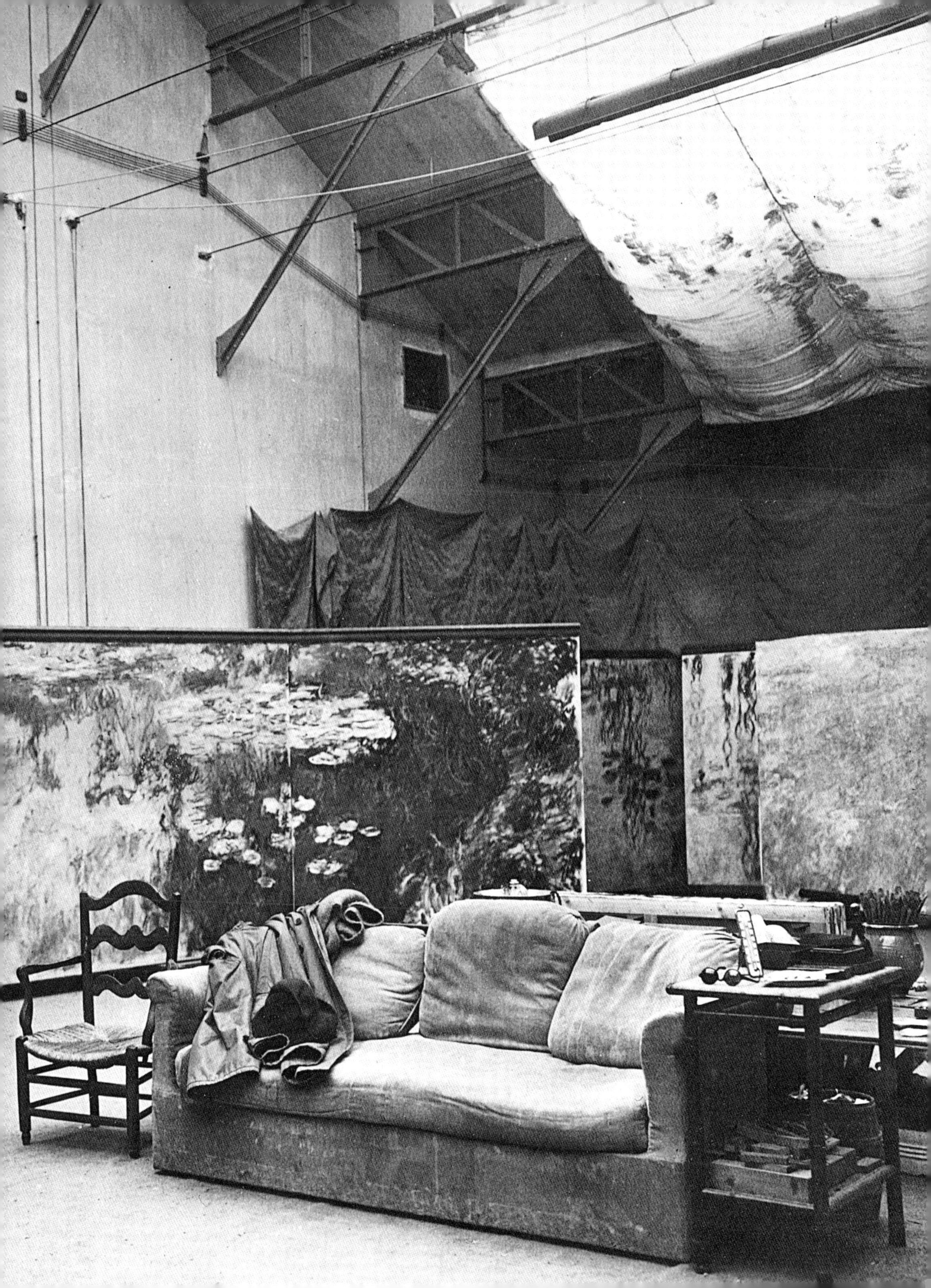

Letters from Claude Monet to Dr. Jacques Mawas

Giverny, near Vernon, Eure
December 8, 1924

Dear Doctor,

I have received the two pairs of glasses from Meyrowitzs—the first white pair is more to my satisfaction than the slightly tinted one.
I waited for a few days before replying to you because one always has to get used to new spectacles.
All things considered, I am very content with the white lenses. I see colors much better and so can work with more confidence.
Just one point is that with both the new glasses, the white as much as the tinted, if I can see better at 10–15 meters or at 50 meters, I can see clearly from 5 or 6 meters.
But perhaps it is a question of getting used to them.
In short, I am really pleased, and glad to be able to tell you this and thank you most, most warmly.
Kind regards,

Claude Monet

Giverny, near Vernon, Eure
March 25, 1925

Dear Doctor,

I am very late in giving you my news and the upshot of my new glasses. They reached me at a very bad time when I was deeply discouraged and did not believe I could improve the results, so that I did not carry on using the spectacles to which I might have perhaps become accustomed, but which disturbed me terribly —fuzzy vision, the least tone separate and outlandish.
As soon as I am in a better mood, I'll try to make a go of them, although I am surer than ever that a painter can never regain his sight. When a singer loses his voice, he retires; the painter operated on for a cataract has to give up painting: and this is what I have proved incapable of doing.
Excuse my frankness and believe that I am most grateful,

Claude Monet

View of the Water-Lily Pond, Giverny
Henri Cartier-Bresson, 1952, Henri Cartier-Bresson Archives, Magnum Photos

Claude Monet's Water Garden at Giverny
Anonymous, 7 × 9¼ in. (18 × 23.5 cm)
Jean-Dominique Rey Archives, Paris

Monet and Clemenceau
Anonymous, 8¾ × 6¾ in. (22.5 × 17 cm)
Jean-Dominique Rey Archives, Paris

Monet in His Garden
Anonymous, c. 1920, 9½ × 6½ in. (24 × 16.5 cm)
Jean-Dominique Rey Archives, Paris

Photograph of Claude Monet in His Large Studio at Giverny
Henri Manuel, c. 1923, Durand-Ruel Archives

FACING PAGE
Letter from Claude Monet to Jacques Mawas
December 8, 1924
Jean-Dominique Rey Archives, Paris

Letter from Claude Monet to Jacques Mawas
March 25, 1925
Jean-Dominique Rey Archives, Paris

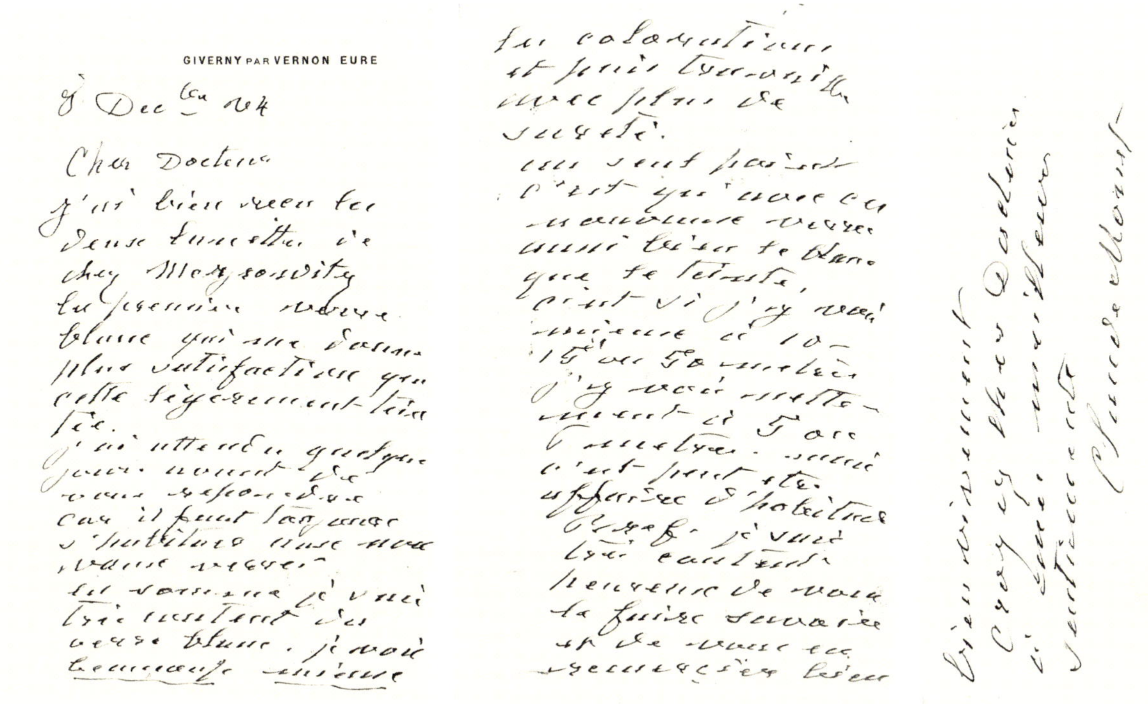

GIVERNY PAR VERNON EURE

8 Décembre 24

Cher Docteur

J'ai bien reçu les deux lunettes de chez Meyrowitz, les premiers verres blancs qui me donnent plus satisfaction que celles légèrement teintées.

J'ai attendu quelques jours avant de vous répondre car il faut longuement s'habituer avec mes nouveaux verres. Cette semaine je suis très content des verres blancs, je vois beaucoup mieux les colorations et puis travaille avec plus de sûreté.

Une seule chose c'est que mon œil [illegible] voit aussi bien le blanc que le [illegible], point si j'y vois mieux à 10-15 ou 20 mètres. J'y vois nettement à 5 ou 6 mètres, mais c'est peut-être affaire d'habitude.

Enfin je suis très content, heureux de vous le faire savoir et de vous en remercier bien vivement.

Croyez cher Docteur à mes meilleurs sentiments

Claude Monet

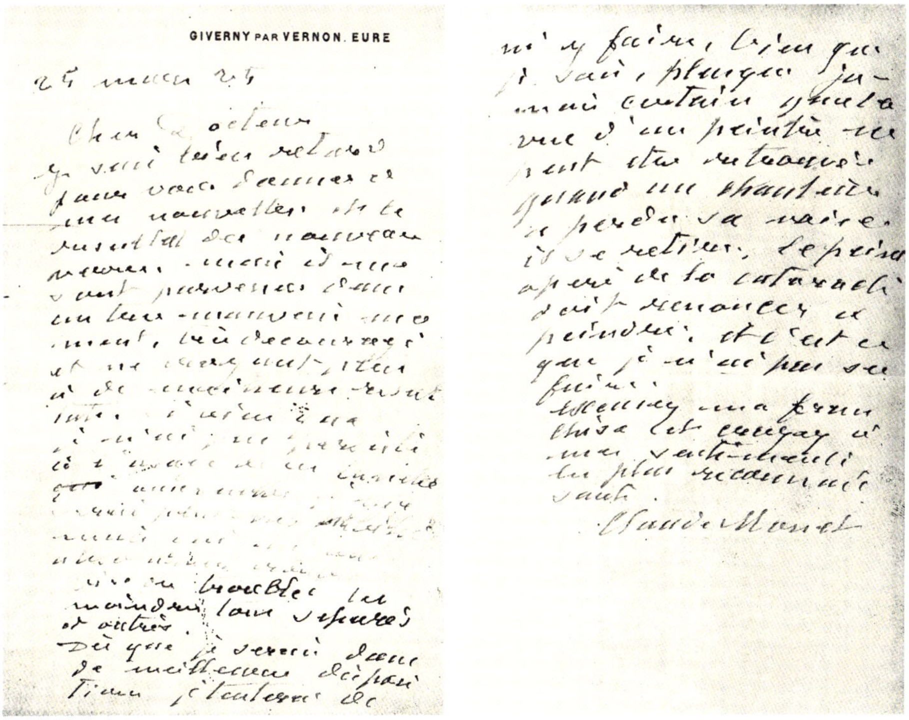

GIVERNY PAR VERNON. EURE

25 mars 25

Cher Docteur

Je suis bien en retard pour vous donner de mes nouvelles et le résultat des nouveaux verres. Mais ils me sont parvenus dans un bien mauvais moment, très découragé et ne marquant rien [illegible] troublés les mains [illegible] et autres. Dès que je serai dans de meilleures dispositions j'essaierai de m'y faire, bien que je sois plus que jamais certain que la vue d'un peintre ne peut être retrouvée. Quand un chanteur a perdu sa voix il se retire, le peintre opéré de la cataracte doit renoncer à peindre, et c'est ce que je n'ai pas su faire.

Excusez ma franchise et croyez à mes sentiments les plus reconnaissants.

Claude Monet

Chronology

1840 **November 14** Claude Monet is born in Paris.

1855 By the age of fifteen he has acquired a reputation as a caricaturist in Le Havre, where he lives with his family.

1858 Monet meets Eugène Boudin, who introduces him to painting in the open air.

1859 **May** Monet spends time in Paris working at the Académie Suisse.

1860 Military service in Algeria. Demobbed at the beginning of 1862, he returns to Le Havre in the summer and works with Boudin.

1863 He paints at Chailly in the forest of Fontainebleau with Renoir, Sisley, and Bazille.

1864 Meets Courbet in Paris. Spends the summer in Honfleur.

1865 Summer in Chailly where he produces studies for *Le Déjeuner sur l'herbe*. Camille Doncieux and Bazille sit for him.

1866 At Ville-d'Avray he paints *Women in the Garden* and at Le Havre *The Terrace on the Seashore, Sainte-Adresse*.

1867 Birth of Jean Monet, his first son, to Camille Doncieux, his companion.

1869 With Renoir, he paints *La Grenouillère* near Bougival.

1870 He marries Camille Doncieux with Courbet as his witness. Trapped at Trouville by the war, Monet heads for London where Daubigny introduces him to the art dealer Paul Durand-Ruel.

1871 Summer at Zaandam in Holland.

1872 Spring at Le Havre, paints *Impression, Sunrise*.

1873 Fits out a floating studio on a boat on the Seine.

1876 **Winter** Begins the *Gare Saint-Lazare* series.

1878 **January** Rents a house at Vétheuil. March: birth of a second son, Michel Monet.

1879 **September** Death of Camille Doncieux. In winter, he starts on the series of *Débacles* ("Ice Floes") featuring ice breaking up on the river, which he pursues until 1881.

1883 **May** Moves to Giverny. December: travels in the south of France with Renoir.

1884 **January-April** Stays at Bordighera, then in Menton.

1886 After a journey to Holland, spends time at Belle-Île.

1888 **January-April** Stays at Antibes.

1890 Series of *Poplars* (1890–91) and *Haystacks* (1890–93).

1892 **February** *Rouen Cathedral* series (1892–94). He marries Alice Hoschedé.

1896 Begins the *Branches of the Seine, near Giverny* series (1896–97).

1899 Begins the *Water-Lily Ponds* series. He stays in London in autumn and starts on the *Thames* series, a theme he continues developing from memory until 1904.

1900 **November 22-December 15** One-man exhibition in Galerie Durand-Ruel, Paris, with thirteen *Water-Lily Ponds*.

1904 Begins a first series of *Water Lilies* that continues until 1908 (approximately sixty paintings)

1908 Falls ill and begins having problems with his eyesight. September–December: stays in Venice.

1909 **May 6-June 5** Shows forty-eight *Water Lilies, Water Landscapes* in the Galerie Durand-Ruel, Paris.

1911 Death of his wife.

1914 Death of Jean Monet, the painter's son.

1915 Clémenceau encourages Monet to start a vast decoration of *Water Landscapes*. Construction in Giverny of a special studio 75 1/4 feet (23 meters) long by 49 1/4 feet (15 meters) wide.

1918 In Clemenceau's presence, Monet agrees to donate these large panels to the French State.

1922 Deed of gift signed at Vernon. Onset of a double cataract.

1923 Cataract operation.

1924 *Water Lilies* exhibited in New York.

1926 **December 26** Monet dies in Giverny.

1927 **May 17** Inauguration of the *Water Lilies* in the Musée de l'Orangerie, Paris.

1956 Exhibition of *Water Lilies* at the Galerie Katia Granoff, Paris.

1957 Further exhibition of *Water Lilies* at the Galerie Katia Granoff, Paris.

1966 The Michel Monet Bequest enters the Musée Marmottan, Paris.

Selected Bibliography

Duret, Théodore. *Le peintre Claude Monet.* Paris: 1880.
Mirbeau, Octave. *Les "Venise" de Claude Monet*. Paris: 1912.
Alexandre, Arsène. *Claude Monet.* Paris: Bernheim-Jeune, 1921.
Geoffroy, Gustave. *Claude Monet, sa vie, son temps, son œuvre*. Paris: Crès, 1922.
Elder, Marc. *A Giverny, chez Claude Monet.* Paris: Bernheim-Jeune, 1924.
Mauclair, Camille. *Claude Monet.* Paris: John Lane, 1925.
Fels, Florent. *Claude Monet.* Paris: Gallimard, 1927.
Fosca, François. *Claude Monet.* Paris: L'Artisan du Livre, 1927.
Gillet, Louis. *Trois variations sur Claude Monet.* Paris: Plon, 1927.
Clemenceau, Georges. *Claude Monet, Les Nymphéas*. Paris: Plon, 1928 and 1965.
Werth, Léon. *Claude Monet*. Paris: Crès, 1928.
Fels, Marthe de. *La vie de Claude Monet.* Paris: Gallimard, 1929.
Grappe, Georges. *Monet*. Paris: Plon, 1941.
Malingue, Maurice. *Claude Monet.* Monaco: Les Documents d'Art, 1943.
Reuterswaerd, Oscar. *Monet.* Stockholm: Bonniers, 1948.
Roger-Marx, Claude. *Monet.* Lausanne: 1949.
Besson, Georges. *Claude Monet.* Paris: Braun, 1951.
Degand, Léon, and Denis Rouart. *Claude Monet.* Geneva: Skira, 1958.
C. Seitz, William. *Claude Monet.* New York: Abrams, 1960.
Hoschedé, Jean-Pierre. *Claude Monet, ce mal connu.* Geneva: P. Cailler, 1960.
Taillandier, Yvon. *Monet.* Paris: Flammarion, 1963.
Cogniat, Raymond. *Monet and His World.* London: Thames & Hudson, 1966.
Kuroe, M. *Claude Monet.* Tokyo: 1970.
Wildenstein, Daniel. *Claude Monet, Catalogue raisonné.* 5 vol., Lausanne: La Bibliothèque des Arts, 1974–91.
Isaacson, Joel. *Claude Monet, Observation and réflexion.* Oxford: Phaidon, 1978.
Lévèque, Jean-Jacques. *Monet.* Paris: Siloé, 1980.
Bortolato, Rossi. *L'œuvre complet de Monet.* Paris: Flammarion, 1981.
Gordon, R., and A. Forge. *Monet.* New York: Abrams, 1983.
Hoog, Michel. *Les Nymphéas de Claude Monet au Musée de l'Orangerie.* Paris: RMN, 1984.
Guillaud, Maurice. *Monet at the Time of Giverny.* New York: Rizzoli, 1985.
Sagner-Duchting, Karin. *Claude Monet "Nympheas."* Hildesheim: Olms, 1985.
Patin, Sylvie. *Monet: "un œil… mais bon dieu quel œil!"* Paris: Gallimard/RMN, 1991.
J. Stuckey, Charles. *Monet, Water Lilies*. London: Park Lane, 1991.
Spate, Virginia. *Claude Monet: The Colour of Time.* London: Thames & Hudson, 1992.
Alphant, Marianne. *Monet, une vie dans le paysage*. Paris: Hazan, 1993.
Moffett, Charles. *Monet at Giverny: Beyond Impressionism.* New York: Abrams, 1998.
Hayes Tucker, Paul. *Monet in the 20th Century.* New Haven: Yale University Press, 1999.
Georgel, Pierre. *Claude Monet: Waterlilies*. Paris: Hazan, 1999.
Temkin, Ann, and Nora Lawrence. *Claude Monet: Water Lilies*. New York: Museum of Modern Art, 2009.
Cogeval, Guy, Sylvie Patin, Sylvie Patry, Anne Roquebert, and Richard Thomson. *Monet (1840–1926)*. Paris: RMN/Musée d'Orsay, 2010.
Mathieu, Marianne, and Dominique Lobstein (eds.). *Impression, soleil levant: L'histoire vraie du chef d'œuvre de Claude Monet*. Paris: Hazan, 2014.

Photographic Credits (t: top; c: center; b: bottom; l: left; r: right; col.: column)

Photo © 2016 Carnegie Museum of Art, Pittsburgh: p. 145 col. 2 b; © 2016 Kunsthaus Zürich: pp. 83, 145 col. 2 4th row; Photo © 2016 Museum Associates/LACMA: pp. 80, 123 col. 2 t; Photo © 2016 Museum of Fine Arts, Boston: p. 126 col. 2 c; © Akg-Images: pp. 12, 22, 37, 39, 43, 47, 49, 115, 110–11, 120 col. 3 b, 121 col. 3 c, 126 col. 3 t, 127 col. 2 t, 131 col. 2 b, 134 col. 2 c, 135 col. 1 t, col. 3 c, 139 col. 3 c, 140 cols. 2–3 2nd row, 142 col. 1 c, col. 2 c, 143 col. 2 c; © Akg-images/Electa: p. 123 col. 2 b; © Akg-images/Erich Lessing: pp. 26, 30 t, 99, 126 col. 3 c, 142 col. 2 b; © Allen Phillips/Wadsworth Atheneum: p. 126 col. 3 b; © All rights reserved: pp. 62, 86 l, 95, 127 col. 3 c, 129 col. 3 b, 138 col. 1 b, col. 3 b, 139 col. 3 t and b, 141 col. 2 t, col. 3 b, 143 col. 1 b; Archives Durand-Ruel © Durand-Ruel & Cie, All rights reserved: pp. 154–55; © Archives J.-D. Rey: p. 157; © Atami MOA: p. 140 col. 1 t; Photo © BPK, Berlin, Dist. RMN-Grand Palais/Elke Walford: p. 30 b; © Bridgeman Images/Christie's: pp. 23, 55, 79, 85 r, 109, 133 col. 2 b, col. 3 t, 134 col. 2 t, 139 col. 2 t and c, 143 col. 1 t; © Bridgestone Museum of Art, Tokyo, Japan, Peter Willi/Bridgeman Images: pp. 87 c, 124 col. 1 c, 129 col. 2 b; © Bruno Scotti: p. 138 col. 1 c; © Buhrle Collection, Zurich, Switzerland/Bridgeman Images: p. 135 col. 3 b; Photo © Centre Pompidou, MNAM-CCI, Dist. RMN-Grand Palais/All rights reserved: p. 107; Photo © Centre Pompidou, MNAM-CCI, Dist. RMN-Grand Palais/Georges Meguerditchian: p. 114; Photo © Centre Pompidou, MNAM-CCI, Dist. RMN-Grand Palais/Philippe Migeat: p. 106; © Christie's Images/Getty Images: pp. 85 l, 100, 124 col. 2 b, 126 col. 1 b, 131 col. 3 t; © Collection Roger-Viollet/Roger-Viollet: pp. 150–51; Courtesy of Sotheby's Picture Library: pp. 44, 93, 125 col. 3 c, 127 col. 3 t, 133 col. 2 c, 142 col. 1 t; © Dallas Museum of Art, gift of the Meadows Foundation Incorporated: p. 131 col. 3 b; Fondation Beyeler, Riehen/Basel, Beyeler Collection, © Akg-Images: p. 142 col. 3 b; © Fondation Beyeler, Riehen/Basel, Beyeler Collection: p. 140 cols. 2–3 t; Fondation Beyeler, Riehen/Basel, © Bridgeman Images: 134 col. 2 b; Fondation Beyeler, Riehen/Basel, Beyeler Collection, © Christie's Images/Getty Images: p. 137 col. 3 b; © Fondation Collection E.G. Bührle, Zurich: p. 145 col. 1, 4th row; © Francis G. Mayer/Getty Images: p. 120 col. 3 c; © Gothenburg Museum of Art, Sweden: p. 128 col. 2 t; © Henri Cartier-Bresson/Magnum Photos: pp. 148–49; © Hulton Archives/Getty Images: p. 121 col. 1 c; © Image Courtesy the Fine Arts Museums of San Francisco: p. 131 col. 2 t; © Laurent Lecat: pp. 25, 35, 146 b; © Minneapolis Institute of Art, MN, USA, Bequest of Putnam Dana McMillan/Bridgeman Images: p. 144 col. 1 t; © Musée Albert-André de Bagnols-sur-Cèze/Bridgeman Images: p. 135 col. 1 c; Photo © Musée de Grenoble: pp. 67, 138 col. 3 t; © Musée de l'Orangerie, Paris, France/ Bridgeman Images: pp. 117, 146 t, 2nd row, and 3rd row, 147; © Musée des Beaux-Arts André Malraux, Le Havre, France/Bridgeman Images: p. 127 col. 2 b; © Musée des Beaux-Arts Nantes, France/Bridgeman Images: p. 141 col. 1 c; © Musée d'Orsay, Paris, France/Bridgeman Images: p. 4, 33 t; © Musée Marmottan Monet, Paris, France/Bridgeman Images: pp. 6, 9, 13, 16–17, 24, 27, 29, 53, 61, 64, 85 c, 87 c, 90, 96, 118, 123 col. 2 c, 125 col. 2 t, col. 3 t, 128 col. 2 b, 129 col. 2 t, 133 col. 2 t, col. 3 b, 134 col. 1 b, 135 col. 1 b, 136 col. 1 t, col. 1 b, col. 2 t, col. 2 c, col. 3 t, 137 col. 2 c, b, col. 3 t, 138 col. 1 t, col. 2 b, 139 col. 2 b, 141 col. 1 b, 142 col. 2 t, col. 3 t, 143 col. 1 c, col. 2 t, col. 3 t and c, and b, 144 col. 1 b, col. 2 t; © Museum of Fine Arts, Boston, Massachusetts, USA, Bequest of Alexander Cochrane/Bridgeman Images: p. 45 b; © Museum of Fine Arts, Boston, Massachusetts, USA, Given in the memory of Governor Alvan T. Fuller/by the Fuller Foundation/Bridgeman Images : p. 89 l, 121 col. 3 t; © Museum of Fine Arts, Houston, Texas, USA, gift of Mrs. Harry C. Hanszen/Bridgeman Images: pp. 86 r, 129 col. 1 t; © National Gallery, London, UK/Bridgeman Images: p. 145 col. 1, 3rd row; © National Gallery of Australia, Canberra/Bridgeman Images: p. 135 col. 3 t; © National Museum of Wales: p. 124 col. 2 t; © National Museum of Wales/Bridgeman Images: pp. 125 col. 2 b, 126 col. 2 t; © Philadelphia Museum of Art/Getty Images: p. 120 col. 2 c; © Portland Art Museum, Oregon, Helen Thurston Ayer Fund Purchase: p. 134 col. 1 t; © Princeton University Art Museum/Art Resource NY/Scala, Florence: p. 120 col. 1 b; Private collection, All rights reserved: pp. 10, 34, 87 l, 113, 121 col. 1 b, 122, 123 col. 1 t, c, and b, 123 col. 3 t, c, and b, 124 col. 1 b, col. 3 t, c, and b, 125 col. 1 t, c, and b, 126 col. 1 b, 127 col. 1 t and b, 127 col. 3 b, 128 col. 3 t and b, 129 col. 1 b, col. 3 t, 130, 131 col. 1 t, c, and b, 132 col. 1 t, c, and b, col. 2 t, c, and b, col. 3 t and c, 133 col. 1 c, 134 col. 3 t, 136 col. 2 b, col. 3 c and b, 137 col. 1 t, c, and b, 139 col. 1 t and b, 140 col. 1 c and b, cols. 2–3 3rd row, col. 2 4th row, col. 3 4th row and b, 142 col. 3 c, 144 col. 2 b, col. 3 t, c, and b; © Private collection/Bridgeman Images: pp. 19, 40, 45 t, 58, 88 l, 112, 120 col. 1 t, 121 col. 1 t, 126 col. 1 c, 127 col. 2 c, 128 col. 1 t, 131 col. 3 c, 133 col. 1 t, col. 3 c, 134 col. 1 c, 135 col. 2 b, 138 col. 3 c, 141 col. 1 t, 144 col. 2 c; Private collection, Photo © Christie's Images/Bridgeman Images: pp. 125 col. 2 c, 138 col. 2 t, 142 col. 1 b; Private collection, Photo © Lefevre Fine Art Ltd, London/Bridgeman Images: pp. 32, 104-5, 138 col. 2 c, 141 col. 3 t; © Private collection Peter Willi/Bridgeman Images: pp. 89 r, 120 col. 2 t, 126 col. 1 t; © Pushkin Museum, Moscow, Russia/Bridgeman Images: pp. 20, 84 l, 120 col. 2 b; Photo © RMN-Grand Palais/Agence Bulloz: p. 153; Photo © RMN-Grand Palais (Musée d'Orsay)/Hervé Lewandowski: pp. 33 b, 84 r, 120 col. 3 t, 121 col. 2 c; © Image courtesy Saint Louis Art Museum, photo Jean Paul Torno: p. 145 tc; © Scottish National Gallery, Edinburgh/Bridgeman Images: p. 48 t; © Sotheby's/Akg-Images: pp. 50, 88 d, 120 col. 1 c, 121 col. 3 b, 141 col. 3 c; Photo © The Art Institute of Chicago: pp. 121 col. 2 b, 124 col. 2 c, 141 col. 2 b; © The Barnes Foundation, Philadelphia, Pennsylvania, USA/Bridgeman Images: p. 38; © The Cleveland Museum of Art, John L. Severance Fund: p. 145 tl; © The Dayton Art Institute, Dayton, Ohio, USA, gift of Mr. Joseph Rubin/Bridgeman Images: p. 124 col. 1 t; © The Israel Museum, Jerusalem, Israel/Bridgeman Images: pp. 86 c, 128 col. 1 b; Photo © The Metropolitan Museum of Art, Dist. RMN-Grand Palais/Image of the MMA: pp. 48 b, 121 col. 2 t, 137 col. 2 t; © The Museum of Modern Art, New York/Scala, Florence: pp. 134 col. 3 b, 144 col. 1 c, 145 2nd row, col. 1 b, col. 2 3rd row; © The National Museum of Western Art, Tokyo: pp. 68, 135 col. 2 c; © The Nelson-Atkins Museum of Art, Kansas City, Missouri/Photo Louis Meluso: p. 145 tr; Photo © The Philadelphia Museum of Art, Dist. RMN-Grand Palais: p.143 col. 2 b; © Tokyo Fuji Art Museum, Tokyo, Japan/Bridgeman Images: p. 125 col. 3 b; © Wally Findlay Galleries International, Inc., All rights reserved: p. 127 col. 1 c; © Photo by Walter Daran/The LIFE Picture Collection/Getty Images: p. 132 col. 3 b, 133 col. 1 b, 134 col. 3 c; © Walter Drayer, Zurich: p. 152; © Winterthur, Kunstmuseum Winterthur, gift of the Galerieverein 1952: p. 135 col. 2 t; © Worcester Art Museum, Massachusetts, USA/Bridgeman Images: p. 131 col. 2 c.

Front cover: *Water Lilies* (detail), 1916, 78 ¾ × 78 ¾ in. (200 × 200 cm), oil on canvas, National Museum of Western Art, Tokyo, inv. P. 1959.151
Back cover: *Monet in His Studio* (detail), Henri Manuel, early 1920s, silver print, Musée Marmottan, Paris, Giraudon / The Bridgeman Art Library - © Henri Manuel
Front endpapers: *The Water-Lily Pond, Green Reflections* (detail), 1914–18, oil on canvas, Musée de l'Orangerie, Paris, inv. 20102
Back endpapers: *The Water-Lily Pond, Sunset* (detail), 1914–18, oil on canvas, Musée de l'Orangerie, Paris, inv. 20103

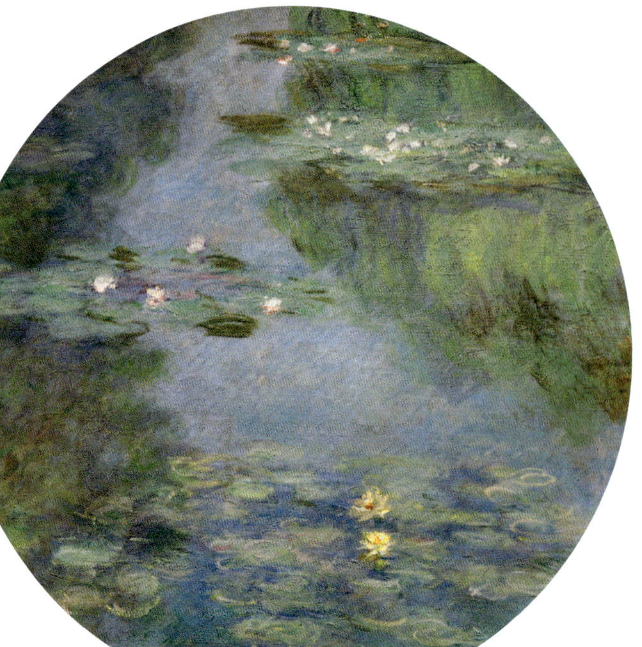

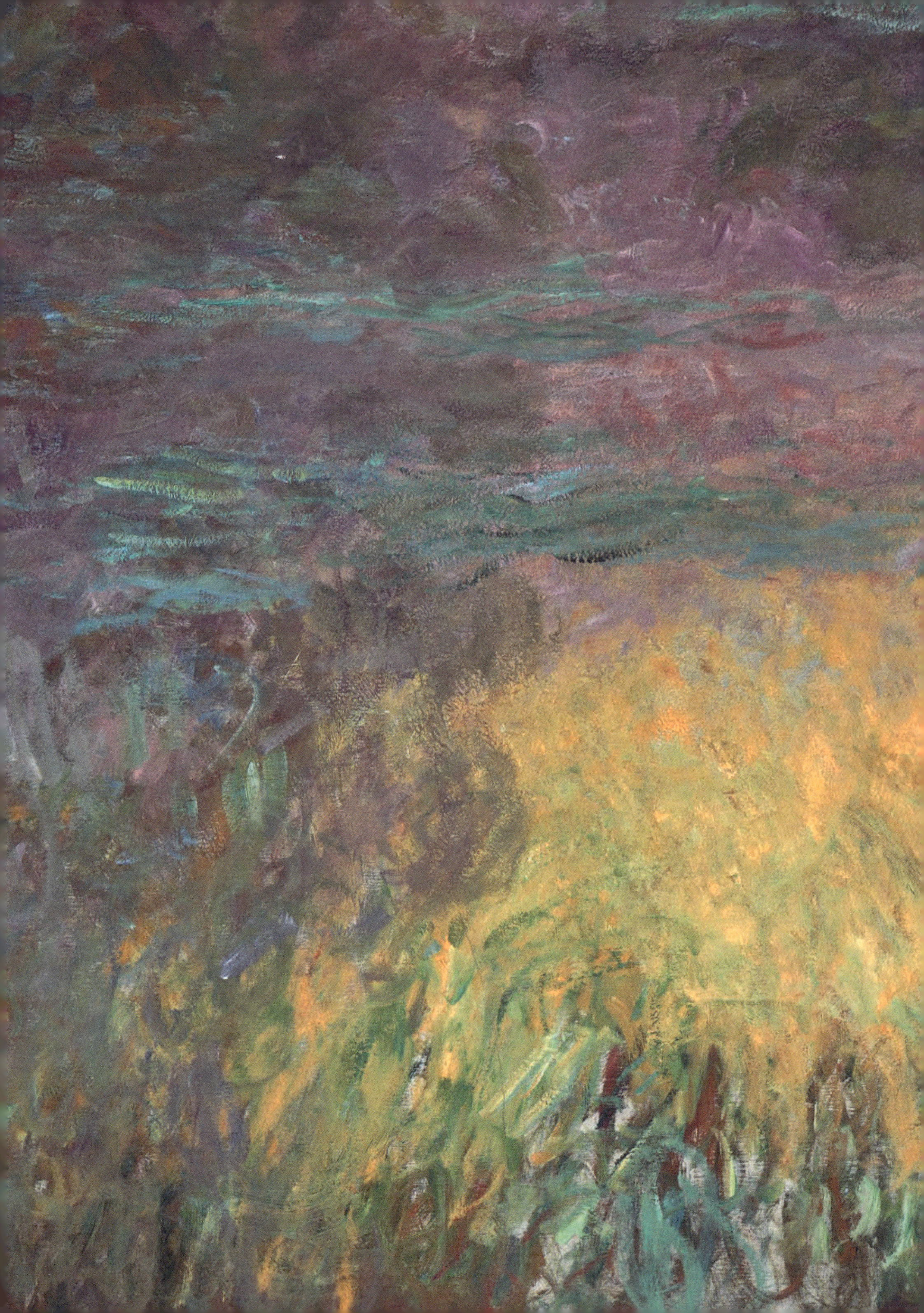